HELLENIC STUDIES SERIES 100

CRITERIA OF TRUTH

Recent Titles in the Hellenic Studies Series

http://chs.harvard.edu/chs/publications

CRITERIA OF TRUTH

REPRESENTATIONS OF TRUTH AND FALSEHOOD IN HELLENISTIC POETRY

Kathleen Kidder

Center for Hellenic Studies

Trustees for Harvard University
Washington, D.C.
Distributed by Harvard University Press
Cambridge, Massachusetts, and London, England
2023

Criteria of Truth: Representations of Truth and Falsehood in Hellenistic Poetry
By Kathleen Kidder
Copyright © 2023 Center for Hellenic Studies, Trustees for Harvard University
All Rights Reserved.
Published by Center for Hellenic Studies, Trustees for Harvard University,
    Washington, D.C.
Distributed by Harvard University Press, Cambridge, Massachusetts and
    London, England
Printed by Gasch Printing, Odenton, MD
Cover Design: Joni Godlove, with original artwork by Steve Kemple
Production: Jen Jackowitz

ISBN: 978-0-674-29242-0
Library of Congress Control Number: 2023933685

the so-called Euphonists, the importance of aesthetic qualities like word choice and arrangement trumped even the meaning of a poem.[20] Yet the heightened emphasis on aesthetic qualities does not hinder the potential of poetry to question notions of truth and falsehood and the means by which they are judged. Such poetic interrogation, however, is often subtle, demanding from the reader awareness of the prior textual tradition. For instance, the Epimenides quotation, as preserved in Paul's *Epistle to Titus* (1.12), runs in full Κρῆτες ἀεὶ ψεῦσται, κακὰ θηρία, γαστέρες ἀργαί ("Cretans are always liars, evil beasts, idle bellies"), thus recalling the Muses' taunt at the beginning of the *Theogony*: ποιμένες ἄγραυλοι, κάκ' ἐλέγχεα, γαστέρες οἶον ("rustic shepherds, base reproaches, mere bellies," 26). This insult prefaces the Muses' boast about their dual ability to tell the truth and falsehoods that are akin to the truth (27–28). As a result, Callimachus' appropriation of the Epimenides' maxim works on two levels, not only discrediting the authority of Cretans but also evoking a famous passage that establishes the difficulty of distinguishing truth and falsehood in poetry.

Related to this issue of truth and falsehood, scholars have detected philosophical dimensions in Callimachus' *Hymn to Zeus*.[21] Zeus, for the Stoics, symbolized the eternal and omnipresent rational principle governing the world.[22] Indeed, they favored the popular etymology that connected the two forms of Zeus' name (Ζην- and Δι-) with the fact that all things live (ζῆν) through (διά) him.[23] Though more obviously playful, Callimachus' *Hymn to Zeus* similarly touches upon these ideas, featuring etymological puns on Zeus' name throughout the narrative.[24] In this hymn, however, Callimachus makes the nature of Zeus subject to questioning, presenting the anthropomorphized god of traditional myth as well as hinting at Zeus the abstract, eternal principle. For this reason, Cuypers observes, "So, while on the surface level of the text Callimachus the

---

[20] Of the Euphonists, whose ideas are preserved in Philodemus' *On Poems*, Heracleodorus argued that the poet's task was not the construction of thought, but the arrangement of words. Pausimachus of Miletus focused on good sound alone. For discussion of these critics, see Janko 2000:143–189 and Gutzwiller 2010:346–354, who finds examples of Euphonist principles in Hellenistic poetry. See also Acosta-Hughes and Stephens 2002:242–244 and Romano 2011:318–322 for discussion of sound in Callimachus.

[21] See, for instance, Kirichenko 2012:188–200.

[22] Such ideas found expression in the *Hymn to Zeus* (preserved in Stobaeus *Anthology* 1.1.12) of the Stoic philosopher Cleanthes (333–262 BCE), as well as the beginning of Aratus *Phaenomena* (1–18). See discussion of these two passages in James 1972:28–38. It is not certain who influenced whom.

[23] For this etymology, see Plato *Cratylus* 396a–c and Chrysippus *Stoicorum Veterum Fragmenta* 2.1062.

[24] The following words, which contain the elements δι-, ζην-, or both, can be viewed as puns on Zeus' names: δίζητο ("searched," 16), Ἀζηνίς (another name for Arcadia, 20), διεροῦ ("moist," 24), δίχα ("in two," 31), διέστη ("was separated," 31), and διάτριχα ("three ways," 61). See Hopkinson 1984:141–142.

narrator embarks on a mythological discussion about the birthplace of Zeus, Callimachus the author allusively introduces theological, cosmological, and ontological—in short, philosophical—questions that make the narrator's strictly mythological frame of reference appear rather naive, and the idea that 'Zeus' might not be the short-fused autocratic philanderer of traditional mythology appear conceivable after all."[25]

Associated with such philosophical questions about the nature of Zeus, moreover, is a political dimension. Just as Zeus establishes order in heaven, so too do kings, such as the Ptolemies, enact order on earth. Consequently, "kings are from Zeus" (ἐκ δὲ Διὸς βασιλῆες), as the narrator states at 79, quoting verbatim the Hesiodic maxim (*Theogony* 96).[26] Indeed, a few lines later, the narrator mentions the current king with ἔοικε δὲ τεκμήρασθαι / ἡμετέρῳ μεδέοντι ("it is reasonable to judge by our ruler," 85–86). Although Callimachus does not specify which Ptolemaic monarch is this ruler, Clauss has assembled evidence to support Ptolemy II. For example, Clauss observes a parallel between Zeus' triumph over Poseidon and Hades (58–59) and Ptolemy II's acquisition of the Egyptian throne over his half-brother, Ptolemy Ceraunus, the son of Ptolemy I's previous wife Eurydice.[27] Furthermore, Clauss interprets allusions to the *Homeric Hymn to Hermes* as reflecting this internecine strife as well as reconciliation.[28] Just as Apollo forgives his brother Hermes for the theft of the cattle (*Homeric Hymn to Hermes* 496–520), so too does Ptolemy II rightfully deserve the throne.

Through this dense web of literary quotations and allusions, Callimachus enables his *Hymn to Zeus* to touch upon a variety of issues. A mythological dilemma provides the starting point to interrogate the tensions between truth and falsehood in poetry, the nature of divinity, and finally the relationship between divinity and kingship.[29] The narrator, though ironic and doubtful,

---

[25] Cuypers 2004b:97.

[26] See Reinsch-Werner 1976:61–63.

[27] Clauss 1986:160. He, of course, notes that this parallel is not exact, as Ptolemy II's ascension was marked by contention. Moreover, since the poem centers around Zeus' birth, Clauss 1986:158 argues that the occasion is Ptolemy II's birthday, which coincided with the Basileia as well as Ptolemy's ascension to joint rule with Ptolemy I in 285/4 BCE.

[28] For an analysis of these allusions, see Clauss 1986:161–166. For instance, ἑσπέριος κεῖνός γε τελεῖ τά κεν ἦρι νοήσῃ / ἑσπέριος τὰ μέγιστα, τὰ μείονα δ', εὖτε νοήσῃ ("in the evening he [our king] achieves what he thinks of in the morning, in the evening the greatest things, the lesser things, whenever he thinks of them," 87–88) echoes the birth of Hermes at the beginning of the *Homeric Hymn*: ἠῶος γεγονὼς μέσῳ ἤματι ἐγκιθάριζεν / ἑσπέριος βοῦς κλέψεν ἑκηβόλου Ἀπόλλωνος ("after he was born at dawn, he played the cithara in the middle of the day and in the evening stole the cattle of far-shooting Apollo," 17–18). Lüddecke 1998:30n58 detects irony in the triple parallel between Zeus, the Ptolemaic king, and Hermes, the god of lies.

[29] In accordance with Egyptian custom, rulers were divine. See Koenen 1993:25–115 for a discussion of Ptolemaic kingship, which involved an amalgamation of Greek and Egyptian ideas. Ptolemy

nevertheless affirms the authority of "Zeus" and by implication his earthly counterpart Ptolemy II.[30] Both monarchs exert their authority to make their will become reality.

2. Criteria of Truth

This reality of the Hellenistic period, as shaped by the monarchs and the intellectuals working in a cultural milieu, profoundly influenced the poetic production during this time and the texts' relationship to truth. Just as rulers drew poets and philosophers from all parts of the world to enrich their courts,[31] so too did poets derive source material from a myriad of fonts. The increasing proliferation of prose texts, some of which were produced by poets, provided as much material as did the poetic sources.[32] The scholarly centers established by the monarchs contained the producers and the results of such activity. Indeed, with its immense collection, the Library of Alexandria was a physical manifestation of the nexuses that connected past and present of the disparate places throughout the Hellenistic world.[33]

Such an accumulation of sources, however, does not simplify the task of judging truth and falsehood. Rather, as is exemplified by Callimachus' dilemma in the *Hymn to Zeus*, it only entangles the issue. When challenged by contradictory sources, how can one determine which piece of information is correct? That is, by what means can a person judge truth and falsehood, whether in dealing with a sense perception, a mythological narrative, or a reading in the text of Homer? In all cases, some standard must be applied to distinguish the real from the spurious, the being from the seeming. In philosophic terms, such a standard was called a criterion (κριτήριον) or a canon (κανών). While the latter referred to a physical stick (straightedge), it, like κριτήριον, could encompass any means of judgment.[34] Epicurus, for instance, wrote a work entitled the *Canon* (Diogenes Laertius 10.14). The Skeptic Timon (325–235 BCE), in a fragment of the *Indalmoi*

II founded a cult for himself and his sister wife Arsinoe II in 272/271 BCE (Fraser 1972.1:215; 2.364–365).

[30] As Hunter and Fuhrer 2002:174 note, "The learned poet can have lots of fun with the absurdities of traditional stories and the inconsistent tales of poets, and yet still expound the realities of power."

[31] For a concise overview of the relationship between literature and kings in the Hellenistic period, see Strootman 2010:32–45; 2017. See also Weber 2011:225–244.

[32] The *Suda* (κ 227), for instance, attests to Callimachus' production of prose treatises. One of the listed titles is *Arcadia*, and it is likely that Callimachus could access similar information for the Arcadian section in the *Hymn to Zeus*. See also Stephens 1998:174.

[33] See Fraser 1972.1:320–335 and Stephens 2010:54–56.

[34] See Striker 1996c:24 [1974].

(842 *SH*), mentions a "straight canon of truth" (ἀληθείης ὀρθὸν ... κανόνα, 2). This concept of a criterion in fact elicited debate among the Hellenistic philosophic schools. Various thinkers grappled with whether a definite criterion of truth exists, and if so, what it is.[35]

Using this notion of a criterion as a heuristic tool, in this study I will explore how five Hellenistic poets represent the task of assessing truth and falsehood. Amid the accumulation and organization of new information, how can one reconcile the problems that arise when contemplating the ordered and the chaotic, the certain and the doubtful, and finally what is apparent and what is hidden? As I will demonstrate, all these issues manifest in the following five Hellenistic poems: Aratus' *Phaenomena*, Nicander's *Theriaca*, Callimachus' *Aetia*, Apollonius of Rhodes' *Argonautica*, and Lycophron's *Alexandra*.

Several reasons motivate the selection of these five works for extended analysis. First, these five poems display a variety of scientific, geographic, and ethnographic information integrated with overtly mythical material. In many cases, the myths of these five poems are aetiological, treating the remote past to rationalize the observable present. Both Aratus and Nicander, for instance, incorporate myths in their scientific catalogues of perceivable phenomena. Conversely, mythic narration predominates the *Aetia, Argonautica, and Alexandra*. The *Aetia* catalogues myths explaining cults and rituals, and the *Argonautica* deals with the Argonauts' expedition for the Golden Fleece. The *Alexandra* encompasses the events before and after the Trojan War, as recounted by the prophetess Cassandra in a prophecy. At the same time, these poems, like Callimachus' *Hymn to Zeus*, include reflections on the validity of the material or the sources (e.g. Callimachus *Aetia* fr. 75.76). Such reflections encourage the reader to consider truth and falsehood of this material. Furthermore, the sizable length of these five poems is conducive for analyzing changes in the treatment of truth and falsehood over the course of each work. Finally, aside from the fragmentary *Aetia*, these poems are extant, thereby facilitating close readings of the poetic language, allusions, personae, and myths. These elements combined, I argue, embody various methods of discovery and evaluation regarding truth about the past, present, and future, about birth, change, and death.

Thus, the aim of this monograph is not merely to catalogue and analyze notions of truth and falsehood in a selection of poems but ultimately to explicate the processes of tackling uncertainty, confronting authority, and detecting patterns of information amid a state of accumulation. In all of this, the philosophical concept of a criterion is a shorthand for conveying these processes of evaluation. Indeed, the various criteria proposed by the Hellenistic schools

---

[35] Concise overviews of these debates can be found in Striker 1996e:150–165 [1990] and Gerson 2009:90–111.

entail mental processes. Epicurus, for instance, listed perceptions (αἰσθήσεις), preconceptions (προλήψεις), and feelings (πάθη) as the criteria for truth (Diogenes Laertius 10.31). Of the three, the first criterion, αἰσθήσεις, receives the most emphasis in later reception of Epicurean epistemology. Indeed, later sources attribute to Epicurus the idea that "all perceptions are true."[36] As the raw data about the world, they are not subject to distortion, which comes only with the addition of opinion.[37] The Stoics, acknowledging the potential for false impressions, specified the φαντασία καταληπτική ("apprehensible presentation") as the criterion for truth.[38] Sextus Empiricus defines the apprehensible presentation as "one caused by an existing object and imaged and stamped in the subject in accordance with that existing object, of such a kind as could not be derived from a non-existent object"(*Against the Mathematicians* 7.248; Trans: Bury). In other words, this presentation must derive from something real, not from a dream or hallucination. This criterion, however, also involves a process, as one must recognize and assent to this presentation (*Against the Mathematicians* 7.151).[39] Such assent in turn leads to apprehension (κατάληψις), the intermediary step between opinion (δόξα) and knowledge (ἐπιστήμη).[40]

[36] These later sources include Plutarch *Against Colotes* 1109b, Aristocles in Eusebius *Preparation for the Gospel* 14.20.5 and Sextus Empiricus *Against the Mathematicians* 7.203–204 and 8.9. However, the wording varies among the authors. For example, Plutarch records the statement that all presentations (φαντασίας) that come through perception (δι' αἰσθήσεως) are true (ἀληθεῖς), and *Against the Mathematicians* 8.9 records the claim that sensation always tells the truth. For the controversy whether ἀληθεῖς means "true" or "real," see Taylor 1980:111 and Striker 1996b:80 [1974]. Epicurus stated that all perception is without reason (ἄλογος) and incapable of memory (μνήμης οὐδεμιᾶς δεκτική). Moreover, the sensations cannot refute one another due to their equal strength (Diogenes Laertius 10.31).

[37] Opinion, in turn, can be judged as true or false (*Against the Mathematicians* 8.9). For an opinion, the criterion of truth is confirmation (ἐπιμαρτύρησις) and no non-confirmation (οὐκ ἀντιμαρτύρησις), while a lack of confirmation and non-confirmation characterize falsehood (*Against the Mathematicians* 7.216).

[38] Diogenes Laertius 7.54 accredits Chrysippus, Antipater, and Apollodorus with this theory. For discussion of the φαντασία καταληπτική and the Academic Skeptics' attacks against this theory (e.g. Arcesilaus; see Sextus Empiricus *Against the Mathematicians* 7.154), see Frede 1987b:151–176. He uses the translation "cognitive impression." Other criteria favored by Stoics include νοῦς ("mind"), αἴσθησις ("perception"), ὄρεξις ("desire"), ἐπιστήμη ("knowledge"), προλήψεις ("preconceptions"), and ὀρθὸς λόγος ("right reason").

[39] As Sandbach 1971:19 points out, this theory raises the question of how the agent can recognize and assent to this presentation. See also Annas 1980, who analyzes the φαντασία καταληπτική in terms of a coherence interpretation and a correspondence interpretation. According to her (87), the former interpretation stresses the act of apprehension, whereas the latter emphasizes the presentation itself. Finding issues in both interpretations, however, Annas concludes (101–104) that this Stoic theory of the criterion of truth failed to consider the Stoic distinction between "the true" (τὸ ἀληθές) and "truth" (ἡ ἀλήθεια). Sextus Empiricus describes the Stoic distinction at *Outlines of Pyrrhonism* 2.81–83.

[40] Cicero *Academica* 1.41 attributes this threefold distinction to Zeno.

Although such criteria seem most applicable for elementary sensory experiences,[41] several factors support applying the philosophic concept of the criterion to exploring the five chosen Hellenistic poems. Indeed, sense perception, despite its potential fallibility, remains a foundation for what constitutes knowledge, particularly scientific information. At the same time, Hellenistic poetry is replete with descriptions of sensations.[42] Several of these descriptions surpass archaic and classical examples in detail and frequency. For instance, in the third book of the *Argonautica*, Apollonius of Rhodes devotes several lines to describing the painful symptoms of Medea's love for Jason (e.g. 3.286–298; 3.755–765).[43] Likewise, Callimachus dwells on the symptoms of Cydippe's malady at *Aetia* fr. 75.12–19. Along with these notable examples of physical suffering, in the *Phaenomena* and *Theriaca*, sense perception is inextricably linked with the scientific subject matter. In cataloguing the constellations and weather signs in the *Phaenomena*, Aratus frequently highlights the act of seeing (e.g. *Phaenomena* 199) and the relative visibility of these signs (e.g. *Phaenomena* 94). For his subject matter in the *Theriaca*, Nicander fixates on the gruesome symptoms of snake-bites (e.g. the bite of the female blood-letting snake, 298–307). Finally, as befits her preternatural prophetic ability, Cassandra in the *Alexandra* sees (e.g. λεύσσω at 52, 86, 216) and even hears the events (253–256) in the prophecy she utters.

Along with these references to sense perceptions in the studied poems, the previously discussed *Hymn to Zeus* shatters a sharp delineation between the two spheres of poetry and philosophy. Philosophic concepts on the nature of divinity can easily slither into verse, and indeed, as I will discuss below, the Stoics viewed poetry as the preferred medium for articulating such information. Finally, the notion of criteria is not foreign to poetry. Amid its shifting functions over time, poetry has always offered itself subject to critique, not just regarding truth and falsehood, but also moral appropriateness and its ability to induce pleasure.

The variety of these views and their subsequent influences on Hellenistic poetry necessitate a condensed excursus into the past. Beginning with Homer and ending with Plato, Aristotle, and the Stoics, I will track how both poets and critics articulated and critiqued the relationship between poetry and truth and falsehood. A judgment of a poem's truth-value simultaneously involves a judgment of truth itself. Along with attesting to the relevance of criteria for poetry,

---

[41] On this fact applied to the Stoic apprehensible presentation, see Frede 1987b:166. He, however, argues that the apprehensible presentation allows for general ideas, and it is for this reason it is the criterion of truth.

[42] For an analysis of sensation in Hellenistic poetry, see Sistakou 2014a:135–156. Specifically, she sees a minimization of the cognitively based emotions preferred by Aristotle in favor of sensation. For instance, in the *Argonautica*, Hypsipyle's love for Jason is motivated by sight (1.774–780).

[43] For discussion of these passages, see Hunter 1989:129–131; 178–180.

such an overview will be useful considering the consistent allusiveness of the Hellenistic poets. In rejecting the Homeric version of Zeus' ascent to power, Callimachus engages in a form of critique with his predecessors, whom he dubs as not "entirely truthful" (οὐ πάμπαν ἀληθέες ἦσαν ἀοιδοί, 60).[44] In the overview of the Hellenistic poets' predecessors, moreover, I will discuss the vocabulary for truth and falsehood. Indeed, evaluating truth and falsehood involves determining what they are in the first place.

3. Background

3.1 Truth and falsehood in early poetry

3.1.1 Homer

The issue of truth and falsehood in Homer's two poems, the *Iliad* and the *Odyssey*, must be regarded as two separate questions: the veracity of the poet and that of the characters he depicts. Throughout the two epics, various characters explicitly emphasize the validity of their utterances. In these contexts, several words denote "true" or "truth": ἔτυμος, ἐτήτυμος, ἐτεός, ἀληθής, νημερτής, and ἀτρεκής. As Krischer observes, the first three words (ἔτυμος, ἐτήτυμος, and ἐτεός) refer to "the real in contrast with the unreal."[45] For instance, at *Odyssey* 19.562–567, Penelope describes the dreams emanating from the Gate of Horn as those "that achieve real things" (ἔτυμα κραίνουσι, 19.567). By contrast, dreams from the Gate of Ivory bring words that will be unfulfilled (ἔπε' ἀκράαντα φέροντες, 19.565) and thus will not correspond to reality.

While the group of related words ἔτυμος, ἐτήτυμος, and ἐτεός covers objective reality, ἀλήθεια and its adjective ἀληθής deal with subjective truth as expressed in oral communication.[46] In particular, characters strive to tell or learn the entire truth, such when Priam asks Hermes about the condition of Hector's body: ἄγε δή μοι πᾶσαν ἀληθείην κατάλεξον ("come now and tell me the whole truth," *Iliad* 24.407). Similarly, νημερτής and ἀτρεκής appear in

---

[44] For the ambiguity of this phrase, see Goldhill 1986:29. The translation "not at all true" is also possible.

[45] Krischer 1965:166.

[46] See Krischer 1965:163, who argues for the role of perception in ἀλήθεια. Cf. Snell 1978:100 and Cole 1983:9. These scholars reject Heidegger's (1927:212) interpretation of ἀλήθεια as *Unverborgenheit* and Detienne's as "non-forgetting" (1967:24–25). Cole 1983:12 rightfully emphasizes the communicative aspect of ἀλήθεια. Aside from one place in a simile (*Iliad* 12.433), the substantive adjective ἀληθέα and the noun ἀληθείη in Homer occur with verbs of speaking, such as ἀγορεύω (*Odyssey* 3.254 and 16.61), μυθέομαι (*Iliad* 6.382; *Odyssey* 11.507, 14.125, 17.15, and 18.342), and καταλέγω (*Odyssey* 7.297, 16.226, 17.108, 21.212, and 22.420).

contexts of oral communication, with νημερτής often connected to prophecy.[47] Aside from their uses in oral communication, ἀλήθεια, νημερτής, and ἀτρεκής share an important commonality: all are expressed via negation. What falls under "truth" or "true" is something not overlooked / forgotten (ἀλήθεια), not missed (νημερτής), and undistorted (ἀτρεκής).[48] In this framework, falsehood (ψεῦδος) constitutes the presence of error, manipulation, or omission, whether intentional or not.[49] Odysseus, for instance, frequently utters falsehoods purposefully, as when he conceals his identity to Penelope in *Odyssey* 19: ἴσκε ψεύδεα πολλὰ λέγων ἐτύμοισιν ὁμοῖα ("he feigned, saying many falsehoods like real things," 19.203).[50]

Despite specifying the truth and falsehood of his characters' utterances, Homer offers no explicit statement regarding the veracity of his own words. To some scholars, the Homeric poet's relationship with the Muses guarantees the truth of his poems.[51] As the daughters of Memory, the Muses supply the poet with accurate information about the deeds of men and gods.[52] Aside from the invocations in both poems (*Iliad* 1.1; *Odyssey* 1.1), this exchange is clear in the poet's request for their aid before the Catalogue of Ships (*Iliad* 2.484–487). Their omniscience counterbalances human limitation: ὑμεῖς γὰρ θεαί ἐστε, πάρεστέ τε, ἴστέ τε πάντα, / ἡμεῖς δὲ κλέος οἶον ἀκούομεν, οὐδέ τι ἴδμεν ("for you are goddesses and are present and know everything, while we hear only report and know nothing," 2.485–486). Similarly, in *Odyssey* 8, the poet Demodocus' relationship with the gods enables him to sing about the events of the Trojan War with utmost accuracy (8.487–491).[53] Indeed, Odysseus comments that Demodocus sang as though he were there himself or had heard from another (*Odyssey* 8.491). In the oral society portrayed in the poems, the attribution of truth to the bard makes sense. A poet like Demodocus ensures the preservation of social memory.

---

[47] For νημερτής with verbs of speaking, see *Iliad* 14.470; *Odyssey* 3.101, 4.314, 4.331, 4.642, 12.112, 15.263, and 22.166. Proteus is called νημερτής (e.g. *Odyssey* 4.384). In Homer, the adverb ἀτρεκέως accompanies the imperative κατάλεξον. See *Iliad* 10.384, 10.405, 24.380, and 24.656; *Odyssey* 1.169, 1.206, 1.224, 4.486, 8.572, 11.140, 11.170, 11.370, 15.383, 16.137, and 24.256.

[48] For etymological analyses of these words, see Chantraine 2009:68 (νημερτής), 129 (ἀτρεκής), and 594 (ἀλήθεια).

[49] Luther 1935:80–90 and Levet 1976:201. Carlisle 1999:90–91 diverges from this observation by arguing that ψευδ- words in Homer refer to variant versions that do not correspond to the material presented as true in the poem. As she observes, characters in Homer tell ψεύδεα in agonistic situations for personal benefits.

[50] See Walcot 1977:1–19 for an analysis of Odysseus' lies.

[51] Detienne 1967:13–16, Rösler 1980:290, 292–293, and Puelma 1989:73.

[52] For discussion of the relationship between the Muses and poets, see Murray 1981:89–91.

[53] For discussions of this passage, specifically the meaning of the phrase λίην ... κατὰ κόσμον (*Odyssey* 8.489), see Adkins 1972:16–17 and Walsh 1984:8–10.

Several objections, however, destabilize the equation between the Homeric poet and truth. As isolated passages, the invocation in *Iliad* 2 and the scene in *Odyssey* 8 do not necessarily speak to the poet's interaction with the Muses throughout the epics.[54] Additionally, some scholars downplay the relevance of truth for Homer, emphasizing rather the importance of pleasure and enchantment.[55] In the case of Demodocus, only Odysseus, who was directly involved in the events, can judge the validity of the words, whereas the rest of the audience is entranced by their beauty and the poet's virtuosity. At the same time, the situation of Odysseus in the *Odyssey* problematizes the veracity of the poet. Not only does Odysseus narrate a large chunk of the poem (books 9–12), Alcinous likens his virtuosity to that of a poet (*Odyssey* 11.367–369).[56] Does this comparison imply the presence of deception in Homeric poetry? Indeed, if the poet boasts skills like the arch-liar Odysseus, how are we the audience to judge?

3.1.2 Hesiod

In the proem of the *Theogony*, Hesiod makes the Muses comment on the truth and falsehood of their words. Appearing to Hesiod as he was tending sheep on Mount Helicon (21–22), they proclaim:[57]

ποιμένες ἄγραυλοι, κάκ᾽ ἐλέγχεα, γαστέρες οἶον,
ἴδμεν ψεύδεα πολλὰ λέγειν ἐτύμοισιν ὁμοῖα,
ἴδμεν δ᾽ εὖτ᾽ ἐθέλωμεν ἀληθέα γηρύσασθαι.

Rustic shepherds, base reproaches, mere bellies. We know how to say many falsehoods like real things, and we know, whenever we wish, how to utter the truth.

Hesiod *Theogony* 26–28

These famous and enigmatic lines have elicited a multitude of interpretations. Scholars disagree about their exact meaning and overall significance for Hesiod's work and for poetry in general.[58] Clear, however, is the distinction between the addressed shepherds and the powerful Muses. After hurling the insults "base

---

[54] According to Bowie 1993:13–14, for instance, the difficulty of recounting all the Greek leaders' names constitutes a special circumstance.
[55] See Pratt 1993:53. See also Halliwell 2011:55. Walsh 1984:13–14 sees pleasure and truth as inextricably linked in the Homeric poems. Ford 1992:53–55 connects the pleasure of Homeric poetry with its vividness.
[56] For this problem and the bibliography, see Goldhill 1991:47–49.
[57] See West 1966:158–161 for a summary of views regarding whether this was a "genuine" epiphany.
[58] For instance, Pucci 1977:13 interprets the Muses' claim in 27 to symbolize the inevitability of distortion caused by discourse. Cf. Ferrari 1988 for a refutation of Pucci's findings.

reproaches" and "mere bellies,"[59] the Muses express their power as a kind of knowledge with the repetition of ἴδμεν ("we know") in 27–28. Although this association of the Muses with total knowledge has a Homeric precedent in the *Iliad* 2 invocation (2.485), the Hesiodic Muses include the telling of many false things as a part of their repertoire. These ψεύδεα, moreover, are described as "like real things" (ἐτύμοισιν ὁμοῖα, 27), an expression recalling *Odyssey* 19.203. Ambiguity, however, suffuses the phrasing in the Hesiodic boast, which lacks the context of the *Odyssey* passage. What kinds of things constitute falsehoods like the real things?[60] Does this similarity involve external appearance or some other shared quality?[61]

Additional questions arise from the second portion of the boast. The Muses, when they wish, can speak the truth (ἀληθέα, 28). What kind of poetry, however, falls under this rubric, and what kind qualifies as falsehoods like real things? Since Hesiod promises to tell his brother Perses ἐτήτυμα in the *Works and Days* (10), some scholars have grouped Hesiod in the camp of truth.[62] Nowhere, however, in the ensuing *Theogony* does Hesiod specify the truth or falsehood of the material learned from the Muses. Instead, he stresses the curative effects of the Muses' song. They delight the mind of their father (*Theogony* 51), and their mother Memory bore them as "forgetfulness from troubles and a rest from woes" (*Theogony* 55). Moreover, they empower their servants (singers) to make mortals forget pain and suffering (*Theogony* 99–103). As was the case with

[59] Svenbro 1976:57–59 reads "mere bellies" as referring to poets who lie because of their desire for profit. Thalmann 1984:146 connects "mere bellies" to the low status of the shepherds living in the wild. Katz and Volk 2000 posit a reference to prophecy, specifically to the type in which a demon possesses a person's belly. They suggest that "mere bellies" represents Hesiod's role as "receptacle for the Muses' inspiration" (127).

[60] Verdenius 1972:234 takes this phrase to mean "deceptive pictures." Pratt 1993:110 proposes that ψεύδεα πολλὰ ... ἐτύμοισιν ὁμοῖα equates to "plausible fictions." See also Bowie 1993:21.

[61] Heiden 2007:155, for instance, disputes the translation of ὁμοῖος as "resembling," arguing that the adjective in Homer never denotes exact likeness, but a shared quality. According to Heiden, Hesiod does not clarify in what respect lies share a quality with reality, thus contributing to the ambiguity of the passage. Heiden prefers the translation "lies equivalent to truth [sc. somehow]." His analysis (170) proposes that the phrase "half is more than the whole" at *Works and Days* 40 qualifies as such a lie. The phrase, while literally false, functions as a "truth." Nagy 2010:153–167, however, assembles usages of ὁμοῖος in Homer to argue that the word in Hesiod means "looking like."

[62] See Luther 1935:125, Puelma 1989:74–75, and Finkelberg 1998:157, who envision a polemical contrast between Hesiod (truth) and Homer (falsehood). West 1966:162 refutes this argument based on the assumption that no Greek ever considered the Homeric poems as fiction. Stroh 1976:110 dismisses a polemical reading by arguing that the scholarly designation of Hesiod as a "didactic poet" does not find support in the ancient evidence. Stroh's analysis (106) considers lying a positive trait and finds in Hesiod's poetry a mixture of truth and falsehoods. For a refutation of Stroh's views, particularly the idea that Hesiod is purposely including lies, see Neitzel 1980:400.

Homer, this emphasis on pleasure and the therapeutic effects of song has led some scholars to argue that truth is not Hesiod's prime concern.[63] Ledbetter in fact contends that the Muses' plausible falsehoods prevent both the poet and the audience from distinguishing the truth.[64] While such an observation may not necessarily apply to the poet, we can see the Muses' boast as twofold in its effects. Despite explicitly proclaiming the possibility of their falsehood, they offer no clarification on how to determine what is false and what is true.

3.1.3 Pindar

Pindar laces his epinician odes with explicit claims to truth, as well as rejections of lies and falsehood.[65] For instance, at the beginning of *Olympian* 10, he invokes Truth (Ἀλάθεια) to ward off the blame of lying.[66] By disassociating his poetry from falsehood, Pindar establishes the authenticity of his praise, which strives to glorify athletes and heroes appropriately.[67] False praise, on the other hand, does not accurately reflect its subject, as Pindar in *Nemean* 7 observes in the case of Odysseus: ἐγὼ δὲ πλέον' ἔλπομαι / λόγον Ὀδυσσέος ἢ πάθαν / διὰ τὸν ἀδυεπῆ γενέσθ' Ὅμηρον ("I expect that the story about Odysseus has become greater than his experience because of sweet-speaking Homer," 20–21). Moreover, this embellished portrayal of Odysseus has eclipsed the fame of Ajax, whom Pindar deems worthier of remembrance.[68] Thus, Pindar shows the damaging effects false praise can wreak, both in rewarding the unworthy and depriving the commendable.

While Pindar frequently addresses truth and falsehood in terms of praise, he also exhibits concern about the veracity of mythological narrative. In *Olympian* 1, he dismisses the story that the gods ate Pelops, attributing the tale to a hateful neighbor (τις αὐτίκα φθονερῶν γειτόνων, 47). Unlike his predecessors, Pindar refuses to depict gluttonous gods: ἐμοὶ δ' ἄπορα γαστρίμαργον μακάρων τιν' εἰπεῖν· ἀφίσταμαι ("I cannot say one of the blessed gods is gluttonous; I stand away," 52). By denying this version, Pindar seeks to shield the majesty of the gods from this hateful lie. Yet the story is a lie because it portrays

---

[63] Heath 1985:262–263.

[64] Ledbetter 2003:44. Belfiore 1985:55, however, notes that not even the Muses know the entire truth. Since they were born after Zeus' succession, they could not have witnessed firsthand the events narrated in the *Theogony*.

[65] See Komornicka 1972 for an overview of truth and falsehood vocabulary in Pindar.

[66] ὦ Μοῖσ', ἀλλὰ σὺ καὶ θυγάτηρ / Ἀλάθεια Διός, ὀρθᾷ χερί / ἐρύκετον ψευδέων / ἐνιπὰν ἀλιτόξενον ("But come Muse, you and daughter of Zeus, Truth, with a correcting hand ward off the charge of harming a guest friend with lies," Pindar *Olympian* 10.4–5).

[67] Park 2013:17–36 argues for a generic connection between praise and truth in Pindar's poetry. Pindar does not want to praise beyond what is right (καιρός). See Pindar *Pythian* 10.4.

[68] See Pindar *Nemean* 8.24–35.

the gods in a negative light.[69] Pindar, moreover, makes a distinction between a true account and stories embellished with variegated lies.[70]

His practice of evaluating his material corresponds to his role as a prophet for the Muses (fr. 150 Snell).[71] Acting as the intermediary through which the Muses' knowledge reaches a mortal audience, he interprets and filters their words. In this role, Pindar aims not only to portray gods, men, and heroes as is befitting, but also to avoid showing examples of criminal behavior. For instance, in *Nemean* 5, he refuses to elaborate on the unjust deed of Phocus, stating that the "whole exact truth is not more profitable when she shows her face."[72] Thus, in suppressing the full truth, Pindar transforms the traditional ἀλήθεια into a new kind of truth: one that he ultimately decides is morally suitable for his audience. Under this new ἀλήθεια, only the worthy are commemorated, while criminal and insignificant deeds are consigned to oblivion.[73]

3.1.4 Parmenides

A new notion of ἀλήθεια plays a central role in Parmenides' hexameter philosophic poem *On Nature*.[74] Aided by a goddess (DK 28 B 1.22), he embarks on a journey to learn of the "unmoved heart of well-rounded Truth" (Ἀληθείης εὐκυκλέος ἀτρεμὲς ἦτορ, DK 28 B 1.29). Contrasted with the truth are the opinions of men, in which there is no genuine belief (DK 28 B 1.29–30). Additionally, he refers to the road of *Peitho* ("Persuasion"), which attends the road of Truth (DK 28 B 2.3–4). As Cherubin has argued, Parmenides creates a new conception of ἀλήθεια.[75] No longer does a person automatically receive the truth through divine revelation or personal experience. Instead, they must exert mental effort and understand the principles of being (τὸ ἐόν, DK 28 B 8.3–9) to discover ἀλήθεια, which has now gained the meaning of reality. As a result, ἀλήθεια can

---

[69] Ledbetter 2003:70.

[70] ἦ θαύματα πολλά, καί πού τι καὶ βροτῶν / φάτις ὑπὲρ τὸν ἀλαθῆ λόγον / δεδαιδαλμένοι ψεύδεσι ποικίλοις / ἐξαπατῶντι μῦθοι ("Yes, there are many wonders, but then too, I suppose, in men's rumors, stories are beyond the true account and deceive, embellished with variegated lies," *Olympian* 1.28–29).

[71] Ledbetter 2003:62.

[72] οὔ τοι ἅπασα κερδίων / φαίνοισα πρόσωπον ἀλάθει' ἀτρεκής (Pindar *Nemean* 5.16–17).

[73] Walsh 1984:60–61.

[74] Parmenides' poem has been divided into the *Proem* (DK 28 B 1.1–28), *Aletheia* (DK 28 B 1.29–8.49), and *Doxa* (DK 28 B 8.50 on). Interpretation of this difficult poem varies widely, as scholars debate the implications of Parmenides' principles. For some sample interpretations, see Tarán 1965:175–201 and Coxon 2009:20–22.

[75] Cherubin 2009:66. See also Long 2011:29.

paradoxically refer to what is concealed from human perception, as well as what is revealed through dialogue or sensory experience.

3.5.5 Summary

In this overview spanning Homer to Parmenides, I have tackled separate but related questions. What are truth and falsehood? How can they be discerned? And finally, what is the relationship between poetry and truth? From this selective—albeit representative—sample, some broader trends are apparent. While initially limited to oral subjective truth in Homer, ἀλήθεια and its adjective ἀληθής assume new senses. Aside from the meaning of "reality," ἀληθής can mean "truthful" or "sincere" when applied to a person."[76] This transformation in meaning coincides with ἔτυμος, ἐτήτυμος, and ἐτεός dissipating from Attic prose usage.[77] At the same time, new words take on the sense of truth and accuracy. ἀκριβής, for instance, supplants ἀτρεκής,[78] while ὀρθός ("straight") and forms from the verb εἰμί ("to be") connote truth and reality.[79] Falsehood similarly undergoes some changes in meaning, acquiring a moral sense when lying constitutes a fault.[80] Indeed, in his epinician poetry, Pindar makes morality central to discerning what is false and what is true. At the same time, in specifying how he discerns the truth, Pindar represents a significant divergence from the practices of Homer and Hesiod. While all three interact with the Muses, only Pindar asserts the confidence to interpret their material. Homer and Hesiod, by contrast, do not overtly display the same level of authorial discernment, even though the Hesiodic Muses hint at the possibility of falsehood. Similarly, Parmenides engages with a divine authority figure, yet one who presents true reality as the object of sustained rational inquiry.

3.2 Sixth- and fifth-century criticism

Homeric and Hesiodic poetry stimulated critical reaction in the sixth and fifth centuries BCE. In this time, poetry, especially that of Homer, occupied a

---

[76] See Levet 2008:143–144, who cites Thucydides 5.45.3 and Herodotus 8.142.5 as examples.

[77] In Ionic prose, however, Democritus features the substantive form ἐτεή in his writings (DK 68 B 9 and DK 68 B 117).

[78] See Levet 2008:297–312. Thucydides, for instance, at 1.22 announces that he will narrate each subject with accuracy (ἀκριβείᾳ) as much as he is able.

[79] Levet 2008:273–280, 282–297. For instance, ὀρθός can mean "exactly" (Aristophanes *Clouds* 228, Aeschylus *Eumenides* 584, and Herodotus 6.53.1). For ὄντως as "in fact," see Aristophanes *Wasps* 997 and *Clouds* 86.

[80] Levet 2008:319. For instance, in Sophocles' *Philoctetes* Neoptolemus assumes that telling lies is shameful (108). To counter this assumption, Odysseus argues that deception can have useful effects (109–111).

central position in the education of elite citizens.[81] As the material memorized by children, Homer's poetry was expected to be morally appropriate and offer some forms of truths. Yet Homer and Hesiod's depiction of fighting and philandering anthropomorphic gods provoked the censure of the thinker and poet Xenophanes (DK 21 B 11). Not only did such portrayals fail to correspond to Xenophanes' conception of the divine (DK 21 B 23),[82] they presented damaging models for human behavior. Indeed, in fragment 1 DK, he extorts symposiasts to avoid speaking of the battles of Titans, Giants, and Centaurs, dubbing these creatures "fabrications of our predecessors" (πλάσματα τῶν προτέρων, 22) and denying their usefulness (τοῖσ' οὐδὲν χρηστὸν ἔνεστι, 23).[83]

Some thinkers, however, employed allegorical interpretation to read poems as articulations of true propositions. Since allegory (ἀλληγορία) means "saying something else,"[84] it enables an interpreter to extract truth from a poem, despite the perceived falsehood of the surface meaning. For instance, the scholion on *Iliad* 20.67 records a method of interpretation that is ascribed to the sixth-century BCE Theagenes of Rhegium. By this kind of interpretation, one can view the Theomachy as a conflict between elemental forces. For instance, Apollo and Helius symbolize fire, while Poseidon and Scamander are water.[85] The passage thus serves as an expression of scientific principles, rather than a literal scene of strife among the gods. In the fifth century BCE, Metrodorus of Lampsacus analyzed heroes as parts of the universe and gods as parts of the human body.[86] Although scholars debate whether an impetus to defend Homer motivated this mode of interpretation,[87] the readings of Theagenes and Metrodorus nevertheless granted Homeric verse the potential to transmit truth.

---

[81] For a discussion of poetry in education, see Ford 2002:197–201.

[82] For Xenophanes' criticism of anthropomorphism, see DK 21 B 15 and DK 21 B 16.

[83] See Ford 2002:56 for discussion of this section.

[84] While I use the term ἀλληγορία here to refer to this type of interpretation, Plutarch (*How the Young Man Should Study Poetry* 19e–f) makes clear that ἀλληγορία was a newer term to convey ὑπόνοια ("under-meaning"). For more on ancient allegory, see Whitman 1987:14–57, Dawson 1992, Ramelli and Lucchetta 2004, and Struck 2004. Dawson 1992:3–4 distinguishes between allegorical reading and allegorical composition. See, more recently, Domaradzki 2017:301, who employs "allegory" to refer to composition and allegoresis for reading and interpretation. Kotwick 2020:1–26 maintains this terminological distinction in her argument that the analysis of Penelope's dream at *Odyssey* 19.535–552 qualifies as the earliest example of allegorical interpretation.

[85] DK 8 A 2. This scholion is attributed to Porphyry.

[86] DK 61 A 3–4. Plato at *Ion* 530 mentions Metrodorus of Lampsacus. For discussion of Metrodorus, see Richardson 2006:67–68.

[87] Tate (1929:142; 1934:105–114) argues that defending Homer was not the prime motivation of allegorical reading. Rather, thinkers used this interpretation to support their own philosophic principles. See Pfeiffer 1968:9–10 for the view that allegory was defensive. See also Morgan

This mode of allegorical interpretation was not just reserved for Homeric poetry. The Derveni Papyrus, discovered in Tomb A in Derveni (1962) and written in a script dated to the 340s BCE, includes an allegorical commentary on an Orphic hexameter cosmogonical poem.[88] The commentator remarks that "the poem is strange and riddling to people, though [Orpheus] himself did not intend to say contentious riddles but rather great things in riddles" (col. VII. 4–7). As Struck and Ford observe, this notion of riddling and enigmas is the operant term for allegory at this stage.[89] In the mind of the Derveni commentator, the Orphic poet has purposely produced enigmatic verse throughout, thereby demanding the analysis of an enlightened reader, who must probe the poem word by word to uncover meaning (col. XIII).[90] For instance, when interpreting αἰδοῖον ("reverend") as "penis," the commentator notes a connection between genitals and the sun, since both have generative power.[91] Through this type of allegorical analysis focused on linguistics, the commentator can read an existing text to match his own cosmogonic principles.

Instead of rejecting certain poetry for its falsity or employing allegorical interpretation, some critics downplay truth as a goal of poetry. For instance, the author of the *Dissoi Logoi* identifies pleasure as the poets' goal, instead of truth (90 DK 3.17). This minimizing of truth enables deception (ἀπάτη) to qualify as a virtue of poetry, rather than a fault or moral failing.[92] Indeed, the same treatise characterizes the best tragedian as the one who creates the greatest illusion of reality (90 DK 3.10). Similarly, the fifth-century BCE Sophist Gorgias attaches positive associations to deception in tragedy, stating that "the deceiver is more just than he who does not deceive, and the deceived is wiser than the one who is not deceived" (DK 82 B 23). Furthermore, in the *Helen*, Gorgias argues that a person deceived by λόγος (speech) should not deserve reproach, since speech can achieve the most divine deeds (θειότατα ἔργα, DK 82 B 11.8). To prove his point, Gorgias cites the ability of poetry, defined by him as λόγος with meter, to induce fear, pity, and longing in the audience. This occurs because the soul experiences

---

2000:64–65. Yet, as Domaradzki 2017:307 argues, apologetic and appropriative motives can coexist.

[88] Since the papyrus features information on rituals as well as cosmogonic principles, there is disagreement concerning the authorship and the primary goals of the text. For a summary of these issues, see Kouremenos, Parássoglou, and Tsantsanoglou 2006:45–59.

[89] Struck 1995:225 and Ford 1999:39.

[90] ὅτι μὲν πᾶσαν τὴν πόησιν περὶ τῶν πραγμάτων / αἰνίζεται κ[α]θ' ἔπος ἕκαστον ἀνάγκη λέγειν ("since he is speaking through the entire poem allegorically about real things, it is necessary to speak about each word in turn," Trans and Text: Kouremenos, Parássoglou, and Tsantsanoglou 2006).

[91] Kouremenos, Parássoglou, and Tsantsanoglou 2006:196. See Kotwick 2020:9–12 for a concise overview of the Derveni commentator's interpretive strategies.

[92] For discussion of ἀπάτη as a positive for Gorgias, see Rosenmeyer 1955:232 and Segal 1962:112–116.

its own response to others' situations "through the speeches" (διὰ τῶν λόγων, DK 82 B 11.9).[93] As is revealed in the subsequent section (DK 82 B 11.10), magic affects an individual in the same way, introducing ψυχῆς ἁμαρτήματα καὶ δόξης ἀπατήματα ("errors of the soul and deceptions of opinion"). In emphasizing ἀπάτη while posing this parallel between discourse and magic,[94] Gorgias exalts the affective potential of λόγος over the veracity of its content.

3.3 Philosophical views toward poetry and truth

3.3.1 Plato

The concerns of sixth- and fifth-century criticism culminate in the works of Plato. In several dialogues, his character Socrates questions poetry's relationship to the truth, the role of *mimesis*, and the effects of poetry on society and the individual. While the complexity and diversity of these dialogues render it difficult to pinpoint a single Platonic conception of poetry, we can see the arguments of Plato's Socrates as responses to the central role that poetry occupied in Greek education and culture. Despite ultimately acknowledging poetry's charm (*Republic* 607a), Socrates denies it any value in the quest for philosophic truth and knowledge.[95] Aside from attacking the poet's authority in possessing technical knowledge (*Ion*),[96] Socrates observes the impossibility of extracting unambiguous meanings from poems regarding ethical matters (*Protagoras* and *Republic* 1). In the *Republic* particularly, a concern about moral corruption underlies such critiques, as Socrates tackles the inappropriateness of traditional mythic stories (*Republic* 2) and the problematic ramifications of *mimesis* (*Republic* 3 and 10).

In two places, Socrates criticizes the use of poetry in arguments concerning ethical matters. After debating Protagoras about the syntax in a Simonides poem concerning virtue in the *Protagoras* (339a–346c), Socrates remarks upon the futility of such an exercise. Poems generate various interpretations from different people (*Protagoras* 347e), and without the poet present it is impossible

93 For analysis of this process, see Segal 1962:99–155 and Ford 2002:175–187. Ford emphasizes the materiality of this language interacting with the listener (180) and thus views Gorgias as engaging with ideas about natural science (186).
94 For discussion of this parallel, see Segal 1962:116. De Romilly 1973:158 considers Gorgias's arguments as pointing to the increased role of the poet's τέχνη in achieving these effects of poetry. Finkelberg 1998:177 views Gorgias' arguments as legitimizing fiction as an autonomous sphere.
95 For instance, Socrates at *Republic* 607b mentions an "ancient quarrel between philosophy and poetry." Kannicht 1988:5 takes the statement as evidence for the ongoing polemic of philosophy and science against poetry. For a doubtful reception of this view, see Ford 2002:46 and Most 2011:1–20. As Most (4–5) points out, Xenophanes did not target Homer and Hesiod for writing poetry, but because of the improper contents of the poetry.
96 For discussion of this dialogue's arguments, see Murray 1996:9.

to figure out what poems mean. Socrates instead prefers live debate, in which all members can offer their own thoughts and be examined. Similarly, Socrates in *Republic* 1 criticizes quoting Simonides to define justice. Simonides, Socrates argues, "spoke in riddles" (ἠνίξατο), by calling justice "returning what is owed" while intending "what is fitting for each" (ἠνίξατο ἄρα, ἦν δ' ἐγώ, ὡς ἔοικεν, ὁ Σιμωνίδης ποιητικῶς τὸ δίκαιον ὃ εἴη. διενοεῖτο μὲν γάρ, ὡς φαίνεται, ὅτι τοῦτ' εἴη δίκαιον, τὸ προσῆκον ἑκάστῳ ἀποδιδόναι, τοῦτο δὲ ὠνόμασεν ὀφειλόμενον, *Republic* 332 b–c). The adverb ποιητικῶς ("poetically") modifying ἠνίξατο suggests that Socrates considers speaking in riddles (ἠνίξατο) a characteristic of poetic language. Yet, whereas the Derveni commentator saw riddling language as a valid medium for communicating truths, Socrates implies that riddling language is antithetical to such a goal. Coupled with the impossibility of knowing the author's intentions, obscurity impedes the use of a poem in establishing a clear definition for a moral concept.

The discussion in *Republic* book two evaluates the role of poetry in terms of the content of mythological stories. The context of this discussion is the education of the future guardians of the ideal state, who require an educational curriculum that inculcates proper behavior within their souls. Due to the impressionable nature of young children's minds (377b), however, Socrates demands the elimination of the traditional stories about the gods recounted by Homer and Hesiod (377d). Such stories earn Socrates' censure not necessarily because they are false, but rather because Socrates considers them examples of "lying not well (377d)." In addition to attributing evil actions to the gods, tales such as Cronus' ascent to power (378a) offer poor models for human behavior. Hearing such stories would hinder harmony among the guardians (378c). By reflecting on the social consequences of poetry, Socrates makes morality a central concern of his criticism, subordinating the issue of truth and falsehood. Indeed, he remarks that such stories should be suppressed, even if true (378a).[97] Moreover, he rejects the possibility of poems having an "under-meaning" (ἐν ὑπονοίαις πεποιημένας), arguing that children cannot discern alternate hidden meanings (378d). Since ὑπόνοια is the word for allegory at this point, we can see Plato's Socrates as denying the practicality of an allegorical interpretation, at least for a young impressionable audience.

The third book of the *Republic* continues the evaluation of the effects of poetry on the young guardians. However, while book two discusses poetry in terms of the subject matter, the focus of book three is on how the contents of poetry are spoken. At 392d, Socrates identifies three possibilities: simple narration (ἁπλῇ διηγήσει), *mimesis* (διὰ μιμήσεως), or a mixture of the two

---

[97] In this curriculum, even lies are acceptable as long they fulfill this purpose.

(δι' ἀμφοτέρων). Unlike simple narration, where the poet speaks as himself, *mimesis* entails a poet assuming the voice of another character.[98] This assimilation of the poet with another character seems problematic to Socrates, who worries that poet who mimics many things (398a) would influence the guardians to represent characters indiscriminately. The guardians should mimic only worthy characters, not lowly individuals such as women, slaves, and cowardly men (395d–396a). In fearing this consequence of *mimesis*, Socrates again dwells on the moral dimensions of poetry. Yet the disapproval here stems from the ability of mimetic poetry to convey a semblance of reality, rather than from the falsity or immorality of traditional mythological stories. Mimetic poetry, when representing real yet unworthy humans, can corrupt the guardians.

In *Republic* book ten, Socrates returns to the problematic nature of *mimesis* by emphasizing the distinction between the products of *mimesis* and truth.[99] To make this point, Socrates constructs an analogy that contrasts a carpenter with a painter. While the carpenter builds a couch in imitation of the ideal couch, the painter produces only an imitation of an imitation (598b). The poet, who imitates human life, corresponds to the painter in the analogy and is thus three levels removed from the truth (599a). Moreover, Socrates condemns tragic poetry for arousing emotions, such as grief (605d). In inducing emotions that Socrates deems unsuitable for a man, tragedy nurtures the lowest portion of the soul, the appetitive part (606d).[100]

Although he emphasizes the corrupting effects of tragic poetry, nowhere does Plato's Socrates doubt its aesthetic charms. In fact, Socrates mentions the "honeyed Muse" (ἡδυσμένην Μοῦσαν, *Republic* 607a) and proposes allowing poetry the chance to defend herself in the *polis* (*Republic* 607d). However, it is this acknowledgment of poetry's beauty that underlies Socrates' attacks and decision to banish mimetic poetry from the *polis*. Through its charm, mimetic poetry overwhelms an audience, causing them to feel strong emotions unsuitable for the rational mind. This suspension of rationality makes poetry unsuitable for the pursuit of philosophic truth.

---

[98] *Mimesis* characterizes the entirety of tragic and comic works (*Republic* 394c), as well as the sections in epic where the poet speaks as another character (*Republic* 394d).

[99] Scholars have struggled to reconcile the discussion of *mimesis* in book ten with book three, where the usage seems to correspond to "impersonation" rather than "representation." For discussion of this issue and arguments for a consistency in Plato's arguments, see Belfiore 2006:87–114. Halliwell 2002:56 proposes that while book three refers to *mimesis* in the dramatic mode, book ten applies the term to all forms of representation in poetry and the visual arts.

[100] As Ferrari 1989:138 observes, this appealing to the appetitive part of the soul implies a descent to the tyrannical personality, which was described in *Republic* 9 (587b–c).

3.3.2 Aristotle

Aristotle's *Poetics* provides a departure from the criticisms raised by Socrates in the Platonic dialogues. While Plato's Socrates deemed most poetry corrupting and thus antithetical to philosophic development, Aristotle seems to cast poetry as a worthwhile pursuit.[101] According to him, all poetry is *mimesis*, along with music and dance (1447a13–17).[102] Of the poetic types, tragedy occupies the bulk of the analysis in the *Poetics*, as Aristotle describes the characteristics of effective tragedies. Well-composed plots induce pity and fear, which together produce *katharsis* for the audience (1449b27–28).[103] In judging these plots, however, Aristotle subordinates the issue of truth and falsehood by offering a new set of criteria to evaluate poetry.[104]

Aristotle assesses poetry by considering the possible objects of *mimesis* (1448a1–5). Like painters, poets can portray those better than us (βελτίονας), those worse than us (χείρονας), and those just like us (τοιούτους). Tragedy represents the βελτίονας, while comedy deals with χείρονας (1448a26–30). In comparing the objects of *mimesis* with the audience ("us"), Aristotle acknowledges the process of recognition involved in the *mimesis*. The audience comprehends characters with reference to themselves. This emotional involvement in turn affects their response, namely the emotions of pity and fear. For instance, while no one would pity a wicked person falling into misfortune (1453a1–3), seeing someone similar to oneself suffering heightens fear (1453a5–6). Indeed, as Nussbaum notes, "In fearing the downfall of a person whom we see as similar to ourselves, we are in effect fearing our own related possibilities."[105] For this reason, Aristotle recommends a character who is outstanding in neither virtue nor vice (1453a7–10). The preference for this middling character does not stem

---

[101] It is unclear to what extent Aristotle is directly responding to Plato's criticisms of poetry. For the view that Aristotle is, see Halliwell 1986:1–2. See Woodruff 1992:73–74 for a critique of this assumption.

[102] For a discussion of the meaning of *mimesis* in Aristotle, see Woodruff 1992:89–91, who eschews translating the word as "imitation," "reproduction," or any other English equivalent.

[103] The exact sense of *katharsis* remains ambiguous. Bernays 2006:158–175 [1857] advanced the idea that it was a technical medical term that Aristotle transferred from the physical sphere to the emotional sphere. *Katharsis* then is the purgation of emotions. Lear 1988:302 attacks this notion of purgation, arguing that emotions like pity and fear cannot be expelled by the tragedies. Moreover, he observes that a virtuous member of the audience would not require such purgation (301). Belfiore 1992:340–341 claims that tragic *katharsis* entails "applying" (like a drug) a tragic emotion to remove shameless emotions.

[104] According to Ford 2002:269, the *Poetics* "inaugurates literary criticism as a technical appreciation of poetry that was distinct from the abundant moral, social, and religious critiques."

[105] Nussbaum 1992:275.

from a desire for realism insomuch as this kind of character has the most potential for the tragic emotions.

At 1460b10–11, Aristotle offers a different division of the objects of *mimesis*. A poet represents "as things were or are" (οἷα ἦν ἢ ἔστιν), "as they say and seem to be" (οἷά φασιν καὶ δοκεῖ), or "as things ought to be" (οἷα εἶναι δεῖ). The quote attributed to Sophocles at 1460b33–34 connects Sophocles and Euripides with the third and first options, respectively, while the second category corresponds to things concerning the gods (τὰ περὶ θεῶν). Of these options, only the first, οἷα ἦν ἢ ἔστιν, would equate with truth. οἷά φασιν καὶ δοκεῖ, on the other hand, would equal δόξα ("opinion"), which could be true or false.[106] Finally, οἷα εἶναι δεῖ does not fall exactly under the rubric of falsehood, but rather represents an ideal. By framing the objects of *mimesis* in this way, Aristotle downplays the truth and falsehood distinction. In fact, Aristotle praises Homer for teaching poets how to convey falsehoods in a suitable manner (1460a18–19).

In eliding the issue of truth and falsehood, Aristotle instead evaluates tragic plots based on their adherence to probability (τὸ εἰκός) or necessity (τὸ ἀναγκαῖον) (e.g. 1451a12–13). In well-constructed plots, events happen because of each other (διὰ τάδε), not simply after each other (μετὰ τάδε) (1452a18–21). For instance, Aristotle cites the arrival of the messenger in *Oedipus the King* as an example of a περιπέτεια ("reversal") happening from probability and necessity (1452a24). In demanding that plots follow the rules of probability and necessity, Aristotle expects plots to possess an internal logic. Such logic does not necessarily correspond to the rules of external reality. In fact, Aristotle prefers an impossible probability to an unpersuasive possibility (1460a26–27). This emphasis on a plot's internal logic and believability has led some scholars to read in Aristotle an articulation of the rules of fiction.[107] While it is perhaps anachronistic to ascribe to Aristotle the concept of fiction as we understand it, Aristotle nevertheless does mark poetry as a separate discourse. Unlike history, which must convey what happened (τὰ γενόμενα), poetry portrays what kind of things could happen (οἷα ἂν γένοιτο). For this reason, Aristotle characterizes poetry as more philosophical and serious: poetry deals with universals, while history with only particulars (1451b4–7).

Despite concentrating on the proper effects of tragedy (pity and fear), nowhere in the *Poetics* does Aristotle specify whether tragedy has cognitive value or is primarily for pleasure. This silence has resulted in varying interpretations. For instance, Ferrari disputes some scholars' emphasis on cognitive

---

[106] As Ford 2015:12 notes, "It is evidently more important that a poem engage the beliefs and even prejudices of its audience than that it be philosophically or theologically correct."
[107] See Rösler 1980:308–319. See also Gill 1993:74–79.

benefits,[108] instead arguing that tragedy for Aristotle entails only an aesthetic response. For him, the tragic emotions of pity and fear work toward the suspense of a plot.[109] According to his argument, the adherence to probability and necessity allows the plot to absorb the audience into the fiction. Yet arguments about the importance of aesthetic experience do not preclude the possibility of cognitive or moral benefits. An audience member easily could extract some sort of general understanding through such emotional absorption in the plot. The plot's relationship to an external reality matters less than its potential for enabling such absorption. For this reason, it does not matter that Homer depicts a doe with horns (1460b18).[110] On the other hand, excessive obscurity (1458a18–26) and inconsistent staging (1455a26–29) receive censure. These are the faults that hinder the proper experience of tragedy, whether that experience is tied to aesthetics, cognition, or moral benefits.

3.3.3 Early Stoics

Despite their different views concerning *mimesis* and the role of poetry in society, both Plato and Aristotle dismiss allegorical interpretation as a strategy for reading and interpreting poetry. Plato's Socrates views "under-meanings" as inadequate for explaining socially inappropriate myths. As Struck notes, enigmas are antithetical to what he dubs Aristotle's "poetics of clarity," which demands refined and lofty language without riddles or barbarisms (1458a18–26).[111] The Stoics, on the other hand, employed allegorical interpretation, perceiving in poetry the potential to convey philosophic ideas.[112] Zeno maintained the truth-value in Homer by instructing that he "composed things in accordance with opinion and some things in accordance with truth" (Dio Chrysostom *Discourses* 53.4–5 = *SVF* 1.274). Cleanthes, in fact, deemed rhythmic arrangements the more effective medium for making a listener contemplate the divine (Philodemus *On Music* col. 28 = *SVF* 1.486). Cleanthes' *Hymn to Zeus* thematizes Zeus as the rational governing principle central to Stoic theology. For instance, the phrase διὰ πάντων ("through all things") in 12 signifies not only Zeus' omnipresence, but also plays on his name Δία.[113]

---

[108] E.g. Halliwell 1992:255–256 and Nussbaum 1992:287.

[109] Ferrari 1999:194.

[110] Aristotle at 1460b15–16 distinguishes between two kinds of flaws: a technical error with respect to the art and an error outside of the art.

[111] Struck 2004:63–67.

[112] For a discussion of the Stoic interest in poetry, see DeLacy 1948:241–271.

[113] Gutzwiller 2010:355.

In their readings of poetry, the early Stoics applied allegorical interpretation consisting of etymological analysis.[114] For instance, Zeno analyzed χάος in Hesiod's *Theogony* as "water," from χέεσθαι ("to pour") (*SVF* 1.103). According to Plutarch (*How the Young Man Should Study Poetry* 31d–e = *SVF* 1.535), Cleanthes read ἄνα Δωδωναῖε ("lord of Dodona") at *Iliad* 16.233 as a single word, explaining that "the air coming as vapor from the earth is ἀναδωδωναῖον because of its rising" (διὰ τὴν ἀνάδοσιν). Through such linguistic analyses of words, the Stoics could detect expressions of their own philosophic principles. Indeed, the Epicurean Velleius in Cicero's *On the Nature of the Gods* (1.41) observes that Chrysippus in his second book on the gods made the ancient poets seem Stoic. Although it is not certain whether the early Stoics viewed intentionality on the part of the poets,[115] their kinds of readings uphold the pedagogical value of Homer and other ancient poets.

3.4 Summary

Two characteristics of poetry, its uncertain veracity and definite charm, provoked a variety of responses from subsequent poets, critics, and thinkers. Faced with fantastic and morally dubious depictions of divine strife, one could adopt three basic approaches in dealing with the truth-value of poetry. Of these, the first is to reject the surface meaning as false. Xenophanes did so while framing his own poetry as the better medium for dealing with the divine. Plato's critiques, articulated by Socrates in various dialogues, attacked not just the authority of poets and the moral impropriety in traditional stories, but ultimately poetry's overwhelming emotional power. Plato's dialogue format, not poetry, supplies a model for finding the truth. The second approach is to reject a false surface meaning of a poem but still maintain the existence of a deeper truth. For this, some critics used allegorical interpretation, which, though rejected by Plato and Aristotle, found favor with the Stoics.

A final strategy for dealing with the possibly false subject matter of poems is to eliminate truth as a criterion for judging poems. Indeed, Gorgias and the

---

[114] Long 2006:234 [1992] argues that this type of etymological analysis does not qualify as allegory. See, however, Struck 2004:113. Other practitioners of allegory include Crates of Mallus (second century BCE), the Stoic philosopher Cornutus (first century CE), and Heraclitus the Allegorist (first or second century CE). Crates of Mallus interpreted Agamemnon's shield at *Iliad* 11.32–40 as a μίμημα τοῦ κόσμου (Σ bT *Iliad* 11.40). Cornutus' *Compendium of Greek Theology* consists of a catalogue of etymological analyses of gods' names. The allegorical readings in Heraclitus' *Homeric Problems* serve to defend Homer from the charge of impropriety. As Russell 2003:221 points out, Heraclitus tends to favor moral allegories over scientific ones.

[115] See Boys-Stones 2003b:189–216 for the argument that the early Stoics did not believe in authorial intention behind their readings.

unnamed author of the *Dissoi Logoi* construed deception as a virtue of poetry. In the *Poetics*, Aristotle minimizes the issue of truth and falsehood in favor of probability and necessity. This minimization of truth as a quality of poetry in fact continued among Hellenistic thinkers. While the Euphonist critics obsessed over the pleasures produced by good sound, the poet and scientist Eratosthenes, as Strabo (1.2.3) reports, contended that the poet aims not for instruction (διδασκαλία) but for enchantment (ψυχαγωγία).[116]

Yet from these diverging views arises a general agreement. Poetry possesses the simultaneous potential for expressing truth and falsehood.[117] At the same time, surface falsehood can still transmit moral, social, and scientific truths. An awareness of such truths, hidden or not, in turn depends on additional factors. What does a reader consider true? By what means does an individual acquire and assess truth and falsehood? Moreover, is absolute certainty even possible, especially in the case of unpredictable deadly creatures (Nicander) or the remote mythical past (Callimachus, Apollonius, and Lycophron)? These are the questions, as I will argue, that underlie the representations of the truth and falsehood in the five studied poems.

4. Methodology

Although truth and poetry do not necessarily converge, we should envision both as processes, rather than simply goals or products. Indeed, acquiring and discerning the truth, if it is possible, is an amalgam of sense perception, logical reasoning, and communication. Poetry, itself an act of communication, entails multiple processes. The poet composes and performs, while an audience, while hearing or reading, engages in interpretation and experiences the poem's effects. The framing of poetry and truth as processes, of course, maps onto the road imagery associated with both poetry and truth. Just as poetry is traditionally a path,[118] so too does Parmenides employ the image of the road on his quest for the Truth. Within this traditional system of metaphor, my heuristic tool of a criterion can similarly participate, even if the official criterion of truth remains associated with philosophy, not poetry. Criteria, such as signs, maps,

---

[116] See Meijering 1987:5–6.

[117] The bT scholion on *Iliad* 14.342–351 lists three ways of considering poetry: "that which imitates the truth" (ὁ μιμητικὸς τοῦ ἀληθοῦς), "in imagination of truth" (ὁ κατὰ φαντασίαν τῆς ἀληθείας), and "surpassing truth and imagination" (ὁ καθ᾽ ὑπέρθεσιν τῆς ἀληθείας καὶ φαντασίας). Fantastic beasts like the Cyclops and Laestrygonians fall into the third category. For discussion of this scholion, see Meijering 1987:67–69.

[118] For instance, οἴμη in Homer refers to the lay of song (*Odyssey* 8.481), and Pindar employs οἶμος for his poetry (*Pythian* 4.248). Asper 1997:21–107 tracks the development of the hodological metaphor.

and personal experience, exist as means of orientation amid diverse and dense bodies of sources and information.

Detailed close reading and intertextuality will form the primary methods of my analysis. Indeed, the major characteristics of the poetry of this period (third and second centuries BCE) include the prevalence of obscure vocabulary and names, an interest in the foundation of cults and cities, and complex allusive engagement with literary predecessors.[119] Connected to this allusive engagement, moreover, is a mingling of generic expectations.[120] Within a work, markers from epic, comedy, lyric, and tragedy could appear. Of the five poems, Lycophron's *Alexandra* represents the most extreme example of these features. Not only does it merge epic and tragic generic conventions, this poem requires an encyclopedic knowledge of mythology, cults, and geographic data to navigate the profusion of the obscure allusions and rare vocabulary.

Three major questions will guide my analysis. In what ways can poetic language replicate these processes of assessing truth? How do the poetic personae respond to their predecessors, who are for them "sources?" Finally, to what extent can we detect subtle influences from philosophers, such as Plato, Aristotle, the Stoics, and the Skeptics? In all cases, I consider the language and the structure of the passage in isolation. What does the poet achieve by juxtaposing certain words or phrases, whether by placing them in the same line or in the same metrical *sedes*? For example, in the *Hymn to Zeus*, Callimachus balances Ζεῦ, σὲ μὲν Ἰδαίοισιν in 6 and Ζεῦ, σὲ δ' ἐν Ἀρκαδίῃ in 7, and Hopkinson reads this structure as reproducing the seeming division between the two options.[121] Moreover, what meaning or emphasis does the repetition of words and sounds in a passage create? As I noted earlier, Callimachus highlights the idea of eternity by repeating the ἀεί sound, both in the adverb (2; 9) and within the verbs ἀείδειν (1) and ἀείσομεν (4). With such repetition, moreover, Callimachus produces wordplay that suggests a connection between the act of singing and eternity: it is through the act of song that subjects become immortal.[122]

After analyzing the passage by itself, I will also look for both intertextual and intratextual parallels. I construe "intertextuality" as the interaction between

---

[119] For discussion of these topics, see Kyriakou 1995 (*hapax legomena* in Apollonius), Cusset 1999 (*hapax legomena* in Hellenistic poetry), Fantuzzi and Hunter 2004:49–51 (aetiology in Callimachus), Giangrande 1967:85–97 (*arte allusiva* in Callimachus and Apollonius), and Hutchinson 1988:6–11 (allusion in Hellenistic poetry in general).

[120] See, for instance, Harder 1998:95–113 for an analysis of generic mixing in the *Aetia*. See Kroll 1924:202–205 for discussion of the *"Kreuzung der Gattungen"* (mixing of genres).

[121] Hopkinson 1984:140.

[122] See Hopkinson 1984:139n5, who cites Theocritus *Idyll* 16.1–4.

texts.[123] An author, by adopting or modifying a word, phrase, sentence, or motif of another text and placing it in a new context, creates new meaning. Although one can focus on intertextuality exclusively in terms of the author's intent, it is ultimately the part of the reader to discover such interactions and determine significance from them. In the case of direct quotations, such as Epimenides' Κρῆτες ἀεὶ ψεῦσται and Hesiod's ἐκ δὲ Διὸς βασιλῆες, the modern reader has the most success in spotting these. However, the interaction can be subtler and more complex, necessitating a deeper knowledge of the original text(s). For instance, Callimachus' ἐν δοιῇ μάλα θυμός, ἐπεὶ γένος ἀμφήριστον (*Hymn to Zeus* 5) is a subtle modification of Antagoras' ἐν δοιῇ μοι θυμός, ὅ τοι γένος ἀμφιβόητον ("my heart is in doubt, since your lineage is far famed"), the first line of Antagoras' *Hymn to Eros* (Diogenes Laertius 4.26–27 = Antagoras fr. 1 Powell), which also questions the nature of a god (Eros).[124] As Stephens points out, the change from ἀμφιβόητον to ἀμφήριστον ("contested") provides an allusion to the rare Homeric word ἀμφήριστον, used twice in *Iliad* book 23 (382, 527) in the context of the funeral games.[125] Cuypers, moreover, detects another intertextual play. Since the adjective ἀμφήριστον contains the *eris*- element, she argues that it recalls the section in Hesiod's *Works and Days* (11–26) devoted to the two kinds of Eris, the good and the bad.[126] Thus, Callimachus, in modifying the Antagoras line, recalls not just Antagoras' philosophic dilemma about the nature of Eros, but also the idea of conflict within Homeric and Hesiodic contexts. Since Homer and Hesiod exerted a profound influence on the Hellenistic poets, I pay close attention to influences from them.

While intertextual analysis situates a passage in the larger tradition, intra-textuality is crucial for determining how passages function within the work as a whole. In particular, I will focus on words that involve truth and falsehood. In fact, not only do the Hellenistic poets revive words that had vanished from Attic prose (e.g. ἐτεός and ἔτυμος), they offer new formations: ἐτητυμίη (Callimachus *Aetia* fr. 75.76), πανατρεκές (Apollonius *Argonautica* 4.1382), and νητρεκῶς (Lycophron *Alexandra* 1).[127] Along with these words, I will consider words or phrases that indicate authority or sources: φασι ("they say," *Hymn to Zeus* 6) and φάτις ("speech," "report," e.g. *Argonautica* 4.984). In using these markers of

---

[123] See Hinds 1998 (esp. 21–25) for a general overview of intertextuality and its application to Latin poetry. Cusset 1999:1–23 discusses the approach specifically for the Hellenistic period. He employs intertextuality as an equivalent of "*réécriture*" (10).

[124] In this *Hymn to Eros*, the speaker deliberates on whether to refer to Eros as the son of Erebus and Nyx or as the child of Cypris.

[125] Stephens 2003:80.

[126] Cuypers 2004b:98.

[127] See, for instance, Giubilo 2009:249–254 for an overview of the adjective ἐτήτυμος in Apollonius and Callimachus.

authority, does the poetic voice exhibit a consistent attitude? For instance, at 65 in the *Hymn to Zeus* the use of ψευδοίμην ("may I lie") picks up ἐψεύσαντο ("lied," 7) and ψεῦσται ("liars," 8). While the wish on its own seems ironic, the irony deepens when we consider that the Cretans' falsehood functioned as evidence against the Cretan version of Zeus' birth. Does this mean that the Cretans lack the capacity to fashion believable falsehoods? Callimachus' wish for believable falsehood possibly evokes Aristotle's praise of Homer (1460a18–19).[128]

5. Case Study: Posidippus AB 63

For further illustration of my methodology, I affix a reading of Posidippus AB 63. This epigram, fragmentary albeit intelligible, appears grouped with other similarly themed epigrams (AB 62–70) under the ἀνδριαντοποιικά heading in the Milan papyrus (*P.Mil.Vogl.*VIII 309).[129] Although an extended treatment of Hellenistic literary epigram falls outside the scope of this monograph,[130] this poem in particular brings up multiple notions of truth when describing a sculpture of the poet Philitas by Hecataeus:

τόνδε Φιλίται χ[αλ]κὸν [ἴ]σọν κατὰ πάν‹θ›{α} Ἐκ[α]ταῖος
    ἀ]κ[ρ]ιβὴς ἄκρους [ἔπλ]αṣεν εἰς ὄνυχας,
καὶ με]γέθει κạ[ὶ σα]ρκὶ τὸν ἀνθρωπιστὶ διώξας
    γνώμο]ν', ἀφ' ἡρώων δ' οὐδὲν ἔμειξ{ε} ἰδέης,
ἀλλὰ τὸν ἀκρομέριμνον ὅλ[ῃ κ]ατεμάξατο τέχνῃ
    πρ]έσβυν, ἀληθείης ὀρθὸν [ἔχων] κανόνα·
αὐδήσ]οντι δ' ἔοικεν, ὅσῳ ποịκịλλεται ἤθει,
    ἔμψυχ]ọς, καίπερ χάλκεος ἐὼν ὁ γέρων·
ἐκ Πτολε]μαίου δ' ὧδε θεοῦ θ' ἅμα καὶ βασιλ‹ῆ›ος
    ἄγκειτ]ạι Μουσέ{ι}ων εἵνεκα Κῷος ἀνήρ.

---

[128] Lombardi 1998:171 discusses the intersections between Callimachus and Aristotle's conceptions of plausibility in poetry.

[129] Heading this collection is the programmatic AB 62, a poem enjoining the audience to eschew the hard style of old in favor of Lysippus' new style. After AB 63, the subjects run as follows: the Idomeneus of Cresilas (AB 64), Lysippus' Alexander (AB 65), Myron's cow (AB 66), Theodorus' miniature chariot (AB 67), Chares' Colossus of Rhodes (AB 68), Myron's Tydeus (AB 69), and a comparison between Polyclitus and Lysippus (AB 70). For analyses of the collection's unity and its interaction with art history discourse, see Gutzwiller 2002b:41–60, Kosmetatou 2004:187–211, Stewart 2005:183–205, Sens 2005:206–225, and Prioux 2017:13–51.

[130] For instance, in Callimachus epigram 13 Pf. (= AP 7.524) a passerby interrogates the tomb of Charidas. While denying the veracity of traditional beliefs about the Underworld (4), this tomb offers a pleasant falsehood as an alternative, proclaiming that a large ox is worth a Pellaean in Hades (6). See Gutzwiller 1998:210–211 for discussion and bibliography about this epigram and its enigmatic final line.

Hecataeus accurately molded this bronze statue like Philitas in all respects, down to even the tips of the nails. By pursuing the standard of what is human in both size and texture, he mingled in no part from the form of heroes. But with his entire art he modeled the exactingly careful old man, while holding a straight canon of truth. The statue seems like someone about to speak, with so much character he is decorated—living, although the old man is made of bronze. On the command of Ptolemy Philadelphus, both god and king, the Coan man is dedicated here for the sake of the Muses.

Posidippus AB 63

As an epigram devoted to a sculptural work, this poem features several conventional elements. Posidippus indicates the work's similarity to its subject matter (τόνδε Φιλίται χ[αλ]κὸν [ἴ]σον, 1), as well as its semblance to life (ἔμψυχ]ος, 10).[131] In this poem, however, Posidippus places stress on the painstaking process that Hecataeus has undertaken to achieve such a complete likeness (κατὰ πάν‹θ›{α}, 1). With utmost accuracy (ἀ]κ[ρ]ιβής, 2), Hecataeus molded even the nails, while focusing on rendering Philitas as a man, not as a hero (3). In this way, Hecataeus can successfully imitate the poet/scholar Philitas and his famous exactingness (ἀκρομέριμνον, 5).[132] Thus, Hecataeus' process has coalesced with its product, and Posidippus conveys this assimilation at the verbal level with the pointed repetition of ἄκρ- in ἀ]κ[ρ]ιβής (2), ἄκρους (2), and ἀκρομέριμνον (5).[133]

Enabling this Hecataean hyper-accuracy is a device dubbed a straight canon of truth: ἀληθείης ὀρθὸν ... κανόνα (6). As I mentioned above, a κανών is both a literal stick and a standard in general. Aside from its philosophical relevance, κανών also referred to the mathematical proportions used by Polyclitus to sculpt the Doryphoros.[134] Thus, in the context of this epigram, κανών works in several ways. Hecataeus would wield a physical rod to measure proportions and a metaphorical one to discern what suits Philitas and what does not. Likewise, the adjective ὀρθός embeds multiple meanings, connoting literal straightness as well as moral rectitude.[135] Finally, as Gutzwiller notes, ἀληθείη takes on a new

---

[131] For a useful overview of ecphrastic epigrams and their conventions, see Gutzwiller 2002a:85–110.

[132] See Angiò 2002:20, Stewart 2005:196, and Sens 2005:210.

[133] For an overview of Philitas' scholarly and poetic production, see Bing 2003:330–348. Due to the tradition of Philitas' extreme thinness (Aelian *Various Histories* 9.14), Bernsdorff 2002:23 assumes that this sculpture was also thin.

[134] Gutzwiller 2002b:47. For further discussion of ἀληθείης ὀρθὸν [ἔχων] κανόνα, see also Prioux 2007:45–48.

[135] See Stewart 2005:203–204, who identifies four modalities of artistic straightness connected with Hecataeus' work. It is "straightforward" in method, "objectively straight," exudes "moral rectitude," and appeals to the viewer in a straightforward way.

dimension, referring to truth as the "similarity between the object depicted and the image."[136] Indeed, the old man, despite being bronze (χάλκεος ἐών, 8), can seem (ἔοικεν, 7) to be about to speak.

In detailing the act of sculpting, Posidippus suggests multiple processes partaken by multiple agents with multiple objects of judgment. The meticulous Philitas exerts judgment to produce careful poetry and scholarship. Hecataeus in turn represents this assiduousness in sculptural form, discerning not just size, appearance, and detail but what is human and what is heroic. Posidippus, in praising this process, does the same, replicating the act of viewing and judgment for himself and for the reader. In all of this, the reader evaluates Posidippus' craft in forging this poem and in doing so can perceive links to other works. ἄκρους (2), for instance, finds analogous formations in other Posidippus epigrams on sculptures: ἄκρως in AB 64.2, ἄκρα in AB 67.4, and ἄκρα in AB 142.3 (= 29 G.-P.).[137] Similarly, the phrase ὅλ[η κ]ατεμάξατο τέχνη in 5 resembles ὅλαν ἀπεμάξατο μορφάν ("he imitated the whole form,") in *AP* 16.120.1 (Asclepiades or Archelaus), an epigram on a Lysippan sculpture of Alexander. While conceding to the impossibility of determining an exact chronology, Sens sees an important relationship between the two poems' subject matter. Whereas Lysippus sculpts Alexander as heroic and even boasting to Zeus (4), Hecataeus' Philitas is wholly human.[138]

Intertextually, the phrase ἀληθείης ὀρθὸν ... κανόνα stirs interest, as it echoes the phrase in Timon's *Indalmoi* (842 *SH*), which I mentioned briefly above in conjunction with discussion of the criteria of truth. The fragment, preserved in Sextus Empiricus (*Against the Mathematicians* 11.20), runs as follows:

ἦ γὰρ ἐγὼν ἐρέω ὥς μοι καταφαίνεται εἶναι
    μῦθον, ἀληθείης ὀρθὸν ἔχων κανόνα
ὡς ἡ τοῦ θείου τε φύσις καὶ τἀγαθοῦ αἰεὶ
    ἐξ ὧν ἰσότατος γίνεται ἀνδρὶ βίος.

Come, I will utter an account, as is evident to me to be, as I hold the straight canon of truth, how the nature of the divine and the good is always the source of the most equable life for a man.

Timon 842 *SH*

---

[136] Gutzwiller 2002b:48.

[137] Angiò 2002:20n7. ἄκρα is particularly fitting in the context of AB 142 (= 29 G.-P.), which consists of a dialogue between a viewer and the allegorical sculpture of Καιρός ("Right Moment") by Lysippus. As befits the constant movement of this god, its sculptural form is rendered on its toes (3). For analyses of this epigram, see Gutzwiller 2002a:95–96 and Prauscello 2006:511–523.

[138] Sens 2005:213–215.

Commentators have struggled with the interpretation of this fragment, which seems to impute a dogmatic stance to Timon's teacher, the supposedly dogma-free Pyrrho.[139] Yet without dwelling on the gamut of interpretations and translations,[140] we can see that this fragment similarly associates the straight canon of truth with a source of authority. This poem's speaker, whether Pyrrho or Timon, wields this criterion to assert his authority, in the same way Hecataeus and by extension Philitas and Posidippus employ the criteria in their respective endeavors. Based on this link between AB 63 and 842 *SH*, Clayman contends that the speaker (Timon) of the poem uses this canon to achieve the greatest semblance of reality, just like Hecataeus.[141] Another similarity, however, binds together these two poems. Both touch upon the question of the divine and its relationship to humanity. According to the μῦθος in the Timon fragment, the nature of the divine brings an equable life for a man (3–4), while Posidippus juxtaposes the godlike Ptolemy (9) with the human Philitas (10).

Finally, the juxtaposition between molding ([ἔπλ]ασεν, 2) and truth in AB 63 finds a parallel in a famous section from Theocritus' *Idyll* 7. There Simichidas voices his hesitancy to vie with the master poets Sicelidas (Asclepiades) and Philitas (40–41). In response to this modesty and imitating the Muses' initiation of Hesiod (*Theogony* 30–32),[142] Lycidas promises him a staff, proclaiming (43–48):

'τάν τοι' ἔφα 'κορύναν δωρύττομαι, οὕνεκεν ἐσσὶ
πᾶν ἐπ' ἀλαθείᾳ πεπλασμένον ἐκ Διὸς ἔρνος.
ὥς μοι καὶ τέκτων μέγ' ἀπέχθεται, ὅστις ἐρευνῇ
ἶσον ὄρευς κορυφᾷ τελέσαι δόμον Ὠρομέδοντος,
καὶ Μοισᾶν ὄρνιχες, ὅσοι ποτὶ Χῖον ἀοιδὸν
ἀντία κοκκύζοντες ἐτώσια μοχθίζοντι.'

"I will gift you this staff," he said, "since you are a sapling fabricated by Zeus entirely for truth. For I greatly despise the builder, who seeks to construct a house equal to the peak of Mount Oromedon, and I greatly

[139] For this issue, see Burnyeat 1980:86–87. Bett 1994:326, however, argues that Timon is the speaker of this fragment and is expressing a view that will be refuted by Pyrrho.
[140] Such issues include the translation of καταφαίνεται ("appears" vs. "is evident") and whether ἀληθείης goes with μῦθον or κανόνα. For καταφαίνεται, Burnyeat 1980:89 favors the meaning "appears," while Clayman 2009:58 adopts the latter meaning of "is evident," following Bett 1994:317. Svavarsson 2002:248 takes ἀληθείης with κανόνα, while also translating μῦθον as "fiction" (250–251). For the third line, the issue is whether the omitted ἐστι/ἔστι is existential (Svavarsson 2002:249) or predicate (Burnyeat 1980:88–92).
[141] Clayman 2009:66.
[142] See, for instance, Puelma 1960:157. The Muses bequeath Hesiod with a scepter of bay. This staff, however, is a crooked one made from wild olive (*Idyll* 7.18–19). As Hunter 1999:164 points out, crookedness is associated with deception and injustice (e.g. *Works and Days* 221).

despise the Muses' roosters who toil in vain while crowing against the Chian singer."

Theocritus Idyll 7.43–48

As Sens observes in his analysis,[143] this pointed contrast between truthfulness and striving for heroic pretensions is analogous to Hecataeus' choice to eschew the heroic and sculpt Philitas as an ordinary human. Indeed, the presence of Philitas in Posidippus AB 63 and Theocritus *Idyll* 7 further attests to a textual relationship between the two poems, both of which feature the language of crafting. However, whereas Hecataeus molds his Philitas sculpture by using a straight canon of truth, Simichidas, according to Lycidas, is "a sapling fabricated by Zeus entirely for truth" (πᾶν ἐπ' ἀλαθείᾳ πεπλασμένον ἐκ Διὸς ἔρνος, 44). Since πλάσσω often implies fabrication and hence falsehood,[144] the collocation of ἀλαθείᾳ and πεπλασμένον appears paradoxical and evokes important questions. What exactly does truth mean here? How can something be wrought for this purpose? How, moreover, can a person qualify as such? To address these crucial and perhaps unanswerable questions, I will return to this section in the concluding chapter.

Consequently, within the span of ten allusive lines, this Posidippus epigram strikes upon multiple notions of truth. A surface praise of sculptural precision embeds deeper interests in philosophical questions about perception and reality, being and seeming, and divinity and humanity. At the same time, questions regarding poetic representation and craft are engrafted in this epigram. In this way, the poem parallels Callimachus' *Hymn to Zeus*, which simultaneously interrogated conflicting poetic accounts regarding Zeus' birthplace, the nature of Zeus' divinity, and the power of his human analogue, Ptolemy II. In rejecting the Cretan version of Zeus' birth and the Homeric account of Zeus' ascent to power, moreover, Callimachus' narrator also wielded his own straight canon of truth.

6. Chapter Overview

In employing the notion of the criterion of truth while analyzing the structure, language, and verbal parallels in selected passages of the *Phaenomena*, *Theriaca*, *Aetia*, *Argonautica*, and *Alexandra*, I consider the effects that poetry can accomplish in tackling notions of truth and falsehood. While a technical prose treatise

---

[143] Sens 2005:210.

[144] For instance, at *Timaeus* 26e, Socrates makes a contrast between a "fabricated tale" (πλασθέντα μῦθον) and a "true account" (ἀληθινὸν λόγον). See *Republic* 485d for the adverb πεπλασμένως juxtaposed with ἀληθῶς. Thus, for Theocritus *Idyll* 7, Segal 1974:132 suggests the translation "fictioned for truth" to bring out the paradox of the statement.

is useful for conveying information,[145] poetic works, I argue, possess rich potential for questioning the same kinds of information. In the five works that I have chosen, however, such interrogation does not occur in the voice of the actual author, as we could assume for a technical prose text, but rather through the filter of poetic personae. In their technical scientific poems, Aratus and Nicander assume the roles of teachers dispensing information for pupils. Callimachus and Apollonius, on the other hand, feature first-person voices that fulfill the function of narrators but sometimes act like characters in the work. Callimachus in the *Aetia*, in fact, features multiple narrators, although I confine my analysis to a single narratorial voice of the Callimachean narrator or a "scholar poet." Finally, Lycophron in the *Alexandra* excludes an external narrator and instead speaks as a messenger, who repeats the utterances of the prophetess Cassandra. In each of these situations, the expectations for truth would be different. Different speakers wield different standards for truth.

At the same time, meter plays a significant role in influencing the poetic personae's treatment of truth and falsehood. The poems of Aratus, Nicander, and Apollonius are composed in dactylic hexameter, the meter used by Homer and Hesiod. As such, dactylic hexameter exuded the air of authority.[146] Callimachus' *Aetia*, on the other hand, is set in elegiac couplets. Although this meter served a variety of poetic functions during the Archaic, Classical, and Hellenistic periods (e.g. symposiastic poetry and epigrams), poems in elegiacs often entailed a personal dimension.[147] As scholars have observed,[148] such a personal dimension is apparent in the *Aetia's* construction of various narrative voices. For the *Alexandra*, Lycophron chose iambic trimeters, the meter of the spoken portions in tragedy and the one most like normal speech (Aristotle *Poetics* 1449a24). By adapting the meter of tragedy, Lycophron evokes its generic

---

[145] Hutchinson 2014:31–51 explores the differences between poetic and prose texts by comparing prose passages with poetic ones not necessarily related (e.g. Polybius 8.20.9–12 and *Argonautica* 2.218–239). In the case of Callimachus, Hutchinson sees Callimachus avoiding obvious derision in the criticism of predecessors at *Hymn to Zeus* 60–65. By contrast, Callimachus "laughs" at his opponents in his work on rivers (fr. 458 Pf.)

[146] For discussion of the authority of Homer and Hesiod in a pan-Hellenic context, see Nagy 1989:32–35.

[147] For discussions of the archaic uses of elegy, see West 1974:10–21 and Bowie 1986:13–35. Unlike West, however, Bowie 1986:34 concludes that the archaic occasions for elegiac poetry were symposia and public festivals. Barbantani 2002/2003:29–47 analyzes a Hellenistic elegy commemorating the defeat of the Galatians (*SH* 958), seeing it as an "example of the standard encomiastic poetry of the Hellenistic period" (47) that would be performed in a court setting.

[148] For consideration of the *Aetia's* status in the elegiac tradition, see Magnelli 2005:203–210 and Harder 2012.1:30–32. Cameron 1992:310 proposes that for Callimachus elegy boasted the "potential for a different sort of narrative and a more personal style." He thus proposes that the quarrel in the *Aetia* Prologue is not concerned with epic, but rather elegy (309).

associations, including its associations with deception (Gorgias DK 82 B 23), excessive emotions such as grief (*Republic* 605d), and depictions of the "lowly" individuals like women and slaves (*Republic* 395d–396a). In the *Alexandra*, not only does Cassandra express intense emotion, but both she and the messenger qualify as such lowly individuals. As a result, these two characters lack the authority attributed to the Muse-inspired poet.

The natural world of the present occupies Aratus' *Phaenomena* and Nicander's *Theriaca*. For this reason, as well as their shared hexameter meter and didactic mode, I discuss these two works together in the second chapter. Acknowledging the impossibility and futility of determining a sincere didactic intent from the actual authors, I regard both poets as constructing a fiction of teaching scientific material. Although Aratus and Nicander acquired such material secondhand from prose sources, it could be theoretically tested by a reader for truth. By looking at the heavens, one can determine whether the stars and signs appear and move as Aratus' persona claims. Likewise, observation in nature could confirm or deny the veracity of Nicander's descriptions of creatures, bites, and remedies. Nicander's persona, however, imparts a body of knowledge characterized by uncertainty, irregularity, and concealment. Such concepts are antithetical to the certain and divinely ordered Stoic universe of Aratus' *Phaenomena*. As I show in this chapter, the two authors' treatments of myths indicate these differences in subject matter. While Aratus employs his myths to emphasize the regularity of a world filled with visible and meaningful signs, his successor Nicander highlights the ambiguity of myth to represent the uncertainty entailed in learning about dangerous and chaotic threats through direct experience.

This dichotomy between certainty and uncertainty figures also in the third chapter, which I devote to an analysis of passages in Callimachus' *Aetia* (elegiac couplets) and Apollonius' *Argonautica* (dactylic hexameter), two poems roughly contemporaneous with each other. While both works are concerned primarily with the distant mythic past, the predominant aetiological focus makes the present relevant as well. In fact, both poets assume narratorial voices that participate in the recounting of the narrative. The Callimachean persona asks the Muses questions about cults and rituals in the first two books of the *Aetia*, while the Apollonian narrator frequently intrudes in the *Argonautica*'s narrative. Several passages, moreover, consist of these narrators commenting on the validity of sources or information. By focusing on these passages, I demonstrate how Callimachus constructs a narratorial persona confident in his ability to collate and evaluate information by employing personal experience as a criterion. The Apollonian narrator, by contrast, boasts a progressively uncertain tone, and in doing so, implies the deficiency of a definite criterion. Even the authoritative Muses are subject to doubt. In this way, Apollonius' epic exhibits influences from Skepticism.[149]

The focus of my fourth chapter, Lycophron's *Alexandra*, deals not with the authority of the author or authorial personae, but rather the authority of two dramatic characters: an unnamed messenger and the Trojan prophetess Cassandra. Although the messenger repeats Cassandra's prophetic speech about the aftermath of the Trojan War, these two characters differ in their relationships to understanding and assessing truth. Lacking Cassandra's omniscience and synoptic view of past, present, and future, the messenger comprehends only surface appearances, interpreting Cassandra's external madness as evidence for the falsity of her utterances. Cassandra, on the other hand, can combine genealogy and personal experience as criteria to understand the true and hidden essence of an entity by realizing the disjunction between appearance and reality. I argue this point by examining Cassandra's representation of three reoccurring characters: Helen of Troy, Odysseus, and the Sirens. Since a rich literary tradition surrounds all three figures, we can clearly see Lycophron's subtle manipulation of the tradition via the representation of Cassandra's riddling voice. While characterizing Helen and Odysseus by falsehood and deception, Cassandra casts the alluring and deadly Sirens as symbols for the hidden truth.

In handling these five works together, I consider how each poet has endeavored to condense a complex body of information in a poetic format. Information about genealogy, aetiology, and etymology is entwined with allusions, riddles, puns, and other poetic techniques. Rather than viewing these poems as exercises in aesthetic virtuosity, I ask how such poetic effects can interrogate the material. Yet, in doing so, I do not presume an actual intent to communicate truth, nor do I attempt to determine whether any material is true or not. In that, I profess the uncertainty that the *Hymn to Zeus* narrator ironically adopts.

---

[149] With this, I adopt the arguments offered by Clayman 2009:174–208, who argues for Skeptic influences in Hellenistic poetry. Unlike her, however, I view these Skeptic influences as evident primarily in Apollonius' *Argonautica*. See also Clayman 2000:33–53. For a discussion of the word Skeptic as applied to the Academics and Pyrrhonists, see Striker 1996d:92n1 [1980].

2

Aratus and Nicander
Myth and Subject Matter

The natural world has long fascinated Greek poets and thinkers. While Homer and Hesiod included descriptions of constellations and creatures in their poetic works,[1] later prose authors (e.g. Aristotle and Theophrastus) produced systematic catalogues of information about the physical world. Amid the proliferation of prose treatises, this trend flourished in the Hellenistic period, and poets like Aratus (ca. 283/282–246 BCE) and Nicander (ca. second century BCE) mined such treatises to compose their dactylic hexameter catalogue poems, which are now classed under the term "didactic" epic.[2] Aratus adapted Eudoxus of Cnidus for the astronomical portions (19–757) of the *Phaenomena*, a poem that deals with signs broadly, including weather signs (758–1141).[3] Similarly, in the *Theriaca*, Nicander used prose sources for the poem's descriptions of deadly creatures, bites, and the appropriate remedies.[4] In doing so, both poets transformed this technical material, subjecting it to the confines of dactylic hexameter while at the same

---

[1] For instance, in the description of Achilles' shield, Homer lists the Pleiades, Hyades, Orion, and the Ursa Major (*Iliad* 18.486–489). See also *Odyssey* 5.272–275 (Pleiades, Bootes, Ursa Major, and Orion). In the *Works and Days* 383–387, Hesiod identifies the rising of Pleiades as the time to start the harvest. Homer's descriptions of creatures can be found primarily in the similes. See, for instance, *Iliad* 22.93–95, where Hector is compared to a snake.

[2] For the issue of "didactic" as a genre of poetry and the various ways to isolate its characteristics, see Toohey 1996:15, Fowler 2000:205–219, Volk 2002:34–43, van Noorden 2015:16–23, and Overduin 2019:266–272. Sider 2014:22, however, argues that didactic was not invented until the Hellenistic period. For the relationship between didactic and epic, see Lausberg 1990:180–188. Indeed, the ancients would not have a felt a strong distinction between epic and what we identify as didactic, since both were composed in dactylic hexameter, the traditional meter of epic poetry.

[3] Hipparchus' (ca. 147–127 BCE) *Commentary on the Phaenomena of Aratus and Eudoxus* indicates Aratus' debt towards Eudoxus by citing parallel passages in the two authors. For discussion of Aratus' sources for the section on weather-based signs, see Kidd 1997:21–23. The material overlaps with pseudo-Theophrastus' *On Signs*.

[4] Schneider 1856:181–201 claimed that the major source for the *Theriaca* was *On Poisonous Animals* (Περὶ Θηρίων) by the third-century BCE writer Apollodorus. The scholia of the *Theriaca* mention this work at 715 and 858. Recent work, however, has attacked the notion of a single major

time interweaving metaphors, allusions, etymological figures, and mythological narratives.[5] Since these elements contribute to the pleasure produced in reading a poem, the communication of truth no longer constitutes the sole goal of the work, if one at all. In fact, the mythological stories integrated by Aratus and Nicander implant doubt amid the presumably true scientific information. Derived from the oral tradition or written sources, such stories cannot be verified by empirical means and thus seemingly undermine the speakers' authority.

Yet, I argue, in inserting this doubt through the mythological stories, both poets represent the processes involved in acquiring and evaluating the truth and falsehood of their respective subject matter. The fundamental differences in the two poets' subject matter necessitate different processes, along with different criteria. For the celestial signs in the *Phaenomena*, visibility and regularity are the primary criteria by which one can comprehend and derive meaning from signs. Aratus' elaborate mythic narratives, which he confines to the astronomical portion of the poem (19-757), not only emphasize the signs' consistency and visibility, but also imitate the circular processes of sign interpretation. Nicander's myths, by contrast, highlight the uncertainty and hiddenness that characterize deadly creatures and remedies. Only through the criterion of direct experience can a person grasp such erratic threats, and likewise Nicander's myths embody this process.

To contextualize my readings of the myths, I begin the chapter with a brief overview of the two poems' respective subject matters, as well as pertinent intellectual trends. Since Aratus precedes Nicander chronologically,[6] discussion of Aratean sections will preface analyses of the *Theriaca* narratives. Additionally, I restrict my focus to the constellation portions of the *Phaenomena*, where Aratus locates the myths. After establishing the major differences between the poets' subject matter, I pair narratives that display similarities in theme, content,

---

source for the *Theriaca*. For a discussion of Nicander's sources, see Touwaide 1991:71–73, Jacques 2002:XLIX–LVIII, and De Stefani 2006:55–65.

[5] For the relationship between prose and poetic texts, see Hutchinson 2009:196–197.

[6] Aratus dates to about the time of Ptolemy Philadelphus (283/282-246 BCE). The evidence for his life comes from four *Lives* preserved in the manuscripts and an entry in the *Suda*. According to *Life* I, Antigonus Gonatas summoned him to Pella in 276 BCE. Although this *Life* includes an account of how Antigonus bid Aratus, a doctor, to write the *Phaenomena* and Nicander the astrologer to compose the *Theriaca*, it is almost certain that Nicander comes after the time of Aratus. Magnelli 2006:185–204 comes to this conclusion based on Nicander's word choice and allusions. However, the dating and identity of Nicander, the author of *Theriaca* and *Alexipharmaca*, is fraught, since multiple sources, which consist of the *Lives*, *Suda*, and a Delphian decree (*Syll. Inscr. Gr.*[3] 452) that confers *proxenia* to Nicander of Colophon, offer different dates and fathers. For discussions and solutions to this issue, see Pasquali 1913, Gow and Scholfield 1953:6, Cameron 1995:194–208 and Massimilla 2000:127–137.

and/or structure.[7] For instance, the second section covers stories placed at the beginning of the works: the catasterism of the Bears (*Phaenomena* 30–35) and the origin of venomous creatures from the Titans' blood (*Theriaca* 8–12). Reading both stories as programmatic passages, I compare the use of similar expressions of doubt (εἰ ἐτεὸν δή, *Phaenomena* 30 vs. εἰ ἐτεόν περ, *Theriaca* 10), as well as the role of Hesiod. In the third section, I analyze two Hesiod-inspired narratives: the Dike excursus (*Phaenomena* 96–136) and the loss of youth (*Theriaca* 343–358). Looking at how the poets track the changes in the relationship between these entities and humans, I argue that the two stories encapsulate different processes of acquiring and judging information.

In the fourth section, I treat narratives that explicitly thematize discovery. While Aratus features a single narrative about the name giver and organizer of the stars (373–382), Nicander includes three stories about the first finders of remedies (501–502, 541–549, and 666–675). As I argue, these three stories together attest to the importance of direct experience and the arbitrariness of naming. Likewise, naming and etymologies bear relevance for the next pair of myths in section five: Aratus' discussion of the Hippocrene (*Phaenomena* 216–224) and Helen's injury of the female blood-letting snake (*Theriaca* 309–319). Aratus, by citing the name Hippocrene ("Spring of the Horse") as the primary evidence for the Horse creating the spring on Mount Helicon, portrays etymology as a valid strategy. Nicander, however, subtly destabilizes the logic of etymology by portraying a beneficent Helen who does not entirely conform to her apparently dire name. These contrasting treatments of names correspond more broadly to the relationship between the poets' subject matter and naming. While names determine identity for constellations, the naming of creatures and remedies is even more arbitrary and variable, not unlike direct experience.

The chapter concludes with a comparison of two versions of the same myth: Orion's death by the Scorpion. While Aratus at *Phaenomena* 636–646 recounts the tale in a repetitive and indirect manner, ostensibly in reverence for Artemis, Nicander (*Theriaca* 8–12) highlights the directness and painfulness of the assaults and in doing so signifies the unexpectedness of his subject matter. At the same time, this myth enables Nicander to distinguish his material from

---

[7]   Although this chapter will treat in detail only the most developed mythological sections in the two authors, other stories (not counting brief allusions) occur at *Phaenomena* 64–66 (Engonasin), 71–73 (Crown), 179–181 (Cepheus), 268–271 (Tortoise of Hermes), and 653–658 (Cassiopeia). The other narratives in the *Theriaca* are 439–440 (Apollo and the Dragon), 484–487 (the metamorphosis of Ascalabus into a gecko), 608–609 (Cadmus and Harmonia as snakes), 685–688 (Heracles vs. the Hydra), 835–836 (the death of Odysseus), and 903–906 (the death of Hyacinthus). By the count of Jacques 2002:LXXIXn175, there are seventy lines in the *Theriaca* devoted to digressions.

that of Aratus' *Phaenomena*. In analyzing these stories together, I elucidate the significance and function of the myths for the poets' respective projects, both of which I construe as fictions of purveying the truth. In such projects, the myths illuminate how the truth of the subject matter can be judged: interpretation of visible and consistent signs for Aratus and direct experience of creatures and remedies for Nicander.

1. Nature of the Subject Matter

1.1 Aratus

In cataloguing the constellations (19–461) and their movements (462–757), Aratus stresses their visibility, regularity, and orderliness. Such characteristics are especially clear in the hymnic invocation to Zeus at the beginning of the poem (1–18).[8] There Aratus describes Zeus' creation of the celestial signs:

αὐτὸς γὰρ τά γε σήματ' ἐν οὐρανῷ ἐστήριξεν,
ἄστρα διακρίνας, ἐσκέψατο δ' εἰς ἐνιαυτὸν
ἀστέρας οἵ κε μάλιστα τετυγμένα σημαίνοιεν
ἀνδράσιν ὡράων, ὄφρ' ἔμπεδα πάντα φύωνται.

Zeus himself fixed the signs in the sky, making them into distinct constellations, and organized the stars for the year to give the most clearly defined signs of the seasons to men, so that everything may grow without fail.

Phaenomena 10–13

While identifying Zeus' role as creator (αὐτός, 10), Aratus offers several pieces of information regarding these creations. As σήματα ("signs," 10), the entities are visible and express meaning. Yet through their placement in the heaven (ἐν οὐρανῷ, 10), the stars are removed from immediate experience. Moreover, such placement is fixed and permanent, as Aratus indicates with the verb ἐστήριξεν ("fixed," 10). Along with affixing the signs' placement, Zeus forms them into distinct constellation groupings (ἄστρα διακρίνας, 11), and in so doing facilitates human comprehension. Constellation groupings not only consolidate multiple stars into a single unit, but one can more easily comprehend these units in a spatial relationship to the others. Indeed, as Aratus later states (375–376; see below), it would be impossible to name and know each star on its own. At the same time, Zeus arranges the stars in temporal terms (ἐσκέψατο δ' εἰς ἐνιαυτόν, 11),

---

8 For analysis of the traditional hymnic elements of the proem, see Fakas 2001b:3–66.

thus allowing comprehension of the seasons. Together such visibility, permanence, ordering, and temporal regularity illuminate objects whose vast distance and immense number should completely confound human comprehension. Wrought by Zeus in this way, such signs evidence his concern for men, as Aratus underscores with the repetition of σήματα (10) and σημαίνοιεν ("to give signs," 12) in this section.

Like Zeus' pervasive presence (*Phaenomena* 1–4), the language and themes of this passage permeate the poem. In addition to the many manifestations of the noun σῆμα and its related verbal forms,[9] Aratus employs several words to emphasize sight and visibility. Befitting the poem's title *Phaenomena*, forms of φαίνω/φαίνομαι abound: φαινομένη (41), φαεινόμενον (76), φαίνεται (135), etc.[10] The constellation descriptions, moreover, often concern the varying brightness of the stars. Some stars are clear and visible (e.g. Helice; καθαρὴ καὶ ἐπιφράσσασθαι ἑτοίμη, 40), while others are hazy (e.g. the nameless stars near the Hare, 385).[11] Finally, the *Phaenomena* contains several verbs dealing with sight and judgment, which often appear in addresses to the audience.[12] Of these verbs, τεκμαίρομαι ("I judge by signs") is especially relevant, as it incorporates the connection between visualization and interpretation. We can observe this verb's significance through the use of the active form τεκμαίρω in the invocation to the Muses (τεκμήρατε, 18).[13] The Muses are to guide Aratus via signs, while Aratus in turn enjoins the reader to judge from these signs.

Likewise, Aratus frequently underscores the permanence and regularity of the constellations. For instance, after the invocation to the Muses, he describes the constellations as eternally moving: οἱ μὲν ὁμῶς πολέες τε καὶ ἄλλυδις ἄλλοι ἐόντες / οὐρανῷ ἕλκονται πάντ᾽ ἤματα συνεχὲς αἰεί ("The stars, all alike, being many and scattered in different directions, are drawn across the sky every

---

9   For σῆμα (singular and plural), see 10, 72, 168, 170, 233, 247, 303, 337, 410, 418, 429, 433, 459, 461, 465, 515, 565, 608, 725, 730, 760, 772, 777, 805, 820, 824, 837, 890, 909, 922, 964, 986, 1001, 1017, 1022, 1037, 1040, 1052, 1061, 1103, 1129, 1141, 1142 (*bis*), 1146, and 1148; for σημαίνω, see 6, 12, 267, 381, 420, 757, 808, 873, 891, and 904; for ἐπισημαίνω, see 248.

10   See also 140, 148, 150, 166, 189, 384, 414, 450, 472, 517, 619, 655, 713, 734, 772, 789, 824, 830, 866, 867, 870, 894, 905, 908, 965, 990, 992, 1043, 1074, 1079, 1141, and 1147.

11   For words indicating visibility, see ἀγαυός (392), ἀγλαός (77, 165, 415), αἴγλη (80, 139), ἀμφαδόν (95), ἀρίδηλος (94), ἀφαυρός (277, 569), εἰσωπός (79), ἐπίοπτος (25), ἐπόψιος (81, 258), καθαρός (383), περίσκεπτος (213), πολύσκεπτος (136), and φαεινός (350, 587, 753). For lack of visibility, see ἠερόεις (276, 317, 349, 630).

12   For examples, see θεάομαι (224, 325, 451), ὁράω (199, 223, 430, 456, 563, 573, 710, 727, 733, and 996), (περι)σκέπτομαι (75, 96, 157, 199, 229, 474, 560, 562, 729, 778, 799, 832, 880, 892, 994, and 1143), (περι)σκοπέω (435, 464, 852, 925, and 987), and (ἐπι)τεκμαίρομαι (38, 142, 170, 229, 456, 801, 802, 932, 1038, 1063, 1104, 1121, and 1129). Bing 1993:99 observes that, apart from the appeal to the Muses in the proem (*Phaenomena* 16) and Dike's address to mankind (*Phaenomena* 123–126), Aratus employs the second person singular.

13   For discussion of this address to the Muses, see Kidd 1997:174, Gee 2000:80–81, and Volk 2012:226.

day continuously forever," 19–20). The Axis, by contrast, is always set fast and unmoving (21–22). Similarly, the repetition of στηρίζω embodies the sense of permanence. Like ἐστήριξεν in 10, the perfect form ἐστήρικται reoccurs four times as the last word in the line (230, 274, 351, and 500), paralleling the regularity of the signs. Such regularity and fixedness suit the stars' status as objects made by Zeus (τετυγμένα, 12), and Aratus in fact integrates numerous evocations of craftsmanship throughout the poem.[14] While irregularity does exist in this well-crafted world (e.g. the planets' movement, 454–461), Aratus ultimately glosses over these aberrations in favor of certainty and regularity.[15]

The regular and ordered world of the *Phaenomena* closely maps onto Stoic conceptions of the universe. For the Stoics, Zeus was the omnipresent guiding divine principle, as Cleanthes demonstrates in his *Hymn to Zeus*.[16] The *Lives* in fact associate Aratus with the Stoic philosophers Zeno (*Life* III) and Persaeus (*Life* IV).[17] For these reasons, it is tempting to interpret the *Phaenomena* through a Stoicizing lens. Nevertheless, scholars have debated the extent of Stoic elements in the *Phaenomena*. While some scholars have belabored the Stoic aspects of the poem, others have minimized the philosophical aspect in favor of the literary dimension.[18] Yet, as I noted in the previous chapter, the philosophical and literary are not mutually exclusive, especially for the Stoics (e.g. Cleanthes), who gravitated toward poetry as a medium for conveying truth.

Likewise, several fundamental aspects of the *Phaenomena* intersect with Stoic interests. The interpretation of signs occupied a major component of Stoic epistemology.[19] Hunter, moreover, observes that the Stoic notion of κόσμος

---

[14] For instance, see *Phaenomena* 529–533, where Aratus compares the world to the product of a skilled craftsperson. See Kidd 1997:367–369 and Volk 2012:211 for discussions of this passage. For discussion of ecphrasis in the *Phaenomena, see* Semanoff 2006a:157–177.

[15] For analyses of Aratus' refusal to discuss the planets' movement, see Martin 1979:92 and Semanoff 2006:313–314. As Kidd 1997:343 observes, the planets have no usefulness for determining the time or seasons.

[16] See Asmis 2007:413–429, who argues that Cleanthes' poem presents a Zeus aligning with both traditional values as well as Stoic ones. For commentary and comparison of Cleanthes' poem and the beginning of the *Phaenomena*, see James 1972:28–38.

[17] For discussion of the *Lives* and Aratus' biography, see Martin 1998.1:XI–XLVIII.

[18] Along with Effe (1970; 1977), Erren 1967:25 and Martin 1979:91–92 emphasize the Stoic elements of the poem. See also Gee 2000:70–81, who argues that Stoic notions reoccur throughout the poem. She identifies these notions as (1) the divinity of celestial bodies, (2) universal sympathy, and (3) the relationship between language and the universe. Both Kidd 1997:12 and Fakas 2001b:19, however, minimize the philosophical aspect in favor of the literary. See also Cusset 2011. While he dismisses the *Lives* as convincing evidence for Aratus' Stoicism, he nevertheless concedes the poem's appeal for Stoic readers. Volk 2010:204 argues that, while Aratus' universe is compatible with Stoicism, it is not discussed in Stoic terms.

[19] For the importance of signs in Stoic thought, see, for instance, Allen 2001:150–158. The Stoics define the sign as an "antecedent proposition in a valid hypothetical premise, which serves to

("order") is central to the *Phaenomena*.[20] Nowhere does this interest emerge more clearly than in the famous and much discussed ΛΕΠΤΗ acrostic at 783–787.[21] At the same time, the poem is replete with puns and etymologies,[22] both of which piqued Stoic interest. Of course, as a poetic technique employed since the beginnings of Greek poetry and one especially popular in Hellenistic poetics,[23] etymological puns do not automatically imply Stoic influence. However, in the case of constellations, names are essential components for identification and comprehension. By imposing names and mythical narratives on the constellations, one can better construe the order of the universe. In a similar way, Stoic interpreters applied their interpretations to etymologies and myths to uncover deeper truths.[24] For these reasons, one can still construe Aratus' subject matter as a Stoic would, even without affirming Aratus' Stoic affiliations or reading an earnest desire to teach Stoic philosophy in the poem.

1.2 Nicander

In contrast to Aratus' ordered universe of visible signs, Nicander in the *Theriaca* portrays a world plagued by irregularity and concealment. Even when boasting to his addressee, Hermesianax,[25] Nicander does not suppress this reality:

ῥεῖά κέ τοι μορφάς τε σίνη τ' ὀλοφώϊα θηρῶν
ἀπροϊδῆ τύψαντα λύσιν θ' ἑτεραλκέα κήδευς
φίλ' Ἑρμησιάναξ, πολέων κυδίστατε παῶν,
ἔμπεδα φωνήσαιμι· σὲ δ' ἂν πολύεργος ἀροτρεύς
βουκαῖός τ' ἀλέγοι καὶ ὀροιτύπος, εὖτε καθ' ὕλην

---

reveal the consequent" (Sextus Empiricus *Outlines of Pyrrhonism* 2.104; *Against the Mathematicians* 8.245, Trans: Bury). For a treatment of signs in the *Phaenomena*, see Bénatouïl 2005:129–144, who (136–138) analyzes Aratus' signs in terms of the distinction between commemorative and indicative signs as described by Sextus Empiricus (*Against the Mathematicians* 8.151–155).

[20] Hunter 2008b:161–164.
[21] The acrostic appears shortly after Aratus states that Zeus has still hidden signs (769–770). For the initial discovery of this acrostic, see Jacques 1960:50–52. For further discussion of this acrostic, see Volk 2012:226–227 and Hanses 2014:609–614.
[22] For discussions of etymologies and puns in the *Phaenomena*, see Pendergraft 1995:43–67 and Cusset 2002:187–196. Bing 1990:281–285 analyzes ἄρρητον ("unmentioned") in 2 as a pun on Aratus' name. As Bing notes, Callimachus seems to have picked up this pun and the ΛΕΠΤΗ acrostic in the praise of Aratus in 26 Pf. (= AP 9.507.3–4): χαίρετε λεπταί / ῥήσεις Ἀρήτου ("hail slender utterances of Aratus"). See also Cusset 2002:188. For examples of naming in the *Phaenomena*, see 66 (Engonasin), 164 (Goat of Zeus), 245 (Celestial Knot), 261 (names of the Pleiades), 315 (Eagle), 331–332 (Sirius), 399 (Water), 444 (Hydra), 476 (Milk), 544 (Zodiac Circle), and 898 (Asses).
[23] For a list of examples, see Kraus 1987:22–41 and O'Hara 1996:7–18.
[24] See Boys-Stones 2003b:189–216.
[25] As the scholiast (Σ *ad* 3; Crugnola 1971:35–36) makes clear, this Hermesianax is not the same as the poet Hermesianax of Colophon. See Overduin 2015:172.

ἢ καὶ ἀροτρεύοντι βάλῃ ἔπι λοιγὸν ὀδόντα,
τοῖα περιφρασθέντος ἀλεξητήρια νούσων.

Easily and securely I might tell you of the appearance of beasts and
their deadly bites that strike unforeseen, and the countering remedy
for the injury, dear Hermesianax, noblest of my many kinsmen. The
hardworking ploughman, the cowherd, and the woodsman, whenever
a beast casts its deadly fang into a person in the woods or at the plow,
would respect you, since you have knowledge of such ways of averting
diseases.

Theriaca 1–7

In making ῥεῖα ("easily") the poem's first word, Nicander exudes a confident
tone, recalling the repetition of this word at the beginning of Hesiod's *Works
and Days* (5–7). There the word refers to the ease with which Zeus wields his
power.[26] Nicander further develops this confident tone with ἔμπεδα ("securely")
beginning the fourth line. Appearing between these two words and opening
the second line, however, is the adjective ἀπροϊδῆ ("unforeseen").[27] With this
word, Nicander alerts the reader to the unpredictable nature of these creatures.
Such creatures often conceal themselves and strike without warning. While this
dangerous reality increases the need for a teacher dispensing such information,
the coordination of ἀπροϊδῆ with ῥεῖα and ἔμπεδα generates a tension. Despite
the inherent uncertainty of this subject matter, the teacher still assumes an air
of confidence regarding the capacity of his verse. Such verse will not only benefit
the addressee, Hermesianax, but also any workers that might fall prey to deadly
creatures and thus require Hermesianax's medical knowledge (*Theriaca* 4–7).

At the same time, Nicander amplifies this friction between uncertainty
and confidence by eschewing indicative verbs in these beginning seven lines.
Rather, he features two optative verbs (φωνήσαιμι in 4 and ἀλέγοι in 5) as well
as one subjunctive (βάλῃ in 6) in an indefinite temporal clause. The combina-
tion of the optative + κε/ἄν (potential optative) conveys less certainty than a
future indicative would, as the construction conveys potentiality as an "opinion
of the speaker" and ranges from "possibility to fixed resolved" (Smyth §1824a).
In the case of ἀλέγοι in 5, the potential optative befits the hypothetical dimen-
sion of Hermesianax's respect, which depends ultimately on his ability to aid

---

[26] See Clauss 2006:162–164. This verbal parallel has led Clauss to detect a parallel between
Nicander's knowledge as poet and the power of Zeus. The *Theriaca*, for Clauss, "embodies a cele-
bration of human knowledge" (182).

[27] For the importance of this word, see Wilson 2015:188. She notes, moreover, that the word occurs
in the same position (first word of second line) as ἄρρητον ("unmentioned") at *Phaenomena* 2.

these supposed workers. The first optative, however, serves another function. Like ῥεῖα in 1, κε + φωνήσαιμι evokes the beginning of Hesiod's *Works and Days*: ἐγὼ δέ κε Πέρσῃ ἐτήτυμα μυθησαίμην ("I should tell Perses true things," 10).[28] Yet while recalling this construction from the *Works and Days*, Nicander has applied some significant changes. While Hesiod categorizes his subject matter as "true things" (ἐτήτυμα), Nicander devotes two lines (1–2) to establish the poem's tripartite division of beasts, bites, and remedies. In the process, Nicander produces a considerable delay between the initial κε in 1 and its accompanying verb φωνήσαιμι in 4. Such a delay in turn parallels the unpredictable nature of these creatures and their bites.

Following this address, Nicander details how concealment and irregularity characterize all three components of his subject matter: the deadly creatures, their bites, and even the remedies for the bites. The appearance and movements of deadly creatures contribute to their dangerousness. Via their smallness, snakes and other creatures can easily hide. For instance, Nicander describes how the διψάς ("thirst-snake") lurks its hole: ὅτε σὺν τέκνοισι θερειομένοισιν ἀβοσκής / φωλειοῦ λοχάδην ὑπὸ γωλεὰ διψὰς ἰαύῃ ("when the unfed thirst-snake sleeps with the children it broods, lurking in the recesses of its hole," 124–125). Additionally, snakes like the ἀσπίς ("cobra") signal their unpredictability by shifting swiftly from lethargy to attack mode (164–168). In fact, while the *Theriaca* does cover non-snake creatures (715–836), serpents serve as the perfect embodiment of uncertainty and chaos. Through their coiling movements, they continuously assume new shapes, and by shedding their old skin, they acquire fresh vitality and lethalness (137–138). At the same time, some snakes can alter their color: the σήψ (*seps*, 148–149; 153–156), the ἀσπίς (172–174), and the αἱμόρροος ("blood-letting snake")(288).[29] These variations in color permit assimilation with their environment. The σήψ disguises itself to match its lair (149), while the ἀσπίς blends in with the mud of the Nile (174–176).[30] In this way, these snakes intensify their dangerousness, further concealing themselves from human sight. Finally, Nicander often problematizes the identification of snakes. Certain species vary in size (viper, 210) or number of horns (κεράστης, "horned viper," 261), while some snakes resemble others; the δρυΐνας ("oak-snake") looks like the water-snake (ὕδρῳ, 421). The δρυΐνας, moreover, also bears the name χέλυδρος (χέλυδρον, 411–412), a name like χέρσυδρος, a

---

[28] On this similarity, see Cazzaniga 1975:180. On this line in Hesiod, see West 1978:142, who reads κε as exerting the force of politeness.

[29] For an overview of Nicander's color vocabulary, see Papadopoulou 2009:95–119.

[30] Cusset 2006b:78 detects a wordplay with ἄσιν ("mud," 176) and ἄσπις.

separate snake described at 359–371.[31] It is no wonder that modern readers and commentators struggle to identify these snakes![32]

Just as the snakes and other deadly creatures fluctuate in their appearance and movements, so too can the symptoms of their bites diverge.[33] For instance, a viper bite can produce bloody or colorless discharge (236). Likewise, the skin can become green, bloody, or bruise-colored (236–238). When bitten by the water-snake, one can discharge either bilious or bloody vomit (435–436). The bite of the wasp spider induces either shaking or weakness (744–745). In noting these variations in symptoms, Nicander points to a wide diversity of human suffering caused by dangerous and unpredictable creatures. Their unpredictability extends even to the symptoms of their bites.

The remedies likewise embody concealment and irregularity. Indeed, reme-dies are by nature hidden. One must not only discover a remedy but also extract the materials from the ground or in some cases from an animal. At the same time, just as Nicander indicates the variations in creatures and bites, he also lists remedies with multiple possible ingredients. For instance, pellitory works when consumed with vinegar, wine, or even water (539–540). Likewise, the remedy described at 907–914 includes an array of remedy options (e.g. tufted thyme or samphire, 909), and is effective with wine, vinegar, water, or milk (913–914). Even the initial prevention of snakes involves multiple options (35–97), including human spit (86).

Consequently, throughout the *Theriaca*, Nicander imparts a profusion of information, some of which is contradictory. This combined data corresponds to the difficulty of his chaotic and strange subject matter. In all cases, direct experience plays an integral role. One must encounter hidden creatures directly in the wild, feel their bites oneself, and consume remedies for salvation. Not only does Nicander simulate many of these possible encounters (e.g. encoun-tering snakes without prior protection, 115–117), he also frequently enjoins the audience to look and consider (φράζεο), paralleling Aratus' commands.[34] Like Aratus, moreover, he also refers to the signs (σήματα) of the bites. Such σήματα, however, are not distant constellations in the sky. Rather these σήματα are expe-rienced directly as wounds and symptoms on the body (282, 360, 716).

---

[31] See Jacques 2002:122–124 for a discussion of the confusion between the χέλυδρος and the χέρσυδρος.

[32] For attempts at classification, see Scarborough 1977:6–9.

[33] For discussions of Nicander's obsession with describing symptoms in gruesome detail, see Toohey 1996:65–68, Spatafora 2005:256–262, Overduin 2009:88–90; 2017:141–155, and Sistakou 2012:200.

[34] For forms of φράζομαι (including compounds), see 70, 157, 234, 438, 541, 589, 656, 715, and 759.

In dealing with the variations of human suffering, Nicander seems to align with the empiricists, a medical sect for whom experience was the sole means of obtaining knowledge.[35] Yet, as is the case regarding the relationship between the *Phaenomena* and Stoicism, scholars have debated Nicander's medical credentials, as well as the actual value of the *Theriaca* as a source of technical information. According to the *Suda* entry (ν 374), Nicander was also a doctor and wrote a metaphrasis of Hippocrates' *Prognostics*. Jacques goes so far to argue that Nicander was a specialist in venomous creatures (θηριακός).[36] On the other side of the spectrum, some scholars see the poem's hyper-focus on aesthetics and internal inconsistencies as evidence for its pseudoscientific status.[37] Yet an intermediate position is possible.[38] Just as philosophy and poetry are not necessarily separate, so too does poetry have usefulness for certain kinds of technical information. Recipes set in verse, for instance, would be more difficult to alter.[39] Additionally, Nicander's other works (e.g. *Alexipharmaca*, *Georgica*) evidence his interest in the natural sciences. Thus, even without working as a doctor, Nicander can still treat subject matter of acute interest to one. By extension, we can also analyze the material of the *Theriaca* via an empiricist method, in the same way that constellations are conducive to a Stoic mode of interpretation.

1.3 Summary

In this overview, I have compared the two poets' portrayal of their respective material. Aside from some exceptions (e.g. the planets at 454–461), visibility, order, and regularity define Aratus' world, while Nicander dwells on invisible and chaotic hostile forces and hidden remedies. These differences lead to

---

[35] See Sistakou 2012:200 for Nicander's relationship with empiricism. She notes, however, that Nicander's knowledge came from written sources. The empiricists were a medical sect active in the first half of the third century BCE and argued against the rationalists, who regarded theory as the basis for medical knowledge. For discussion of the empiricists, see Frede 1987c:245–249.

[36] Jacques 2006:30.

[37] Observing the various inconsistencies, such as the claim that human spit can ward off snakes (*Theriaca* 86), Overduin 2009:92 argues that the poem fails if the primary goal is to articulate clear scientific knowledge concerning bites and remedies. For him, the *Theriaca* is a pseudo-scientific treatise, and Nicander's interest is more in exciting and poetical writing, rather than scientific accuracy. Toohey 1996:67 detects a "pronounced dissonance between sensationalism and dry technicality."

[38] For instance, Papadopoulou 2009:117 proposes that Nicander's color vocabulary strives simultaneously to add poetic flavoring and achieve scientific accuracy. For views on Nicander's role as poet and scientist, see also Hatzimichali 2009:33–39. Wilson 2018a:278 reads these simultaneous interests in Nicander's description of viper births (132–136). As she argues, by describing the baby vipers bursting from their mother's womb and avenging their father, Nicander evokes tragic paradigms of vengeance.

[39] On this point, see Hutchinson 2009:209–210, who cites Galen's praise of employing verse for this reason (e.g. *On Antidotes* 14.32).

differing processes of understanding. Aratus' distant and visible signs involve the act of interpretation. One must recognize the appearance of stars and their regularity to derive meaning. By contrast, Nicander's subject matter of creatures, symptoms, and remedies demands direct experience. These two processes in turn roughly correlate to broader intellectual trends: Stoicism for Aratus' material and medical empiricism for the *Theriaca*. Yet, in linking the two works with these intellectual trends, I do not argue for the poets' strict association with any school. In fact, it is impossible even to ascertain the poets' actual prior knowledge and experience of their material before the poetic transformations.[40] Nor can we judge the seriousness of their claims to teach practical information for an audience.[41] In fact, although both poets refer to possible beneficiaries of their teachings, the density of poetic allusions and difficult poetic language exclude such individuals as a likely audience.[42] For these reasons, it is best to construe both the *Phaenomena* and *Theriaca* as fictions of instruction. In these fictions, the personae's intent to teach is sincere, in the same way that the material is presented as true.

2. Myths

Let us turn now to the focus of this chapter, the use of myth in the *Phaenomena* and the *Theriaca*. Just as myths serve numerous functions in society,[43] the mythological digressions fulfill several purposes in the *Phaenomena* and the *Theriaca*. Most obviously, these narratives offer diversions from the technical material.[44]

[40] Cicero, for instance, famously denies that either poet possessed knowledge of their subject matter (*On the Orator* 1.69), while nevertheless conceding to the stylistic prowess of both. For discussion of Hipparchus' criticism of Aratus, see Possanza 2004:90–91.

[41] Effe 1977:26–39 bases his typology of didactic on this notion of authorial intent. While Effe identifies the actual theme of the *Phaenomena* to be an expression of the power of Stoic Zeus, he argues that Nicander has primarily aesthetic concerns. Thus, the *Phaenomena* is an example of "transparent didactic," while the *Theriaca* is a "formal" didactic. See Effe 2005:27–34 for further discussion of this typology.

[42] In the *Phaenomena*, these targeted people are sailors (42, 419) and farmers (7–9), both of whom use constellations and signs. Nicander refers to farmers, cowherds, and carpenters (*Theriaca* 4–5) as those in possible need of remedies. For views that the actual audience is the *literati*, see Ludwig 1963:448 (for Aratus) and Touwaide 1991:91 (for Nicander).

[43] See Edmunds 1990b:1–20 and Brillante 1990:91–138 for an overview of ancient and modern approaches to Greek myth. Brillante discusses the relationship between myth and history. See also Veyne 1988:59–70.

[44] See Kidd 1997:9 for Aratus' stories. For Nicander's stories, see Effe 1977:63 and Overduin 2015:57–59. Effe 1988:403–407 compares the narratives of Aratus and Nicander. Fakas 2001a:481 proposes that the mythological stories allow Aratus to respond to Aristotle's criticism at *Poetics* 1447b17 that didactic poetry (like that of Empedocles) does not qualify as poetry because it lacks *mimesis*. Hutchinson 1988:216–224 discusses how Aratus treats the "interplay" between the stars as visible objects and mythological figures.

Indeed, Effe has observed that Nicander's myths appear in strategic locations in the poem.[45] At the same time, the narratives are fertile areas for displaying poetic virtuosity. Nicander, for instance, embeds his acrostic in the myth at *Theriaca* 343–358, while Aratus' Myth of Dike (*Phaenomena* 96–136) is a lengthy and complex reworking of Hesiod's Myth of the Ages (*Works and Days* 106–201). Finally, such tales bear thematic significance. While a symbolic function emerges clearly from an analysis of Aratus' extended Dike section, Nicander's myths likewise boast thematic potential, specifically for exposing the wickedness of deadly creatures.[46] As a result, my readings will feature consideration of these various functions. At the same time, I consider how these narratives intersect with the technical portions of the poem.

2.1 Origins stories

At the beginnings of their works, Aratus and Nicander incorporate mythological stories that explain the origins of their respective subjects. Describing the catasterism of the Bears (*Phaenomena* 30–35), Aratus narrates the childhood of the infant Zeus, whom the Bears protected on Crete. Since Zeus established the signs that make up Aratus' catalogue in the *Phaenomena* (10–13), the god himself is essential to Aratus' topic.[47] Nicander similarly deals with the topic of mythical birth, recounting how dangerous creatures originated from the blood of the Titans. Both stories, moreover, contain similar expressions that question the veracity of the narrative. Aratus employs εἰ ἐτεὸν δή ("if it is indeed true," *Phaenomena* 30) to introduce the story, while Nicander adapts this phrase to interrogate the truthfulness of Hesiod: εἰ ἐτεόν περ ... Ἡσίοδος κατέλεξε ("if Hesiod recounted truly," *Theriaca* 10, 12). As Kidd observes in his commentary on the *Phaenomena*, the adjective ἐτεός ("true") in Homer occurs in genealogical contexts and is thus particularly suited for a story about Zeus' childhood.[48] Yet the exact effects of these phrases remain ambiguous. Do they serve to provide an objective tone, as Stinton suggests for Aratus,[49] or is the effect to add doubt? Furthermore, to what extent does Nicander's use differ from Aratus'? Focusing on these expressions and the role of Hesiod, I argue that these two programmatic passages establish how to understand the two poets' respective topics.

---

[45] See Effe 1974a:57 for the placement of 343–358.
[46] Touwaide 1991:90 and Spatafora 2008:50.
[47] For the role of Zeus in the *Phaenomena*, see Rostropowicz 2003:219–228.
[48] Kidd 1997:184. For the use in Homer, see Homer *Odyssey* 3.122, 9.529, and 16.300.
[49] Stinton 1976:63–64. Cf. Kidd 1997:185.

2.1.1 Aratus' care Bears: *Phaenomena* 30–35

Aratus begins the catalogue of the northern constellations with a description of the two Bears (25–30). He then features a mythological story that explains their ascent into the sky:

> εἰ ἐτεὸν δή,
> Κρήτηθεν κεῖναί γε Διὸς μεγάλου ἰότητι
> οὐρανὸν εἰσανέβησαν, ὅ μιν τότε κουρίζοντα
> Δίκτῳ ἐν εὐώδει, ὄρεος σχεδὸν Ἰδαίοιο,
> ἄντρῳ ἐγκατέθεντο καὶ ἔτρεφον εἰς ἐνιαυτόν,
> Δικταῖοι Κούρητες ὅτε Κρόνον ἐψεύδοντο.

> If it is indeed true, those Bears ascended from Crete to heaven by the will of great Zeus, because, when he was then a boy in fragrant Dicton,[50] near Mount Ida, they deposited him in a cave and nurtured him for a year, while the Dictaean Curetes were deceiving Cronus.

Phaenomena 30–35

In describing Zeus' childhood, Aratus has drawn from the account in Hesiod's *Theogony*, signaling this influence with an array of verbal parallels. For instance, Διὸς μεγάλου ("of great Zeus") in *Phaenomena* 31 echoes Ζῆνα μέγαν in *Theogony* 479, and ἔτρεφον ("nurtured") in *Phaenomena* 34 recalls τρεφέμεν in *Theogony* 480. Furthermore, ἄντρῳ ("cave") occupies the same *sedes* at the beginning of the line in *Phaenomena* 34 and *Theogony* 483. [51] Yet in drawing a narrative from Hesiod, a literary source, Aratus is no longer treating the visible world of the sky, but rather a mythical narrative not subject to direct testing on visual grounds. Indeed, as Hunter points out, εἰ ἐτεὸν δή in 30 "marks the first introduction of what cannot be seen, but must be narrated."[52] As a result, in the context of a catalogue of visible constellations, the truth-value of this story appears problematic. Aratus in fact further calls the story's truth-value in question by identifying the Bears as Zeus' nurses on Crete. In doing so, he deviates not only

---

[50] Like Martin 1998.1:79–91, I maintain the reading of the MSS Δίκτῳ, taken by the scholion in MDΔKVUA to be the equivalent of Δίκτη. However, the scholiast (Σ *ad* 30–33; Martin 1974:85), as well as Strabo (10.4.12), criticizes Aratus for an error, on the grounds that Mount Dicte is more than a thousand stades from Ida. To eliminate this error, Kidd 1981:358 defends Grotius' conjecture Λύκτῳ, since the mountain appears at *Theogony* 477 and 482 as the place where Zeus was sent for hiding on Crete. This emendation would thus make Aratus adhere to Hesiod. Kidd posits paleographic corruption caused by the proximity of Δικταῖοι in 35.

[51] The bipartite structure of the *Phaenomena* is a reworking of the structure of the *Works and Days*. Porter 1946:158–170 argues that Aratus followed Hesiod's metrical practices.

[52] Hunter 2008b:182.

from his model, Hesiod (*Theogony* 477–484), but also from the other versions of the Bears myth.[53] At the same time, as was the case for Callimachus' *Hymn to Zeus*, the reference to Crete (Κρήτηθεν, 31) exudes connotations of falsehood, recalling Epimenides' paradoxical dictum Κρῆτες ἀεὶ ψεῦσται ("Cretans are always liars").[54] Aratus, by juxtaposing an expression concerning truth (εἰ ἐτεὸν δή) with a location famed for dishonesty (Κρήτηθεν), signals the possibility of falsehood entailed in the story.

Along with implying the story's potential falsehood, Aratus interweaves several paradoxes within the narrative. As both Effe and Fakas observe,[55] a paradox arises from the story's portrayal of Zeus. The description of Zeus as a child (μιν τότε κουρίζοντα, 32) conflicts with the image of Zeus in the proem, where Aratus employed traditional hymnic elements to depict him as a force pervading the universe and responsible for all things (*Phaenomena* 1–4). Aratus further suggests this all-powerful Zeus with the phrase Διὸς μεγάλου ἰότητι ("by the will of great Zeus," 31). Yet, by coordinating it with the participle κουρίζοντα ("when he was a boy," 32), Aratus makes the story present two contradictory versions of Zeus: one, an omnipotent deity, who can generate new constellations through his will, and the other, a child who was once dependent on the Bears for protection and nourishment. That Aratus places εἰ ἐτεὸν δή in the same position as κουρίζοντα and ἰότητι highlights this paradox.

This contradictory version of Zeus generates another paradox. As a deity, Zeus exerts his power through signs, which are characterized by their visibility (*Phaenomena* 6, 771–772). In the story, however, he is hidden in a cave (ἄντρῳ, 34), while the Curetes were deceiving Cronus (Δικταῖοι Κούρητες ὅτε Κρόνον ἐψεύδοντο, 35). Such deception took place over the span of the year (εἰς ἐνιαυτόν, 34), and this prepositional phrase echoes ἐσκέψατο δ' εἰς ἐνιαυτόν ("he organized for the year," 11). There (10–13), Aratus describes how Zeus fixed the constellations to follow a yearly and orderly cycle and thus allowed mortals consistency in their lives. The repetition of this phrase, which connoted regularity and visibility, in this context, however, is ironic, since it refers only to a single year of action (as opposed to a yearly cycle) and deals not with visible signs, but rather concealment and deception. Indeed, Aratus calls attention to this inconsistency by making ἐνιαυτόν mirror the placement

---

[53] Kidd 1997:185 and Martin 1998.2:166 both comment that Aratus seems to be the first to give a version of this myth. Elsewhere (e.g. Callimachus *Hymn to Zeus* 48–49), the goat Amaltheia is Zeus' nurse on Crete, while the Great Bear is the Arcadian nymph Callisto, assaulted by Zeus, but subsequently changed into a bear and then catasterized. See Martin 1998.2:162–166.

[54] Epimenides fr. 5 Kinkel. The quotation appears at Callimachus *Hymn to Zeus* 8. See Kidd 1997:185 for discussion of the quotation and the relationship of this section to Callimachus' *Hymn to Zeus*.

[55] Effe 1977:52 and Fakas 2001b:183.

of ἐψεύδοντο. Yet at the same time, the repetition of εἰς ἐνιαυτόν for both Zeus and the mythic Bears suggests a parallel between the two. Just as Zeus shows concern for men, so too did the Bears nourish (ἔτρεφον, 34) him. Furthermore, the Bears' depositing of Zeus in the cave corresponds to Zeus' placement of them in the heavens, and Aratus implies this analogy through the parallel placement of the verbs εἰσανέβησαν ("they ascended," 32) and ἐγκατέθεντο ("they deposited," 34).

Aratus further develops this parallel between Zeus and the Bears in the subsequent lines, where he again focuses on them as constellations:

καὶ τὴν μὲν Κυνόσουραν ἐπίκλησιν καλέουσιν,
τὴν δ᾽ ἑτέρην Ἑλίκην. Ἑλίκῃ γε μὲν ἄνδρες Ἀχαιοὶ
εἰν ἁλὶ τεκμαίρονται ἵνα χρὴ νῆας ἀγινεῖν.
τῇ δ᾽ ἄρα Φοίνικες πίσυνοι περόωσι θάλασσαν.
ἀλλ᾽ ἡ μὲν καθαρὴ καὶ ἐπιφράσσασθαι ἑτοίμη
πολλὴ φαινομένη Ἑλίκη πρώτης ἀπὸ νυκτός,
ἡ δ᾽ ἑτέρη ὀλίγη μέν, ἀτὰρ ναύτῃσιν ἀρείων,
μειοτέρη γὰρ πᾶσα περιστρέφεται στροφάλιγγι.
τῇ καὶ Σιδόνιοι ἰθύντατα ναυτίλλονται.

Now they call one of them Cynosura by name, and the other Helice. By Helice, Greek men at sea judge where it is suitable to steer ships, while the Phoenicians cross the sea trusting in the other. And the one, Helice, appearing large at the beginning of the night, is clear and easy to recognize, while the other is small, but better for sailors, for it revolves entirely in a smaller circle. By this one, the Sidonians sail the straightest.

Phaenomena 36–44

Helice is said to guide Greek sailors because it appears clear (καθαρή, 40), easy to recognize (ἐπιφράσσασθαι ἑτοίμη, 40), large (πολλή, 41), and at the beginning of the night (πρώτης ἀπὸ νυκτός, 41). For the Phoenician sailors, Cynosura, although small (ὀλίγη, 42), allows for the straightest (ἰθύντατα, 44) sailing. In connecting the constellations' appearance in the sky with their usefulness for navigation, Aratus again underscores the protecting function of the Bears. Just as they nurtured Zeus on Crete, they prevent sailors from becoming lost at sea. Yet, unlike the mythical Bears, the constellations benefit humans through their visibility, and it is through this visibility that they parallel Zeus, the omnipotent Stoic god, who first established the visible signs and whose status as source of order in the universe in fact mirrors the Bears' placement at the beginning of the pole.[56] Thus, in constructing this parallel between Zeus and the Bears, Aratus demonstrates how both qualify as "sources," that is, they are starting points with which humans can begin to comprehend the order of the universe.

In addition to serving as sources, both Zeus and the Bears have two manifestations: a mythical as well as a scientific manifestation. Indeed, as Hutchinson has observed, throughout the *Phaenomena*, Aratus vacillates between treating Zeus as a benevolent force, the figure of myth, and an another word for the "sky."[57] While the scientific manifestations of Zeus (the benevolent force and the sky) and the Bears (the constellations) are defined by their visibility, the mythic Bears are associated with concealment, since they hid the child Zeus. Motifs of hiding and concealment suit mythic narration, since myths account for things that cannot be perceived directly and are thus concealed from human knowledge. At the same time, myths involve sentient beings that purposely hide things, just as the gods hid men's livelihood according to *Works and Days* 42. Yet, as scholars have noted,[58] Aratus, by portraying Zeus as a deity whose signs are evident for all, transforms this image of a concealing Zeus. Aratus thus reworks Hesiod's Zeus, in the same way he has modified the Hesiodic account of Zeus' childhood to integrate the Bears.

Such a reworking of Hesiodic myth is an act of interpretation. After beginning with visible signs (the Bear constellations), Aratus attributes their origin to a mythic scenario that he suffuses with elements of falsehood, concealment, and paradox—all concepts antithetical to the visible and ordered world of the *Phaenomena*. In fact, Aratus' choice to return to the Bears as constellations (36–44) implies a subordination of the myth to the scientific concerns of the poem. Yet it is through the myth that the analogous functions of the Bears and Zeus as protectors becomes clearer. The myth, like the stars whose origin it explains, acts as the starting point for recognizing the order of the universe.

2.1.2 Nicander's creepy-crawlies: *Theriaca* 8–12

As in the *Phaenomena*, the first mythological story in the *Theriaca* appears at the beginning of the work, immediately after the proem (*Theriaca* 1–7). Describing the origin of deadly creatures, this tale combines verifiable scientific information with a dubious story:

Ἀλλ' ἤτοι κακοεργὰ φαλάγγια, σὺν καὶ ἀνιγρούς
ἑρπηστὰς ἔχιάς τε καὶ ἄχθεα μυρία γαίης

---

[56]   Erren 1967:33. See also Possanza 2004:86.
[57]   Hutchinson 1988:215. For Zeus meaning "sky," see *Phaenomena* 224, 253, 293, 899, and 936.
[58]   Kidd 1997:12. See also Kaibel 1894:84, Solmsen 1966:127, and Fantuzzi and Hunter 2004:230.

Τιτήνων ἐνέπουσιν ἀφ' αἵματος, εἰ ἐτεόν περ
Ἀσκραῖος μυχάτοιο Μελισσήεντος ἐπ' ὄχθαις
Ἡσίοδος κατέλεξε παρ' ὕδασι Περμησσοῖο.

But you know, they say that malicious spiders, along with painful reptiles and vipers and the countless burdens of the earth, are from the blood of the Titans, if indeed the Ascraean Hesiod recounted a catalogue truly on the banks of the secluded Melisseeis by the waters of the Permessus.

Theriaca 8–12

The first two lines consist of a catalogue of dangerous creatures: spiders (φαλάγγια, 8), reptiles (ἑρπηστάς, 9), vipers (ἔχιας, 9), and the "countless burdens of the earth" (ἄχθεα μυρία γαίης, 9). In listing these creatures, Nicander places emphasis on their potential for causing harm. The adjective κακοεργά ("malicious," 8), in particular, typically connotes purposeful intent,[59] and Nicander further highlights this idea of deadliness with the adjective ἀνιγρούς ("painful," 8), a rare word also found in a Callimachus fragment where it refers to an illness (Callimachus *Aetia* fr. 75.14). Since Nicander's persona previously mentioned "means of warding of diseases" (ἀλεξητήρια νούσων, 7), it makes sense to see here a parallel between diseases and deadly creatures. As is the case with diseases, the symptoms caused by the bites of deadly creatures are directly experienced by humans, such as the farmer, cowherd, and carpenter mentioned in the proem (4–5), all of whom confront the creatures while in the woods (καθ' ὕλην, 5). Indeed, Nicander notes the creatures' habitat in the earth with ἄχθεα μυρία γαίης (9), a poeticized phrase that combines the Homeric ἄχθος ἀρούρης ("burden of the land") with Empedocles' ἔθνεα μυρία θνητῶν ("countless races of mortals").[60] In addition to indicating the creatures' habitat in the ground, this phrase suggests the damage caused by creatures. The χ in ἄχθεα repeats the continuing string of gutturals (κακοεργά, φαλάγγια, ἀνιγρούς, ἔχιας), mimicking the harshness of bite.

While the contents of 8–9 consist of information that can be directly experienced, namely the effects and habitats of dangerous creatures, the subsequent information about their origins from the blood of Titans cannot be. Indeed, the mention of Titans in 10 brings the mythical sphere into play, specifically the primeval time of creation and overthrow.[61] With the verb ἐνέπουσιν ("they say,"

---

[59]   See Theocritus *Idyll* 15.47 (applied to a robber) and *Phaenomena* 131 (applied to a brigand's knife).
[60]   For ἄχθος ἀρούρης, see *Iliad* 18.104 and *Odyssey* 20.379. For ἔθνεα μυρία θνητῶν, see Empedocles DK 31 B 35.7 and 35.16.
[61]   See Sistakou 2012:198.

10), Nicander attaches this Ur-myth to an unspecified "they." It is impossible to determine whether this "they" refers to folk wisdom or to specific prose or poetic sources. Nevertheless, Nicander associates this unnamed group with a named source, Hesiod (12). Due to the association of the verb κατέλεξε (12) with catalogue verse,[62] we can assume that Nicander is referring to Hesiod producing a catalogue. At the same time, by bringing up the Titans, Nicander evokes the *Theogony*, the Hesiodic catalogue in which the Titans and their struggles with Zeus featured predominantly (674–731). Similarly, the geographic markers in 11–12 point to the *Theogony*. Περμησσοῖο in 12, for instance, appears in the same *sedes* as in *Theogony* 5. There, Hesiod describes how the Muses wash their skin in the stream of Permessus on Mount Helicon.[63] Moreover, the scholiast explains Μελισσήεντος ("Melisseeis," 11) as the place where the Muses manifested to Hesiod.[64]

Scholars have interpreted these references as signaling Hesiod's authority for Nicander's adaptation of catalogue verse.[65] Indeed, Hesiod, for Nicander, is a source, in the same way that the Titans' blood has engendered the deadly creatures. Yet the absence of this exact story in Hesiod has confounded both the scholiast and modern scholars. While the scholiast accuses Nicander of an error,[66] Cazzaniga and Knoefel and Covi have posited various explanations for Nicander associating this story with Hesiod.[67] Although it is impossible to know whether Nicander's "error" was intentional or not, the use of εἰ ἐτεόν περ further complicates the Hesiod citation. If taken literally, such a phrase implies the possibility of Hesiod not uttering the truth in his catalogues. By this logic, Hesiod's credibility is weakened, not just for the narrated story, but for anything that derives from his works. In fact, the famous initiation by the Muses in the *Theogony* already insinuates the possibility of Hesiod's falsehood.

---

[62] Kühlmann 1973:23–28.

[63] καί τε λοεσσάμεναι τέρενα χρόα Περμησσοῖο ("washing their delicate skin in the Permessus," *Theogony* 5).

[64] Σ *ad* 11c; Crugnola 1971:39: <Μελισσήεντος> Μελισσήεντα δέ φησιν τὸν τόπον τοῦ Ἑλικῶνος, ἐν ᾧ εὗρε τὰς Μούσας, ὃς οὕτως ἐκλήθη ἀπὸ Μελισσέως βασιλεύσαντος τοῦ τόπου ("of the Melisseeis: He says that the Melisseeis is a place on the Helicon, in which he [Hesiod] discovered the Muses. It was called so because of Melisseus who was king of the region").

[65] See Effe 1974b:120, Hunter 2014:26, and Overduin 2015:185.

[66] Σ *ad* 12a; Crugnola 1971:39. The scholiast then provides other authors' accounts of dangerous creatures' origins, citing Acusilaus (*FGrHist* 2 F 14) and Apollonius of Rhodes (fr. 4 Powell, *Foundation of Alexandria*), who identified the blood of Typhon and Medusa, respectively, as the source of snakes. See also *Argonautica* 4.1513–1517. See, moreover, Jacques 2002:78, who provides an overview of these sources.

[67] Cazzaniga 1975:178 proposes that Nicander had identified a *Titanomachia* as a work of true Hesiodic authorship. Knoefel and Covi 1991:53 hypothesize that Nicander saw the snake-legged Giants on the Altar of Zeus at Pergamon and conflated Giants with the Titans.

Hesiod's inspirers, the Muses, can tell "many falsehoods like real things" (ψεύδεα πολλὰ ... ἐτύμοισιν ὁμοῖα, *Theogony* 27), as well as the truth. Since the geographic markers Περμησσοῖο and Μελισσήεντος recall this encounter with the Muses, we can see εἰ ἐτεόν περ as similarly evoking this scene. An evocation of this scene inevitably brings up the problematic implications of the Muses' dual abilities for Hesiod's veracity.[68]

Thus, in pairing Hesiod's name with an expression of doubt while also recalling this encounter with the Muses, Nicander has infused his model with a mixture of authority and uncertainty, in the same way that the story blends verifiable scientific information (snakes' painfulness) with dubious mythical elements (the Titans). The absence of the exact story in Hesiod's works only increases the ambiguity of the Hesiod citation. Nevertheless, Hesiod's *Theogony* does feature a similar story of birth from blood:

> ὅσσαι γὰρ ῥαθάμιγγες ἀπέσσυθεν αἱματόεσσαι,
> πάσας δέξατο Γαῖα· περιπλομένου δ᾽ ἐνιαυτοῦ
> γείνατ᾽ Ἐρινῦς τε κρατερὰς μεγάλους τε Γίγαντας,
> τεύχεσι λαμπομένους, δολίχ᾽ ἔγχεα χερσὶν ἔχοντας...

> For Gaea received all the bloody drops that gushed forth. As the years went by, she begat the mighty Furies and the great Giants, who gleamed with their armor, holding long spears in their hands...

> *Theogony* 183–186

While Nicander deviates from the Hesiodic story with respect to mythological figures, he preserves the essential point of the narrative. Blood from an act of vengeance results in the creation of many harmful beings: the Furies and Giants after Uranus' castration by Cronus and deadly creatures from the Titans' blood. In fact, the Furies and Giants share many similarities with the deadly creatures described by Nicander. Like snakes and spiders, the Furies and Giants are chthonic beings, sprung from the earth both literally (from the ground) and figuratively (born from the goddess Gaea). Moreover, Furies, Giants, and deadly creatures all pose threats to the established order. Just as the Furies and Giants battle Zeus and the Olympians,[69] so too do deadly creatures, as Spatafora observes, undermine the social stability guaranteed by human exertion.[70] Indeed, Nicander frequently depicts such creatures as sentient evils incessantly menacing humans with their

---

[68] Cf. Overduin 2019:278n58, who is agnostic about the seriousness of εἰ ἐτεόν περ.
[69] For the rivalry between the Olympians and the Furies, see, for instance, Aeschylus *Eumenides* 225–234.
[70] Spatafora 2008:58.

bites.[71] Consequently, this variation of the Hesiodic narrative is appropriate. An oblique comparison with mythical paradigms of vengeance and violence (Furies and Giants) elucidates the deadly creatures' harmfulness and thus the incessant need for vigilance. The story, then, despite its dubiousness and apparent absence in Hesiod's works, nevertheless communicates a truth, but one that must be grasped by weighing Nicander's version against a Hesiodic version of births from divine blood. By instilling doubt regarding Hesiod's authority with εἰ ἐτεόν περ, Nicander, I suggest, urges the reader to undertake this process of discovery.

At the same time, εἰ ἐτεόν περ invites comparison with Aratus' phrase εἰ ἐτεὸν δή and its accompanying narrative. Both mythical stories appear at the beginning of their respective works and entail the origin of their poems' major subjects: Zeus for Aratus and dangerous creatures for Nicander. While the narrative at *Phaenomena* 30–35 illustrates Zeus' continued and manifest concern for mankind, Nicander's story emphasizes the vengeful hostility of dangerous creatures toward men. As a result, we can see that both narratives impart a truth, albeit obliquely, employing mythical paradigms that shed light on discernible phenomena.

Nicander's presentation of his story, however, differs from Aratus' treatment in several respects. In the *Phaenomena*, the phrase εἰ ἐτεὸν δή precedes the story about the Bears and Zeus. Nicander, on the other hand, uses εἰ ἐτεόν περ with reference to Hesiod, a literary source, as opposed to the story. In doing so, Nicander injects a greater amount of doubt into his mythological account. Questioning Hesiod's veracity not only problematizes the pertinent story, but undermines anything derived from Hesiod, who is himself a source for the format of catalogue verse. Moreover, unlike Aratus, who follows his story with a return to the visible world (*Phaenomena* 36–44), Nicander shifts to another mythological story about the creation of the scorpion (*Theriaca* 13–20; discussed below). The effect of these choices is significant. By returning to the visible world, Aratus can "confirm" the truth in his story, drawing a parallel between the protective functions of the constellation Bears and the mythical Bears. Nicander's transition to another myth, by contrast, leaves the issue of Hesiod's veracity unanswered. Such uncertainty surrounding Hesiod's veracity in fact suits the *Theriaca*'s subject matter. Just as one cannot know whether Hesiod recounted truly or falsely, or even if the story is in his oeuvre, so too is it difficult to anticipate the actions of hidden, evil creatures.

At the same time, Nicander has inverted Aratus' treatment of Hesiod and the Muses. Whereas Aratus modifies a Hesiodic story by featuring the Bears as Zeus' protectors, Nicander explicitly names Hesiod, albeit in connection with

---

[71] For examples of personification, see Overduin 2015:98–101.

a seemingly non-Hesiodic narrative. Additionally, in contrast with Aratus' clear request for the Muses' assistance (*Phaenomena* 16–18), Nicander neither addresses nor mentions them explicitly. Instead, Nicander merely hints at their encounter with Hesiod on Mount Helicon. Scholars have interpreted this suppression of the Muses as reflecting an increased emphasis on the poet as a source of knowledge.[72] Yet the absence of the Muses produces another consequence. Without the Muses to bestow knowledge as they do to poets traditionally (*Iliad* 2.484–487) or to guide by signs as at Aratus' *Phaenomena* 18, the uncertainty is only amplified, not just for the speaker, but also for the audience.

3. Myths of Decline and Loss

3.1 Introduction

As aetiological myths influenced by Hesiod, Aratus' Dike narrative (*Phaenomena* 96–136) and Nicander's story about the loss of youth (*Theriaca* 343–358) explain a phenomenon by narrating the decline and folly of mankind.[73] The wickedness of the Bronze Age triggers the goddess Dike's catasterism, while the loss of youth results in mankind's experience of old age, the thirst induced by the thirst-snake's bite, and the sloughing of skins by serpents. This loss occurs after humans foolishly relinquish youth to a donkey. Since both passages stand out as the most elaborate sections in their respective works,[74] they invite careful analysis of language and structure. Yet, as Schiesaro advises in the case of Aratus' Dike narrative, [75] the tales should not be read in isolation from their larger works. Analysis of the two passages reveals that each poet likens the story's respective subject to objects of scientific inquiry. Aratus' goddess Dike receives the attributes of a star, while Nicander portrays youth like a drug. As a result, both passages can reflect the processes of learning about the poems' respective subject matter. Via her visibility and regularity as a sign, Dike is a marker of truth, but one that men must interpret. The gift of youth, in being "lost,"

---

[72] See, for instance, Overduin 2019:278–280. See also Fakas 2001b:63n190 and Magnelli 2006:196–197.

[73] In Aratus' myth the progressive worsening of humanity over three generations recalls the Hesiodic Myth of Ages (*Works and Days* 106–201), which envisioned decline over five generations. Dike's departure from Earth in Aratus mimics the flight of Nemesis and Aedos (*Works and Days* 197–201). For a discussion of Aratus' imitation and revision of Hesiod in this passage, see Kaibel 1894:85–86, Ludwig 1963:440–442, Schwabl 1972:336–356, Landolfi 1996:1–21, and Fakas 2001b:151–175. Nicander's reference to Prometheus, who is obliquely called the "fire-thief" (πυρὸς ληΐστορ', 347), evokes Hesiod's version of the myth at *Theogony* 521–616 and *Works and Days* 47–58.

[74] Gow and Scholfield 1953:177.

[75] Schiesaro 1996:9.

symbolizes the concealment of knowledge, which one must recover through direct experience when encountering unexpected threats.

3.1.1 Disappearance of Dike

Aratus prefaces his lengthy narrative about Dike with a reference to the Maiden constellation, which he describes as located beneath the feet of Bootes and holding the dazzling Spica in her hands (96–97). In the subsequent lines, however, Aratus turns to an issue appropriate for a personified goddess, namely the Maiden's paternity. For this question, Aratus presents two possibilities: Astraeus or "some other" (τευ ἄλλου, 99). Since Hesiod identifies Zeus as the father of Dike (*Theogony* 902 and *Works and Days* 256), whom Aratus is equating with the Maiden constellation, we may read ἄλλου as an oblique reference to Zeus.[76] This choice to suppress Zeus, the traditional father of Dike, as the unnamed other parent places more attention on the first option, Astraeus, whose name is connected etymologically to his status as father of the stars (ἄστρων ἀρχαῖον πατέρ᾽, 99). By emphasizing Astraeus, the star father, as Dike's possible parent, Aratus implies her eventual transformation into a constellation.

The subsequent narrative continues these hints of a starlike Dike, as Aratus focuses on her changing location and visibility over the course of the Golden, Silver, and Bronze Ages. The regularly accessible Golden Age Dike is transformed into a constellation, who, despite her distance, remains as regularly visible as her Golden Age counterpart and attests to the existence of Justice. For this reason, van Noorden argues that the story of Dike's departure from earth "describes the origin of the poem's underlying principle that viewers must independently deduce meanings from signs."[77] Adopting van Noorden's emphasis on the importance of sign interpretation, I will propose further that Aratus' representation of a cyclical and starlike Dike, achieved by his ordered poetic language, reflects the circular processes of thought entailed in the interpretation of signs.

Aratus introduces his story as "another one that is current among men" (λόγος γε μὲν ἐντρέχει ἄλλος / ἀνθρώποις, 100–101).[78] The initial description of

---

[76] See Solmsen 1966:124n4. According to the scholiast (Σ *ad* 96; Martin 1974:126), the Maiden was also identified as Demeter, Isis, and Tyche.

[77] van Noorden 2009:260.

[78] ἄλλος with λόγος evokes ἕτερον ... λόγον at *Works and Days* 106 (the introduction to the Myth of the Ages). However, as Gee 2013:25–26 notes, Hesiod's other story succeeds the Myth of Prometheus, while Aratus gives no other version.

the Golden Age, moreover, continues this focus on humans, as Dike is initially
always available to them:

> ὡς δῆθεν ἐπιχθονίη πάρος ἦεν,
> ἤρχετο δ᾽ ἀνθρώπων κατεναντίη, οὐδέποτ᾽ ἀνδρῶν
> οὐδέποτ᾽ ἀρχαίων ἠνήνατο φῦλα γυναικῶν,
> ἀλλ᾽ ἀναμὶξ ἐκάθητο καὶ ἀθανάτη περ ἐοῦσα.
> καί ἑ Δίκην καλέεσκον· ἀγειρομένη δὲ γέροντας
> ἠέ που εἰν ἀγορῇ ἢ εὐρυχόρῳ ἐν ἀγυιῇ
> δημοτέρας ἤειδεν ἐπισπέρχουσα θέμιστας.

How actually she used to dwell on earth, and came face to face with
men, and never did she refuse the tribes of ancient men and women.
But she sat in their midst, even though she was immortal. And they
called her "Justice." Gathering the elders either in the agora or on the
broad street, she used to chant, urging them on to judgments favorable
to the people.

Phaenomena 101–107

Despite the goddess's immortal status (ἀθανάτη περ ἐοῦσα, 104), Aratus depicts
her as both visible and accessible. While she resided on earth (ἐπιχθονίη, 101),
never did she refuse these ancient men or women. Since the gods in Greek liter-
ature are typically concealed from normal mortal vision,[79] the depiction of an
accessible and visible goddess is remarkable, but nevertheless fits the extraordi-
nariness of this prelapsarian state, in which men and gods could mingle. Aratus
highlights this extraordinary situation by making the adjective ἀθανάτη occupy
the same metrical position as ἐπιχθονίη in 101. Along with κατεναντίη ("face
to face," 102), which also occurs in this position, these two adjectives feature
consonance (dentals and nus), as well as assonance. With this artful arrange-
ment of similarly sounding adjectives, all of which modify Dike, Aratus symbol-
izes the regularity of her availability during the Golden Age. She appears in the
same place in the line, just as she would manifest regularly on earth. Indeed,
even the participles ἀγειρομένη ("gathering," 105) and ἐπισπέρχουσα ("urging,"
107) are situated in similar positions in the line. By such regularity, Dike resem-
bles a star, and like a star, moreover, she receives a name. In this case, men name

[79] For example, at *Iliad* 1.198, Athena appears to Achilles alone. Hesiod describes his Dike as being
"cloaked in air" (ἠέρα ἑσσαμένη, *Works and Days* 223). The same description applies to the
immortal guardians who watch over mortals (*Works and Days* 255). Since Dike is mentioned in
this passage (*Works and Days* 256), Hunter 2008b:178 proposes that Aratus read these immortal
watchers as the stars.

her Justice (καί ἑ Δίκην καλέεσκον, 105). Yet, as van Noorden notes, it is not until men call her Dike that she becomes Dike.[80] In noting this fact, Aratus thus signals the importance of humans in establishing the identity of Dike.

During the Silver Age, this regular availability of Dike diminishes, as she no longer favors humans:

> ἀργυρέῳ δ᾽ ὀλίγη τε καὶ οὐκέτι πάμπαν ἑτοίμη
> ὡμίλει, ποθέουσα παλαιῶν ἤθεα λαῶν.
> ἀλλ᾽ ἔμπης ἔτι κεῖνο κατ᾽ ἀργύρεον γένος ἦεν,
> ἤρχετο δ᾽ ἐξ ὀρέων ὑποδείελος ἠχηέντων
> μουνάξ, οὐδέ τεῳ ἐπεμίσγετο μειλιχίοισιν...

She was accompanying the Silver Race only a little and no longer entirely readily, longing for the ways of the ancient men. But nevertheless, she was still with that race. She used to come from resounding mountains near the evening time, alone, and she did not engage anyone with friendly words...

Phaenomena 115–119

Aratus indicates this change of a formerly constant goddess by disrupting the pattern established by the previous lines, situating the adjectives that modify Dike, ὀλίγη ("a little," 115) and ἑτοίμη ("readily," 115), in locations different than the fourth *sedes*. At the same time, the combination of these two adjectives recalls the descriptions of the constellations Cynosura and Helice (ἑτοίμη at 40, ὀλίγη at 42) and thus expand this notion of a starlike Dike. However, in repeating these adjectives for Dike, Aratus calls attention to the differences between the Bears and the Silver Age Dike. While ὀλίγη and ἑτοίμη occurred in a discussion of the Bears' utility for sailors, the words for Dike attest to her decreased helpfulness toward humans. No longer (οὐκέτι, 115) is she ready, and unlike the Bears, her visibility is reduced.

Aratus expands on Dike's reduced visibility in the subsequent lines. For instance, when upbraiding men for their wickedness (121), she threatens never to appear when they call (οὐδ᾽ ἔτ᾽ ἔφη εἰσωπὸς ἐλεύσεσθαι καλέουσιν, 122), and after abandoning them in the hills, she leaves all the people still looking toward her (τοὺς δ᾽ ἄρα λαοὺς / εἰς αὐτὴν ἔτι πάντας ἐλίμπανε παπταίνοντας, 127–128). As Schiesaro observes,[81] Aratus, in making humans (πάντας ... παπταίνοντας, 128) the passive recipients of Dike's verbal action, indicates the shift from the mutual relationship between the two parties during the Golden Age. Such

[80] van Noorden 2009:263.
[81] Schiesaro 1996:11.

a mutual relationship involved her regular visibility and accessibility, and in altering her visibility, Dike becomes, in one sense, less like a constellation. Yet by absconding into the hills (ὀρέων ἐπεμαίετο, 127) and limiting her approachability, Dike veers to her eventual constellation status. Like a constellation, she is distant from men; her absence forces men to exert effort in finding her, and Kidd notes that the verb παπταίνοντας (128) implies wistful sadness.[82]

The advent of the Bronze Age (129–132) finalizes Dike's withdrawal from mankind and ascent into the stars, since she despises their wicked ways:

καὶ τότε μισήσασα Δίκη κείνων γένος ἀνδρῶν
ἔπταθ' ὑπουρανίη, ταύτην δ' ἄρα νάσσατο χώρην
ἧχί περ ἐννυχίη ἔτι φαίνεται ἀνθρώποισι
Παρθένος ἐγγὺς ἐοῦσα πολυσκέπτοιο Βοώτεω.

Dike, then coming to hate the generation of those men, flew into the sky. So, she settled in that region where she still appears at night for men as the Maiden, near conspicuous Bootes.

Phaenomena 133–136

The phrase ἔτι φαίνεται ("still appears," 135) responds to ἔτι πάντας ἐλίμπανε παπταίνοντας ("she left all still looking," 128), marking the contrast between her current visibility and her former absence during the Silver Age. Since she now dwells in the sky, in a fixed location, no longer must men search longingly for her. Indeed, Aratus suggests this regularity at the verbal level by coordinating the words μισήσασα ("coming to hate," 133), ὑπουρανίη ("into the sky," 134), and ἐννυχίη ("at night," 135), mimicking the artful parallel arrangement of adjectives featured in the Golden Age section. Yet, unlike the Golden Age version, this Dike in the sky is merely an object of viewing, rather than a personified goddess always available to men and their needs. In this form, she no longer speaks directly to humans, either kindly or cruelly.[83] Rather, her presence in the sky necessitates interpretation from the part of the viewer, who must equate the goddess Dike of the narrative with the Maiden in the sky. Aratus calls attention to this fact by filling 136 with echoes from 96–97, where he introduced the Maiden constellation. Occupying the same *sedes*, παρθένος in 136 echoes παρθένον in 97, and the genitive Βοώτεω ends lines 96 and 136. The adjective

---

[82] Kidd 1997:228.

[83] For the changes in Dike's modes of communication, see Volk 2012:224–225. As scholars have emphasized, Dike is the only figure in the *Phaenomena* who speaks directly. Wilson 2018b:324–327 analyzes Dike's changes in terms of performance and education. For discussions of Dike's voice, see also Faulkner 2015:75–86 and Cusset 2018:93–95.

πολυσκέπτοιο ("conspicuous," 136), moreover, recalls the verb σκέπτοιο ("you may regard") in 96. With the repetition of these words, which emphasize the constellation's visibility, the passage forms a ring composition.[84]

Such a circular structure, while attesting to the overall artfulness in the passage, serves a larger goal, mirroring the circular progression of Dike's transformation, whereby, as a goddess, she began with the aspects of a constellation, only to conclude as one. At the same time, the circular structure of the passage represents the circularity of thinking involved in interpreting a sign. For a sign to have a meaning, it must be constant and regular (like a constellation), but a preconceived notion from the interpreter is required. In this case, the viewer must have previously equated the Maiden with Dike. Thus, the agent who perceives is crucial in determining meaning.[85] Aratus, in his account of Dike, in fact emphasized the role of human beings as perceivers, beginning the story with the dative ἀνθρώποις ("among humans," 101) and ending the story with another dative ἀνθρώποισι (136). By pairing ἀνθρώποις with λόγος ... ἄλλος (100) and ἀνθρώποισι with φαίνεται ("appears," 135), Aratus demonstrates how it is ultimately the task of humans to perceive a visible phenomenon and apply a rational account upon it.

3.1.2 Disappearance of youth

While Aratus labels his Dike narrative as an "another account" (λόγος ... ἄλλος, 100) current among men, Nicander characterizes his tale, which he inserts in a discussion of the διψάς ("thirst-snake"), as an ancient μῦθος: ὠγύγιος δ' ἄρα μῦθος ἐν αἰζηοῖσι φορεῖται ("so a very ancient tale is current among men," 343). Since μῦθος can mean "fable," as well as a mythological narrative,[86] the word is fitting for a story that narrates the interaction between anthropomorphized animals, the donkey and the snake.[87] Both animals trigger the loss of youth, when the thirsty donkey trades the snake youth for a drink of water (*Theriaca* 350–354). In subtly likening youth to a drug, as I will argue, Nicander allows this ornamental passage featuring the famous acrostic at 345–353 and replete with kennings to encapsulate the larger scientific concerns of the *Theriaca*. Specifically, this narrative attests to the role of direct experience in

---

[84] For an analysis of the ring composition featured in the passage, see Gatz 1967:63 and Schwabl 1972:345.
[85] As van Noorden 2015:190 notes, "Her status as a 'sign' means that she can be appropriated differently by different viewers, depending on the resources they bring to bear on interpretation."
[86] For μῦθος as "fable," see van Dijk 1997:84–88.
[87] According to Aelian (*On the Nature of Animals* 6.51), Sophocles (fr. 362 Radt) and Ibycus (fr. 342 *PMGF* Davies) recounted this narrative, as did Deinolochus, Aristias, and Apollophanes.

encountering hidden and pernicious threats. At the same time, the profusion of riddling language compels the reader to reenact this process of discovery.

Nicander establishes the physicality of youth in the opening lines of the story, when he tells how Zeus first granted the gift to mortals only for them to waste it:

> ὡς, ὁπότ᾽ οὐρανὸν ἔσχε Κρόνου πρεσβίστατον αἷμα,
> νειμάμενος κασίεσσιν ἑκὰς περικυδέας ἀρχάς
> ἰδμοσύνῃ νεότητα γέρας πόρεν ἡμερίοισι
> κυδαίνων· δὴ γάρ ῥα πυρὸς ληΐστορ᾽ ἔνιπτον.
> ἄφρονες, οὐ μὲν τῆς γε κακοφραδίης ἀπόνηντο·
> νωθεῖ γὰρ κάμνοντες ἀμορβεύοντο λεπάργῳ
> δῶρα· πολύσκαρθμος δὲ κεκαυμένος αὐχένα δίψῃ
> ῥώετο· γωλειοῖσι δ᾽ ἰδὼν ὀλκήρεα θῆρα
> οὐλοὸν ἐλλιτάνευε κακῇ ἐπαλαλκέμεν ἄτῃ
> σαίνων· αὐτὰρ ὁ βρῖθος, ὃ δὴ ῥ᾽ ἀνεδέξατο νώτοις
> ᾔτεεν ἄφρονα δῶρον, ὁ δ᾽ οὐκ ἀπανήνατο χρειώ.

How, when the eldest offspring of Cronus acquired the heavens, he distributed illustrious realms separately to his brothers, and in his wisdom, he bestowed youth as a gift for mortals, honoring them. For indeed, they denounced the fire-thief. Thoughtless ones! In their sense-lessness, they did not benefit from it! In their weariness, they handed over the gifts to the sluggish white-coated one. And that one, its throat burning with thirst, rushed off with many leaps. And when it saw the deadly trailing beast in its hole, it fawned and begged that one to ward off the terrible plight. But the snake asked the foolish one for a gift, the load that it carried on its back. The donkey did not refuse the request.

Theriaca 344–354

Along with forming a pun that plays on the similarity between γέρας ("gift") and γῆρας ("old age"),[88] the juxtaposition of νεότητα ("youth," 346) and γέρας attributes a material form to the concept of youth. Although the text does not explicitly indicate the shape and appearance of youth, Overduin proposes that youth could be a herb. His evidence for this claim is based on the parallel in the *Epic of Gilgamesh,* in which a snake steals a plantlike coral of rejuvenation.[89] In Aelian's version (*On the Nature of Animals* 6.51), moreover, youth is called "a drug that wards off old age" (φάρμακον γήρως ἀμυντήριον). Applying this idea

---

[88] See Reeve 1996–1997:246 and van Dijk 1997:135.
[89] Overduin 2015:316–317.

to the story is attractive, since a significant portion of the *Theriaca* concerns the properties of herbs and plants and their roles in healing.[90] In fact, Nicander also refers to youth as a βρῖθος ("load," 353). Since the noun βρῖθος occurs at two other places in the *Theriaca* in the context of recipes for remedies, specifically two recipes that involve animal parts,[91] its use here strongly implies that Nicander is imagining youth as a kind of drug. The story, thus, recounts how men originally possessed knowledge of a remedy, but ultimately lost it in their folly (κακοφραδίης, 348).

This loss of youth occurs at the hands of a donkey and a snake, both of whom are designated by allusive kennings. The donkey is a "sluggish white-coated one" (νωθεῖ ... λεπάργῳ, 349),[92] and the snake is the "deadly trailing beast" (ὁλκήρεα θῆρα / οὐλοόν, 351–352). The use of such riddling language is appropriate for the fable format. Indeed, Nagy notes that αἶνος, the archaic word for fable, in Homer denotes "an allusive tale containing an ulterior purpose."[93] Here, the kennings contribute to the overall theme of the concealment of youth, while also working in conjunction with the famous ΝΙΚΑΝΔΡΟΣ acrostic embedded in 345–353.[94] Like the acrostic, the kennings demand decipherment from the reader to determine the identity of the animals.

---

[90] The section detailing the herbs and remedies against snakebites begins at 493 and continues until 714. The remedies against other creatures are listed in 837–956.

[91] For βρῖθος, see lines 102 and 712. The former recipe is a prophylactic ointment against snakebites, consisting of two snakes mating in the crossroads, the marrow of a freshly killed stag, and rose oil. At 700–713, the final recipe against snakebites, Nicander describes a mixture of sea-turtle blood, wild cumin, and the curd from a hare's stomach.

[92] Following Hopkinson 1988, Jacques 2002, and Overduin 2015, I adopt the dative singular, as opposed to the nominative plural νωθεῖς, which Gow and Scholfield print and take to modify humans. The strongest evidence for reading the adjective as dative to modify the donkey is an allusion to *Iliad* 11.558–559, where the adjective is also applied to an donkey. λεπάργῳ is a modification of Callimachus' πελαργός ("stork," fr. 271 Pf.). See Hopkinson 1988:145.

[93] Nagy 1999:237 and van Dijk 1997:79–82.

[94] See Lobel 1928:114 for the discovery of the acrostic. For a summary of the functions of Nicander's acrostic, see Overduin 2015:312–315. The acrostic can act as a seal (σφραγίς), a reminder for the reader of Aratus' ΛΕΠΤΗ acrostic at *Phaenomena* 783–787, and as a means of preserving the poet's immortal fame. This wish for immorality is especially pertinent in the context of the loss of youth. Sullivan 2013:241–242 argues that Nicander's other acrostic at *Alexipharmaca* 266–274, which can be read with Jacques' emendation of ἀσκηροῦ ("a type of chestnut") for the MSS καστηνοῦ ("chestnut") in 269, represents the antidote to the loss of youth. In these lines, Nicander gives the recipe against the deadly ἐφήμερον. In addition to having the acrostic with Nicander's name, both passages feature verbal similarities, such as the verb ὀπάζει (*Alexipharmaca* 270 and *Theriaca* 356), as well as a reference to Prometheus (*Alexipharmaca* 273 and *Theriaca* 347). Since the *Alexipharmaca* passage describes the remedy against a deadly poison, Sullivan (241–242) argues that "the poet transforms the 'victory over man' in the *Theriaca* acrostic into a 'victory of man' in its *Alexipharmaca* passage, and a double victory for the man himself, ΝΙΚΑΝΔΡΟΣ."

Through these allusive kennings, Nicander elucidates the dangerousness of both the donkey and the snake, constructing a parallel between the two parties. For instance, in referring to the donkey's sluggishness with νωθεῖ (349), Nicander recalls previous uses of the word for the movement of snakes. At 165 Nicander relates how the cobra sluggishly throws off sleep from its body (νωθρὴ μὲν ἀπὸ ῥέθεος βάλεν ὕπνον).[95] Similarly, νωθής appears in the discussion of the viper, modifying the noun ὁλκῷ: νωθεῖ δ' ἔνθα καὶ ἔνθα διὰ δρυμὰ νίσεται ὁλκῷ ("with its sluggish coil, it moves here and there through the thickets," 222). By using an adjective that he applied previously to snakes, Nicander implies a connection between snakes and the donkey of the story. Like the cobra and the viper, the donkey seems innocuous due to its normal sluggishness. Yet, as Nicander makes clear with πολύσκαρθμος ("with many leaps," 350) and ῥώετο ("rushed off," 351), the donkey, its throat burning with thirst (κεκαυμένος αὐχένα δίψῃ, 350), quickens its movement and becomes active.[96] In this way, the donkey of the story compares to the cobra, which, when perceiving a new sight or sound, "raises its bristling head in a terrifying manner" (λευγαλέον δ' ἀνὰ μέσσα κάρη πεφρικὸς ἀείρει, 167). It is in this aroused state when the cobra becomes dangerous. In this story, the donkey, while not purposely malicious and dangerous on its own, does harm humans. Its suffering and foolishness (ἄφρονα, 354) make it relinquish the precious remedy of youth, instigating the loss of the gift from mankind.

While νωθεῖ generates an implicit parallel between the donkey and snakes, Nicander's description of the snake as the "trailing and deadly beast" (ὁλκήρεα θῆρα / οὐλοόν, 351–352) in the fable matches the poem's general depiction of snakes. With the two adjectives ὁλκήρεα ("trailing") and οὐλοόν ("deadly"), Nicander indicates two important aspects of the snake: its movement and its lethalness. Additionally, the dative noun γωλειοῖσι ("in its hole," 351) refers to the snake's habitat, a topic frequently mentioned by Nicander in his treatment of individual snakes.[97] As I noted above (section 2), the hidden abodes of snakes increase their deadliness. Thus, in referring to this aspect here, Nicander anticipates the snake's harmfulness toward mankind. Ultimately, the snake's acceptance of youth cements the loss of this gift from mankind.

---

[95] νωθρός is a variant of νωθής. Jacques 2002:15 prints the nominative νωθρή, preserved in Parisinus suppl. gr. 247. Gow and Scholfield 1953:38 print νωθῆ, taking the adjective to agree with ὕπνον.

[96] Due to the donkey's quick movement in the story, Hopkinson 1988:145 prefers to translate νωθής as "stupid." However, as Jacques 1969:48 contends, the adjective πολύσκαρθμος is not a natural characteristic, but rather indicates the ass's current movement.

[97] The word occurs earlier in a description of the habitat of the thirst-snake: ὅτε σὺν τέκνοισι θερειομένοισιν ἀβοσκὴς / φωλειοῦ λοχάδην ὑπὸ γωλεὰ διψὰς ἰαύῃ ("when the unfed thirst-snake sleeps with the children it broods, lurking in the recesses of its hole," 124–125).

In the final four lines of the section, Nicander summarizes the ramifications of this exchange:

ἐξότε γηραλέον μὲν ἀεὶ φλόον ἑρπετὰ βάλλει
ὀλκήρη, θνητοὺς δὲ κακὸν περὶ γῆρας ὀπάζει·
νοῦσον δ' ἀζαλέην βρωμήτορος οὐλομένη θήρ
δέξατο, καί τε τυπῇσιν ἀμυδροτέρῃσιν ἰάπτει.

From this point, trailing serpents always cast aside their coverings in old age, and baneful old age attends mortals. The deadly beast received the disease of thirst from the brayer and transmits it with its feeble blows.

Theriaca 355–358

As with the portrayal of youth, Nicander presents abstract physiological states like old age and thirst as physical objects subject to exchange. Serpents discard their senescence in the form of their sloughed skin, and old age attends (ὀπάζει, 356) men. Moreover, Nicander frames thirst as a disease (νοῦσον, 357) that can be received (δέξατο, 358), just as the donkey had received (ἀνεδέξατο, 353) youth on its back. The thirst-snake can in turn transfer this thirst via its feeble bites. In emphasizing the physicality of these states, Nicander signals the imminence of such phenomena. Old age and thirst, while not literal exchangeable objects, nevertheless wreak perceivable changes on a body.

At the same time, Nicander continues the kennings in these concluding lines. Here the donkey is "the brayer" (βρωμήτορος, 357) and the snake the "deadly beast" (οὐλομένη θήρ, 357). While the former designation refers to the donkey's unpleasant sound, the latter phrase reaffirms the threatening nature of the thirst-snake, as οὐλομένη (357) echoes οὐλοόν (352). Through this sustained use of riddling language, Nicander further represents the persistent need for discovery amid the constant threats of snakes and deadly creatures. The permanent transference of youth, from men to snakes, has only magnified this danger. Not only do men now lack the remedy of youth, but they must deal with snakes' constant shedding and regeneration, as well as the bites of the thirst-snake. Such is the consequence of human folly combined with the foolishness of the donkey and the wickedness of the snake.

By falling into the possession of serpents, the gift of youth differs greatly from the subject of *Phaenomena* 96–136: the star / goddess Dike / Maiden. As a distant constellation in the sky, Dike does not directly affect humans. In fact, her departure from earth still allows men to enjoy her as a visible sign, albeit one that must be interpreted and identified as one. Gee, moreover, points out,[98] "By

---

[98] Gee 2013:24.

turning Dike into a star, Aratus makes Hesiod's open-ended narrative of decline into a closed loop in which the notion of cyclicality replaces the Hesiodic time-line." In this way, Aratus employs this Dike λόγος to counteract the pessimism inherent in Hesiod's Myth of the Ages. In Nicander's μῦθος, by contrast, the movement of youth follows a linear progression of decline more akin to Hesiod's pessimistic world.[99] Initially a remedy bestowed by Zeus, youth becomes forever lost from humans, perceived only in the exuviae of serpents. Additionally, whereas Aratus tracked the upward shift from a goddess residing on earth to a constellation in the sky, Nicander demonstrates how a gift from heaven became assimilated into the earthborn snake. In inverting Aratus' progression, Nicander further reveals the concealment of his subject matter. Such concealment in turn breeds greater uncertainty.

4. Narratives of Discovery

While *Phaenomena* 96-136 and *Theriaca* 343-358 concern the loss of entities (Dike and youth), both poems also contain narratives that deal with the act of discovery by first finders. At *Phaenomena* 373-382, Aratus recounts how an unnamed person ordered and named the stars. Nicander, by contrast, inserts three stories about first finders (501-502, 541-549, 666-675) in the first remedy portion of the poem (493-714). As I will demonstrate, not only do these stories present various modes of discovery, they also clarify the relationship between names and the poets' respective subject matter. Whereas names, appearance, and identity are intricately linked for constellations, the naming of herbs is based on multiple possibilities.

4.1 Finder of the stars

Aratus' narrative of discovery appears after a description of the nameless stars (367-373). Whirling between the Argo's Rudder and Cetus and under the Hare's flanks, they are small, dim, and form no distinct shape (367-371). Other constel-lations, however, bear a name, thanks to the efforts of an unnamed finder:[100]

> τά τις ἀνδρῶν οὐκέτ' ἐόντων
> ἐφράσατ' ἠδ' ἐνόησεν ἅπαντ' ὀνομαστὶ καλέσσαι
> ἤλιθα μορφώσας· οὐ γάρ κ' ἐδυνήσατο πάντων
> οἰόθι κεκριμένων ὄνομ' εἰπέμεν, οὐδὲ δαῆναι.
> πολλοὶ γὰρ πάντη, πολέων δ' ἐπὶ ἶσα πέλονται

99 For a similar point, see Wilson 2015:181.
100 For discussion of this finder's identity, see Effe 1970:182, who posits that this person might be one of the early discoverers discussed by Persaeus (Cicero *On the Nature of the Gods* 1.15.38).

μέτρα τε καὶ χροιή, πάντες γε μὲν ἀμφιέλικτοι.
τῷ καὶ ὁμηγερέας οἱ ἐείσατο ποιήσασθαι
ἀστέρας, ὄφρ᾽ ἐπιτὰξ ἄλλῳ παρακείμενος ἄλλος
εἴδεα σημαίνοιεν. ἄφαρ δ᾽ ὀνομαστὰ γένοντο
ἄστρα, καὶ οὐκέτι νῦν ὑπὸ θαύματι τέλλεται ἀστήρ.

One of the men who no longer exist marked the constellations and planned to call them all by name, forming them into compact shapes. He would not have been able to utter the names of them all distinguished individually, or to comprehend them. Because there are many everywhere, the size and color of many are alike, while all revolve. For this reason, he decided to assemble the stars, so that different stars arranged in order next to each other could signal shapes. After that, the named constellations came to be, and now no longer does a star rising cause us amazement.

Phaenomena 373–382

In reading this important passage, scholars have fixated on two major issues. The first of these is the meaning of the verb ἐφράσατο in 374. Does this verb mean only that the unnamed person "observed" the constellations, or does it imply that he also "devised" them?[101] Pendergraft, moreover, deems this section contradictory to the claim that Zeus formed the constellations (*Phaenomena* 10–13) and to the catasterism narratives (e.g. 30–35; 96–136).[102] Yet there is no inherent contradiction between Zeus' initial organization and the contributions of this discoverer. Indeed, for Zeus' signs to convey meaning, humans must recognize this order through distinct constellation groupings.[103]

This passage, in fact, expands and clarifies the earlier section describing Zeus' role in creating signs. Not only do both passages address the organization of the universe, verbal parallels attest to an intratextual relationship. For instance, σημαίνοιεν ("signal," 381) echoes σημαίνοιεν in 12. τις ἀνδρῶν ("one of the men," 373) corresponds to ἀνδράσιν in 13, and κεκριμένων ("distinguished," 376) recalls διακρίνας (11). Yet, whereas in the earlier passage Aratus highlights Zeus' role in creation and frames humans as recipients, here the unnamed human is the perceiver and thus the "creator" of the constellations. In contrast with the named and immortal Zeus, however, this person is emphatically anonymous and exists no longer. By effacing the identity of this mortal finder, Aratus

---

[101] Martin 1998.1:22 (2:310) favors the former translation (*"a observées"*), citing *Iliad* 23.450. Kidd 1997:320 opts for the latter translation.
[102] Pendergraft 1990:104. For discussions of this passage, see Kidd 1997:320 and Volk 2012:220–222.
[103] For this interpretation, see Volk 2012:220.

can instead stress the usefulness of his contributions, as he does by highlighting the impossibility of identifying each star on its own (375–378).

At the same time, the structure of this passage exhibits a ring composition organization analogous to that displayed in the Dike passage.[104] For instance, the adverb οὐκέτι ("no longer") appears in both 373 and 382. Likewise, Aratus presents the information in a circular fashion. The mention of naming (ὀνομαστὶ καλέσσαι, 374) precedes the description of organizing the constellations (ἤλιθα μορφώσας, 375). Aratus then refers to these acts again in 379–382. Together τῷ καὶ ὁμηγερέας οἱ ἐείσατο ποιήσασθαι / ἀστέρας (379–380) and ὄφρ' ἐπιτὰξ ἄλλῳ παρακείμενος ἄλλος / εἴδεα σημαίνοιεν (380–381) restate and expand ἤλιθα μορφώσας (375), while ὀνομαστὰ γένοντο (381) corresponds to ὀνομαστὶ καλέσσαι (374). The result is a chiastic structure (name, shape, shape, name), through which Aratus suggests the close link between the shaping and the application of the name. Indeed, both inform the other.

The chiastic structure and the emphasis on names continue in the three following lines, where Aratus returns to the nameless stars beneath the Hare:

ἀλλ' οἱ μὲν καθαροῖς ἐναρηρότες εἰδώλοισι
φαίνονται, τὰ δ' ἔνερθε διωκομένοιο Λαγωοῦ
πάντα μάλ' ἠερόεντα καὶ οὐκ ὀνομαστὰ φέρονται.

So those stars appear fixed in clear shapes, but those beneath the pursued Hare are all carried along quite hazily and without a name.

Phaenomena 383–385

In these three lines, Aratus presents a contrast between the distinct, named stars and the dim and nameless ones beneath the Hare. With οὐκ ὀνομαστά ("without a name," 385), Aratus recalls not only ὀνομαστά in 381, but also νώνυμοι in 370. Likewise, as in 367–368, Aratus refers to the dimness of the nameless stars with πάντα μάλ' ἠερόεντα in 385. By referring to these stars' dimness in conjunction with their namelessness, he further implies the close correlation between appearance and naming.

So great is this link between the naming and shape of constellations that deviations necessitate justification. For instance, the Pleiades, described earlier at 254–267, pose a difficulty for Aratus. Although there are seven Pleiades according to the mythic narrative (257), Aratus counts only six as clear to the eyes (258).[105] Proclaiming that no star has ever been lost since the beginning

---

[104] On this chiasmus, see Kidd 1997:318, Gee 2000:85, and Semonoff 2006a:172.

[105] For discussion of this difficult passage, see Kidd 1997:274–278, Martin 1998.2:263–268, and Hunter 2008b:184–185. Hipparchus (1.6.14), however, criticized Aratus for failing to notice the

of the oral tradition and thereby discounting the narratives in which one star vanishes,[106] Aratus nevertheless names all seven Pleiades (262–263). At the same time, he affirms the stars' famousness as well as usefulness for agriculture:

αἱ μὲν ὁμῶς ὀλίγαι καὶ ἀφεγγέες, ἀλλ' ὀνομασταὶ
ἦρι καὶ ἑσπέριαι, Ζεὺς δ' αἴτιος, εἰλίσσονται
ὅ σφισι καὶ θέρεος καὶ χείματος ἀρχομένοιο
σημαίνειν ἐπένευσεν ἐπερχομένου τ' ἀρότοιο.

They are all alike, small and faint, but famously they revolve at dawn and in the evening, with Zeus responsible, he who sanctioned them to signal the beginning of summer and winter and the arrival of plowing time.

Phaenomena 264–267

Unlike the dim and nameless stars beneath the Hare, these faint stars are famous (ὀνομασταί, 264). Zeus ensures this fame by assigning these stars to signal (σημαίνειν, 266) the beginnings of summer, winter, and the time to plow. By attaching their fame to this signifying function, Aratus yet again poses a correlation between name and appearance. In this case, the ambiguities stem less from the faded appearance of these stars than from a complicated mythic tradition, which allows for the disappearance of one star. For the purposes of farmers relying on the Pleiades, the visibility of six or seven stars does not matter.[107]

4.2 Chiron's herb

Like Aratus, Nicander also treats the discovery of his subject matter. In the *Theriaca*, the first discovery narrative occurs shortly after the transition from snake-bites to remedies (493–496). The narrative itself is brief, wedged between an initial description of the discovered plant and additional details about appearance, location, and intake method:

πρώτην μὲν Χείρωνος ἐπαλθέα ῥίζαν ἑλέσθαι
Κενταύρου Κρονίδαο φερώνυμον, ἥν ποτε Χείρων
Πηλίου ἐν νιφόεντι κιχὼν ἐφράσσατο δειρῇ.

---

seventh star.

[106] For instance, elsewhere (Σ ad 259; Martin 1974:206), Aratus narrated that Electra vanished from the sky when grieving over the destruction of Troy. See also Ovid *Fasti* 4.171–178.

[107] As Possanza 2004:96 points outs, Aratus does not provide enough information regarding when the Pleiades rise and set. This omission contrasts with Hesiod in the *Works and Days* (383–387), who specifies forty days of invisibility.

τῆς μὲν ἀμαρακόεσσα χυτὴ περιδέδρομε χαίτη,
ἄνθεα δὲ χρύσεια φαείνεται· ἡ δ' ὑπὲρ αἴης
ῥίζα καὶ οὐ βυθόωσα Πελεθρόνιον νάπος ἴσχει
ἣν σὺ καὶ αὐαλέην, ὁτὲ δ' ἔγχλοον ὅλμῳ ἀράξας
φυρσάμενος κοτύλῃ πιέειν μενοεικέος οἴνης·
παντὶ γὰρ ἄρκιός ἐστι· τό μιν πανάκειον ἔπουσιν.

First, choose the curative herb of Chiron, which bears the name of the
Centaur son of Cronus. Chiron once observed after he came upon it in
the snowy peaks of Pelion. Luxuriant foliage, like marjoram, surrounds
it, and its flowers appear gold. The root grows at the surface and not
deep in the vale of Pelethronius. Crush it in a mortar, dried and or when
fresh, and mix it in a cup of pleasant wine and drink. It is suitable for
everything. They call it all-heal.

Theriaca 500–508

In introducing this root (centaury), Nicander first conveys its name with the
genitive Χείρωνος ("of Chiron," 500). In doing so, he establishes the passage's
sustained interest in naming, one that is continued with the periphrastic appo-
sitional phrase Κενταύρου Κρονίδαο φερώνυμον ("which bears the name of the
Centaur son of Cronus," 501). Following this phrase, Nicander inserts an explan-
atory relative clause: the Centaur Chiron unearthed it while traversing his
native region of Mount Pelion.[108] Yet aside from tagging Chiron as the πρῶτος
εὑρητής, ("first finder"), this brief narrative illustrates the relationship between
direct experience and discovery. Chiron's "coming upon" (κιχών, 502) the herb
triggered his observation (ἐφράσσατο, 502) regarding its appearance, which
Nicander details in 503–505.[109] Additionally, since the verb φράζομαι reoccurs
throughout the poem and applies to the audience (e.g. 70, 157, etc.), the use here
suggests a parallel between Chiron's actions and those of the audience. That is,
Chiron's initial discovery in the mythical past serves as an exemplar for any
present and future discoveries of this herb.

At the same time, ἐφράσσατο in 502, the same verb employed by Aratus
at *Phaenomena* 374, invites comparison with *Phaenomena* 373–382. Indeed, both
passages cover the relationship between discovery and naming. Like Aratus at
Phaenomena 381–382, moreover, Nicander concludes this section with another
reference to naming: παντὶ γὰρ ἄρκιός ἐστι τό μιν πανάκειον ἔπουσιν ("It
is suitable for everything. They call it all-heal," 508). This name πανάκειον

---

[108] For Chiron's association with the Pelion mountain range, see *Iliad* 16.143–144. Overduin 2015:
375–376 collates other instances that mention Chiron's connection to this place.
[109] See Spatafora 2005:237–238 for discussion of the poetic language in this section.

reflects the herb's all-healing ability, as Nicander emphasizes with the word-play of παντὶ γὰρ ἄρκιός and πανάκειον.[110] Key differences, however, distinguish Nicander's treatment of centaury from the discovery of the constellations in the *Phaenomena*. Most obviously, unlike the constellations treated by Aratus, this herb exists on earth, visible only in the areas where it grows.[111] Additionally, whereas Aratus refers to an anonymous human of the past as the organizer and name giver, the discoverer of this herb is an emphatically named Centaur, whose name appears three times in the span of two lines: twice as Chiron and once as the patronymic kenning Κενταύρου Κρονίδαο. Despite belaboring the herb's name and finder, Nicander does not specify whether Chiron was the name giver himself. Similarly, Nicander does not identify the subject of ἔπουσιν in 508. In not disclosing a name giver amid this emphasis on names, Nicander implies the complexity involved in naming plants and remedies. That is, who is responsible for naming a plant? What, moreover, constitutes a suitable name? In this case, the herb itself possesses two names: centaury and all-heal, which reflect its finder and its effects, respectively. These multiple names in fact fit the multiplicities embodied by this herb: As an all-heal, its uses are manifold, and as with other remedies, it can be consumed multiple ways, either dried or fresh (506).

4.3 Alcibius narratives

Just as herbs can have multiple names, so too can multiple herbs possess the same name. Such is the case with Alcibius' herb. Situated strategically in the first remedy section (493–714),[112] two separate narratives highlight his eponymous herbs. In contrast to the brief centaury narrative, both sections feature greater detail about the context of discovery. The first narrative runs as follows:

ἐσθλὴν δ' Ἀλκιβίου ἔχιος περιφράζεο ῥίζαν
τῆς καὶ ἀκανθοβόλος μὲν ἀεὶ περιτέτροφε χαίτη,
λείρια δ' ὡς ἴα τοῖα περιτρέφει· ἡ δὲ βαθεῖα
καὶ ῥαδινὴ ὑπένερθεν ἀέξεται οὐδεΐ ῥίζα.
τὸν μὲν ἔχις βουβῶνος ὕπερ νεάτοιο χαράξας

[110] See Overduin 2015:377. He, however, suggests that this is a quality rather than another name. Nicander also calls marjoram all-healing: πανάκτειόν τε κονίλην (*Theriaca* 626). Clauss 2006:177–179 sees the word play at *Theriaca* 508 as allusion to *Works and Days* 80–82. There Hesiod describes the naming of Pandora, connecting it with everyone on Olympus bestowing her with gifts. For this reason, Clauss suggests that the πανάκειον is an answer to Pandora.

[111] According to Theophrastus (*Enquiry into Plants* 9.11.1), centaury favors fertile places.

[112] Overduin 2013:108 observes that the first Alcibius narrative (541–549) occurs 48 lines after the beginning of this section, while the second Alcibius narrative (666–675) begins 48 lines before the end of this section.

ἄντλῳ ἐνυπνώοντα χυτῆς παρὰ τέλσον ἅλωος
εἶθαρ ἀνέπνευσεν καμάτου βίῃ· αὐτὰρ ὁ γαίης
ῥίζαν ἐρυσάμενος τὸ μὲν ἕρκεϊ θρύψεν ὀδόντων
θηλάζων, τὸ δὲ πέσκος ἑῷ περὶ κάββαλεν ἕλκει.

Consider the excellent root of the Alcibius' bugloss. Prickly foliage always grows thickly upon it, and flowers like violets bloom in clusters. The root grows deep and slender beneath them in the ground. A male viper struck Alcibius above the lowest part of his groin, as he slumbered in a corn heap next to the border of piled threshing floor. At once, it awakened him in the violence of the struggle. But Alcibius extracted the root from the earth, and crushed it in the confines of his teeth, suckling it. He cast the skin around his wound.

Theriaca 541–549

Nicander focuses first on the plant's excellent quality as well as its name: Alcibius' bugloss (Ἀλκιβίου ἔχιος, 541). This double name indicates the finder Alcibius of the herb and its usefulness as a remedy against vipers. By employing ἔχιος (from ἔχις) instead of the typical designation for bugloss, ἔχιον,[113] Nicander anticipates the accompanying aetiological narrative, which pits Alcibius against a male viper (ἔχις, 545). While depicting this encounter, Nicander not only pinpoints the painful and embarrassing location of the bite (the groin, 545), he highlights Alcibius' vulnerable state sleeping. In doing so, he stresses the suddenness of this attack and thus the danger of the male viper. In fact, Nicander further conveys the snake's erratic behavior by omitting the reason for the attack. As the reported progeny of the Titans' blood (8–9), the malicious snakes of the *Theriaca* do not require definite grounds to wreak harm.

At the same time, as in the brief Chiron story, this narrative also exemplifies the relationship between discovery and direct experience. Had the viper not randomly attacked him, Alcibius would not have needed to uncover the remedy and apply it. Moreover, Nicander couples the description of the attack with a systematic account of Alcibius' multistep process of intake. Extraction is followed by chewing, suckling, and topical application to the skin (548–549). Such steps demonstrate Alcibius' mastery of the herb and by extension his worthiness as its namesake. By embedding this information within the narrative, rather than before or after, Nicander effaces the boundaries between narrative digression

---

[113] Overduin 2013:106n2.

and technical cataloguing. In this way, Alcibius, like Chiron, can function as a mythological *exemplum* of learning by direct experience.

Likewise, the second Alcibius narrative thematizes the correlation between experience and discovery:

ἄλλην δ' Ἀλκιβίοιο φερώνυμον ἄργεο ποίην
δράχμα χερὸς πλήσας, παύρῳ δ' ἐν νέκταρι πίνειν
τὴν μὲν ὑπὸ σκοπέλοισι Φαλακραίοισιν ἐπακτήρ,
Κρύμνης ἂμ πεδίον καὶ ἀνὰ Γράσον, ἠδ' ἵνα θ' Ἵππου
λειμῶνες σκυλάκεσσιν Ἀμυκλαίῃσι κελεύων
κνυζηθμῷ κυνὸς οὔλῳ ἐπήϊσε θυμολέοντος
ὅς τε μεταλλεύων αἰγὸς ῥόθον ἐν στίβῳ ὕλης
κανθῷ ἐνὶ ῥαντῆρι τυπὴν ἀνεδέξατ' ἐχίδνης
καὶ τὴν μὲν κλάγξας ἀφ' ἑκὰς βάλε, ῥεῖα δὲ ποίης
φύλλα κατέβρυξεν, καὶ ἀλεύατο φοινὸν ὄλεθρον.

Take the other herb bearing Alcibius' name. Fill your hand full and drink it in a little wine. While he was hunting beneath Phalacra's cliffs, on Crymna's plain and around Grasus and where lie the Horse's meadows, and was shouting commands to his Spartan dogs, he perceived the grass by the baneful [or "repetitive"] whimpering of his lion-hearted hound. While searching after a goat's trail on a forest path, it received a female viper's bite in the watering corner of its eye. Yelping, it cast the viper away and with ease chomped on the leaves of the herb and avoided deadly destruction.

Theriaca 666–675

With the collocation Ἀλκιβίοιο φερώνυμον ("bearing Alcibius' name," 666), Nicander again signals the importance of naming, echoing the words' respective placements in the Chiron story (φερώνυμον, 501) and the previous Alcibius narrative (Ἀλκιβίοιο, 541). Yet, in contrast to those two narratives, Nicander here does not specify the appearance of the grass. Instead, after devoting a single line to the mode of intake (667), Nicander details the situation of discovery in eight lines. Whereas Alcibius one was sleeping (546), Alcibius two is awake, hunting with his dogs (668–670). Additionally, although lending his name to this herb,[114] paradoxically Alcibius two does not find it first. Rather, one of his dogs fulfills this role, after suffering the bite of a female viper in its eye. In undergoing the

---

[114] Although Nicander is silent on this etymological dimension, the scholiast (Σ *ad* 666b; Crugnola 1971:247) connects the name Alcibius to the fact that herb "gives aid" (ἀλκεῖ, ἤγουν βοηθεῖ) to the person who uses its power for a remedy.

process of suffering and fortuitous discovery, the dog parallels Alcibius in the previous narrative and thus qualifies as the actual "first finder."

Although the dog is the actual first finder, Alcibius two still learns about the herb's existence and efficacy. Alcibius' awareness, however, derives not from sight or touch, but through sound. In fact, the verb used to indicate the discovery (ἐπήϊσε, 671) boasts the primary meaning of "hearing."[115] Overduin, however, rejects this meaning, favoring instead the translation "discovered by chance." As he argues, "Alcibius deduces the root's curative powers from observing his dog's behaviour."[116] The dog's behavior, however, consists in the production of sounds, and it by this οὔλῳ ("baneful" or "repetitive") whimpering that Alcibius perceives the herb.[117] For this reason, it is not unreasonable to see this sonic sense as still present in the verb ἐπήϊσε. Indeed, aside from the alliterative κνυζηθμῷ κυνός ("whimpering of the dog," 671), Nicander further indicates this emphasis on sound with three other words beginning with kappa that pertain to sound: κελεύων ("shouting commands," 670), κλάγξας ("yelping," 674), and κατέβρυξεν ("chomped," 675). Amid this interest in sound and physical pain, it is fitting that Nicander glosses over the herb's appearance. Additionally, since the viper bites the dog in the eye, we might posit that even the dog fails to see the herb. In pain, the dog would have reflexively closed both eyes as it quickly consumed the herb. Consequently, the narrative still touches upon the role of direct experience in discovery. However, in ironically framing the herb's namesake—Alcibius—as the secondhand discoverer, Nicander points to the multistep process required in uncovering this cure. In this case, a human must decode the dog's noisy suffering and subsequent salvation.

Read together, the two Alcibius narratives reveal the multiplicity of personal experiences. Snakes can attack any animal (man or dog), in any state (sleeping or awake), on any part of the body (groin or eye), and in any outdoor context. Both farmers and hunters are equally vulnerable.[118] Moreover, by casting a male and a female viper as the antagonists of the respective Alcibius narratives,

---

[115] LSJ ἐπαΐω (I.1).

[116] Overduin 2015:427. Gow and Scholfield 1953:73 adopt the translation "discovered," while Jacques 2002:52 renders the verb "*l'avait reconnue.*"

[117] For the purposeful ambiguity of the adjective οὔλῳ, see Coughlan forthcoming. As he argues, the meaning "destructive" or by extension "baneful" does not fit the outcome of story, as the dog does live. Rather, the meaning "repetitive" or "frequent" emerges as the more appropriate meaning. For a similar ambiguity in meaning of οὔλῳ, see *Theriaca* 233, where the adjective refers to the female viper's bite. Both the meanings "whole" and "deadly" are appropriate. For other discussions of the adjective οὖλος in Nicander, see Jacques 2002:20 and Overduin 2015:427. Both commentators, however, favor the meaning "shrill" at 671, citing *Iliad* 17.576 and 17.579, where the adjective refers to the cries of jackdaws and starlings.

[118] For these variations between the two Alcibius narratives, see Overduin 2015:424.

Nicander shows the equal danger of both genders, recalling his earlier discussion of viper reproduction (*Theriaca* 130–136).[119] At the same time, the narratives exemplify the complexity of naming and identifying remedies. Despite sharing the same name, the herbs are different and vary in methods of application. Whereas the first herb entails an oral and topical mode of intake, the second Alcibius herb is consumed orally. The addressee, however, is to drink the first herb with wine, while the dog merely chews the leaves of the second herb. Both narratives, moreover, lack information necessary for identifying these herbs. While the Alcibius one narrative includes a physical description the plant (542–544), in that section Nicander features no geographic markers. In the second Alcibius narrative, by contrast, Nicander eschews a physical description of the herb, instead including a string of allusive geographic designations to indicate Troy (668–670).[120] In highlighting the geographic dimension at the expense of this herb's appearance, Nicander subtly implies the necessity of one journeying to Troy oneself to unearth this herb.

4.4 Summary

Through these narratives about discoverers, Aratus and Nicander represent the processes of learning the truth of their respective subject matters. For constellations, a person must perceive them in the sky, order them together, and know their names, repeating the efforts of the initial unnamed finder. By contrast, the act of finding a herb differs from "discovering" the constellations. Unlike the visible stars in the sky, a herb must be found in a more limited area, extracted from the ground, and tested for its medicinal properties. The process, for both the original finder and any future finders, is a direct and bodily one. In some cases, a painful and nearly deadly encounter precipitates this discovery.

At the same time, these narratives depict the relationship between naming and identity. For constellations, the name and the outward appearance are tightly linked. That is, if one were to add or subtract stars in a constellation, the name would presumably need to change in order to reflect the new shape. Even alternate names, like "Wagons" for the Bears (*Phaenomena* 27), still derive from the constellations' outward appearance, in this case their

---

[119] After mating, female vipers bite off the heads of the males, only to be later killed when their progeny burst from their belly. See Herodotus *Histories* 3.109 and Aristotle *History of Animals* 622b28. For discussion of this passage in Nicander, see Wilson 2018a:257–280.

[120] The scholiast (Σ *ad* 668–672; Crugnola 1971:248) explicates these geographic markers as near Troy. Phalacra is a peak, while Crymna and Grasus are plains in Troy. The scholiast interprets the Horse as the Trojan Horse.

wheeling motion.[121] The naming of herbs, however, is a thornier matter. A plant's name(s) can stem not only from its appearance, but also its effect (e.g. all-healing) or finder (centaury or Alcibius). In this way, an even greater degree of arbitrariness surrounds the naming of herbs. Nicander in fact points to such arbitrariness when he lists the multiple names of herbs. For instance, the treacle clover (τρίσφυλλον, 520) is called "brief-flower" (μινυανθές, 522) and "trefoil" (τριπέτηλον, 522, 907), while pellitory (ἑλξίνην) is also dubbed κλύβατις (537).[122] Yet, in contrast with the constellations, a radically different name would have no effect on the identity of a plant.

5. Myths and Etymology

Along with these overt narratives concerning discovery and names, both Aratus and Nicander feature an aetiological myth in which etymology plays a role. Just as aetiological myths offer rationalizations for the current state of the world, etymology tries to uncover the true explanation (ἔτυμος λόγος) behind a name.[123] At *Phaenomena* 216–224, Aratus goes to great lengths to rationalize the name Hippocrene, since he equates the Horse constellation with the horse responsible for creating the spring. As I will demonstrate, Aratus makes etymology the prime evidence for this aetiological myth, and in doing so portrays the technique of etymology as an adequate means of grasping his subject matter of constellations. In *Theriaca* 309–319, the issue of etymology is less overt, as the story concerns Helen's disfigurement of the female blood-letting snake in Egypt. Yet, in concentrating on Helen, Nicander treats a complex figure, whose name was ripe for etymological analysis. Despite initially introducing an evil Helen with the name Αἰνελένη (309), Nicander ultimately destabilizes this logic of etymology by showing Helen's beneficence to humans in this circumstance. Such an undercutting, I will propose, connects to the confusion involved in naming creatures and plants.

---

[121] See Possanza 2004:84–85. These two constellations, moreover, also bear the names of the Bears (Cynosura and Helice).

[122] Horehound bears two similar names (μελίφυλλον and μελίκταιναν) because of its attractiveness to bees (554–555).

[123] The *Cratylus* of Plato features a discussion concerning etymologies and etymological analysis. At 435c Socrates suggests that names were originally divine in origin and significant but became corrupted over time. For a discussion of the *Cratylus*, see Silverman 1992:25–71. As Sedley 2003:28 argues, "The etymologies are, broadly speaking, *exegetically* correct, in that they do recover the original beliefs of the name-makers, but it remains a moot point whether they are also *philosophically* correct, that is whether ... the beliefs they recover for us are true beliefs."

5.1 Aratus and the Hippocrene

After describing the Horse constellation's appearance in the sky (204–215), Aratus shifts to a story about the creation of the Hippocrene (the Spring of the Horse):

κεῖνον δὴ καί φασι καθ᾽ ὑψηλοῦ Ἑλικῶνος
καλὸν ὕδωρ ἀγαγεῖν εὐαλδέος Ἱππουκρήνης.
οὐ γάρ πω Ἑλικὼν ἄκρος κατελείβετο πηγαῖς·
ἀλλ᾽ Ἵππος μιν ἔτυψε, τὸ δ᾽ ἀθρόον αὐτόθεν ὕδωρ
ἐξέχυτο πληγῇ προτέρου ποδός, οἱ δὲ νομῆες
πρῶτοι κεῖνο ποτὸν διεφήμισαν Ἱππουκρήνην.

That one, they say, from the heights of Mount Helicon brought forth the fine water of the nourishing Hippocrene. For not yet was the peak of Helicon flowing with springs, but the Horse struck it, and from that very place a flood of water gushed out with the stroke of his front foot. The shepherds were the first to call that drink the Hippocrene.

Phaenomena 216–221

Unlike the constellation fixed in the sky, this Horse's involvement in the spring's creation cannot be subjected to direct visual confirmation. Rather, as Aratus signals with the third person plural verb φασι ("they say," 216), the story's truth is based on the authority of an unspecified "they," which could refer either to the oral tradition in general or to specific literary sources, such as Hesiod. Although the *Theogony* features both the Hippocrene (6) and the horse Pegasus (281),[124] Hesiod does not credit Pegasus with the creation of the spring. Kidd as a result posits that the story is an invention on Aratus' part, similar to the story of the Bears (*Phaenomena* 30–35).[125] For this mythical story, however, Aratus appeals not only to the authority of the oral tradition, but also to the name itself, placing Ἱππουκρήνης emphatically at the end of 216. This name, which literally means "spring of Horse," implies a close connection between the Horse and the water of the spring, and Aratus highlights this connection by coordinating κεῖνον ("that one") at the beginning of 216 with καλόν ("fine," 217), the adjective that modifies ὕδωρ ("water," 217). This adjective, moreover, along with εὐαλδέος ("nourishing," 217) emphasizes the spring's corporality. Despite the

---

[124] According to Hesiod, Pegasus' name comes from the fact that he was born next to the streams (πηγάς) of the Ocean (*Theogony* 282). Kidd 1997:262 proposes that πηγαῖς in 218 recalls this etymology. Cf. *Aetia* fr. 2.1, where Callimachus obliquely calls the Hippocrene the "footprint of the swift horse" (ἴχνιον ὀξέος ἵππου).

[125] Kidd 1997:261.

impossibility of confirming the story through perception, these qualities of the water can be observed presently on Mount Helicon, just like the Horse constellation in the sky. Thus, in focusing on the visibility and materiality of the spring, Aratus strengthens the parallel between the Horse and the water as is embodied by the name Hippocrene.

The emphasis on the name, as well as the connection between the Horse and spring, is further developed in 218–221, in which Aratus restates and expands the content of 216–217. Each line in the section corresponds to an element in 216–217. Ἑλικὼν ἄκρος ("the peak of Helicon") in 218 picks up ὑψηλοῦ Ἑλικῶνος ("the heights of Helicon") in 216, repeating the focus on the location, while the Ἵππος ("Horse") and ὕδωρ ("water") reoccur in 219–220, where Aratus specifies that the Horse yielded the water by kicking the ground with its front foot. Finally, Ἱππουκρήνην at the end of 221 mirrors Ἱππουκρήνης in 217. By mentioning the name again, this time with reference to the act of naming by the shepherds, Aratus demonstrates how the name was a consequence of the narrated phenomenon, and as such, represents a piece of evidence for the story. Yet, in reusing the name as evidence, Aratus makes the passage exhibit a circular structure. The name, invoked in both the introduction and the conclusion of the story, serves as both a source for the story and what justifies it. Indeed, at the verbal level, this circularity manifests through the chiastic arrangement generated by ὕδωρ (217), Ἱππουκρήνης (217), Ἵππος (219), and ὕδωρ (219). Combined, these words reinforce the connection between the Horse and the water and thus the name Hippocrene.

The circular structure of the section culminates in the final lines, in which Aratus concludes by again referring to the spring and the Horse constellation as visible entitites:

ἀλλὰ τὸ μὲν πέτρης ἀπολείβεται, οὐδέ τοι αὐτὸ
Θεσπιέων ἀνδρῶν ἑκὰς ὄψεαι, αὐτὰρ ὅ Ἵππος
ἐν Διὸς εἱλεῖται, καί τοι πάρα θηήσασθαι.

But it flows from the rock, and you will never see it far from the men of Thespiae. But the Horse revolves in the realm of Zeus, and it is possible for you to behold.

Phaenomena 222–224

Not only does Aratus emphasize the spring and Horse's visibility with the verbs ὄψεαι ("you will see," 223) and θηήσασθαι ("to behold," 224), he also focuses on their movement. ἀπολείβεται ("flows," 222) responds to κατελείβετο ("was flowing," 218) to indicate the contrast between present and past, while εἱλεῖται ("revolves," 224) refers to the constant circular motion of the constellation. As Hunter comments, the visibility of the spring in Boeotia and the Horse in the heavens seem mutually reinforcing.[126] However, despite this shared visibility, nothing about their physical existence necessitates a direct relationship between the two. Indeed, Aratus presents a contrast between the two entities, noting their separate locations. While the spring exists in the realm of men (Θεσπιέων ἀνδρῶν, 223), the Horse moves in the heavenly sphere of Zeus (ἐν Διός, 224). In mentioning this distance between the spring and Horse, Aratus somewhat undercuts the image of their closeness, as was developed by the myth and particularly the name Hippocrene, upon which the myth ultimately hinges. Yet, in doing so, Aratus points to the logic underlying aetiological myth as well as the etymology. Both processes impose a relationship between two separate objects, creating order to facilitate understanding.

The overall importance of naming and etymology to Aratus' subject matter of constellations explains the centrality of the name Hippocrene to the myth. Since, as I have shown, the name serves as the primary evidence for the story as well as its proof, Aratus' treatment of the myth reflects how information can be extracted from names and how in turn this information can receive confirmation through visual means. Although the citation of the Horse and spring as visual objects seems to support this story on the surface, Aratus' reliance on circular argumentation and the mythical tradition throws doubt on the story's validity. Yet, as with the other myths, we must not consider truth in literal terms, but rather how this story can be construed as symbolically true. Despite their physical distance from each other, the spring and Horse constellation are both subject to Zeus' influence. According to the hymnic proem (1–18) and to Stoic philosophy (e.g. Cleanthes *Hymn to Zeus*), Zeus' influence pervades all things. As a result, there exists a logic behind the name Hippocrene, since it conceptualizes the affinity between the Horse and the spring.

5.2 Bane Helen vs. the blood-letting snake

Just as the etymology of the Hippocrene figures in the story at *Phaenomena* 216–224, Nicander also addresses the issue of etymology at *Theriaca* 309–319, which describes Helen's wounding of the αἱμορροῒς θήλεια ("female blood-letting snake"). The narrative in fact deals not just with the name Helen, but also Canobus, who lends his name to the Egyptian settlement and region.[127] In the

---

[126] In Fantuzzi and Hunter 2004:245.
[127] For the naming of Canopus, see Hecataeus *FGrH* 1 F 308 and Strabo 17.1.17.

first three lines, Nicander establishes this Egyptian context, while also introducing Helen with a baneful name:

εἰ ἔτυμον, Τροίηθεν ἰοῦσ' ἐχαλέψατο φύλοις
Αἰνελένη, ὅτε νῆα πολύστροιβον παρὰ Νεῖλον
ἔστησαν βορέαο κακὴν προφυγόντες ὁμοκλήν...

If it is true, while coming from Troy, Bane Helen became angry at the species when the crew beached the ship next to the tempestuous Nile, after they fled the terrible onslaught of the North Wind.

Theriaca 309–311

As a combination of the αἰν- root and Helen, the appellation Αἰνελένη ("Bane Helen," 310) embodies Helen's destructive qualities,[128] alluding to her status as *casus belli* for the Trojan War (see chapter 4.2). The chorus in Aeschylus' *Agamemnon* in fact famously puns on her name by interpreting the root ἑλ- as "destroying." As suits her name, Helen is a destroyer of ships, men, and the city (ἑλένας ἕλανδρος ἑλέ- / πτολις, 688–689). In placing νῆα ("ship") near Αἰνελένη, Nicander seems to be recalling this pun.

At the same time, Nicander in these lines evokes alternate strands of Helen's mythic tradition. Aside from introducing the subsequent section as a myth,[129] εἰ ἔτυμον is reminiscent of ἔτυμος in the fragment of Stesichorus' *Palinode* (fr. 192 *PMGF* Davies) quoted at *Phaedrus* 243a: οὐκ ἔστ' ἔτυμος λόγος οὗτος, / οὐδ' ἔβας ἐν νηυσὶν εὐσσέλμοις / οὐδ' ἵκεο πέργαμα Τροίας ("This story is not true; you did not go in the benched ships, you did not reach the citadel of Troy"). Similarly, the clustering of Τροίηθεν (309) and νῆα (310) echoes Τροίας and νηυσίν in Stesichorus. By denying Helen's presence in Troy, Stesichorus absolved her culpability for the war.[130] According to Socrates in the *Phaedrus*, moreover, Helen's retributive blinding of Stesichorus stimulated this composition. Similarly, Nicander's narrative envisions an image of a powerful and vengeful Helen. The blood-letting snake, like the slanderous Stesichorus, incurs an injury for its transgression. Yet, in mentioning Helen's return from Troy (Τροίηθεν,

---

[128] This compounded name occurs in a fragment of the *Epyllion of Diomedes* (*Epica Adespota* 2.11 *CA*). In the *Agamemnon* (712), the adjective αἰνόλεκτρον ("ill-wedded") describes Paris (cf. Lycophron *Alexandra* 820, where the adjective refers to Helen). For Αἰνόπαρις, see Alcman fr. 77 Davies and Euripides *Hecuba* 945. Euripides has the compound Δυσελέναν at *Iphigenia at Aulis* 1316 and *Orestes* 1388. For Δύσπαρι, see *Iliad* 3.39 and 13.769.

[129] Overduin 2015:297.

[130] For discussions of the *Palinode*, see Bassi 1993:51–75 and Austin 1994:90–117. For some discussions of the rich tradition surrounding Helen, see also Naddaff 2009:73–97 and Blondell 2013.

309), Nicander contradicts Stesichorus' emphatic denial of her presence in Troy. Despite this deviation, the analogous narrative element (an injury caused by Helen) and the similar language signpost Nicander's reworking of Stesichorus and by extension the possibility of the revised Stesichorean Helen motivating this portrayal. That is, in recalling Stesichorus and his Helen, Nicander presents a Helen who is vengeful, but not for humans.

Finally, by situating Helen in Egypt in this story (πολύστροιβον παρὰ Νεῖλον, 310), Nicander recalls the traditions that set her in Egypt: Homer's *Odyssey* 4.351–592, Herodotus book two, and Euripides' *Helen*. Of these, Euripides' *Helen* offers the most radical rehabilitation of her character. Not only did this play depict a guiltless Helen who never went to Troy, but one who acted as an exemplary wife.[131] At the same time, the play includes an etymology of her name that reflects this innocent Helen. In the *deus ex machina*, Castor proclaims that the island which received Helen will be dubbed hereafter "Helene," because the island took her when she was stolen (κλοπὰς <σάς>, 1675). As Allan observes, the etymology casts Helen as a passive victim, with the root ἑλ- in her name interpreted in the passive sense "taken."[132] Thus, Euripides' reformulation of Helen entails not only a change in the myth, but also in how to understand her name. Construed in this way, Helen's name signals her innocence.

Consequently, in the span of three lines, Nicander has elicited multiple versions of Helen: an evil Helen, a vengeful yet innocent one, and a good Helen in Egypt. This variegated and contested portrayal problematizes the initial use of the ominous name Αἰνελένη. It thus becomes difficult to conceptualize a straightforward correlation between a name and thing. Aside from evoking this varied tradition in 309–311, Nicander's subsequent portrayal of Helen further undermines the appropriateness of Bane Helen. Unlike some of her previous manifestations, this Helen is not evil, but beneficial for humans, as she neutralizes the malicious blood-letting snake, a dangerous threat to mankind.

As in his other narrative digressions (e.g. 541–549), Nicander does not suppress the brutal details of the encounter between Helen and the snake:

ἦμος ἀποψύχοντα κυβερνητῆρα Κάνωβον
Θώνιος ἐν ψαμάθοις ἀθρήσατο· τύψε γὰρ εὐνῇ
αὐχέν' ἀποθλιφθεῖσα καὶ ἐν βαρὺν ἤρυγεν ἰόν
αἱμοροῒς θήλεια, κακὸν δέ οἱ ἔχραε κοῖτον.
τῷ δ' Ἑλένη μέσον ὁλκὸν ἐνέθλασε, θραῦσε δ' ἀκάνθης
δεσμὰ πέριξ νωταῖα, ῥάχις δ' ἐξέδραμε γυίων·

---

[131] On this version of Helen, see Holmberg 1995:19–42.
[132] Allan 2008:344

ἐξόθεν αἱμορόοι σκολιοπλανέες τε κεράσται
οἷοι χωλεύουσι κακηπελίῃ βαρύθοντες.

... when she beheld the helmsman Canobus fainting in the sands of Thonis. For the female blood-letter struck him on the neck in his bed, after it was crushed, and it belched forth heavy venom and inflicted an evil sleep upon him. For this reason, Helen crushed the middle of the coil and broke the ligatures of the back surrounding the spine, and the backbone popped out from the body. From this point, only blood-letting snakes and crooked wandering horned vipers limp, burdened by their injury.

Theriaca 312–319

In this story, the snake and Helen play analogous roles, both harming their targets in an act of vengeance. The snake kills Canobus after he had crushed it, and Helen consequently injures the snake in retaliation for Canobus' death. Nicander in fact stresses the violence of these actions through the accumulation of thetas used for both figures: ἀθρήσατο ("beheld," 313), ἀποθλιφθεῖσα ("crushed," 314), θήλεια ("female," 316), ἐνέθλασε ("crushed," 316), θραῦσε ("broke," 316), and ἀκάνθης ("spine," 316). The repetition of this harsh sound reproduces the image of violent crushing. Such violence, however, is not equivalent. Whereas Helen causes an injury to avenge another's death, the snake kills in retribution for its own injury. Helen's actions are not self-serving, but in solidarity with the remainder of her crew, who have suffered the loss of their second helmsman.[133]

Nicander further attests to Helen's helpfulness for men by heightening the maliciousness of this snake. Indeed, in assaulting Canobus in his bed, the snake assails a victim who is vulnerable while sleeping. In the narrative, however, the exact timeline of the events is unclear. Canobus could have crushed the snake while sleeping, thus triggering an instantaneous attack in self-defense.[134] Overduin, on the other hand, interprets the snake as waiting for the best moment to strike, in retaliation for an earlier injury.[135] The adoption of this latter option infuses the snake with intent, a human trait that amplifies its malice and dangerousness. As Jacques notes, moreover, the verb for the snake, ἔχραε ("inflicted," 315), mirrors the language of *Odyssey* 5.396: στυγερὸς δέ οἱ

---

[133] The first helmsman, Phrontis, was slain by Phoebus while sailing past Sounion (*Odyssey* 3.278–283). See Overduin 2015:301–302 for instances of the death of the helmsman trope.

[134] For instance, Gow and Scholfield 1953:176 propose that εὐνῇ ... ἀποθλιφθεῖσα could mean "crushed by his bedding."

[135] See Overduin 2014:633–634; 2015:302.

ἔχραε δαίμων ("a hateful god attacks him").[136] Jacques interprets this verbal parallel as Nicander likening the snake to a malevolent spirit. Combined with the poem's pervasive anthropomorphism of snakes as sentient evils, this language substantiates the snake's maliciousness. The snake does not simply kill Canobus, but rather punishes him as a resentful spirit would.

At the same time, a comparison with *Argonautica* 4.1502–1526, Nicander's model for this passage, further illuminates the wickedness of the female blood-letter. As in Nicander's narrative, a man, the seer Mopsus, dies while marooned with his crew in a foreign land (Libya). He steps on a snake, which subsequently bites and kills him. Additionally, several verbal parallels bind together these two passages. For instance, the phrase ἰὸν ἐνείη in 305 replicates the phrase at *Argonautica* 4.1508. Since αἰνός is an equivalent of δεινός, Αἰνελένη very likely recalls δεινὸς ὄφις ("terrible serpent") at 4.1506, especially since both sit in the same *sedes* and match in metrical shape.[137] Yet in contrast to Nicander's female blood-letter, Apollonius specifies the general reluctance of the snake to attack: νωθὴς μὲν ἑκὼν ἀέκοντα χαλέψαι, / οὐδ' ἂν ὑποτρέσσαντος ἐνωπαδὶς ἀίξειεν ("It is too sluggish to attack willingly an unwilling person, nor would it dart head-on against a person escaping," 4.1506–1507). It is only Mopsus' treading on the snake that provokes the attack (4.1518–1521). The reference to this snake's customary reluctance and the description of its pain (πέριξ ὀδύνησιν ἑλιχθείς, 4.1520) portray its attack as a desperate measure. In the *Theriaca* narrative, Nicander mentions neither the snake's reluctance nor does he emphasize its pain, confining the description of the injury to the participle ἀποθλιφθεῖσα (314), while also dedicating more space to describe the attack on Canobus (τύψε γὰρ εὐνῇ ... κακὸν δέ οἱ ἔχραε κοῖτον, 313–314). In downplaying the snake's agony while highlighting its ferociousness, Nicander further implies the hostility of this snake.

Just as Nicander's blood-letting snake diverges from Apollonius' snake in its overt hostility and aggressiveness, so too does Helen contrast with the female figure involved in the *Argonautica* section: Medea. Indeed, Helen and Medea possess numerous similarities. Both abscond from home with outsider men (Paris and Jason, respectively), generate conflict for this reason, and boast

---

[136] Jacques 2002:26. Jacques 2002:116 also brings up an alternate version of the myth in which some god casts sleep upon Canobus. This would have been to punish Canobus for spurning the love of Theonoe (Conon in Photius *Bibliotheca* 186.132a24). See Maass 1892:362–363 for a reconstruction of these events. The scholiast to Nicander (Σ *ad Theriaca* 309–317; Crugnola 1971:138) does specify that Canobus fell asleep unwillingly (ἄκων).

[137] Other verbal echoes include ἐχαλέψατο in 309 (cf. χαλέψαι, 4.1506), ψαμάθοις in 313 (cf. ψαμάθοισι, 4.1505), ἀκάνθης in 316 (cf. ἄκανθαν, 4.1518), and πέριξ in 317 (cf. πέριξ, 4.1520). Noting Nicander's debt to this Apollonian passage, Hunter 2015:286 posits that εἰ ἔτυμον in 309 points the reader back to this specific scene.

skills in magic and making drugs.[138] Yet despite displaying her magic powers elsewhere in the *Argonautica*, as in her defeat of Talus (4.1654–1688), Medea in this section absconds with her handmaidens (ἀτὰρ Μήδεια καὶ ἄλλαι / ἔτρεσαν ἀμφίπολοι, 4.1521–1522). She neither confronts the snake nor attempts to offer relief to Mopsus as he perishes. Helen in the *Theriaca*, on the other hand, although unable to save Canobus, is willing to take immediate action on his behalf. Although it is not specified, she could have stepped on the snake just like Mopsus. In doing so, she exposes herself to potential harm, since the snake could have bitten her as well while she broke its spine. By depicting Helen as more beneficial in a situation than her counterpart Medea, Nicander further promotes the image of a Helen who is helpful for men.

At the same time, the choice to highlight Helen with an extended narrative potentially carries wider significance for the *Theriaca's* subject matter of plants and remedies. Although Nicander does not explicitly refer to her association with plants in this narrative,[139] Helen possesses pharmaceutical skills. Indeed, in *Odyssey* 4, she drugs Menelaus and Telemachus with a pain-alleviating substance (4.219–221).[140] Her drugs, moreover, come from Egypt, gifted by Polydamna the wife of Thon (4.227–232). Nicander in fact recalls this narrative with the designation Θώνιος ἐν ψαμάθοις ("in the sands of Thonis," 313).[141]

Aside from *Odyssey* 4, two other narratives associate Helen with plants in Egypt. Although preserved in later sources, these two tales nicely overlap with *Theriaca* 309–319, as both deal with snake encounters. According to a tale featured in Aelian (*On the Nature of Animals* 9.21), ἑλένιον (elecampane; *Inula helenium*) receives Helen's name after she employs this plant to purge the isle of Pharos of snakes. The *Etymologicum Magnum* (328.17–19) preserves an account even more pertinent to this *Theriaca* narrative: elecampane sprung from Helen's tears after the female blood-letter killed Canobus. While we cannot confirm exactly where or if Nicander included these narratives in other now-lost works,[142] the two narratives together attest to a close connection between Helen, Egypt, plants, and snakes. Such an association in turn deepens the reading of *Theriaca* 309–319. That is, Helen not only serves as an antagonist against snakes in human form,

---

[138] See Hunter 1993:67.

[139] Aside from the Spartan tree cult described by Theocritus in *Idyll* 18.43–48, Helen was worshipped on Rhodes as Helen Dendritis (Pausanias 3.19.11). See Clader 1976:63–80 for discussion of Helen's worship.

[140] For discussion of this passage, see Suzuki 1989:66–67 and Bergren 2008a:118.

[141] Thonis is a place at the Canopic mouth of the Nile. In Herodotus (2.114), Thonis is a guard who meets Helen and Paris and sends word to Proteus. See Gow and Scholfield 1953:176.

[142] See Gow and Scholfield 1953:176, 204 and Jacques 2002:117.

she can continue warding off snakes via her eponymous plant. In this way, Helen anticipates Alcibius' eponymous herbs (541–549, 666–675).

Consequently, over the course of the story, Nicander has revised the notion of the traditional baneful Helen. When compared with the evil blood-letting snake, Helen seems benign, as her wrath does not adversely affect humans. Unlike Medea in Apollonius' Mopsus narrative, Helen acts, facing a snake even more aggressive than Apollonius' δεινός yet reluctant ὄφις. In challenging this initial impression of Helen, Nicander signals the role of experience in determining the relationship between an entity's name and its true essence. In this case, Helen's actions in the story attest to the inability of a single name to capture completely something's essence, especially a figure as debated and multifaceted as Helen. By switching from Bane Helen in 310 to Helen in 316, Nicander implies the level of arbitrariness involved in the act of naming. This switch to the less ominous version, that is, without the damning αἰν-, encourages the reader to interpret her disfigurement of the snake as an act of salvation for humans. The Helen in this story is not a destroyer of men, their ships, and cities à la Aeschylus' *Agamemnon*, but instead an avenger of a man and a bane only for snakes.[143]

5.3 Summary

In reading *Phaenomena* 216–224 and *Theriaca* 309–319, I have focused on the issue of names and etymologies. In the former tale, etymology pervades, as Aratus justifies the aetiological narrative by citing the name Hippocrene. This name embodies the affinity between separate entities, both subject to Zeus' influence. At the same time, the emphasis on the name corresponds more broadly to the importance of names for constellations. By contrast, Nicander's etymological investigation is subtler. By evoking the multiple traditions regarding Helen while depicting an ultimately helpful one in this encounter, he points to the difficulty of assigning a single name for such a complex figure. Helen's complexity is in fact analogous to Nicander's subject matter of snakes, plants, and remedies. Like a remedy, Helen's harmfulness or benevolence must be put to the test.

Aside from these contrasting treatments of etymologies, these two narratives correspond to the two poets' broader use of myth. For instance, in describing the Horse and the spring, Aratus emphasizes their shared visibility

---

[143] Overduin 2015:299 also makes this observation by stating "Helen is thus not αἰνή per se, but she is a terrible destroyer (αἰνό- and ἑλ-) when it comes to the *haimorrhoos*, whose spine she violently crushes." See also Malomud 2015:537. Since Callimachus uses αἰνός for the Python (*Hymn to Apollo* 101), she interprets Αἰνελένη to mean "destroyer of dire creatures (i.e. snakes)."

(*Phaenomena* 223–224). Nicander, on the other hand, suffuses the passage with descriptions of physical suffering (*Theriaca* 312–317), replicating the immediacy and violence of this encounter between Canobus, the snake, and Helen. At the same time, the passages display significant differences in narrative content. Indeed, while the act of striking (ἔτυψε at *Phaenomena* 219; τύψε at *Theriaca* 313) occurs in both stories, the consequences radically diverge. In the *Phaenomena*, the strike of the horse's hoof strike generates a nourishing spring, specifically one connected to poetic inspiration via Hesiod's *Theogony*.[144] The strike of the female blood-letter, however, brings death for Canobus and by extension the loss of its spine for itself and its descendants. The consequence of this painful loss, disjointed sidewinding, contrasts with the regular circular movement of the Horse constellation. In this way, we may interpret sidewinding as the antithesis to the genesis of the Hippocrene. Whereas the latter is a productive process, the former is violent, destructive, and disjunctive, as suits Nicander's chaotic and concealed subject matter.

6. Scorpion Myths

6.1 Aratus' Scorpion

A comparison between the two poets' Scorpion stories further elucidates the poets' respective presentations of myth in relation to the subject matter. In both versions, Artemis summons the Scorpion to punish Orion for an attempted sexual assault. By adapting Aratus' Scorpion myth (*Phaenomena* 634–646), Nicander (*Theriaca* 13–20) signals a clear literary debt to Aratus.[145] Yet Nicander's version diverges from Aratus' in several respects. Whereas Nicander places his myth toward the beginning of the work, Aratus' narrative occurs later in the *Phaenomena* as the last extended myth:

> καμπαὶ δ' ἂν Ποταμοῖο καὶ αὐτίκ' ἐπερχομένοιο
> Σκορπίου ἐμπίπτοιεν ἐϋρρόου ὠκεανοῖο·
> ὃς καὶ ἐπερχόμενος φοβέει μέγαν Ὠρίωνα.
> Ἄρτεμις ἱλήκοι· προτέρων λόγος, οἵ μιν ἔφαντο
> ἑλκῆσαι πέπλοιο, Χίῳ ὅτε θηρία πάντα
> καρτερὸς Ὠρίων στιβαρῇ ἐπέκοπτε κορύνῃ,
> θήρης ἀρνύμενος κείνῳ χάριν Οἰνοπίωνι.
> ἡ δέ οἱ ἐξαυτῆς ἐπετείλατο θηρίον ἄλλο,

---

[144] For the literal and metapoetic fertility of the Hippocrene, see Toohey 1996:58.

[145] Effe 1974b:120. See also Clauss 2006:174–176 for discussion of the relationship between these two passages.

νήσου ἀναρρήξασα μέσας ἑκάτερθε κολώνας,
σκορπίον, ὅς ῥά μιν οὖτα καὶ ἔκτανε πολλὸν ἐόντα
πλειότερος προφανείς, ἐπεὶ Ἄρτεμιν ἤκαχεν αὐτήν.
τοὔνεκα δὴ καί φασι περαιόθεν ἐρχομένοιο
Σκορπίου Ὠρίωνα περὶ χθονὸς ἔσχατα φεύγειν.

The windings of the River will immediately fall into the fair-streaming Ocean when the Scorpion comes. As it approaches, the Scorpion makes even powerful Orion retreat. Be propitious, Artemis! This account belongs to my predecessors, who said that strong Orion dragged her by her robes. At that time on Chios he was striking all the creatures with his sturdy club, while acquiring a hunting gift for that Oenopion. Immediately, she split the middle of the island's hills on both sides and commanded another creature for him—the scorpion. It wounded and killed him, strong as he was, because it turned out to be stronger. This was because Orion had upset Artemis herself. For this reason too they say that, when Scorpion comes over the horizon, Orion bolts around the furthest edges of the earth.

Phaenomena 634–646

As in the Dike (96–136) and Hippocrene (216–224) narratives, this story follows a circular structure, both in thought and language. Aratus not only prefaces the narrative with a description of Orion retreating from the Scorpion (635), but he restates this movement in 645–646, echoing the language of the initial description. ἐρχομένοιο ("coming," 645) points back to ἐπερχομένοιο (634) and ἐπερχόμενος (636), while Σκορπίου (646) mirrors σκορπίον in 635 and Σκορπίου in 643. φασι ("they say," 645), moreover, corresponds to προτέρων λόγος ("this account belongs to my predecessors") and ἔφαντο ("said") in 637, which together introduce the tale in indirect discourse. Additionally, Aratus refers to Orion's large size and strength three times with μέγαν (636), καρτερός (639), and πολλόν (643), implying a connection between Orion's prodigious size and the visibility of the Orion constellation.

At the same time, Aratus infuses this specific passage with a sense of narratorial distancing. Indeed, a traumatizing narrative about Artemis' assault could potentially elicit her distress and fury.[146] For this reason, Aratus couples the initial propitiation (Ἄρτεμις ἰλήκοι, 637) with an attribution of the λόγος to his unnamed predecessors. In this way, like Pindar (e.g. *Olympian* 1.47–53), he seemingly divests himself of responsibility for this tale. Aratus enhances the

---

[146] On this propitiation, see Kidd 1997:397, who observes an affectation of "coyness."

distancing effect with the accumulation of subordinate clauses. For instance, he conveys the attempted rape in indirect discourse embedded within a relative clause (οἵ μιν ἔφαντο / ἑλκῆσαι πέπλοιο, 637–638). Following this oblique description, Aratus then devotes two and half lines to a temporal clause detailing Orion's hunting obligation (638–640). Likewise, the violent scorpion attack is confined to a relative clause (ὅς ῥά μιν ... 643), after which Aratus again refers to Orion's transgression with a causal clause (ἐπεὶ Ἄρτεμιν ἤκαχεν αὐτήν, 644). The ordering of these subordinate clauses creates a disjointed pull back in time (see Table 1), one that precludes narrative linearity and thus further contributes to the circularity characterizing the passage.

The passage's circularity and the narratorial distancing combined accomplish multiple functions. On the one hand, the repetition of the language and thought parallels the perpetual movement of the Orion and the Scorpion constellations. Indeed, the constellations themselves function as endless repetitions of the initial attack recounted in the aetiological myth. Likewise, just as Aratus ostensibly distances himself from the distasteful contents of the narrative, so too does Orion forever eschew the Scorpion in the sky. At the same time, the circularity of the narrative corresponds to the circular process involved in imposing myths on constellations. That is, by asking the audience to envision the Scorpion pursuing Orion, Aratus already has the narrative in mind. The narrative in turn elucidates an image it has already presupposed. In this way, the myth and the visible phenomenon are tightly bound. Yet the imposed myth is disconnected in many ways from the constellation. Not only does this narrative come from unnamed predecessors (637), it treats a remote mythical past in which Giants like Orion roamed the earth and interacted with the gods. The myth is thus unprovable, unlike the present and visible constellations.

6.2 Nicander's Scorpion

While Aratus' Scorpion tale is the last major myth in the *Phaenomena*, Nicander's rendition appears at the beginning of the *Theriaca*, immediately after the Hesiod reference (*Theriaca* 8–12; see above). Indeed, as both a creature on earth and a constellation,[147] the Scorpion forms the perfect link between the *Phaenomena* and the *Theriaca*:

τὸν δὲ χαλαζήεντα κόρη Τιτηνὶς ἀνῆκε
σκορπίον ἐκ κέντροιο τεθηγμένον, ἦμος ἐπέχρα

---

[147] Aside from the dual status of the Scorpion as a constellation and a deadly creature, it is possible that Nicander gravitated towards *Phaenomena* 634–646 because of the emphatic clustering of θηρία (638), θήρης (640), and θηρίον (641).

Βοιωτῷ τεύχουσα κακὸν μόρον Ὠαρίωνι
ἀχράντων ὅτε χερσὶ θεῆς ἐδράξατο πέπλων.
αὐτὰρ ὅγε στιβαροῖο κατὰ σφυρὸν ἤλασεν ἴχνευς
σκορπίος ἀπροϊδὴς ὀλίγῳ ὑπὸ λᾶι λοχήσας·
τοῦ δὲ τέρας περίσημον ὑπ' ἀστέρας ἀπλανὲς αὔτως
οἷα κυνηλατέοντος ἀείδελον ἐστήρικται.

The Titanian maiden sent forth the frost-biting scorpion with its
whetted stinger, when she attacked, contriving an evil fate for
Boeotian Orion, after he grabbed in his hands the untouched robes of
the goddess. But that scorpion, which had lurked unobserved beneath
the tiny rock, struck him in the ankle of his mighty foot, but Orion's
sign is set prominent, fixed there among the stars, as of one hunting,
glittering to see.

Theriaca 13–20

Aside from the shared subject matter, Nicander closely adapts Aratus' vocabu-
lary. πέπλων ("robes," 16) and στιβαροῖο ("mighty," 17) echo πέπλοιο (*Phaenomena*
638) and στιβαρῇ (*Phaenomena* 639), and σκορπίον (14) and σκορπίος (18) mirror
the placement of the words in Aratus' passage. However, in describing the scor-
pion, Nicander elides the details of its creation by Artemis: ἀνῆκε ("sent forth,"
13) condenses *Phaenomena* 641–642. Instead Nicander dwells on the scorpion's
ability to cause pain. The adjective χαλαζήεντα ("frost-biting," 13) refers to its
ability to produce shivering with its stings,[148] while ἐκ κέντροιο τεθηγμένον
("with its whetted stinger," 14) clarifies its mode of attack. Indeed, as Sistakou
observes, in contrast with Aratus, "Nicander highlights, through sensation and
visualization, the amazing and horrifying dimension of nature as observed
by the man of science."[149] At the same time, in contrast with Aratus' circu-
itous account, Nicander does not omit the gruesomeness of both attacks, the
attempted assault and the scorpion's slaying of Orion. ἀχράντων ὅτε χερσὶ θεῆς
ἐδράξατο πέπλων ("after he grabbed in his hands the untouched robes of the
goddess," 16) expands Aratus' terse and oblique ἑλκῆσαι πέπλοιο (*Phaenomena*
638), and the combination of ἀχράντων, χερσί, and ἐδράξατο offer an emphasis
on touching. Likewise, as in later descriptions of attacks by creatures (Canobus'
neck, 314; Alcibius one's groin, 545; the dog's eye, 673), Nicander specifies where
Orion is struck: the heel of his mighty foot (17). The use of στιβαροῖο (17) for his
penetrated body part (instead of his damaging club as in Aratus) is pointed and

---

[148] For a discussion of the meaning of this word, see White 1987:3–7.
[149] Sistakou 2012:200.

highlights Orion's vulnerability when faced with this deadly foe. Additionally, whereas Aratus' Scorpion appears large (644), Nicander's hides beneath a small rock (ὀλίγῳ ὑπὸ λᾶι λοχήσας, 18). Nicander has downsized Aratus' gargantuan scorpion to allow for a sneak attack.

This evocation of Aratus continues in 19–20, as Nicander refers to Orion's transformation into a constellation (τέρας, 19).[150] Here, Nicander stresses the constellation's visibility and brightness (περίσημον, ἀείδελον), as well as its fixedness: ἀπλανές ("fixed," 19) and ἐστήρικται ("is set," 20). As commentators have noted,[151] ἐστήρικται occurs in the same *sedes* in Aratus and thus further cements the reworking of Aratus. Yet in recalling Aratus' content and language, Nicander ultimately distances himself and his chosen material from the visible ordered universe of his predecessor.[152] Specifically, Orion *qua* constellation is the complete inversion of the scorpion on earth. The former is conspicuous and fixed, while the latter was concealed and unforeseen. Nicander clarifies this contrast with a string of verbal correspondences: περίσημον (19), for instance, responds to ἀπροϊδής (18), while ὑπ' ἀστέρας ("among the stars," 19) matches ὀλίγῳ ὑπὸ λᾶι ("beneath the tiny rock," 18). ἀπλανές (19) and ἐστήρικται (20) combined oppose ἤλασεν ("struck," 17) and λοχήσας ("lurked," 18). The scorpion's lurking and subsequent attack are the opposite of visible fixed movement.

In posing this contrast between the scorpion and the Orion constellation, Nicander further illuminates the deadly creature's hiddenness and unpredictability. Indeed, ἀπροϊδής parallels ἀπροϊδῆ in the second line. By repeating this word, Nicander makes the scorpion's attack the first example of the deadly encounters hypothesized in the beginning lines. By calling Artemis a Titanian maiden (κόρη Τιτηνίς, 13), moreover, he evokes again the Titans (10) and their association with begetting deadly creatures. Just as Titan blood bred snakes and spiders, so too does a Titan descendant, Artemis, engender the scorpion. Additionally, this attack anticipates the elements of the other encounters narrated by Nicander. For instance, like Orion, Canobus also perishes unexpectedly and becomes a star,[153] although Nicander is silent on Canobus' catasterism in 309–319. Similarly, Artemis' retribution anticipates the punishments enacted by Helen and Demeter. Helen punishes the female blood-letting snake, while Demeter turns Ascabalus into a gecko (484–487). Orion's appearance as a hunter

---

[150] Aside from the meaning "portent," "sign," etc., τέρας can mean "monster" (LSJ τέρας II).

[151] Effe 1974b:120.

[152] See Wilson 2018a:277, who observes, "At first, Nicander appears self-deprecating in his contrast between the mighty hunter and the lowly scorpion, but who triumphs? The passage makes a clear distinction between the hunter himself and the constellation in the sky; we can infer that Nicander's scorpion killed the original Orion, for all the hunter's strength."

[153] For Canobus' catasterism, see Eudoxus fr. 75a–b and pseudo-Eratosthenes *Catasterisms* 37 MG.

(κυνηλατέοντος, 20) also foreshadows Alcibius two's hunting (668). Finally, just as Orion perishes by the scorpion's sting, so too does Odysseus purportedly die from a stingray barb (835–836). In adapting these elements and reapplying them in his other narratives, Nicander depicts a world marked simultaneously by consistency and variety. That is, while creatures can always attack suddenly, such strikes will vary.

7. Conclusion

In comparing Aratus and Nicander's poems as practical sources of technical information, Gow and Scholfield claim, "The difference between the two poets is that whereas the uninstructed reader may learn a good deal of astronomy from Aratus, the victim of snake-bites or poison who turned to Nicander for first-aid would be in sorry plight."[154] Such an assessment does not consider the fundamental differences between the poets' topics. Since celestial signs are fixed and regular, it is significantly easier to learn about them than small unpredictable creatures. Even the weather signs, which can differ in meaning depending on the perceiver, display some level of regularity.[155] Nicander's world, by contrast, swarms with variation, which emerges in the appearances of creatures, their movements, and even their names. The concealment of remedies and their effects only augments this difficulty.

Correspondingly, the two poets' extended myths indicate two different processes of perceiving and assessing truth about the physical world. For Aratus, the myths explicate how the constellations came to be in the sky. However, as products of the oral and poetic tradition (e.g. Hesiod), these narratives are not confirmable by the criterion of visibility. In some cases (the Pleiades, 254–263), what is seen clashes with what is said. At the same time, as in the beginning story, paradox characterizes these myths. How could Zeus have been a dependent child yet also an omnipotent, eternal pervading force? A similar paradox applies to all the constellations, whose eternal status should preclude any origin story. Nevertheless, despite their dubious and paradoxical nature, Aratus' myths demonstrate several important key truths: Zeus' evident concern for men (*Phaenomena* 30–35), the continued existence of Justice (*Phaenomena* 96–136), and a logical relationship between names and things (*Phaenomena* 216–224). In this way, the myths themselves serve as signs conducive for interpretation. In the *Theriaca*, by contrast, the uncertainties and multiplicities inherent in myth are

---

[154] Gow and Scholfield 1953:18.

[155] For instance, flocks of birds distress the farmer, but please the goatherd since they can indicate abundant milk in goats (*Phaenomena* 1094–1100).

appropriate for the poem's hidden and chaotic subject matter. For this reason, Nicander not only highlights the dubiousness of his myths (εἰ ἔτυμον, 309), but even queries the veracity of Hesiod, his model for catalogue verse (εἰ ἐτεόν περ, 10). In doing so, he reproduces the doubt inherent in learning through direct experience. It is only through experience that names come to describe things, that men are bitten by unpredictable beasts, and that they are saved.

3

Callimachus and Apollonius
Voices, Sources, and Stories

The perceptible world of the present occupied the scientific poems of Aratus and Nicander. Yet both poets delved into the distant past through their myths. Such interest in the past, however, abounded in Hellenistic poetry, as aetiology (the study of causes) pervaded the works of Callimachus and Apollonius of Rhodes.[1] Exploiting the resources of the Library of Alexandria, Callimachus and Apollonius, like Aratus and Nicander, scoured prose sources for information on the origins of places, names, rituals, and customs.[2] In integrating this material into their poems, these two poets attempted to forge a link between the remote past and the contemporary world.[3]

Information about the past, however, entails difficulties. Unlike the scientific information catalogued in the *Phaenomena* and the *Theriaca*, the reasons for a place name cannot be directly tested, either by the reader or by the poet (if he

[1] For the characteristics of aetiology in Greek poetry, see Fantuzzi 1996:369–371. Hunter (Fantuzzi and Hunter 2004:49) points out that aetiology is more prominent in Hellenistic and Roman poetry than in archaic and classical Greek poetry.

[2] With a career lasting from the 270s to the 230s BCE under the reigns of Ptolemy Philadelpus (283/282–246 BCE) and Ptolemy Euergetes (246–222 BCE), Callimachus of Cyrene composed a variety of poetic works, such as the *Hymns*, *Iambi*, a short hexameter poem the *Hecale*, and epigrams, as well as numerous works in prose. As Krevans 2004:175–179 has observed, both Callimachus' prose and poetic works showed an interest in aetiology and paradoxography. Additionally, Callimachus produced the *Pinakes*, a 120-book catalogue of all Greek literature. For the relevance of Callimachus' scholarly activity, see also Blum 1991:124–181 and Kwapisz and Pietruczuk 2019:221–247. According to the *Suda* (α 3420), Apollonius of Rhodes lived during the reign of Ptolemy Euergetes and served as head librarian at the Library of Alexandria. Fragments of foundation poetry attest to his interest in the origins of cities, and Krevans 2000:78 deduces on the basis of these fragments a mix of obscure erotic myth, aetiology, and legendary history. For the topic of the supposed quarrel between Callimachus and Apollonius of Rhodes, see Lefkowitz 1980:1–19.

[3] For the political implications of the poets' aetiologies, see Stephens 2000:208 (for Apollonius), who connects aetiology with the colonizing dimension of Ptolemaic rule. For the relationship between the *Aetia* and Ptolemaic ideology, see Asper 2011:155–159 and Acosta-Hughes and Stephens 2012:170–196.

cared to substantiate his prose sources). Even though the narrators created by Callimachus and Apollonius can cite the current existence of a ritual or name as evidence for the truth of the claim,[4] the temporal distance necessitates that the information come from sources, whether written or oral, not from immediate perception. As a result, the question of truth and falsehood becomes even more tangled. The evaluation of information must also depend on a critique of the sources' credibility.

In this chapter, I examine how these two poets' personae grapple with the truth and falsehood of their information. I restrict my focus to Callimachus' *Aetia* and Apollonius of Rhodes' *Argonautica*, two poetic works replete with aetiological concerns. While Aratus and Nicander employed a primarily descriptive mode for conveying their subject matter, Callimachus and Apollonius integrated information within a narrative frame, separating their poems into four books.[5] For instance, Callimachus, whose elegiac *Aetia* collates αἴτια ("causes") concerning the origins of cults and rituals, structures the first two books as a dialogue between the narrator and the Muses, who answer the narrator's questions.[6] Apollonius of Rhodes inserts numerous aetiological digressions in the *Argonautica*, an epic poem recounting the Argonauts' expedition to Colchis to retrieve the Golden Fleece.[7] In both cases, the narrative mode of the works makes the question of truth and falsehood more difficult. Is the narrated information true? If not explicitly for instruction, then what purpose does the information serve within the work, and how would it affect a reader?

During the Hellenistic period, not only did increasing aesthetic concerns, particularly those espoused by the Euphonists, further problematize the truth-status of poetry, but schools like the Academics doubted the possibility of completely distinguishing truth from falsehood via a "criterion of truth."[8] The

---

[4] For instance, the phrase ἔτι νῦν ("still now") emphasizes the relevance to the present. For this phrase in the *Argonautica*, see 1.1061 (the tomb of Cyzicus), 2.526–527 (the sacrifices made by Cean priests), and 4.480 (the bones of Apsyrtus still lying in the ground).

[5] The *Aetia* and the *Argonautica* feature an overlap in the choice of myths. For instance, Callimachus includes two Argonaut stories in the *Aetia*: the Argonauts' rituals on Anaphe (fr. 7c–21) and the anchor at Cyzicus (fr. 108). In the *Argonautica* (1.953–960), the anchor at Cyzicus appears at the beginning of their expedition, while the rituals at Anaphe occur at the end (4.1711–1730). Callimachus' choice to invert the order of these events and place them at key points in the *Aetia* (Anaphe at the beginning and Cyzicus towards the end) may suggest a dialogue with Apollonius. See Harder 2010:100.

[6] This device drops out in the second two books, which, as Parsons 1977:49 has demonstrated, are framed by poems dealing with Berenice II, the *Victoria Berenices* and *Coma Berenices*. For an overview of the four books of the *Aetia*, see Massimilla 2011:40–56. For the generic associations of the *Aetia*, see Harder 1998:95–113, who identifies influences from epigram, epinician, epic, and hymns.

[7] For a list of the aetiologies in the *Argonautica*, see Valverde Sánchez 1989:309–311. See also Harder 1994:22–29.

[8] For the problems with the criterion of truth, see Striker 1996c:22–51 [1974].

narrators in Callimachus and Apollonius in fact allude to such difficulties, as they do not simply transmit information but rather portray the task of knowing the truth as an active process. Indeed, unlike Aratus and Nicander, Callimachus and Apollonius present narrators with more personalized voices that seem to align closely with the author. Both narrators demonstrate a conscious awareness of their sources, the credibility of their information, and the limitations involved both in acquiring and transmitting the truth.

To determine the effect of these distinct voices on the question of critiquing truth and falsehood, I first offer an overview of the narratorial voices, considering the relationship between narrator and text. Although there are multiple narrative voices at play in the *Aetia* (e.g. the deceased Simonides in fr. 64 and Berenice's Lock in fr. 110), in this chapter I restrict my discussion to passages that feature either the Callimachean narrator (books 1–2) or a persona very close to him (fr. 67–75), whom Harder has dubbed a "scholar-poet." [9] The second section covers the narrators' treatment of their sources, particularly the Muses. Finally, I closely analyze a passage from each work, *Aetia* fr. 75.4–9, which features an ironic refusal by the Callimachean narrator to divulge the reasons for the marriage rites on Naxos, and *Argonautica* 4.982–992, the origins of the name Drepane. Together these two passages encapsulate Callimachus and Apollonius' narratorial voices and approaches to critiquing information.

From these readings, I demonstrate that Callimachus constructs a narrator who displays a confident attitude in his ability to collect and critique information. Specifically, personal experience constitutes his criterion, as his narrator evokes and recreates scenes of direct oral communication. Apollonius, on the other hand, portrays a narrator often riddled with uncertainty and doubt. In attempting to use and evaluate the Muses, whom he presents as sources, this Apollonian narrator reveals an increasing inability to trust them completely, despite their presumed omniscience and his status as epic narrator. From this and his frequent expressions of uncertainty, the Apollonian narrator implies the lack of a firm criterion by which truth and falsehood can be judged.

1. Narrators

1.1 Narratorial types

Due to the predominance of the narratorial voices in the *Aetia* and *Argonautica*, a streamlined outline of narratological theory and its application to Callimachus and Apollonius is necessary. In her introduction to the volume on ancient

---

[9] Harder 2004:68. For discussions of the multiple narrative voices, see Lynn 1995 and Harder 2004.

narrators, de Jong defines the narrator as the figure who recounts the story. While the narrator is a creation of the author, the two are not necessarily the same.[10] Additionally, narratological theory distinguishes narrators by their involvement in the narrative. A narrator who participates as a character in the story is an internal narrator, while one who does not is an external narrator.[11] This same distinction of internal/external applies to the narratees, the recipients of the narration.

Since narrators can embed narration given by another, we may also characterize narrators as primary (existing at the first level of narration and reporting the main story) and secondary (a character who narrates in the main story).[12] By these categories, the Callimachean narrator qualifies as an internal narrator due to his participation in the conversation with the Muses. At the same time, because the primary narrator reports the conversation as occurring in a dream when he was young (2d Harder = Σ *Flor.* 15–20), the Callimachean narrator and the Muses act as secondary narrators, as well as narratees.[13] By contrast, the Apollonian narrator's lack of direct participation in the *Argonautica* makes him an external narrator, as well as a primary one.

In addition to their identity (internal vs. external) and status (primary vs. secondary), narrators vary in the degrees of their self-consciousness, the amount of their knowledge, and the distance between them and the narrated events.[14] Since both the *Aetia* and the *Argonautica* focus on the happenings of the distant mythical past, there spans a sizable disjunction between the narrator and the recounted material.[15] Such a temporal distance affects what information can be known. At the same time, this distance contributes to the high degree of self-consciousness that scholars have detected in the Callimachean and Apollonian

---

[10] De Jong 2004:1.

[11] De Jong 1987:33. In addition to the narrator, there is also the "focalizer," the one who sees and interprets the events of a narrative. The narrator, however, can be distinct from the "focalizer," since a narrator can report the interpretation of someone else. For the sake of ease, I focus solely on the personae as "narrators."

[12] De Jong 2004:2.

[13] Harder 1988:9.

[14] De Jong 2004:2–3.

[15] Harder 2012.1:25, comparing the *Aetia* with the *Argonautica*, observes, "In Apollonius Rhodius' *Argonautica*, the journey of the Argonauts results in a wide range of monuments, rituals, and other traces along their route. The approach is different from that in the *Aetia* if only because in Apollonius the starting point is the Argonauts' adventures in the past, which leave traces that 'even now' people can observe, whereas in the *Aetia* the starting point is the present in which the narrator is confronted by traces from the past which he seeks to explain." See also Harder 2003:290–306 for a discussion of past, present, and future in the *Aetia*. For time more broadly in both authors, see Klooster 2007:63–80 (for Apollonius) and Harder 2007a:81–96 (for Callimachus).

narratorial voices.[16] Indeed, such self-consciousness can also be tied to the authors' simultaneous statuses as scholars and poets.[17] Both professions involve different concerns. While a scholar aims to collate and evaluate data from various sources, a poet composing a narrative poem is concerned with selecting and organizing the material so that it contributes to the poem in meaning and poetic effect. As I show in my subsequent summary of the Callimachean and Apollonian narrators, both concerns are present, even though the voices differ in how they critique the sources and the information. In handling the information, Callimachus' narrator assumes a tone of confidence, while the Apollonian narrator has frequent expressions of doubt that become more obvious, particularly in the fourth book of the *Argonautica*.

1.2 The Callimachean narrator

Callimachus introduces his first-person narrator in the prologue to the *Aetia*. This passage deals with the narrator's quarrel with the so-called Telchines, who are depicted as criticizing the narrator's song: πολλάκ]ι μοι Τελχῖνες ἐπιτρύζουσιν ἀ₍οιδῇ, ("often the Telchines grumble at me for my song," fr. 1.1).[18] According to the narrator, this group chastises him for not having completed "one continuous song of kings and heroes in many thousand lines" (fr. 1.3–4).[19] In response, the narrator poses a series of metaphors that express the superiority of short over long works (fr. 1.9–16), poetic innovation ("untrodden paths") as opposed to the common road (fr. 1.23–28), and the sweet sound of cicadas

---

[16]   Cf. Goldhill 1991:285 (for Apollonius) and Harder 1990:309; 2004:80 (for Callimachus).

[17]   Scholars (e.g. Pfeiffer 1968:125) have construed fr. 612 Pf. (ἀμάρτυρον οὐδὲν ἀείδω, "I sing of nothing unattested") as emblematic of Callimachus' use of scholarship in poetic production. Due to the lack of a definite context for this fragment, I am hesitant to overstate the significance of this quotation. For analysis of this phrase along with bibliography of the varying scholarly opinions, see Meyer 1993:319–324, who advises against reading the fragment as a programmatic statement about Callimachus' information. Callimachus, however, does extract information about the nautilus from Aristotle's *History of Animals* (542b4–17) in epigram 5 Pf. See Prescott 1921:329–332 and Gutzwiller 1992:195–197. Although noting the Peripatetic character of Callimachus' prose production, Brink 1946:11–16 sees Callimachus and Aristotle as diametrically opposed with regards to literary criticism.

[18]   The Telchines, a mythical group of metalworkers residing on Ceos and Rhodes, were known for their envy. See *Aetia* fr. 75.65. Among the Telchines listed in the fragmentary Florentine scholia on fragment 1 (fr. 1b Harder) are Asclepiades, Posidippus, and Praxiphanes.

[19]   οὐχ ἓν ἄεισμα διηνεκὲς ἢ βασιλη[η / ......]ας ἐν πολλαῖς ἤνυσα χιλιάσιν / ἢ .....] ους . ἥρωας. See Cameron 1995:342–343 for an overview of the varying interpretations of ἓν ἄεισμα διηνεκές. The adjective διηνεκές involves telling a story completely from beginning to end; see *Odyssey* 7.241. As Asper 1997:221 contends, the adjective refers only to narrative continuity, not to meter or content. As Harder 2012.2:21 notes, the *Aetia* is not διηνεκές since it lacks completeness and is not in chronological order. See also van Tress 2004:31–38 for discussion of this word.

over the braying of asses (fr. 1.29–30).[20] These statements combined have been interpreted as a general reflection of the aesthetics of Callimachus the poet.[21] While Callimachean poetry does exhibit such characteristics of being refined, we should not, as Schmitz observes, assume a direct overlap between this narrator and the actual poet Callimachus, nor should we construe the quarrel in the prologue as a specific reference to a historical feud.[22] Rather, such explicit pronouncements contribute to the characterization of the persona. In emphasizing the superiority of his own preferences, this persona exudes a confident attitude. Such an attitude in turn empowers him to establish a certain criterion for judging σοφίην ("wisdom," fr. 1.18). It is not the "Persian measure" (σχοίνῳ Περσίδι, fr. 1.18), but skill (τέχνη, fr. 1.17).[23]

Along with this confident attitude, the narrator associates himself with childhood and youth in the prologue. For instance, he claims that the Telchines reproach him for composing like a child: ἔπος δ᾽ ἐπὶ τυτθὸν ἑλ[ίσσω / παῖς ἅτε ("I turn around the words in my mind a little, like a child," fr. 1.5–6).[24] Yet this association of the narrator with a child is ironic, as the narrator indicates immediately that he is of some age: τῶν δ᾽ ἐτέων ἡ δεκὰ‚ς‚ οὐκ ὀλίγη ("although the decades of my years are not a few," fr. 1.6). Later, he expresses a wish to toss off the burden of old age (fr. 1.35–36).[25] At the same time, childhood should imply a lack of knowledge and skill, especially since an association with children qualifies as an insult in Homer.[26] Yet in associating a childlike method of composition with his preferred poetic principles, the narrator reformulates

---

[20] For an overview of these lines, see Acosta-Hughes and Stephens 2002:242–246. See Steiner 2007:195–205 for an analysis of the avian imagery in the prologue.

[21] See, for instance, Schwinge 1986:20–23. On the relationship between the prologue and Greek literary criticism, see Clayman 1977:27–34.

[22] Schmitz 1999:156. Schmitz, however, while not denying the possibility of connections to the real world, stresses, "Callimachus is not making a plain statement of his poetological principles. Instead, he uses these principles and their proclamation as a means to secure his audience's concurrence and sympathy." For a similar assessment, see Asper 2001:89.

[23] For the philosophical implications of σοφίη and τέχνη, see Andrews 1998:10. She notes (1998:8), "The position Callimachus takes on deliberation seems directly to repudiate the Pyrrhonists' suspension of judgment."

[24] Following Harder 2012, I adopt the reading ἑλίσσω, taking it to mean "turning around in the mind." For an overview of the various suggestions, see Harder 2012.2:26–27.

[25] As Acosta-Hughes and Stephens 2002:240 and Hutchinson 2003:49 note, the antithesis between youth and old age reoccurs throughout the *Aetia*. The childlike Callimachus represents an antithesis to the aged Telchines. Whether this claim of old age applies to the actual poet Callimachus at the time of writing remains subject to debate. Pfeiffer 1928:302–341 took the statement as evidence that the prologue was affixed later in life for a second edition of the *Aetia*.

[26] For instance, at *Iliad* 2.337–338, Nestor insults the Achaeans by likening them to infantile children.

childhood as a virtue.[27] Indeed, it was when he first put the tablet on his knees that Apollo manifested to teach him the important poetic precepts: καὶ γὰρ ὅτ‚ε πρ‚ώ‚τιστον ἐμοῖς ἐπὶ δέλτον ἔθηκα / γούνασι‚ν, Ἀπ[ό]λλων εἶπεν ὅ μοι Λύκιος ("for when I first set the writing tablet on my knees, Apollo Lycius said to me," fr. 1.21–22). Consequently, for the Callimachean narrator, childhood is not a time of ignorance, but rather enlightenment.

This emphasis on childhood corresponds to the Callimachean narrator's voice in the *Aetia*. Aside from the confident air, this voice exhibits a persistent eagerness to learn, as one would expect from a child. We can detect such eagerness most clearly in the dialogue structure of the first two books. This dialogue format invites comparisons with the Platonic dialogue.[28] Yet, as Hutchinson points out, whereas the Platonic dialogues involve a superior engaging with inferiors about ideas, in the first two *Aetia* books, a supposed inferior (the Callimachean narrator) probes the Muses, his superiors.[29] By interrogating his superiors, the narrator displays the extent of his desire for knowledge as well as his confidence. Combined, this eagerness and confidence allow for an inversion of typical knowledge hierarchies.

The beginning of *Aetia* fragment 43 attests to the values and pleasures of learning:

κα‚ὶ γὰρ ἐγὼ τὰ μὲν ὅσσα καρή‚ατι τῆμος ἔ‚δωκα
    ξα‚νθὰ σὺν εὐόδμοις ἁβρὰ λίπ‚ῃ στεφάνο‚ις,
ἄπνο‚α πάντ' ἐγένοντο παρὰ χ‚ρέος, ὅσσα τ' ‚ὀδόντων
    ἔνδοθ‚ι νείαιράν τ' εἰς ἀχάριστον ἔ‚δυ,
καὶ τῶν ο‚ὐδὲν ἔμεινεν ἐς αὔρι‚ον· ὅσσα δ' ‚ἀ‚κουαῖς
    εἰσεθέ‚μην, ἔτι μοι μοῦνα πάρεσ‚τι τάδ‚ε.

For my part as well, everything I set on my head on that occasion—the soft golden oils with the fragrant garlands—died at once, and everything that went down into my teeth and my ungrateful stomach, none

---

27 For the role of childhood in Callimachus' poetry in general, see Ambühl 2005. For discussion of childhood in the prologue, see Ambühl 2005:385–408.
28 For the influences of Plato on the *Aetia* prologue, see Acosta-Hughes and Stephens 2012:31–47, who identify two important passages from Plato: *Phaedo* 60c8–61b7 and *Phaedrus* 259b5–d8. In the *Phaedo*, Socrates recounts how a dream induced him to compose poetry, a situation that parallels Apollo's commands to the Callimachean narrator. In the *Phaedrus*, Socrates describes how men who abstained from food and devoted themselves to poetry became cicadas sacred to the Muses. The Callimachean narrator wishes to become a cicada (fr. 1.32–36) and shed off his old age. See also Hunter 1989b:1–2, who compares this wish with the description of a winged poet in the *Ion* (534c).
29 Hutchinson 2003:48.

of those too remained the next day. But everything I admitted to my ears, only these are still with me.

fr. 43.12–17

The mention of the oils and garlands suggests attendance at a symposium, where participants would partake in food, wine, and conversation. In this passage, however, the narrator treats conversation as the most superior aspect. Unlike oils, garlands, food, and wine, all of which bring about temporary pleasure because of their transitory nature, only what is received in the ears (16) remains: ἔτι μοι μοῦνα πάρεσ͵τι τάδ͵ε ("these alone are still with me," 17). In placing the personal pronoun μοι ("me") next to the adjective μοῦνα ("alone"), which modifies the relative clause ὅσσα δ' ἀ͵κουαῖς / εἰσεθέ͵μην ("everything I admitted to my ears," 16–17), Callimachus signifies the proximity between the narrator and the information he has received. Such information has become part of him, so to speak. At the same time, by emphasizing the information's placement in the ears, Callimachus emphasizes the oral nature of this transmission.

Along with boasting this enthusiasm to learn, the narrator flaunts an enthusiasm for exhibiting knowledge that he already possesses. For instance, later in fragment 43 ("the Sicilian Cities"),[30] he brags to the Muses:

οἶδα Γέλ͵α͵ ποταμο͵ῦ͵ κεφαλ͵ῇ ἔπι κεί͵μεγ͵ιον ἄστυ
   Λίνδοθεν ἀρχαίη [σ]κιμπτ[όμενο]ν γενε[ῇ,
Μινῴη[ν] καὶ Κρῆσ[ο]αν, ἵ[να ζείο]γτα λοετ[ρὰ
   χεῦαν ἐ[π'] Εὐρώπης υἱέϊ Κ[ωκαλί]δες·
οἶδα Λεοντίνους [.] δεδρα[.........].....[
   καὶ Μεγαρεῖς ἔτερ[οι] τοὺς ἀ[πέ]νασσαν ἐκεῖ
Νισαῖοι Μεγαρῆες, ἔχω δ' Εὔβοιαν ἐνισπε[ῖν
   φίλατο κα[ὶ] κεστ[ο]ῦ [δ]εσπότις ἦν Ἔρυκα·

I know of the town that lies upon the mouth of the river Gela, which boasts of its ancient lineage from Lindus, and of Cretan Minoa, where the daughters of Cocalus poured seething water on Europa's son. I know of Leontini ... and of the Megarians, whom the other Megarians, from Nisa, sent there as colonists. I can speak about Euboea and Eryx, which the mistress of the girdle loved.

fr. 43.46–53

---

[30] This section recalls Thucydides' excursus on the Sicilian cities (Thucydides 6.2–5). For discussion of how Callimachus evokes yet alters Thucydides' methods and interests, see Greene 2017b:34–38.

With the repetition of οἶδα ("I know") in 46 and 50, Callimachus emphasizes the extent of his narrator's knowledge.[31] Such knowledge consists not only in an awareness of the places in Sicily, but also their lineage (Gela's descent from Lindus) and a tale about mythical violence (the daughters of Cocalus pouring water on Minos).[32] Furthermore, the narrator is familiar with cultic activity, as he marks the city of Eryx as the one loved by Aphrodite (the mistress of the girdle). While the Muse Clio offers a reply about the founding of Zancle in 58–83, the Callimachean narrator nevertheless displays an impressive array of details, as would suit the scholarly persona. Yet such a display is ironic in the context of the exchange. We would expect the person asking questions to profess ignorance in some respect, or at least to not possess such a great amount of preexisting knowledge.[33]

In asserting this previous knowledge, the Callimachean narrator reveals a confident attitude about his existing abilities. At the same time, he indicates his eagerness to supplement this information. Indeed, when Clio's speech ends, the narrator craves to learn more: ὣ[ς] ἡ μὲν λίπε μῦθον, ἐγὼ δ' ἐπὶ καὶ τ[ὸ πυ] θέσθαι / ἤ]θελον—ἦ γάρ μοι θάμβος ὑπετρέφ[ε]το—("thus she ended her tale, but I wanted to learn this too, for truly my wonder was fed," fr. 43b1–2). Cozzoli in fact connects this feeling of wonder to what she dubs a "poetics of childhood" in Callimachus. As she argues, "The poetics of childhood, then, involves a recalibration of the persona of the poet in its entirety, redefining him as philologist and scientist as well as bard. Curiosity, stupefaction, wonder, and imagination are shared by both the child and scientist, because they constitute the conditions of any desire to discover or learn."[34] No matter what, the Callimachean narrator, like an overly inquisitive child, always wants to uncover more. It is not pedantry as much as an enthusiastic desire to learn that drives the plot of the *Aetia*.[35]

---

[31] See Harder 2012.2:324.

[32] Prioux 2009:128 connects this story with Callimachus' research on wonders, as he refers to the boiling water of Camicus (Call fr. 407 Pf.).

[33] As Harder 1988:11 observes, "It is striking that 'Callimachus himself' is here offering a great deal of information and that it is a catalogue too."

[34] Cozzoli 2011:423. While Fantuzzi and Hunter 2004:59 observe the childishness of the impulse to know more, they also associate this feeling of wonder to the preliminary conditions for philosophy, as described by Plato and Aristotle (*Metaphysics* 1.982b12–17). Additionally, Priestly 2014:105–106 proposes a parallel between Callimachean and Herodotean wonder.

[35] For analysis of knowledge as a central theme in the *Aetia*, see Hutchinson 2003:49.

1.3 The Apollonian narrator

Like the Callimachean narrator, Apollonius' narrator speaks in the first person, promising that he "will recall the glorious deeds of men born long ago" (παλαιγενέων κλέα φωτῶν / μνήσομαι, 1.1–2). In announcing such a subject, that of epic, as his theme, the narrator brings in the expectations of an epic narrator like Homer.[36] The voice of such a narrator is not clearly aligned with the historical author, and his knowledge stems from the omniscient Muses (*Iliad* 2.484–287). The Apollonian narrator, however, diverges from his Homeric model in many respects. While both poets alternate between the narratorial voice and the characters' voices, the Apollonian narrator employs his own voice at a greater frequency,[37] while also interlacing the epic with numerous addresses to the characters and to the implied reader. In doing so, he exhibits a high level of emotional investment in the events of the narrative.[38] Berkowitz, in fact, sees the *Argonautica* as displaying elements of a dialogue.[39] Since the epic begins with an address to Apollo (ἀρχόμενος σέο Φοῖβε, 1.1), we may read the whole work as an exchange between the narrator and the god Apollo, who fulfills a crucial role in the narrative by delivering the prophecy that initiates the Argonauts' quest (1.5, 1.8).[40] By extension, the narrator, in interacting with this crucial character, participates in the narrative, despite seeming to serve as an external narrator.

Aside from addressing Apollo, the narrator participates in the narrative via the act of narration. As Beye and Wray have observed,[41] Apollonius fashions an analogy between narration and the journey. For instance, after describing Heracles slaughtering Hylas' father Thiodamas (1.1213–1219), the narrator remarks that "such things would lead me far from the song" (ἀλλὰ τὰ μὲν τηλοῦ κεν ἀποπλάγξειεν ἀοιδῆς, 1.1220) before subsequently returning to the narrative.[42] Similarly, at the very end of the poem, the narrator announces his arrival at the end of the Argonauts' journey: ἤδη γὰρ ἐπὶ κλυτὰ πείραθ' ἱκάνω / ὑμετέρων καμάτων ("for now I have come to the famous end of your struggles,"

---

[36] For the generic expectations of παλαιγενέων κλέα φωτῶν / μνήσομαι, see Hunter 1993:8.
[37] Based on the word count of Cuypers 2005:37, the Homeric narrator speaks 54.3% of the words in the *Iliad* and 31.4% in the *Odyssey*. The Apollonian narrator, on the other hand, is responsible for 70.4% of the words.
[38] For a list and discussion of the places where the narrator addresses the narratee, see Byre 1991:215–227, who argues that these direct addresses "posit a hypothetical world in which the narratee perceives and reacts to the events, characters, and objects of the fictional world" (227). See also Gummert 1992:126 and Klooster 2013:159–166.
[39] Berkowitz 2004:96.
[40] DeForest 1994:37 and Albis 1996:25.
[41] Beye 1982:14, Goldhill 1991:287, and Wray 2000:244.
[42] For discussion of this line, see Clare 2002:282.

4.1775–1776).[43] In recounting the Argonauts' deeds, the narrator too has encountered their toils.

At the same time, the narrator's voice often resembles that of his characters. In particular, the narrator overlaps with Orpheus and Phineus, whose respective roles of poet and seer correspond to that of a narrator.[44] At 2.317–407 Phineus functions like a narrator by relating the obstacles and places that the Argonauts will encounter on their journey to Colchis. As a seer inspired by the gods, Phineus should possess the omniscience that would suit an epic narrator. Yet, as Phineus makes explicit, his reverence for Zeus hinders a full revealing of the future for the Argonauts: οὐ μὲν πάντα πέλει θέμις ὔμμι δαῆναι / ἀτρεκές, ("it is not right for you to know all things exactly," 2.311–312). For this reason, Phineus provides information that produces false expectations. For instance, at 2.334–345, Phineus implies that the Argonauts' safe crossing through the Symplegades will come from the strength of their rowing. In reality, Athena's intervention (2.598–600) achieves their salvation.[45]

This strategy of misdirection corresponds to the techniques of the Apollonian narrator. Despite his presumed and expected omniscience, this narrator frequently often withholds information, expresses uncertainty, and gives conflicting interpretations.[46] All these tendencies culminate in what Cuypers describes as "a Protean narrative persona: an amalgam of (at least) the Homeric singer of epics, the hymnic and Pindaric singers of praise, the Herodotean historian, and the Callimachean scholar."[47] Like Pindar in his epinician poetry, the Apollonian narrator breaks off in the middle of a story, citing the information as too long or irrelevant.[48] The narrator's Herodotean characteristics can be observed in ethnographic digressions such as the discussion of the Tower Dwellers at 2.1015–1029.[49] At the same time, the Apollonian narrator assumes the inquisitive stance of a historian. An aspect of this persona manifests in the narrator's use of που ("I guess, I suppose"), a particle that suggests a narrator

---

[43] Albis 1996:119 and Clare 2002:284.

[44] For instance, at 2.708–709, the narrator apologizes to Apollo with ἰλήκοις· αἰεί τοι, ἄναξ, / ἄτμητοι ἔθειραι, / αἰὲν ἀδήλητοι ("be propitious, lord, may your hair always be unshorn, always unharmed"), echoing Orpheus' prayer to Apollo at 2.693: ἀλλ᾽ ἵληθι ἄναξ, ἵληθι φαανθείς ("so be propitious, lord, be propitious, you who have appeared"). As the first character listed in the Catalogue of Heroes (1.23–34), Orpheus is a crucial figure. For discussion of Orpheus' role and powers in the poem, see, for instance, Clare 2002:231–240, Klooster 2011:82–91, and Murray 2018:209–220.

[45] See Berkowitz 2004:14–16.

[46] Byre 2002:11.

[47] Cuypers 2004a:43.

[48] Cuypers 2004a:49. See *Argonautica* 1.648–649.

[49] See Morrison 2007:274n18 for a list of ethnographic discussions in the *Argonautica*.

does not want to be "pinned down."[50] As Cuypers concludes, the Apollonian narrator, by adopting this doubtful tone in his roles as an epic-inspired bard and a researcher of customs and myths, presents a paradoxical situation.[51] In aiming to establish his credibility to express the truth, he undermines such authority.

At the same time, by assimilating himself with the characters of the epic, the narrator renders himself subject to the same limitations and uncertainties they face. Indeed, as Clayman has observed in her examination of the Skeptic influences in Hellenistic poetry, characters in the *Argonautica* undergo states of ἀπορία and ἀμηχανία.[52] Jason displays these characteristics, whenever he struggles to establish a course of action. For instance, after learning about the disappearance of Heracles and Hylas, Jason is "overcome by helplessness" (ἀμηχανίῃσιν ἀτυχθείς, 1.1286) and sits in silent brooding.[53] According to Sextus Empiricus, ἀπορία and ἀμηχανία are the results of ἐποχή ("suspension of judgment"), the strategy employed by the Pyrrhonists to account for the equal strength of opposites (ἰσοσθένεια).[54] Timon, for instance, states that he could not claim that honey was sweet, only that it seemed so (Diogenes Laertius 9.105).[55]

Of course, the later Skeptic terminology from Sextus Empiricus does not map exactly onto the manifestations of ἀπορία and ἀμηχανία in the *Argonautica*. Nevertheless, the experience is not dissimilar, for both the characters and the

---

[50] Cuypers 2005:41. The particle που is particularly useful for sections where the narrator analyzes characters' motivations, such as the assumption that the grisly murder of Apsyrtus induced Zeus' wrath: αὐτόν που μεγαλωστὶ δεδουπότος Ἀψύρτοιο / Ζῆνα, θεῶν βασιλῆα χόλος, λάβεν οἷον ἔρεξαν ("after Apsyrtus fell dead in his tall stature, I suppose, wrath seized Zeus himself, king of the gods, for what they did," 4.557–458). See also Byre 2002:55n5.

[51] Cuypers 2004a:49–50.

[52] Clayman 2000:35–39. For places where characters are at a loss or deal with unsolvable situations, see also 1.460, 1.638, 1.1053, 1.1233, 2.410, 2.578, 2.681, 2.860, 2.885, 2.1140, 3.126, 3.423, 3.432, 3.504, 3.772, 3.893, 3.951, 3.1157, 4.107, 4.692, 4.825, 4.880, 4.1049, 4.1259, 4.1308, 4.1318, and 4.1527. See Vian 1978:1025–1041 for a discussion of Jason's feelings of helplessness in context.

[53] See Klein 1983:125 for an association between Jason's helplessness and Skepticism. Hunter 1988:436n6 rejects this suggestion, while also doubting the existence of a formal philosophy of Skepticism in the early third century BCE. While Klein goes too far in calling the author Apollonius a Skeptic, influences from Pyrrho and Timon are possible.

[54] For ἀπορεῖν and ἀμηχανεῖν as characteristics of Skepticism, see Sextus Empiricus *Outlines of Pyrrhonism* 1.7.

[55] For a summary of Timon's views, see Diogenes Laertius 9.76. Brunschwig 1999:249 proposes that Timon attributed his own epistemological views to Pyrrho, who left no writings. The other important source is Aristocles in Eusebius *Preparation for the Gospel* 14.18.1–5. See Long and Sedley 1987:1.16–17 for a discussion of this passage. According to them, Pyrrho is not arguing against the criterion of truth, but rather denying truth and falsehood to any sensations or opinions. However, even if the early Skeptics were not directly dealing with the criterion, their noncommittal stance is by implication a rejection of a criterion.

narrator.[56] Like Jason, the Apollonian narrator's indecisiveness and uncertainty sometimes hamper the progression of the narrative, especially in places in the fourth book (e.g. *Argonautica* 4.1–5). Such debilitating doubt, in the context of epic, the most authoritative genre, is surprising. Indeed, not only should the typical epic narrator record the achievements of heroes and not their difficulties and indecisions, but he himself should be able to accomplish the function of narrator.

1.4 Summary of narratorial voices

Through their distinct personal voices, the narrators in both works act like characters, rather than one-dimensional omniscient narrators detached from the action. The Callimachean narrator is in fact a character in the narrative, at least in the first two books of the *Aetia*. The Apollonian narrator, on the other hand, although not directly involved in the story he recounts, absorbs elements of his characters' experiences—not only their emotions, but also their uncertainties. A crucial difference, however, lies in the ways the authors associate the narrators with the characters. Whereas the Callimachean narrator's interactions in the narrative empower him to acquire more knowledge from the Muses and thus eventually abandon them in *Aetia* books three and four, the more the Apollonian narrator interferes in the narrative, the more his uncertainty becomes apparent. As a result, he must rely more heavily on the Muses. Yet, as I will demonstrate, the Muses do not function as unquestionable sources for the Apollonian narrator's inquiries. Through the different treatment of their sources, the Callimachean and Apollonian narrators offer two alternate processes of interrogating truth and falsehood. For the confident Callimachean narrator, the personal experience of researching and learning provides a means of having some amount of surety. The uncertain narrator of the *Argonautica*, on the other hand, only deepens his doubt amid more information and experiences.

2. Sources

2.1 Callimachean sources

In the extant fragments of Callimachus' *Aetia*, we can identify three different kinds of sources. The first two, the Muses and Theogenes, are characters who interact with the narrator in the narrative. Materializing in a dream, the Muses meet a younger version of the narrator, whose questions about the origins of various rituals guide the structure of the first two books of the *Aetia*. Theogenes,

---

[56] Clayman 2000:39.

whom the narrator encounters at a symposium in fragment 178, fulfills a similar function, replying to the narrator's inquiry about the customs on Icus. In these two cases, Callimachus evokes scenes of oral communication, albeit in a written poetic form. The third type of source, however, is written ones. In addition to the brief citation at fr. 92,[57] Callimachus' narrator devotes special attention to the prose author Xenomedes, the source for the story of Acontius and Cydippe (fr. 67–75). In representing these sources, Callimachus frames them in terms of proximity and distance. As a result, he recalls the immediacy of oral communication even though such material has been transmitted through written texts and thus not directly perceived by either the author or his poetic persona. Despite this distance, however, Callimachus makes his confident and eager narrator boast an intimate connection with these sources, stressing the personal aspect of information accumulation.

2.1.1 Callimachus' Muses

Since the Muses are predominant in the first two books of the *Aetia*, their complex presentation has occupied a good deal of Callimachean scholarship.[58] According to Bing, who stresses the increased role of writing in poetic production during the Hellenistic period, the Muses lose their traditional status as anthropomorphic inspirers of poets, becoming instead symbols of the dense literary tradition. The Muse had "learned to write."[59] Although Bing is correct to observe the increased association between writing and the Muses, the Muses in the *Aetia* nevertheless retain some characteristics of their personified forms. Indeed, in two places in the *Aetia* prologue, Callimachus represents the relationship with the Muses as one of friendship. For instance, the narrator, when attacking his critics, the Telchines, states νήιδεϛ οἳ Μούσης οὐκ ἐγένοντο φίλοι ("who, ignorant of the Muse, were not born her friends," fr. 1.2). By associating ignorance with the absence of the Muses' friendship, Callimachus emphasizes the personal dimension of the Muses' favor. Moreover, as is stated later in the prologue, such a relationship with the Muses does not cease with old age: Μοῦσαι γ̣ὰρ ὅσους ἴδον ὄθμα̣ι̣τ̣ι̣ παῖδας / μὴ λοξῷ, πολιοὺϛ̣ οὐκ ἀπέθεντο φίλους ("whomsoever the Muses did not look upon with a slanting eye when they are children, they do not reject as friends when they are old," fr. 1.37–38).[60] While this reference to the

---

57 Leandrius of Miletus is cited at *Aetia* fr. 92.2 (Ino and Melicertes). For discussion of this citation, see Krevans 2004:179, Harder 2012.2:727–728, and Greene 2017a:31.

58 For instance, see Harder 1988:1–14 and Morrison 2011:329–348.

59 Bing 1988b:27.

60 See Crane 1986:270, who notes that πολιοὺϛ̣ οὐκ ἀπέθεντο (fr. 1.38) recalls *Homeric Hymn to Aphrodite* 228. However, unlike Eos, who abandons Tithonus in his old age, the Muses are steadfast in their friendship.

love from the Muses finds parallels in Greek literature (e.g. *Theogony* 96–97), we may interpret a close relationship with the Muses, in the context of the literate Hellenistic milieu, as a kind of capability for collecting information as well as casting it in poetic form.

The Muses themselves appear in the next fragment, now called the *Somnium*: ποιμένι μῆλα νέμιοντι παρ' ἴχνιον ὀξέος ἵππου / Ἡσιόδιῳ Μουσέων ἑσμοὶς ὅτ' ἠντίασεν ("when the swarm of Muses met the shepherd Hesiod as he was tending his flocks next to the footprint of the swift horse," fr. 2.1–2).[61] This meeting with the Muses evokes the *Dichterweihe* of Hesiod's *Theogony*.[62] Callimachus alludes to this famous encounter not only with the explicit naming of Hesiod (Ἡσιόδιῳ, fr. 2.2) and his occupation as shepherd (ποιμένι μῆλα νέμιοντι, fr. 2.1), but also with the phrase παρ' ἴχνιον ὀξέος ἵππου ("next to the footprint of the swift horse," fr. 2.1), an oblique periphrasis for the Hippocrene (see Chapter 2.5.1). Since the meeting with the Muses initiated the contents of the *Theogony*, Callimachus' reworking of this scene exudes programmatic qualities, marking Hesiod as Callimachus' predecessor.[63] Indeed, like Hesiod in the *Theogony*, Callimachus composes a catalogue poem, specifically one of αἴτια.[64] At the same time, both poetic personae recount information received by the Muses personally. Callimachus signifies the closeness of Hesiod's relationship with the Muses by juxtaposing Ἡσιόδιῳ with Μουσέων ἑσμοὶς ("swarm of the Muses," fr. 2.2),[65] a noun pairing linked together by the series of sigmas and the repeated rough breathings in Ἡσιόδιῳ and ἑσμοὶς.

A crucial difference, however, distinguishes the context of Callimachus' meeting with the Muses. According to the Florentine scholia, this run-in with the Muses took place in a dream when the narrator was a young man.[66] The

---

[61]   Scholars have struggled with establishing the transition between the prologue and the *Somnium*. Noting two lemmata in the commentary in *P. Oxy.* 2262 fr. 1a 24–25, Kerkhecker 1988:16–24 proposed an invocation to the Muses, which either concluded the prologue or was sandwiched between the prologue and the *Somnium*. Through this invocation, the Callimachean narrator requested the Muses to recall their answers. See also Bing 1988a:274, who expands on Kerkhecker's observations to claim that Callimachus requested the Muses to recall also his questions posed. However, as Krevans 1991:21 points out, the verb ἀμνήσαιτε (fr. 2c2 Harder) is not necessarily addressed to the Muses. For discussion of this transition, see also Harder 1993b:11–13. Cameron 1995:132 argues that the *Somnium* presupposes the prologue, as both share the themes of childhood and friendship with the Muses.

[62]   Kambylis 1965:122.

[63]   Χάεος γενεο[in fr. 2.3 recalls *Theogony* 116. Additionally, τεύχωιν ὡς ἑτέρῳ τις ἑῷ ικακὸν ἥπατι τεύχει at fr. 2.5 is a reworking of *Works and Days* 265. See Fantuzzi and Hunter 2004:53.

[64]   Harder 1998:95.

[65]   For discussion of ἑσμός, see Scully 2015:128, who proposes an allusion to *Theogony* 83–84.

[66]   [ὡς κ]ατ' ὄναρ σ(υμ)μείξας ταῖς Μούσ[αις ἐν Ἑ-][λι]κῶνι εἰλήφοι π(αρ' α)ὐτ(ῶν) τ(ὴν) τ(ῶν) αἰτίων [ἐξήγη-] [σιν ἀ]ρτιγένειος ὤν ("that when he met the Muses on Mount Helicon in a dream, he received from them the explanation of the causes, when he was a young man," fr. 2d Harder

situation of the dream functions as a filter, and although Callimachus removes the immediacy of the Hesiodic encounter, he in fact makes it an even more personal one. As Harder points out, "Although in the sequel their (the Muses') stories are quoted in direct discourse, they are always subject to the narrator's control and may be understood as an extension of the narrator rather than as an outside force."[67] Thus, the Muses and the narrator are not just "friends," but the Muses are a part of him.[68]

A clear example of this relationship emerges in the first αἴτιον that spans fragments 3–7. The narrator's inquiry involves the absence of wreaths and flutes during sacrifices to Graces on Paros. Although the fragments themselves are scanty, the scholiast (7a Harder = Σ *Flor.* 21–37) supplements our understanding, as well as citing Callimachus' sources (Agias and Dercylus). According to the Muse Clio, Minos discovered his son Androgeus' death while sacrificing to the Graces and in his grief discarded the wreaths and ceased flute playing. Aside from this information, Clio also specifies the parents of the Graces as Dionysus and Coronis, in response to the three genealogies proposed by the narrator (Zeus and Hera, Zeus and Eurynome, and Zeus and Euanthe). From this exchange, we can see several processes at work. The narrator activates the aid of the Muse to improve his knowledge of Parian rituals. At the same time, the Muse Clio acts as the corrector to a genealogical dispute, exercising her authority to dispel the narrator's previously held uncertainty. Yet, since the Muses are figments of the narrator's dream, Clio's correction ultimately derives from the narrator himself.[69]

In fragment 112, identified as the epilogue to the *Aetia*, the Muses reappear, giving the work a ring composition.[70] Callimachus repeats the language of fragment 2, again alluding to the Muses' meeting with Hesiod:

= Σ *Flor.* 15–20). See also *AP* 7.42. See Pretagostini 1995:170–172 and Sistakou 2009b:222–224 for a discussion of the differences between Callimachean and Hesiodic scenes. Sistakou 2009b:223 points out that Callimachus, unlike Hesiod (*Theogony* 22), does not name the narrative persona.

[67] Harder 2012.2:94.

[68] See Nisetich 2001:XLI.

[69] On this passage, see Fantuzzi and Hunter 2004:56, where Hunter states, "The open acknowledgement of competing authorities both sets the poem in a context of agonistic scholarship and ironises ... the very pursuit of 'truth.'" Priestly 2014:107 compares the strategy of three versions followed by the correct one with the beginning of Herodotus *Histories*, where Herodotus offers his own reason for the Greek and Persian conflict after those of the Persians, Phoenicians, and Greeks. Greene 2017a:26 emphasizes the significance of Callimachus choosing a local version from Deryclus' *Argolica* over Panhellenic versions. Eurynome and Zeus are the parents of the Graces according to Hesiod *Theogony* 907–909.

[70] Agreeing with Parsons's 1977 suggestion that Callimachus later in life affixed the second two books of the *Aetia* to the first two, Knox 1993:175–178 argues that fragment 112 originally concluded the first two books of the *Aetia* but was subsequently moved by an editor to the end of book four.

κεῖν.. τῷ Μοῦσαι πολλὰ νέμοντι βοτὰ
σὺν μύθους ἐβάλοντο παρ' ἴχν[ι]ον ὀξέος ἵππου·
χαῖρε, σὺν εὐεστοῖ δ' ἔρχεο λωϊτέρῃ.
χαῖρε, Ζεῦ, μέγα καὶ σύ, σάω δ' [ἐμὸ]ν οἶκον ἀνάκτων·
αὐτὰρ ἐγὼ Μουσέων πεζὸν [ἔ]πειμι νομόν.

[Hesiod] to whom the Muses, when he was tending many animals, contributed stories, next to the footprint of the swift horse; farewell, and come with even better prosperity. A great farewell to you too, Zeus, and preserve the house of my lords. I, however, will go to the pedestrian pasture of the Muses.

Aetia fr. 112.5–9

In this section, Callimachus refers to Hesiod obliquely with the participial phrase πολλὰ νέμοντι βοτά ("shepherding many animals," fr. 112.5), which echoes ποιμ̣ένι μῆλα νέμ̣ιοντι in 2.1. The phrases παρ' ἴχν[ι]ον ὀξέος ἵππου (fr. 112.6) and Μουσέων (fr. 112.9) both occur in the same metrical *sedes* as they did at 2.1 and 2.2, respectively. Additionally, by situating the genitive Μουσέων after the emphatic personal pronoun ἐγώ, Callimachus symbolizes the close connection between his persona and the Muses, as he did through the juxtaposition of Ἡσιόδ̣ι̣ῳ and Μουσέων in fr. 2.2. However, the narrator frames his own relationship with the Muses differently than the one between Hesiod and the Muses. While the Muses met Hesiod (ἠντίασεν, fr. 2.2) and contributed stories (σὺν μύθους ἐβάλοντο, fr. 112.6), it is the narrator himself who will embark in their "pedestrian pastures": πεζὸν [ἔ]πειμι νομόν (fr. 112.9).[71] In the former situation, the participant (Hesiod) plays a passive role, as the Muses appear to him and bestow their wisdom in the form of stories. The Callimachean narrator, by contrast, assumes an active role in his relationship with the Muses, taking the initiative to sustain his connection with them.

Combined with the dream narrative, these final lines support the impression that the Callimachean narrator in fact controls the Muses, his supposed superiors. Indeed, by posing the questions in *Aetia* 1–2 the narrator shapes the discourse. At the same time, as is clear from fr. 3–7 and his boast at fr. 43.46–53, his questions evidence his vast prior knowledge. Similarly, when inquiring about the use of scurrilous language by the Anaphaeans and of profane speech by the Lindians (fr. 7c1–2), he demonstrates an awareness of these customs. The

---

[71] What exactly Callimachus means by πεζὸν ... νομόν remains subject to debate. For the argument that this phrase refers to the *Iambi*, which follow the *Aetia* in *POxy.* 7.1011 and the *Diegesis*, see, for instance, Barigazzi 1981:105–107 and Clayman 1988:277–286. See Hutchinson 2003:58n31 for the claim that the "pedestrian pastures" means prose.

Muses in turn serve to deepen this awareness by explicating the reasons for these rituals. In using the Muses in this way, the narrator attests to his mastery of the source material.

2.1.2 The Ician Theogenes

Aside from the Muses, another character, the Ician Theogenes, fulfills the function of answering questions. Fragment 178 preserves a portion of this exchange, which takes place at a symposium.[72] The Callimachean narrator asks about certain Ician rituals, such as the worship of Peleus and how Ician customs are like Thessalian ones.[73] Before this interrogation, however, the narrator goes to great pains to establish Theogenes' character, emphasizing not only Theogenes' Ician origin, but also the similarities between himself and Theogenes. In doing so, the narrator engages in a form of source criticism, representing how a person can successfully identify another individual as a credible font of information. Such a strategy makes sense. As Greene has observed, Callimachus' presentation of Theogenes encourages interpreting the figure as a written source (or sources) in human form.[74]

After alluding to the Attic wine festivals in 1–4, Callimachus establishes the context for the meeting with Theogenes:

ἐς δαίτην ἐκάλεσσεν ὁμηθέας, ἐν δέ νυ τοῖσι
  ξεῖνον ὃς Α[ἰ]γύπτῳ καινὸς ἀνεστρέφετο
μεμβλωκὼς ἴδιόν τι κατὰ χρέος· ἦν δὲ γενέθλην
  Ἴκιος, ᾧ ξυνὴν εἶχον ἐγὼ κλισίην...

He summoned people with similar habits to a dinner, and among them
was a foreigner who, having just arrived, was staying in Egypt, since he

---

[72] Due to the sympotic context of the fragment, Zetzel 1981:32 argues that fragment 178 should be placed at the beginning of book two, coming before the beginning of fragment 43, which also suggests a symposium. We know from Athenaeus 11.477c that the host's name was Pollis. If this fragment occurs in the context of the conversation with the Muses, then the Callimachean narrator would be recalling it to them.

[73] Μυρμιδόνων ἐσσῆνα τ[ί πάτριον ὔ]μμι σέβεσθαι / Πηλέα, κῶς Ἴκῳ ξυν[ὰ τὰ Θεσσαλι]κά ("Why is it your custom to revere Peleus, king of the Myrmidons, and how are Thessalian customs connected with Ician ones?" fr. 178.23–24).

[74] Greene 2017a:22. "The pleasure of the Callimachean narrator at meeting and hearing the (presumably) ancient tale of the new Ician serves as a metaphor for the poet's appreciation of the historical text that he is using both for information and inspiration." For the relevance of Theogenes, see also Depew 2007:161–162.

had come for some personal business. He was an Ician by birth, and I
shared a couch with him.

Aetia fr. 178.5–8

With the adjective ὁμηθέας ("with similar habits," fr. 178.5), Callimachus provides
the first indication of the similarity between the narrator and Theogenes. Both
are spending time in the company of people like their host. In the subsequent
lines, Callimachus specifies Theogenes' background, marking his status as a
foreigner staying in Egypt (ξεῖνον ὃς Α[ἰ]γύπτῳ καινὸς ἀνεστρέφετο, fr. 178.6),
as well as his Ician lineage (γενέθλην / Ἴκιος , fr. 178.7–8). In making Theogenes'
lineage the first part of the characterization, Callimachus points to its relevance
for Theogenes' status as a source regarding Ician rituals. Indeed, Theogenes'
proximity to the place grants him authority on such matters.

At the same time, as a foreigner in Egypt, Theogenes, is displaced,[75] and
Callimachus stresses this displacement by coordinating ξεῖνον and Ἴκιος at
the beginning of their respective pentameter lines. This displacement from
Icus not only enables Theogenes to participate in this symposium in Egypt,
but also renders him like Odysseus, whose wanderings imparted knowledge of
many peoples and customs (*Odyssey* 1.3).[76] Callimachus in fact implies a parallel
between Theogenes and Odysseus with the verb ἀνεστρέφετο ("was staying"
fr. 178.6), which recalls ἀναστρέφομαι in *Odyssey* 13.[77] There Odysseus express
to Athena a suspicion that he is currently in a land different from Ithaca: οὐ
γὰρ ὄϊω / ἥκειν εἰς Ἰθάκην εὐδείελον, ἀλλά τιν' ἄλλην / γαῖαν ἀναστρέφομαι
("for I do not think I have come to well-seen Ithaca, but I am roaming in some
other land," 13.324–326). As in the *Aetia* passage, the verb in Homer occurs in
the context of a place different than an individual's place of origin. Yet while
Odysseus only supposes he is currently in a foreign land, Theogenes in fact is
and for this reason can transmit knowledge of his local customs to others, like
the Callimachean narrator.

References to the *Odyssey* continue in the description of Theogenes, as
Callimachus cites a Homeric saying to explain the reason for the couch shared
between his narrator and Theogenes:

οὐκ ἐπιτάξ, ἀλλ' αἶνος Ὁμηρικός, αἰὲν ὁμοῖον
ὡς θεός, οὐ ψευδής, ἐς τὸν ὁμοῖον ἄγει.

---

[75] For the theme of displacement in Callimachus' poetry, see Selden 1998:289–412. For this scene as
evidence for Alexandria's placement in a Greek "network", see Harder 2014:265–266.
[76] See Harder 2002:212–217 for a discussion of the reminiscences of the *Odyssey* in this passage. See
also Dettori 2004:44–52.
[77] See Harder 2012.2:965.

καὶ γὰρ ὁ Θρηϊκίην μὲν ἀπέστυγε χανδὸν ἄμυστιν
ζωροποτεῖν, ὀλίγῳ δ' ἥδετο κισσυβίῳ.

Not by prearranged seating, but the Homeric saying, that the god always brings like to like, is not untrue. For he despised to drink wine neat in Thracian drafts with lips wide open but took pleasure in the tiny cup.

Aetia fr. 178.9–12

The maxim that "the god brings like to like" occurs in *Odyssey* 17, when Melanthius rebukes Eumaeus for escorting the disguised Odysseus: νῦν μὲν δὴ μάλα πάγχυ κακὸς κακὸν ἡγηλάζει, / ὡς αἰεὶ τὸν ὁμοῖον ἄγει θεὸς ὡς τὸν ὁμοῖον ("now in truth, a base man leads a base man, as always, the god brings like to like," 17.217–218).[78] As with the other *Odyssey* allusion, the citation of this phrase is here transformed. While in Homer the phrase is uttered by the disreputable figure Melanthius, who mistakenly perceives Odysseus as a base man, Callimachus has his discerning narrator reclaim the saying to substantiate an actual similarity between two elegant and refined gentlemen.

In 11–12, Callimachus provides proof for the veracity of the Homeric statement, specifying how his narrator and Theogenes are similar. Like the narrator, Theogenes detests immoderate Thracian drinking and instead was "delighting in the tiny cup" (ὀλίγῳ δ' ἥδετο κισσυβίῳ, fr. 178.12). As Cameron notes, this antithesis between big and small recalls the aesthetic principles espoused in the *Aetia* prologue, where Callimachus' narrator expressed preference for shorter works over longer works.[79] Theogenes' drinking habits, by the narrator's judgment, signify the deeper similarities between the two, namely their ability to engage in refined discourse and thus exchange information. These similarities with the narrator render Theogenes an appropriate source.

After determining Theogenes' suitability, the narrator addresses him to strike up conversation:

τῷ μὲν ἐγὼ τάδ' ἔλεξα περιστείχοντος ἀλείσου
    τὸ τρίτον, εὖτ' ἐδάην οὔνομα καὶ γενεήν·
'ἦ μάλ' ἔπος τόδ' ἀληθές, ὅ τ' οὐ μόνον ὕδατος αἶσαν,
    ἀλλ' ἔτι καὶ λέσχης οἶνος ἔχειν ἐθέλει.
τὴν ἡμεῖς—οὐκ ἐν γ[ὰ]ρ ἀρυστήρεσσι φορεῖται
    οὐδέ μιν εἰς ἀτ[ενεῖ]ς ὀφρύας οἰνοχόων
αἰτήσεις ὁρόω[ν] ὅτ' ἐλεύθερος ἀτμένα σαίνει—

---

[78] For discussion of this citation, see Fabian 1991:150–151.
[79] Cameron 1995:136. For the preference for smallness, see *Aetia* fr. 1.10–12.

βάλλωμεν χαλεπῷ φάρμακον ἐν πόματι,
Θεύγενες· ὅσσ[α] δ' ἐμεῖο σ[έ]θεν πάρα θυμὸς ἀκοῦσαι
ἰχαίνει, τάδε μοι λ[έ]ξον [ἀνειρομέν]ῳ·

I said these things to him as the goblet was passing by for the third time,
after I learned his name and lineage. "Indeed, this saying is quite true,
that wine wants to have not only a portion of water, but also of conver-
sation. Let us throw this as a drug into the harsh drink, Theogenes, for
it is not carried in ladles, nor will you ask for it while looking toward
the strained eyebrows of wine-pourers at the time when a free man
fawns upon a slave. Everything my heart yearns to hear from you, tell
me when I ask."

Aetia fr. 178.13–22

The key point of the narrator's appeal is the importance of conversation (λέσχη)
amid drinking wine. To make this point, Callimachus' narrator invokes another
truism (ἔπος τόδ' ἀληθές, fr. 178.15), one that calls for the equal need for water
and conversation. Like water, conversation is crucial for alleviating the effects
of drinking. As the narrator exhorts in 20, he and Theogenes should cast conver-
sation in as a drug for the harsh drink: βάλλωμεν χαλεπῷ φάρμακον ἐν πόματι.
With this language, Callimachus recalls yet another scene from the *Odyssey*.
There Helen laces the wine drunk by Telemachus and Menelaus with a drug to
induce forgetfulness of their sorrows:[80]

ἔνθ' αὖτ' ἄλλ' ἐνόησ' Ἑλένη Διὸς ἐκγεγαυῖα·
αὐτίκ' ἄρ' εἰς οἶνον βάλε φάρμακον, ἔνθεν ἔπινον,
νηπενθές τ' ἄχολόν τε, κακῶν ἐπίληθον ἁπάντων.

Then Helen, daughter of Zeus, thought of a different plan. At once she
cast a drug into the wine, which they were drinking, a drug that dulls
pain and anger and makes them forget all evils.

Odyssey 4.219–221

As Hunter observes, the allusion to this scene is ironic, since the drug envi-
sioned by Callimachus will bring not forgetfulness, but memory.[81] Moreover,
conversation is something in which the narrator and Theogenes can purposely
partake, and as the narrator notes in the aside in 17–19, conversation does not
depend on the labor of enslaved people.

---

[80] For this allusion, see Malten 1918:161 and Massimilla 1996:412.
[81] Hunter 1996a:23.

Consequently, this sharing of information in a conversation is what enables the narrator and Theogenes to transcend their surroundings, the festival context of the Aeora, for which solitary imbibing was the norm and whose origins are based in excessive drinking.[82] Eschewing this solitary immoderation, Callimachus' narrator instead advocates for shared moderation and so quotes bits of Homeric wisdom, extracting these sayings from their original questionable contexts (Melanthius' insults and Helen's forgetfulness-inducing drugs) to a contemporary setting of a refined symposium in Egypt. In making a symposium the setting for the narrator's inquiry, moreover, Callimachus replicates one of the most traditional ways of obtaining information: hearing it from another person.[83] Although receiving secondhand information is not as direct as perceiving something firsthand, a real-life meeting, as portrayed in this fragment, enables a more reliable evaluation of a person's credibility than acquiring information from a written source. Indeed, by observing Theogenes' drinking habits firsthand, the Callimachean narrator can deduce that the pair's similarities will result in stimulating conversation.

2.1.3 Xenomedes

While the scene with Theogenes represents an instance of oral communication, Xenomedes, cited in fragment 75 as the source for the Acontius and Cydippe story, is a written source.[84] Callimachus' narrator, however, still infuses the depiction with elements of orality, claiming that he heard (ἐκλύομεν) about Acontius' love from Xenomedes:[85]

Κεῖε, τεὸν δ' ἡμεῖς ἵμερον ἐκλύομεν
τόνδε παρ' ἀρχαίου Ξενομήδεος, ὅς ποτε πᾶσαν
νῆσον ἐνὶ μνήμῃ κάτθετο μυθολόγῳ,

---

[82] See Harder 2012.2:958–964 for an overview of the festivals mentioned by Callimachus. The Aeora commemorated Erigone's suicide by hanging, which occurred after a drunken herdsman, given wine by Dionysus, murdered her father, Icarius. Scodel 1980:39 notes that whereas wine causes sorrow for Erigone, "for Callimachus, antiquarian conversation averts the chief danger in the drinking of wine, tedium."

[83] Additionally, the symposium setting evokes philosophical symposia, such as those dramatized by Plato and Xenophon. See Acosta-Hughes and Stephens 2012:74–78 for a discussion of parallels with Plato's dialogues. Most obviously, the recommendation for moderate wine consumption recalls the decision taken by the participants in the *Symposium* (176e). Similarly, the like-to-like maxim appeared as a topic of debate in the *Lysis* (214a–215e).

[84] For discussion of Xenomedes, see Huxley 1965:235–245. Harder 2013:101 suggests that this citation and reworking of Xenomedes could have encouraged readers to look for Xenomedes in the library for themselves.

[85] See Meyer 1993:333 and Bruss 2004:54.

Cean, we heard about this love of yours from ancient Xenomedes, who once set down the whole island in a mythological record.

Aetia fr. 75.53–55

By inserting the personal pronoun ἡμεῖς ("we," fr. 75.53) between τεόν and ἵμερον ("this love of yours," fr. 75.53), Callimachus illustrates the closeness between his narrator and the subject matter, and indeed the choice to address Acontius directly in 53 heightens the subjective qualities. Such subjectivity and closeness are ironic, especially since the narrator does not participate in the narrated story, but rather has acquired it from another source, Xenomedes. Xenomedes' status as an "ancient" one (ἀρχαίου, fr. 75.54) increases this distance between receiver and source.[86] At the same time, despite the ostensible suggestion of oral communication with the verb ἐκλύομεν, the narrator has assembled this information from a written work, as Callimachus indicates in the relative clause ὅς ποτε πᾶσαν / νῆσον ἐνὶ μνήμῃ κάτθετο μυθολόγῳ ("who once set down the entire island in a mythological record," fr. 75.54–55) and with γέρων ἐνεθήκατο δέλτ[οις ("the old man set in his tablets," fr. 75.66). Yet, along with ἐκλύομεν, the phrasing ἐνὶ μνήμῃ κάτθετο μυθολόγῳ also suggests orality, as it echoes Calliope's command to the narrator during the conversation with the Muses: π]ρῶτ[ον ἐνὶ μ]νήμῃ κάτθεο καὶ Μινύας ("first set also the Minyans in your memory," fr. 7c6).[87] In likening the process of receiving a written work to that of direct hearing, Callimachus presents the process as a more personal and involved one.

After giving a detailed summary of the contents of Xenomedes' work in 56–74, the narrator concludes by readdressing Acontius:

εἶπε δέ, Κεῖε
ξυγκραθέντ᾽ αὐταῖς ὀξὺν ἔρωτα σέθεν
πρέσβυς ἐτητυμίῃ μεμελημένος, ἔνθεν ὁ πα[ι]δὸς
μῦθος ἐς ἡμετέρην ἔδραμε Καλλιόπην.

And he spoke, Cean, about your passionate love mixed in [with these towns], the old man, devoted to truth, from where the child's story ran to our Calliope.

Aetia fr. 75.74–77

---

[86] Since Xenomedes dates to the middle of the fifth century, Greene 2017a:33 deems the designation of Xenomedes as "ancient" to be hyperbolic.

[87] See Harder 2012.2:635.

Chapter 3

With the verb εἶπε ("he spoke," fr. 75.74), Callimachus again evokes orality. The emphasis on Xenomedes' old age (πρέσβυς, fr. 75.76) suggests his authority as a source, as does the participial clause ἐτητυμίῃ μεμελημένος ("devoted to truth," fr. 75.76). Morrison, however, detects irony produced by this phrase.[88] How can Xenomedes be devoted to truth (ἐτητυμίῃ, fr. 75.76) when his account is a mythological one (μυθολόγῳ, fr. 75.55), specifically one that unites fantastical narratives like the story of Acontius' love with the foundation of cities (fr. 75.70–74)? Indeed, Callimachus refers to the story as a μῦθος in 77, insinuating its possible falsity. Yet another question arises. What happens to the truth-status of the story when it has run over to "our Calliope," a word that has been taken to indicate "poetry?"[89] Does the veracity remain the same, or does it undergo some change?

Callimachus, I suggest, subtly implies the latter option, doing so with the coordination of the noun ἐτητυμίη with the adjective ἡμετέρην ("our," fr. 75.77). Since ἡμετέρην repeats and rearranges the letters of ἐτητυμίη (the eta, mu, epsilon, and tau), we can see the coordination of these two words as reflecting the change involved in transferring knowledge from prose into poetry. Like the letters in both words, the raw elements of prose remain the same in poetry, but become rearranged in an artful way that befits Callimachean verse. Indeed, the Callimachean narrator has just condensed Xenomedes' record of the whole island (πᾶσαν / νῆσον, fr. 75.54–55) into a selective summary that has thematic implications for the Aetia as a whole.[90] For instance, at fr. 75.65 the Telchines are mentioned, recalling their appearance in the prologue (fr. 1.1). At the same time, the narrator has extracted the tale of Acontius and Cydippe, which was mixed (ξυγκραθέντ', fr. 75.75) in Xenomedes' work, devoting an extended treatment to the tale. In this treatment, moreover, the narrator features his voice frequently.[91]

[88] Morrison 2007:197. For discussion of these lines, see also Hutchinson 1988:30–32 and Giubilo 2009:254–257. Noting that the adjective ἐτήτυμος is used in genealogical contexts, Giubilo 2009:257 interprets this phrase as an allusion to Xenomedes' carefulness in reporting the genealogy of the Acontidae on Ceos.

[89] Harder 2012.2:657. For discussions of this phrase, see Hutchinson 1988:45 and Cameron 1995:108. Sistakou 2017:7 points out that ἡμετέρην is a deictic expression and implies the Muse Calliope's presence.

[90] Fantuzzi and Hunter 2004:64–65. As Krevans 2004:181 concludes, "The praise of Xenomedes as a Muse, the epithets 'old' and 'truthful,' and the similarity of the topics treated in his history of Ceos to other stories in the Aetia force the readers of the poem to see Xenomedes as a version of Callimachus, and to acknowledge the importance of Callimachean prose in the creation of Callimachean poetry." Magnelli 2005:208 proposes that Callimachus aims to compose an elegiac catalogue not like other long Hellenistic ones.

[91] For instance, Harder 1990:300 sees the address to Acontius at fr. 75.44–49 as an example of the narrator injecting a subjective element. According to the narrator, Acontius would not have exchanged that night with Cydippe for the ankle of Iphicles or the wealth of Midas.

As Harder has argued, this prominence of the Callimachean personal voice, especially in this fragment, is what most distinguishes Callimachus from Homer.[92] This personal voice and its evaluative language define the Callimachean Calliope as unique.

2.1.4 Summary of Callimachean sources

In his depiction of these various sources (the Muses, Theogenes, and Xenomedes), Callimachus' narrator emphasizes his personal connection with them. The Muses come to Callimachus' narrator in a dream, Theogenes is like the narrator, and finally Xenomedes' work is transmitted to "our Calliope." Even when discussing a source written by Xenomedes, Callimachus employs words that recall hearing and direct communication. Such a conceit of direct communication, while ironic given the highly literate nature of the *Aetia*, symbolizes the narrator's deep understanding of his sources. He has absorbed them in such a way that he is confident enough of his existing knowledge to engage all three (even the Muses) in dialogues. Yet, as replications of personal experiences, such dialogues are ultimately controlled by him.

2.2 The Muses of Apollonius

2.2.1 Ὑποφήτορες?

Apollonius of Rhodes' *Argonautica* also includes the Muses, the traditional inspirers of epic. Yet, as was the case with his narratorial voice, Apollonius' portrayal of the Muses diverges in many ways from Homer.[93] Indeed, the choice to invoke the god Apollo at the beginning of the poem (ἀρχόμενος σέο Φοῖβε, 1.1) instead of the Muses represents a major distinction between the *Argonautica*

---

[92] Harder 1990:309. According to her, while the Homeric narrator works in the background, the Callimachean one is "very self-conscious and very prominent, unashamedly interfering with his own story and imposing a great deal of rhythm and emphasis on it, taking great care his readers do not lose sight of him and directing their emotional response in unexpected ways!" See also Lynn 1995:237, who concludes that Callimachus makes the narrative "his own." Sistakou 2019:339 sees the Callimachean narrator as merging his perspective with Xenomedes.

[93] For an overview of the Muses' appearances in the *Argonautica*, see Fusillo 1985:365–374, Wheeler 2002:45–47, Clare 2002:265–268, Klooster 2011:217–225, and Kyriakou 2018:367–391. In addition to the passages that I will discuss in detail, see *Argonautica* 2.845, where the narrator remarks on his obligation to the Muses to mention Idmon's tomb for the Muses.

and the Homeric epics.[94] Rather, Apollonius' narrator calls upon the Muses several lines later:

νῆα μὲν οὖν οἱ πρόσθεν ἔτι κλείουσιν ἀοιδοί
Ἄργον Ἀθηναίης καμέειν ὑποθημοσύνῃσι.
νῦν δ' ἂν ἐγὼ γενεήν τε καὶ οὔνομα μυθησαίμην
ἡρώων δολιχῆς τε πόρους ἁλὸς ὅσσα τ' ἔρεξαν
πλαζόμενοι· Μοῦσαι δ' ὑποφήτορες εἶεν ἀοιδῆς.

And so, the earlier singers still celebrate in their songs how Argus built the ship following Athena's instructions, but I now wish to recount the lineage and names of the heroes, and their journeys on the vast sea, and as many things they achieved as they wandered. May the Muses be the interpreters of the song!

Argonautica 1.18–22

After mentioning the construction of the Argo, as sung by previous singers,[95] the narrator promises to recount the lineage, names, routes, and deeds of their heroes in their wanderings. For this task, the Muses are to act as ὑποφήτορες (1.22) of the song. While the exact meaning of this word ὑποφήτορες has been subject to scholarly debate,[96] previous uses of the similar word ὑποφήτης suggest that word means "interpreters."[97] Yet, in what way would the Muses act as interpreters, and what exactly do they interpret? González, noting the oracular context of the noun ὑποφῆται in Homer, argues the word deals with interpretation as a revelatory activity.[98] According to him, Apollonius' Muses are the interpreters of Apollo, who is preeminent in the narrative, both as the god first addressed (1.1) and as the source of the oracle that initiates the Argonauts'

---

[94] In particular, the language of the first line has been compared to a hymn (cf. *Homeric Hymn to Selene* 18–19). See De Marco 1963:351, Goldhill 1991:287 and Clauss 1993:16.

[95] For discussion of these lines, see Goldhill 1991:290, Clauss 1993:20, and Clare 2002:28. Murray 2005:88–106, by contrast, construes these lines as polemic against Apollonius' predecessors. Whereas the predecessors cast Argus as the builder aided by Athena's instructions, later in the *Argonautica*, characters present Athena as the prime fabricator and Argus as the helper (1.111–114, 1.722–724).

[96] Vian and Delage 1974:239, for instance, argues that it refers to "inspirers of the song." Green 1997:202–203 also adapts this translation. Paduano Faedo 1970:378, taking ὑποφήτορες in 1.22 as "*ministre*," sees in the *Argonautica* an inversion of the traditional relationship between poet and Muse. Garriga 1996:110 adopts the translation "interpreters." See Borgogno 2002:5–21 and Cerri 2007:159–165 for an overview of the possible interpretations of this word.

[97] See LSJ ὑποφήτης.

[98] González 2000:276. ὑποφῆται appears at *Iliad* 16.235 in Achilles' request for Patroclus' safe homecoming and refers to the oracular priests of Zeus at Dodona. See also Theocritus *Idyll* 16.29, 17.115, and 22.116.

quest (1.8). Due to the traditional association between the Muses and Apollo (e.g. *Theogony* 94–95), González's argument carries weight. As interpreters, the Muses are divine mediators, assisting the narrator in constructing the verse.

The Muses' assistance is invaluable, as the subject matter of the *Argonautica* comprises a wide array of topics. Aside from the traditional exploits of heroes, the poem features numerous aetiologies, geographic excurses,[99] and detailed descriptions of psychological states, particularly Medea's love for Jason in book three.[100] Since each of these topics would be critiqued differently with regards to truth and falsehood, the variety of this material necessitates that the narrator employ his sources (the Muses) in different ways. For this reason, it makes sense that Apollonius does not depict a static relationship between the narrator and the Muses, as Hunter and Feeney have observed in examining the invocations in books one, three, and four.[101] In treating the book three and four invocations, Hunter claims that the "brash, modern self-confidence of the opening proem now retreats for safety to an archaic dependence upon the Muse."[102] Morrison connects this increased reliance on the Muses to the Apollonian narrator's growing uncertainty.[103] While agreeing with Morrison's assessment about the narrator's uncertainty, I will extend the argument by contending that, despite the increased use of the Muses in book three and especially book four, the narrator problematizes their roles as sources, particularly for the complex subject matter (i.e. Medea and her motivations) that occupies those two books.[104] Such a problematization in turn reflects the difficulties of completely establishing the truth, while also implying the deficiency of a definite criterion.

2.2.2 Book three invocation

The beginning of book three features an invocation to the Muse Erato:

> εἰ δ' ἄγε νῦν, Ἐρατώ, παρά θ' ἵστασο καί μοι ἔνισπε
> ἔνθεν ὅπως ἐς Ἰωλκὸν ἀνήγαγε κῶας Ἰήσων
> Μηδείης ὑπ' ἔρωτι. σὺ γὰρ καὶ Κύπριδος αἶσαν

---

[99] For an overview of Apollonius' presentation of geography, see Hunter 1996b:13–27, Hurst 1998:279–288, and Meyer 2008:267–285. Sistakou 2014b:161–180 focuses on "counterfactual" geography, discussing, for example, supernatural places, areas belonging to different temporal and spatial realms, and places of the past.

[100] Zanker 1979:52–75 analyzes the love theme throughout the epic.

[101] Hunter 1987:134 and Feeney 1991:90–91.

[102] Hunter 1993:105. Cf. Kyriakou 2018:386.

[103] Morrison 2007:310.

[104] For a similar assessment, see Klooster 2011:224–225, who offers a comparison between the Muses and the documents in the Museum. Both the Muses and documents might not always offer clear information about the distant past.

ἔμμορες, ἀδμῆτας δὲ τεοῖς μελεδήμασι θέλγεις
παρθενικάς· τῶ καί τοι ἐπήρατον οὔνομ᾽ ἀνῆπται.

Come now, Erato, stand next by and tell me how from here Jason
brought the fleece to Iolcus with the help of Medea's love. For you
also have received a portion of Cypris' power and enchant unmarried
maidens with your love-cares. For this reason, a lovely name has been
attached to you.

Argonautica 3.1–5

In contrast to the polite optative of wish ὑποφήτορες εἶεν ἀοιδῆς in 1.22, the
imperatives ἵστασο ("stand," 3.1) and ἔνισπε ("tell," 3.1) inject a greater sense of
immediacy.[105] The first-person personal pronoun μοι (3.1) emphasizes the prox-
imity desired between the narrator and Muse. The Muse's closeness qualifies as
a more active role.[106] This particular subject matter of the third book, that is, the
prominence of Medea's love (Μηδείης ὑπ᾽ ἔρωτι, 3.3), necessitates this role from
Erato, since the desire of a young woman represents a topic especially foreign
to a male perspective. The narrator appoints Erato specifically for this task,
due to her association with love matters,[107] and indeed, the narrator explicitly
comments on Erato's appropriateness in 3–5, observing the connection between
her enchantment of young maidens and her name: τῶ καί τοι ἐπήρατον οὔνομ᾽
ἀνῆπται. The adjective ἐπήρατον ("lovely") in 5 echoes not only her actual name
Ἐρατώ in 1, but also ἔρωτι in 3. By remarking on the relevance of this name, that
is, by citing an etymology, the narrator is engaging in a form of source criticism.
Since love is expressed in her name, Erato qualifies as the best source for this
information.

Yet Erato is not only a source for the information of the narrative, but the
events themselves. Like Cypris, Erato can induce young women like Medea to act
under the influence of *eros*, and this *eros* enables the completion of the narra-
tive, that is, the conveyance of the Golden Fleece to Iolcus, as Apollonius makes
clear with the expression Μηδείης ὑπ᾽ ἔρωτι. Significantly, the verb applied to
Erato, θέλγεις ("you enchant," 3.4), is often associated with the allures of poetry
(e.g. *Odyssey* 12.40). The verb appears, for instance, at *Argonautica* 1.27 and 1.31,

---

[105] Albis 1996:69 detects a sense of anxiety in εἰ δ᾽ ἄγε.

[106] Hunter 1989a:95 considers this a more equal role. Clauss 1997:151 sees Apollonius as setting the
Muse on the same level. Spentzou 2002:105 compares this request to the one posed by Pindar in
Pythian 4.1–4, a poem that features Medea heavily. Asper 2008:172 likens this physical proximity
to the Callimachean claim to friendship with the Muses (*Aetia* fr. 1.2).

[107] Campbell 1983:3 notes that this association was first seen at Plato's *Phaedrus* 259c.

referring both times to the objects charmed by Orpheus' song.[108] The word also carries associations with deception and, as Albis notes, this verb occurs in the third book to describe Eros' effect on Medea.[109] Since Eros' enchantment of Medea results in the dissolution of her rational self (3.284–298), we can see θέλγεις here in this proem evoking similar connotations. Campbell, moreover, perceives the suggestion of violence with the combination of the adjective ἀδμῆτας ("untamed," 3.4) and the noun μελεδήμασι ("love-cares," 3.4).[110] By framing his source, Erato, as a destructive force with the potential to disrupt young girls' rationality, the narrator infuses her with two contradictory aspects. In being asked to speak (ἔνισπε, 3.1), Erato represents an obviously authoritative source regarding love. Yet her authority on such matters renders her liable to deceive and thus untrustworthy for the narrator who must now rely on her.

2.2.4 Book four appearances

In the proem to the fourth book, the narrator again invokes a Muse, this time as an unnamed goddess (θεά):[111]

αὐτὴ νῦν κάματόν γε θεὰ καὶ δήνεα κούρης
Κολχίδος, ἔννεπε Μοῦσα, Διὸς τέκος· ἦ γὰρ ἔμοιγε
ἀμφασίη νόος ἔνδον ἑλίσσεται, ὁρμαίνοντι
ἠέ μιν ἄτης πῆμα δυσίμερον ἦ τό γ' ἐνίσπω
φύζαν ἀεικελίην ᾗ κάλλιπεν ἔθνεα Κόλχων.

Now, goddess, you yourself speak of the struggle and the wiles of the Colchian maiden, Muse, child of Zeus. Truly for me at least, my mind whirls inside me in speechlessness, as I ponder whether I am to call this a lovesick affliction of infatuation or a shameful flight, by which she abandoned the Colchian peoples.

Argonautica 4.1–5

---

[108] See 1.26–27, αὐτὰρ τόνγ' ἐνέπουσιν ἀτειρέας οὔρεσι πέτρας / θέλξαι ἀοιδάων ἐνοπῇ ποταμῶν τε / ῥέεθρα ("and they say he enchanted the hard boulders in the mountains and the course of the rivers with the sound of his songs"), and 1.30–31, ἃς ὅγ' ἐπιπρό / θελγομένας φόρμιγγι κατήγαγε Πιερίηθεν ("the ones he led forth down from Pieria, enchanted by his lyre").

[109] Albis 1996:68. Cf. 3.85–86 and 3.143.

[110] Campbell 1983:2.

[111] As Livrea 1973:3 observes, θεά recalls *Iliad* 1.1, while ἔννεπε Μοῦσα is reminiscent of the first line of the *Odyssey*. Acosta-Hughes 2010:40–44 argues that these Homeric resonances distinguish this Muse from Erato in the book three invocation. Whereas lyric images (e.g. untamed maidens) define Erato, this Muse of book four is closer to the traditional epic Muse. For the assumption that this Muse is Erato, see Hunter 1987:134 and Berkowitz 2004:83–86.

The combination of αὐτή ("you yourself," 4.1) and νῦν ("now," 4.1) continues the sense of immediacy featured in the proem to book three, and the imperative ἔννεπε ("speak," 4.2), the same verb used in *Odyssey* 1.1, looks back to ἔνισπε (3.1). Unlike the proem to 3, however, here Apollonius does not focus on the Muse's authority concerning the subject matter as much as the limitations of the narrator, who is distinguished from the Muse with the emphatic personal pronoun ἔμοιγε (4.2).[112] As Apollonius describes in 2–3, the narrator's mind "is whirling" (ἐλίσσεται, 4.3) in "speechlessness" (ἀμφασίη, 4.3). Such a state of speechlessness is antithetical to the function of an epic narrator to verbalize the events of the past. Rather, speechlessness befits the characters in the narrative, whose limited knowledge makes them uncertain and terrified about the future.[113] Medea, for instance, also experiences such whirling in the previous book (εἰλιχθεῖσα, 3.655), as she agonizes about the proper course of action to take in her lovesickness. Yet, as Hunter observes, in the case of the beginning of book four, the narrator's issue is not a lack of knowledge, but rather a difficulty with interpretation.[114] The narrator knows that Medea abandoned the Colchians (κάλλιπεν ἔθνεα Κόλχων, 4.5), but struggles to ascertain her exact motivations, wavering between calling it a "lovesick affliction of infatuation" (ἄτης πῆμα δυσίμερον, 4.4) or "a shameful flight" (φύζαν ἀεικελίην, 4.5).

These two options in turn map onto evaluations of Medea's character. If her impetus for leaving her family and native land derives from a painful love for Jason, she seems more sympathetic. She is merely a lovesick young girl, unable to control herself when overcome by passion, and as a result is not entirely culpable for her mistake. Indeed, Apollonius' choice to call her a maiden (κούρης) in 1 implies a sense of youthful foolishness. The noun δήνεα ("wiles," 4.1), however, suggests intention and at the same time culpability.[115] Acknowledgment of her guilt corresponds with the second option: φύζαν ἀεικελίην. According to this option, Medea flees in fear of her father's wrath and thus knows she has

---

[112] Hurst 1967:135 notes that the importance of the narrator is stressed through the use of the same verb ἔννεπε for the narrator (ἐνίσπω, 4).

[113] For ἀμφασίη applied to characters, see 2.409 (the Argonauts), 3.284 (Medea), 3.811 (Medea), and 3.1372 (Aeëtes). See Albis 1996:94–95 for discussion of the narrator's assimilation to the characters. Phillips 2020:71–73 likens this presentation of an anxious narrator with the Platonic description of the poet assuming the emotions of characters, as described in Plato's *Ion* 535b–c.

[114] Hunter 1987:134. See also Priestly 2014:176n48, who classifies this examination of motivations as "Herodotean" in that it follows some Herodotean examples. Sens 2000:188, however, views this confession of uncertainty as disingenuous, arguing that the particle ἤτοι in 4.6 reasserts the narrator's control over the material.

[115] Hunter 2015:84 prefers the translation "intentions." Acosta-Hughes 2010:43 considers the combination of κάματον and δήνεα to be evocative of Odysseus.

committed wrong. Her motivations stem less from loving and protecting Jason than on a desperate need for self-preservation.

This struggle to define Medea's motivations makes sense. No longer is Apollonius' narrator dealing with easily known pieces of information like the lineage and names of heroes, as in the Catalogue of Heroes in book one, but instead is focusing on internal states like Medea's κάματον and δήνεα. For such inner states, the consequences can be directly perceived, but not the actual source. While neither of the two options necessarily precludes the other,[116] the narrator does not establish a definite choice, either here in the proem or in the remainder of the book, where the depiction of Medea vacillates between a desperate helpless girl and a homicidal witch.[117] Even though at 4.411–413 Medea admits her error in helping Jason and blames the gods, she still consciously incites Jason to murder her brother Apsyrtus (4.420). For such a heinous deed, the narrator explicitly blames the god Eros, calling him a μέγα πῆμα ("great ruin," 4.445) and accusing him of implanting "hateful outrage" in her mind (στυγερὴν φρεσὶν ἔμβαλες ἄτην, 4.449). With πῆμα and ἄτην, the narrator recalls the first option (ἄτης πῆμα δυσιμέρον, 4.4), thus suggesting that Medea's actions are due to obsessive love. Medea's aunt, Circe, however, refers to the second option (φύζαν ἀεικελίην, 4.5) when at 4.748 she disapproves of Medea's βουλὰς ("plots") and ἀεικέα φύξιν, which acts as a synonym for φύζαν ἀεικελίην. For Circe, Medea is culpable, and as Natzel observes, "Kirke spiegelt die Meinung der Gesellschaft wider, d.h. die konventionelle Beurteilung eines Vergehens, dessen sich Medea schuldig gemacht hat."[118] The narrator's inability to provide a definitive assessment of Medea's behavior and motivations evidences not only his limitations as narrator, but also the limitations of his source. Even though he has requested the Muse's direct help at the beginning of the book, she never fully dispels the doubt.

After the brutal murder of Apsyrtus (4.464–481) and the Argonauts' trek into Hyllean land (4.522–551), the narrator entreats the Muses again, this time asking a series of questions regarding the Argonauts' journeys in the west:

ἀλλά, θεαί, πῶς τῆσδε παρὲξ ἁλός, ἀμφί τε γαῖαν
Αὐσονίην νήσους τε Λιγυστίδας, αἵ καλέονται
Στοιχάδες, Ἀργῴης περιώσια σήματα νηὸς

[116] On this point, see Byre 2002:110–111. As Priestly 2014:176 points out, in both cases, Medea leaves willingly. Kyriakou 2018:383 sees the narrator as "implicitly privileging fear" as the correct reason for Medea's flight, since right after the proem the narrator describes Hera's implanting of fear (*Argonautica* 4.11).

[117] For an overview of Medea's character in the *Argonautica*, see Phinney 1967:327–341, Beye 1982:132–142, Hunter 1987:129–134, Dyck 1989:455–470 and Clauss 1997:149–177.

[118] Natzel 1992:86.

νημερτὲς πέφαται; τίς ἀπόπροθι τόσσον ἀνάγκη
καὶ χρειώ σφ᾽ ἐκόμισσε; τίνες σφέας ἤγαγον αὖραι;

Now, goddesses, how is it that beyond this sea, around the Ausonian land and the Ligystian Islands (which are called the Stoechades), countless signs of the Argo are infallibly seen? What necessity and obligation brought them so far away? What winds conveyed them?

Argonautica 4.552–556

As in the previous invocation, this request deals with the reasons for journeying. Specifically, what external forces impelled the Argo to travel and subsequently leave its numerous marks in these far-flung regions of the sea? Several key differences, however, distinguish this passage from the invocation dealing with Medea's motivations. Whereas the narrator previously only summoned a single goddess (θεά, 4.1), he here calls upon the Muses as a collective (θεαί, 4.552). Similarly, the requested topic is plural in nature. Not only does the narrator emphasize the multiplicity of the Argo remnants with the adjective περιώσια ("countless," 4.554),[119] he refers to the Argonauts as a collective twice with the pronouns σφ᾽ and σφέας in 4.556. In focusing on the ship and its collective crew, the narrator departs from his singular focus on Medea and her ambiguous motivations. At the same time, the narrator minimizes his role as well as his feelings of doubt. Highlighted instead are the Argo's signs (σήματα, 4.554), described with the adverb νημερτές ("infallibly," 4.555).

The infallibility of such signs, however, raises an important question. Why does the narrator summon the Muses for a topic so relatively straightforward? Indeed, he is not dealing with unknowable motivations, but rather physical objects and the reasons for their placement. At the same time, unlike Medea's motivations, this question does receive an answer in the subsequent sections. Medea and Jason travel to Circe's island to expiate for the crime of slaughtering Apsyrtus (4.557–561; 4.580–591). In explaining this invocation to the Muses, scholars have offered various solutions. Albis and Klooster, for instance, propose that the multiplicity of the Argo's return routes necessitates the Muses' aid in resolving the discrepancies.[120] In his reading, Berkowitz sees the Muses as resuming their role as interpreters (ὑποφήτορες, 1.22) of the source material.

---

[119] Fränkel 1968:501 translates περιωσια as "*noch vorhandene.*"

[120] According to Albis 1996:97, "The expression νημερτὲς πέφαται underscores that the poet is thinking about other treatments of the Argonaut story." See Klooster 2012:63, who states, "On a metapoetic level, explicitly marked by this invocation of the Muses, the passage draws attention to the stitching together of different poetic traditions." See also Beye 1982:17.

No longer are the Muses acting as the primary sources, as Erato was for Medea's actions and emotions in book three.[121]

Yet, I argue, this section contains an ambiguity that destabilizes the Muses' ability to interpret the material. As scholars and commentators have observed, the verb of the first question, πέφαται (4.555), can derive from either φαίνομαι ("I appear") or φημί ("I say").[122] Both verbs are appropriate for the context. φαίνομαι would make sense, since σήματα connotes visibility and thus appearances. For instance, the word appears earlier (in the same *sedes*) when referring to the oak trees charmed by Orpheus' songs (1.28).[123] The adverb νημερτές ("infallibly"), however, points to πέφαται deriving from φημί. The word νημερτές occurs in contexts of oral communication in the *Argonautica*, as in the Homeric epics.[124] Additionally, the other two occurrences of πέφαται in the *Argonautica* are forms of φημί.[125] Since both φαίνομαι and φημί are feasible in the context, the narrator's question is tinged with uncertainty. Underlying this uncertainty, I suggest, is a deeper skepticism regarding the identity of these signs. If he is asking how the σήματα are visible (from φαίνομαι), he acknowledges their existence, albeit without affirming their attribution to the Argo and its associated narratives. However, in inquiring how the signs "are said" infallibly (from φημί), the narrator makes the existence of the signs subject to uncertainty. Both their existence and attribution derive from the tradition, not from direct experience. Indeed, by emphasizing the geographic expanse of the Argonauts' journey with ἀπόπροθι τόσσον (4.555), the narrator implies that he has never seen such signs firsthand. Rather, his knowledge stems from the conflicting tradition.

From this reading, multiple ambiguities plague the narratorial voice. The tradition is problematic, not only for its divergences concerning the Argo's return route, but the narrator allows for the possibility of the signs' nonexistence through his ambiguous questioning. The vagueness of the inquiry counteracts the infallibility of the signs. At the same time, this ambiguous question impedes the Muses' assistance. Indeed, when posed with this vague question, the

[121] Berkowitz 2004:88.
[122] See Rengakos 1994a:148 and Hunter 2015:157. For a summary of the issue in translation and bibliography, see Thalmann 2011:31n24, who concedes the possibility of both meanings co-existing simultaneously.
[123] For discussion of this passage, see Klooster 2012:63. For other appearances of σήματα (plural) in the *Argonautica*, see 1.145 (Idmon's ability to interpret signs), 1.1141 (the signs appearing after the ritual to Rhea), 2.853 (the tombs of Idmon and Tiphys), and 4.1620 (the signs of the Argo). See Barnes 2003:89–100 and Thalmann 2011:31–32 for discussion of signs in the *Argonautica*.
[124] The usages in contexts of oral communication are: 1.797 (ἐξερέω νημερτές, "I will speak truly"), 4.810 (τινά τοι νημερτέα μῦθον ἐνίψω, "I will tell you a true account"), 4.1184 (νημερτέα βάξιν, "true report"), and 4.1565 (νημερτὲς ἀνειρομένοισιν ἔνισπε, "tell truly to us asking").
[125] See *Argonautica* 1.988 and 2.500.

Muses would expend more effort interpreting the wording (seen, said, or both?) than answering the question. In this way, they serve as interpreters, but of the narrator's language, not the sources.

This ambiguous question regarding the σήματα invites a contrast with both Aratus and Callimachus. For the former, σήματα are markers of certainty, as the κόσμος functions rationally and consistently via Zeus' visible signs. The σήματα of the Argo, by contrast, lie in distant lands, possibly misattributed to the Argo and possibly nonexistent. At the same time, the Apollonian narrator's mode of questioning contrasts with the methods of the Callimachean persona. Whereas the questioning here reflects the Apollonian narrator's uncertainty, interrogation for Callimachus demonstrates confidence and deep erudition. Indeed, such as was the case at *Aetia* fr. 7c1–2: κῶς δέ, θεαί, . .[. . .] μὲν ἀνὴρ Ἀναφαῖος ἐπ' αἰσ[χροῖς / ἡ δ' ἐπὶ δυ[σφήμοις] Λίνδος ἄγει θυσίην ("Why is it, goddesses, that a man from Anaphe sacrifices with insults and a man from Lindos with shameful words?"). There the Callimachean speaker inquires about the insult rituals on Anaphe and Rhodes. As commentators have noted,[126] the question at *Argonautica* 4.552–556 resembles this question, both verbally and thematically. Both questions feature forms of the interrogative πώς (κώς in Callimachus) and involve the Argonauts. Even if the exact chronology of the two poems is difficult to determine,[127] the textual relationship is clear. For the Apollonian narrator, the Argonaut journey is one steeped with uncertainty and difficulty.

Over the course of book four, further difficulties arise for the narrator and the characters. Not only do the Argonauts traverse far-flung regions (e.g. Libya), but they encounter mist, darkness, and desolation.[128] The Muses figure two more times. The first occurs when the narrator reports an unsavory tale about Drepane (discussed below). The second occurs in the most extreme example of the Argonauts' struggle. During this episode, which is also recorded in Pindar's Fourth *Pythian* (25–27), the Argonauts are forced to carry the boat across the Libyan desert:

> Μουσάων ὅδε μῦθος, ἐγὼ δ' ὑπακουὸς ἀείδω
> Πιερίδων. καὶ τήνδε πανατρεκὲς ἔκλυον ὀμφήν,
> ὑμέας, ὦ πέρι δὴ μέγα φέρτατοι υἷες ἀνάκτων,

---

[126] Vian and Delage 1981:94n2.

[127] For discussion of the dating between the authors, see Köhnken 2008:73–94, who argues for dating Apollonius after Callimachus. It is impossible from the poems, however, to give a definitive answer on who is influencing whom, and as a result, it is most reasonable to posit mutual influence over an extended amount of time. See Harder 1993a:110. See also Murray 2014:266, who pinpoints the constellations depicted in the *Argonautica* as dating to the year 238 BCE.

[128] For the prevalence of darkness and obscured visibility in *Argonautica* 4, see Sistakou 2012:120–130 and Lovatt 2018:107–108.

ἦ βίη, ἦ ἀρετῇ Λιβύης ἀνὰ θῖνας ἐρήμους
νῆα μεταχρονίην ὅσα τ' ἔνδοθι νηὸς ἄγεσθε
ἀνθεμένους ὤμοισι φέρειν δυοκαίδεκα πάντα
ἤμαθ' ὁμοῦ νύκτας τε.

This story comes from the Muses. I sing obedient to the Pierian
goddesses, and I heard this account entirely accurately, that you, O
strongest sons of kings by far, through your power and through your
excellence, hoisted high in the air the ship and all that you carried
within the ship upon your shoulders and transported it over the
isolated sands of Libya for twelve full days and nights.

Argonautica 4.1381–1387

In contrast to the previously discussed mentions of the Muses (1.21–22, 3.1–4,
4.1–5, and 4.552–556), the narrator is not requesting the Muses for aid at the
current moment, but rather is treating them as a source of a story that he heard
in the past (ἔκλυον).[129] As a result, we can read a sense of distance between the
narrator and this story, even though the narrator claims to have received it
"entirely accurately" (πανατρεκές, 4.1382).[130] Since the Muses are the source of
the story, the story's truth should be ensured, and Apollonius emphasizes the
Muses by including two versions of their name: Μουσάων (1381) and Πιερίδων
(1382). Indeed, the parallel placement of their names at the beginning of their
respective lines reflects their status as originators of the tale.

Why does the narrator ascribe this particular tale to the Muses? What does
the use of them here say about the evaluation of truth and falsehood? Why,
moreover, does the narrator here characterize himself as obedient (ἐγὼ δ'
ὑπακουός, 1381)? Such an admission of obedience has been read as his subordi-
nation to the Muses and thus a complete inversion from the role of the Muses
as "interpreters."[131] Some scholars think that the incredibility of the tale has
induced the narrator to call in the Muses for authentication.[132] Deeming this
rationalization unsatisfying because of the poem's several fantastical stories
(e.g. Medea's subjugation of Talus, 4.1654–1688) without any Muse attribution,
Albis proposes that the Muse citation marks Apollonius' use of Pindar *Pythian*

---

[129] Berkowitz 2004:93: "The passage is significant in that it evokes a conversation that the Muses
had before the commencement of the public narrative."

[130] ἀτρεκέως occurs in the context of knowledge at 1.661 (Hypsipyle about the Argonauts' knowl-
edge) and 2.312 (Phineus refusing to let the Argonauts know everything).

[131] Feeney 1991:91.

[132] E.g. Fränkel 1968:596–597, Grillo 1988:27, and Green 1997:344.

4 for this tale.[133] Other scholars connect the emphasis placed on this story to Greek colonization in North Africa and to Libya's geopolitical significance for Ptolemaic rule.[134]

Aside from these suggestions, the depiction of extreme struggle can function as a parallel for the difficulties of narration and by extension the difficulties of determining truth.[135] This proposal finds support not only in the overarching analogy between a journey and the act of narration,[136] but also by the immediate context. Just like the Apollonian narrator, who relies on the Muses for the story, Peleus concocts the plan to escape the Libyan desert with the help of the similarly omniscient Libyan Heroines.[137] Such an effort to determine a plan of action is analogous to the narrator's grappling with the past, especially in a place as unknown and remote as Libya. Indeed, the narrator suggests the desolation of this environment with Λιβύης ἀνὰ θῖνας ἐρήμους ("over the isolated sands of Libya," 4.1384). The desolation of this environment contributes not only to the Argonauts' struggles carrying the ship for such an extended amount of time, but also those of the narrator, who participates in this struggle through the act of narrating.

In the final lines of the section, the narrator explicitly remarks on the difficulty of recounting this tale:

> δύην γε μὲν ἢ καὶ ὀιζὺν
> τίς κ' ἐνέποι τὴν κεῖνοι ἀνέπλησαν μογέοντες;
> ἔμπεδον ἀθανάτων ἔσαν αἵματος, οἷον ὑπέσταν
> ἔργον ἀναγκαίῃ βεβιημένοι. αὐτὰρ ἐπιπρό
> τῆλε μάλ' ἀσπασίως Τριτωνίδος ὕδασι λίμνης
> ὣς φέρον, ὣς εἰσβάντες ἀπὸ στιβαρῶν θέσαν ὤμων.

> But who could speak of their agony and misery, which those men endured as they labored? Surely, they were of the blood of immortals; for what a deed they achieved, as they were compelled by necessity. And as happily as they were transporting it far toward the waters of the

---

[133] See Albis 1996:95 for this point.

[134] See Mori 2008:13–18 and Thalmann 2011:81.

[135] See Hunter 2008a:124–125, who proposes that the entire Libyan episode can function as an extended exploration of the limits of epic.

[136] Beye 1982:14 and Wray 2000:244.

[137] As Apollonius describes in 4.1308–1331, the Heroines appear to Jason, telling him that the Argonauts are to "pay back their mother" (τότε σφετέρῃ ἀπὸ μητέρι τίνετ' ἀμοιβήν, 4.1327). To solve the Argonauts' quandary, Peleus must interpret this cryptic prophecy to mean "carry the ship," in addition to discerning that the tracks of the horse omen lead to water (4.1377–1379). For the omniscience of the Heroines, see 4.1319–1321, which Hunter 1993:126 compares to the Sirens (*Odyssey* 12.189–191). Additionally, the all-knowing Heroines are also like the Muses (*Iliad* 2.485).

Tritonian lake, so happily they strode in the water and placed it down from their burly shoulders.

Argonautica 4.1387–1392

With the particle combination γε μέν in 1387, which suggests an opposition,[138] the narratorial voice reappears, asking who could speak about their struggle (τίς κ' ἐνέποι). By including this conditional question, the narrator insinuates the extreme difficulty of this task and in doing so points to his limitations as narrator.[139] Yet this question appears ironic, as the narrator has just articulated the story, albeit in a condensed manner in *oratio obliqua* dependent on the "report" (ὀμφήν, 4.1382) of the Muses, the ultimate progenitors of the tale. Does such a question then signal the Muses' limitations as well? Are they also liable to repeat stories that are not entirely true?

In the subsequent lines, the narrator seems to support the story's truth, noting the heroes' divine ancestry (ἔμπεδον ἀθανάτων ἔσαν αἵματος, 4.1389) and thus recalling previous claims in the epic (2.1223). The adverb ἔμπεδον ("surely") exerts an authenticating force. Yet, these lines can be read with a tone of incredulity. Although, as the narrator makes clear in 4.1390–1392, the Argonauts do achieve this endeavor, the choice to restate this fact multiple times with τὴν κεῖνοι ἀνέπλησαν μογέοντες (1388) and οἷον ὑπέσταν / ἔργον ἀναγκαίη βεβιημένοι (1389–1390) signals a level of uncertainty. It is not sufficient to tell the story or even to cite the Muses as sources, and in referring to the completion of the event multiple times, the narrator implies an inability to accept this story without reservation.[140] He must strive to convince both himself and the reader of the story's validity. In the process, he undermines the authority he sought to achieve by mentioning the Muses.

2.2.5 Overview of Apollonius' Muses

This mention of the Muses marks their last appearance in the epic, over the course of which the narrator has employed them for various uses. The Muses are requested to serve as "interpreters" (ὑποφήτορες), describe Medea's love, determine Medea's motivations, and explain the Argo traces in the west. Finally, the narrator cites them as the source of a μῦθος. Yet, instead of alleviating his doubt, the narrator's increased use of the Muses only intensifies it. Erato, as a source of

---

[138] Vian and Delage 1981:194. See Denniston 1950:387.

[139] Cf. Kyriakou 2018:387, who rejects a view of the narrator's serious inability here. Rather, she connects this clause to the Homeric narrator's declaration at *Iliad* 2.488–490, where his limits are caused by physical and temporal factors.

[140] Lovatt 2018:101, however, sees this passage as emphasizing the credentials of both the Argonauts and the narrator.

deception, cannot be trusted completely, nor can a single evaluation of Medea's actions be established via the Muses' aid. Similarly, the ambiguity of the question at 4.552–556 hampers the Muses' help in clarifying a contradictory tradition. Even the μῦθος emphatically assigned to the Muses at 4.1381–1392 exudes an air of incredibility. As a result, Apollonius' narrator, even while attempting to draw the Muses closer to him, maintains a distance from them. As his interpreters, helpers, or the source for a story, the Muses never become a part of him, unlike the Muses portrayed by Callimachus. For this reason, the Apollonian narrator can never attain the level of confidence that the Callimachean narrator exudes. Too great are the uncertainties in both the subject matter and sources.

3. Evaluating Stories

In addition to critiquing the credibility of their various sources, the narrators of Apollonius and Callimachus also evaluate their information. Their evaluations, however, not only examine the truth of the information, but also its appropriateness. For instance, the Apollonian narrator refuses to disclose inappropriate information such as the rites on Samothrace (1.916–921) and Medea's rites to Hecate (4.248–252).[141] Scholars have compared the Medea section in particular to a passage in the *Aetia*, in which the Callimachean narrator breaks off before revealing the origins behind the marriage ritual on Naxos.[142] In both cases, the narratorial voices exert control over their material, framing piety as their ostensible reason for silence. In this way, the two narrators evoke Pindar, for whom appropriateness constituted a criterion of truth, allowing him to discount unseemly narratives as false.[143] While we can tie moral and social concerns to Pindar's use of silences, the question becomes more complicated for the narrators of Callimachus and Apollonius. Indeed, scholars have viewed Callimachus' self-reproach of too much knowledge at fr. 75.4–9 as the epitome of Callimachean irony and playfulness.[144] Although I agree with this assessment, I will argue that the passage also reflects the centrality of personal experience as a criterion for truth, albeit ironically in the context of a lament about the dangers of too much knowledge. For comparison, I discuss a passage in the *Argonautica* that deals with an inappropriate narrative (4.982–992) while juxtaposing two differing mythological stories about the island Drepane. Yet, in establishing neither as true, the narrator implies the lack of a definite criterion.

---

[141] For discussion of Apollonius' reference to the Samothrace rituals, see Schroeder 2012:320–324.
[142] Hunter 2008a:120.
[143] For instance, see Pindar *Olympian* 1.52–53. Fuhrer 1988:63–64 compares the breaking off in *Aetia* fr. 75 to Pindar *Olympian* 9.35–41, where Pindar refuses to speak of Heracles fighting the gods.
[144] Meyer 1993:329.

3.1 Too much knowledge

The beginning of *Aetia* fragment 75, the longest section of the Acontius and Cydippe story (fr. 67–75),[145] deals with the various failed attempts to marry off Cydippe. Before describing these attempts and the illnesses that prevent the marriage (fr. 75.12–19), the narrator refers to the Naxian marriage ritual in which Cydippe participated. This ritual consists of a maiden spending the night before her wedding sleeping with a young boy who has two living parents (fr. 75.1–3). Although initially beginning a digression explaining the origins of this ritual, the narrator instead breaks off mid-utterance for a different sort of digression:

> Ἥρην γάρ κοτέ φασι—κύον, κύον, ἴσχεο, λαιδρὲ
>   θυμέ, σύ γ᾽ ἀείσῃ καὶ τά περ οὐχ ὁσίη·
> ὤναο κάρτ᾽ ἕνεκ᾽ οὔ τι θεῆς ἴδες ἱερὰ φρικτῆς,
>   ἐξ ἂν ἐπεὶ καὶ τῶν ἤρυγες ἱστορίην.
> ἦ πολυιδρείη χαλεπὸν κακόν, ὅστις ἀκαρτεῖ
>   γλώσσης· ὡς ἐτεὸν παῖς ὅδε μαῦλιν ἔχει.

> For they say Hera once—dog, dog, restrain yourself, impetuous heart,
> you will sing even what is not sanctioned to sing. You are very lucky
> because you did not see the rites of the dread goddess, since you would
> have vomited out an account of even those things. Indeed, knowledge
> of many things is a terrible evil for whoever cannot control his tongue.
> How truly this man is a child with a knife!

> *Aetia* fr. 75.4–9

With the phrase Ἥρην γάρ κοτέ φασι ("for they say Hera once," fr. 75.4), the narrator identifies Hera's involvement in the ritual's origin. The decision to discontinue this statement with the insult κύον, κύον ("dog, dog"), however, implies the unsuitability of divulging the content of this φασι clause. Since the narrator characterizes these things as not sanctioned (τά περ οὐχ ὁσίη, fr. 75.5), it has been assumed that the Callimachean narrator is referring to Zeus and Hera's premarital sex, which Homer mentions at *Iliad* 14.294–296.[146] This racy subject matter about the gods is not proper for a mortal to articulate, inducing the narrator to address his heart (θυμέ, fr. 75.6). The narrator targets his heart

---

[145] For analysis of these fragments from a narratological point of view, see Lynn 1995:192–238. See also Harder 2012.2:541–659 for commentary and bibliography.

[146] See Cameron 1995:18–22 for the argument that these lines allude to the incestuous marriage between Ptolemy Philadelphus and Arsinoe II. Cameron also detects an allusion to Sotades fr. 16, agreeing with Pretagostini 1984:146.

for reproach, since, as Callimachus indicates at fr. 178.21–22, it yearns to know. Even though the narrator has managed to check himself in this case, the heart tends to say too much: σύ γ᾽ ἀείσῃ καὶ τά περ οὐχ ὁσίη ("you will sing even what is not sanctioned to sing," fr. 75.5). By placing the limiting particle γε after σύ, the narrator acknowledges that such a tendency is one particular to him. The statement, as a result, evidences the narrator's self-awareness about his own knowledge.

The second-person address continues in the next two lines (fr. 75.6–7), where the narrator remarks on what would have occurred had he seen the rites of the terrifying goddess (the Eleusinian Mysteries).[147] Instead of restraining himself, he would have uncontrollably vomited out an inquiry: ἐξ ἂν ἐπεὶ καὶ τῶν ἤρυγες ἱστορίην. The verb ἐξερεύγομαι ("I vomit") generates an amusing image of uncontrollable utterance, which Callimachus further represents through various formal devices: the disjointed word order produced by the tmesis of the verb, the delay of ἐπεί to the third word, and the separation between the genitive καὶ τῶν and the noun ἱστορίην. By referring to this hypothetical situation in which uncontrolled speech is the consequence of seeing (ἴδες), the Callimachean narrator implies the importance of sight and personal experience as ways of determining and authenticating truth. Indeed, by placing ἱστορίην in the line after ἴδες, Callimachus calls attention to the etymological connection between the words.[148] When relying only on hearsay (φασι) about Hera for an account, the narrator can suppress his urge to blurt out forbidden information, but in the case of information acquired firsthand, his heart would not be able to help itself.

Callimachus follows the second-person reproach and the hypothetical situation of the narrator's divulging of the Eleusinian Mysteries with two statements that confirm the dangers of possessing too much information. The first statement explicitly characterizes much knowledge without restraint of speech as an evil: ἦ πολυιδρείη χαλεπὸν κακόν, ὅστις ἀκαρτεῖ / γλώσσης ("indeed, knowledge of many things is a terrible evil, for whoever cannot control his tongue," fr. 75.8–9). With the rare noun πολυιδρείη, a combination of πολύ and ἰδρείη, Callimachus alludes to the Heraclitan saying that "knowledge of many things does not teach sense" (πολυμαθίη νόον ἔχειν οὐ διδάσκει, DK 22 B 40). At the same time, πολυιδρείη picks up ἴδες and ἱστορίην, again suggesting the association between knowing and seeing firsthand. In fact, the word's sole occurrence in the *Odyssey* appears in the context of Eurycleia faithfully watching over all of

---

[147] Harder 2012.2:588 points out that this line offers a contrast with the *makarismos* of those who have beheld the Eleusinian Mysteries (*Homeric Hymn to Demeter* 480).

[148] Chantraine 2009:751–752.

Odysseus' possessions (*Odyssey* 2.346). Yet, whereas the word in Homer denotes a positive trait for a prudent character, Callimachus' associates the word with the possibilities of a negative experience. For a person who cannot control his tongue, πολυιδρείη qualifies as a "terrible evil" (χαλεπὸν κακόν). Since the adjective κακός occurs later in the description of Cydippe's paleness (fr. 75.12), we can see this description as evoking a disease. Indeed, Callimachus implies such an image with the vivid metaphor of belching out (ἤρυγες) the account. In this way, when combined with an uncontrollable tongue, πολυιδρείη can qualify as an αἴτιον for a disease. In remarking on the side effects of πολυιδρείη, the narrator demonstrates an understanding of cause and effect, perhaps hinting at a previous experience of saying too much and suffering the consequences.

The subsequent saying restates the risks of excessive knowledge, this time through the saying of a child wielding a knife: ὡς ἐτεὸν παῖς ὅδε μαῦλιν ἔχει ("how truly this man here is a child with a knife," fr. 75.9). Like ἀληθές at fr. 178.15, the adverb ἐτεόν asserts the validity of this generalized statement. With the deictic pronoun ὅδε Callimachus makes this statement specific to the narrator, recalling the previous association between the Callimachean persona and a child (*Aetia* fr. 1.6). At the same time, the narrator's reference to himself in the third person produces an ironic distancing effect. After addressing his heart in the previous lines, the Callimachean narrator has stepped back to offer an external assessment of himself, explicitly commenting on his playful and child-like persona. Of course, since the narrator is only like a child and not really one, the authenticating force of ἐτεόν is undermined. By employing this statement, however, the narrator demonstrates his ability to manipulate a piece of wisdom to correspond to his personal experiences and his understanding of what and what not to tell.[149]

In this highly self-conscious digression, Callimachus' narrator inserts himself into the narrative, handling the idea of personal experience in a variety of ways. Observing his propensity for saying too much, he reveals an awareness of what is proper to say and to include in the narrative. Through a hypothetical situation about beholding the Eleusinian Mysteries, the narrator implies that personal experience represents a crucial criterion for truth and in his case, an uncontrollable urge to blurt out an account. Finally, to support this ironic scenario, the Callimachean narrator applies two generalized statements that have particular relevance for his situation. Both statements frame too much knowledge as harmful. In warning about such dangers, the narrator indicates

---

[149] See Lelli 2011:402, who states, "Like a child holding the knife, Callimachus too is aware of but fascinated by the danger of the powerful weapon of language. And the efficacy of the image is increased because it is proverbial."

that too much knowledge is indeed possible. For him, the difficulty lies not in determining what is true or false, but rather what should or should not be said, especially for the overly eager child that is this persona.

3.2 The sickle beneath Drepane

Apollonius' narrator also faces this issue of distasteful narratives when discussing the island Drepane, home of the Phaeacians (4.982–992).[150] This digression, which appears before the Argonauts' arrival on the island, simultaneously tackles the issues of geography, etymology, and genealogy, as the narrator addresses the reason why the island has received the name Drepane ("Sickle"). Two versions are offered, the first of which induces the narrator to ask for the Muses' forgiveness:

> ἔστι δέ τις πορθμοῖο παροιτέρη Ἰονίοιο
> ἀμφιλαφὴς πίειρα Κεραυνίῃ εἰν ἁλὶ νῆσος,
> ᾗ ὕπο δὴ κεῖσθαι δρέπανον φάτις—ἵλατε Μοῦσαι,
> οὐκ ἐθέλων ἐνέπω προτέρων ἔπος—ᾧ ἀπὸ πατρός
> μήδεα νηλειῶς ἔταμε Κρόνος.

> There is an expansive and fertile island, in front of the Ionian strait in the Ceraunian sea, under which it is said a sickle lies—be gracious, Muses, not willingly do I speak this account of my predecessors—the sickle with which Cronus pitilessly cut off his father's genitals.

> *Argonautica* 4.982–986

In the first two lines, the narrator avoids indicating the island's name, instead focusing on its location and its geographic characteristics, namely its size (ἀμφιλαφής)[151] and fertility (πίειρα). It is not until the end of 983 that the narrator indicates that he is discussing an island (νῆσος), and the hyperbaton between τις in 982 and νῆσος generates a sense of distance. Furthering this sense of distance is the disjointed structure of 984–986. After first mentioning the rumored existence of the sickle beneath the island with a subordinate clause (ᾗ ὕπο δὴ κεῖσθαι δρέπανον φάτις, 4.984), the narrator breaks in with a direct address to the Muses (ἵλατε Μοῦσαι, 984) to admit his unwillingness to utter this story of his predecessors (προτέρων ἔπος). The story itself (Cronus castrating

---

[150] This island is the Homeric Scherie, home of the Phaeacians in the *Odyssey* and identified as Corcyra. Hellanicus (*FGrHist* 4 F 77) provides the first attestation of the name Drepane. See Vian and Delage 1981:29–33 for a discussion of the varying traditions.

[151] The scholiast (Σ *ad* 983; Lachenaud 2010:483) interprets the adjective ἀμφιλαφής as meaning "having a harbor on both sides."

his father) then appears in another subordinate clause, introduced by ᾧ ("with which," 4.985) and dependent on δρέπανον. That the clause stretches over two lines contributes to the disjointed structure, and indeed the line break occurs right at πατρός ("father") and μήδεα ("genitals"), thus replicating the image of bodily separation.

Through this halted and staccato presentation, the narrator signifies his unwillingness to report this offensive tale, distancing himself from the contents by ascribing the tale to unnamed predecessors.[152] Such narratorial distancing suits not only the tale's morally repugnant character, but also the story's mythological status. Since the sickle lies beneath (ὕπο δὴ κεῖσθαι, 4.984) the island, awareness of its existence comes not from direct sight, but from rumor (φάτις, 4.984). Dependent on this φάτις is the ἔπος ("account"), which explains the reason for the rumored sickle. Apollonius, in fact, suggests a relationship between φάτις and ἔπος by placing them in the same metrical *sedes*. In alluding to this multilayered tradition, the narrator suggests the complexities of dealing with the tradition; neither the φάτις nor the dependent ἔπος can be subject to direct testing. At the same time, the difficulties are amplified, as the narrator does not attach a named source nor does he cite the Muses as sources.

Likewise, the narrator ascribes the alternate and less offensive version to an unnamed group of "others":

> οἱ δέ ἑ Δηοῦς
> κλείουσι χθονίης καλαμητόμον ἔμμεναι ἅρπην·
> Δηὼ γὰρ κείνῃ ἐνὶ δή ποτε νάσσατο γαίῃ,
> Τιτῆνας δ' ἔδαεν στάχυν ὄμπνιον ἀμήσασθαι,
> Μάκριδα φιλαμένη.

> Others, however, say that it is the reaping scythe of native Deo, for indeed Deo once dwelled in that land, and she taught the Titans how to reap the nourishing grain, out of love for Macris.

> *Argonautica* 4.986–990

By coordinating the genitive expressions πατρός (4.985) and Δηοῦς (4.986), Apollonius makes the narrator form a contrast between two different types of "sources" for the rumored sickle: Cronus' father Uranus (the victim of the sickle)

---

[152] Fränkel 1968:550 detects a parallel at Aratus *Phaenomena* 637: Ἄρτεμις ἱλήκοι· προτέρων λόγος, οἵ μιν ἔφαντο. The story of Cronus castrating his father occurs at *Theogony* 174–182. Callimachus *Aetia* fr. 43.70–71, however, places this sickle at Zancle in Sicily. Klooster 2011:224n70 points out that the Apollonian narrator's distaste for this narrative is a reference to *Republic* 377e, where Socrates advises against narrating Cronus' castration.

and Demeter (the owner of the sickle). As is indicated in 987, Demeter employed her sickle for reaping grain (καλαμητόμον, 4.987), as opposed to cutting flesh (μήδεα νηλειῶς ἔταμε, 4.986). Indeed, Demeter's use of the sickle for agriculture differs from Cronus' by the fact that it leads to fertility and production, instead of precluding it, as is the case with castration. At the same time, Demeter's habitation on the island resulted in her teaching the Titans such skills (Τιτῆνας δ' ἔδαεν στάχυν ὄμπνιον ἀμήσασθαι, 4.989), thereby leading to a civilized state. Consequently, the two stories represent a dichotomy between primeval violence and Olympian civilization.[153] The task then becomes determining which of the two fits better for rationalizing the rumor (φάτις) of the sickle under the island. By what criterion can the narrator evaluate these stories?

Based on the criterion of appropriateness and his unwillingness, the narrator could eliminate the first story about the castration as false. Indeed, Pindar in *Olympian* 1 evoked such a standard to dismiss the tale that Demeter accidentally consumed a part of Pelops. Rather, since one must speak well of the gods (ἔστι δ' ἀνδρὶ φάμεν ἐοικὸς ἀμφὶ δαιμόνων καλά, *Olympian* 1.35), Pindar announces that he will speak differently from his predecessors (σὲ δ' ἀντία προτέρων φθέγξομαι, *Olympian* 1.36). Likewise, the Apollonian narrator, in offering a second version, could insinuate his rejection of the first rendition. At the same time, the narrator devotes more space to the second option, including a γάρ clause with an indicative verb (νάσσατο, "dwelled," 4.988). This clause, along with the subsequent clause about her teaching the Titans, not only explains but also carries an authenticating force. The details validate the claim that the sickle belongs to Demeter, not to Cronus. In fact, a story about Demeter teaching agriculture fits with the agricultural reality of the island, namely its fertility (πίειρα, 4.983), as mentioned at the beginning of the section.[154]

Although the narrator seems to favor the second option, the final lines of the section do not point to a definitive choice:

Δρεπάνη τόθεν ἐκλήισται
οὔνομα Φαιήκων ἱερὴ τροφός· ὣς δὲ καὶ αὐτοί
αἵματος Οὐρανίοιο γένος Φαίηκες ἔασιν.

Since then, it has been called Drepane by name, the sacred nurse of the Phaeacians, and thus the Phaeacians themselves come from the blood of Uranus.

Argonautica 4.990–992

---

[153] See Byre 2002:140 and Thalmann 2011:178.
[154] Williams 1991:251.

With Δρεπάνη τόθεν ἐκλήϊσται ("Since then, it has been called Drepane by name," 4.990), the narrator finally reveals the island's name as Drepane, thus indicating that the juxtaposition of the two stories serves as a discussion of an etymology. Yet, for the purpose of explaining the name, both stories could work. The only thing that matters is the supposed existence of the sickle, not which god owned it for what purpose. The description of the island as the "sacred nurse of the Phaeacians" (Φαιήκων ἱερὴ τροφός, 4.991) appears to corroborate the second option, as the phrase connotes fertility. However, the observation that the Phaeacians descend from the blood of Uranus (αἵματος Οὐρανίοιο γένος Φαίηκες ἔασιν, 4.992) looks back to the castration story. As the products of this act of primordial bloodshed, the Phaeacians, by their genealogy, would evidence the truth of the castration tale.[155]

Consequently, in this passage, the narrator deals with the sources on multiple topics: two different sources of the story (the predecessors vs. the others), the source of the island's name, and finally the genealogical origin of the people, the Phaeacians. Two mythological stories, differing in the appropriateness of their content, qualify as possible options for the island's name. Yet, despite distancing himself from the first version, the Apollonian narrator does not explicitly privilege one tale over the other. Nor does he directly call for the Muses to help resolve this issue. Rather, they must be gracious and passively accept the narrator's reporting of the castration tale, which, as he makes clear with οὐκ ἐθέλων ἐνέπω (4.985), he does not want to recite.

Why then does the narrator include the two stories in the first place? Hunter observes that the castration tale carries echoes of the murder of Apsyrtus, which, since it was planned by his sister Medea, also qualifies as an example of kin murder.[156] The second story, by contrast, through its emphasis on fertility and love, looks forward to the coming marriage of Jason and Medea, which will occur on Drepane and in particular in the cave of the nymph Macris (4.1131–1132), mentioned here as the recipient of Demeter's love.[157] This marriage on Drepane, however, is not entirely marked by joy and love. The ceremony takes place after Arete informs Jason that Alcinous will allow Medea to remain with

---

[155] Such a violent association, however, contrasts with the Phaeacians' peaceful and hyper-idealized representation, as depicted in Homer (e.g. *Odyssey* 6.270–272), as well as their subsequent kind treatment of the Argonauts (*Argonautica* 4.995–997). See Knight 1995:244–255 for comparison between Apollonius' and Homer's Phaeacian episodes.

[156] Hunter 1993:69.

[157] The scholiast (Σ *ad* 4.1131; Lachenaud 2010:495) notes that this was the cave where the nymph Macris reared Dionysus.

him only if the two are married (4.1111–1127). Moreover, at 4.1168–1169 the narrator describes how their lovemaking is tinged by fear about the future.[158]

As a result, the juxtaposition of the two aetiological stories reflects the uncertainty of the characters on this island. George, for instance, detects a parallel between the narrator's difficulty dealing with the castration story and Medea's troubles on Drepane after the arrival of the Colchians.[159] Just as the narrator begs the Muses to be propitious with ἵλατε (4.984), so too does Medea employ this plea (ἵλαθι) when supplicating Arete at 4.1014.[160] That both the narrator and Medea request help from external forces (the Muses and Arete, respectively) sharpens this parallel between the narrator and Medea, both of whom are beset by uncertainties. Indeed, Medea and her motivations produce the most uncertainties for the narrator, necessitating his invocations to the Muse in books three and four. Book four, in fact, posed a similar dichotomy between love and violence, as Medea's motivations for leaving Colchis correlate with the evaluation of her character as either loving or vicious. In both cases, the narrator offers a firm solution to neither question.[161] Instead, Medea is simultaneously a girl in love and a murderous witch. In this same way, the island Drepane connotes both fertility and bloodshed, both in its primordial past and its present role in the narrative, where Medea and Jason's future becomes subject to uncertainty. That the narrator imbues single entities with two contradictory aspects points to an inability to choose between two options.

3.3 Summary

In both passages, the respective narrators assess pieces of information, not explicitly for truth and falsehood, but rather for appropriateness and suitability. Nevertheless, truth remains a concern, since some information, even if true, should not be divulged, especially regarding religious matters. While the Callimachean narrator manages to check himself before disclosing the story about Hera, Apollonius' narrator reports the morally unsavory tale, albeit with hesitation, affixing a milder version as an alternative. For Callimachus' narrator,

---

[158] γλυκερῇ περ ἰαινομένους φιλότητι / δεῖμ' ἔχεν εἰ τελέοιτο διάκρισις Ἀλκινόοιο ("even though they were melting in sweet love, fear held them both, about whether Alcinous' decision would be completed").

[159] George 1977:362.

[160] γουνοῦμαι, βασίλεια· σὺ δ' ἵλαθι, μηδέ με Κόλχοις / ἐκδώῃς ᾧ πατρὶ κομιζέμεν ("I beg you queen, be propitious and do not hand me over to the Colchians to take me to my father"). Moreover, Medea's μὴ μὲν ἐγὼν ἐθέλουσα ("not willingly") at 4.1021 echoes the narrator's οὐκ ἐθέλων at 4.985.

[161] Cf. Kyriakou 2018:380, who argues the narrator here does not lack control and is merely asserting his distaste for the first narrative.

the refusal to impart information paradoxically points to his erudition.[162] This narrator makes the reader aware that he has this knowledge, as well as the sense to restrain himself, despite his propensity for saying too much. Apollonius' narrator, on the other hand, does say too much, and in doing so, signals his uncertainty. Not only is he unable to suppress the first story, he does not verify which of the two tales is correct, thus revealing an inability to judge which is true. Not only do both stories adhere to the realities of the island, namely its fertility and the genealogical origin of the people, but the motifs of love and violence characterize the complex character of Medea.

4. Conclusion

Within their respective poetic works, the *Aetia* and the *Argonautica*, Callimachus and Apollonius incorporate a variety of aetiological information: the foundation of cities (*Aetia* fr. 43), cultic rituals (the marriage ritual in *Aetia* fr. 75), the names of places (Drepane in the *Argonautica*), and even love narratives (Acontius and Cydippe and Jason and Medea). Yet, despite the seeming diversity of this subject matter, all share one common trait: the relevance of humans and their relationships with the physical landscape, the gods, and each other. It is this underlying importance of human interaction that may explain why Callimachus and Apollonius portray their narrators as so involved and connected to the narratives, as well as to sources like the Muses. Their narrators are not simply instructors describing the present happenings in the natural world, but appear engaged directly in comprehending the complex webs that tie the past with the present and that connect the disparate and remote places of the Hellenistic world.

For Callimachus, this task is achieved by the juxtaposition of disconnected narratives, framed initially by a conversation with the Muses in *Aetia* 1 and 2. Imbuing his narrator with a confident, eager, and childlike persona, Callimachus represents how the extraction and evaluation of information are achieved through personal experience: the Muses in a dreamtime conversation, Theogenes at a symposium, and finally the experience of receiving Xenomedes' chronicles. In such intimate encounters, the narrator flaunts his ability to discern the credibility of these sources, evaluating this authority with respect to himself and his existing knowledge. Indeed, since the Muses and Theogenes are similar to the narrator, they are appropriate sources to answer the questions that the narrator poses. Likewise, Xenomedes, in his devotion to truth,

---

[162] Fuhrer 1988:64. As Kaesser 2005:105 observes, "It is remarkable that in the single passage where the poet talks at all about the communication of his knowledge, he does so in terms of restraining himself from spreading it. The trope of the teacher-poet is thus wholly reversed." See Krevans 1984:263, who considers this refusal to discuss "anti-aetiological."

has his μῦθος assimilated to Callimachus' Calliope. In depicting a close relation-ship between the narrator and sources, Callimachus symbolizes how deeply the narrator (and by extension poet) has absorbed this information; it has become a part of him. As a result, the narrator can manipulate how he articulates the information. Instead of a continuous narrative or a straightforward catalogue, he juxtaposes disparate stories that feature thematic links.[163] In so doing, he demonstrates that his erudition consists not only in collating and evaluating facts, but in understanding the stories' importance and relevance to one another. It is a "truth" that is not encompassing and total, but selective and controlled, created and shaped by the Callimachean narrator's personal experience.

Apollonius' narrator, by contrast, recounts the Argonauts' circuitous journey in chronological order, albeit ending abruptly before the Argonauts reach Iolcus. The numerous digressions, which disrupt the linearity of this plot, provide a variety of information about peoples, places, and customs. While Apollonius the poet used prose sources for such information, he nevertheless still treats the Muses in the epic as sources. Yet, as I have shown, the narrator's treatment of them reveals their possible fallibility, at least for certain kinds of information. Not only does the narrator struggle with grasping the love and motivations of Medea, he even expresses uncertainty regarding the particular story about the Argonauts' valor, which I construed as a metaphor for the diffi-culties of narration. The difficulties of narration and knowing the truth pervade the epic through the narrator's uncertain voice. As narrator, he can only say how some things seem or seemed, not how they actually are or were, as is the case for the evaluation of Medea's actions in the fourth book. Moreover, he does not decide on the correct reason for the name Drepane, thus mimicking the indecision and uncertainty frequently experienced by his characters.

These narrative voices, as a result, model two different ways of assessing truth and falsehood when encountering numerous and often conflicting sources. One can rely on one's own personal judgment and select only the best infor-mation and sources, like Callimachus' narrator of the *Aetia*. Or, like Apollonius' narrator, one can soften one's assertions of truth with markers of doubt, aware that one cannot always establish a definitive truth from an array of conflicting traditions and interpretations. While they lack the explicit didactic frame of the *Phaenomena* and *Theriaca*, we can instead say that the *Aetia* and the *Argonautica* are poems that thematize the processes of learning and discovery, not only for the narrators, but for the readers as well.[164]

---

[163] Harder 2012.1:20 identifies some of the reoccurring themes as hospitality towards strangers (for instance, fr. 25, Heracles and Thiodamas), crime and punishment (fr. 44, Busiris), and movement and expansion (fr. 43, the Sicilian cities).

[164] See Harder 2007b:44–45, who comes to a similar conclusion for the *Aetia*. She argues that the text "activates" the readers to use their own minds and other resources.

4

Lycophron
A Deeper Understanding

The future, in contrast with the present and the past, entails the most difficul-
ties for uncovering and assessing the truth. To attempt to forecast the future
requires an understanding of both present and past, and even then, the exis-
tence of too many possibilities often precludes an accurate prediction. For this
reason, in ancient Greece, knowledge of the future was reserved for those select
individuals inspired by the gods. Yet with such knowledge came madness,[1] and
nowhere is this confluence of prophetic truth and madness more apparent than
in the case of Cassandra, the prophetess of Troy blessed with the gift of foresight
by Apollo but subsequently cursed with an inability to persuade her listeners.[2]
Her prophecies concerning the aftermath of the Trojan War make up the subject
of the *Alexandra*, a 1474-line poem in iambic trimeters ascribed to Lycophron
of Chalcis.[3] Yet, what qualifies as the future for Cassandra and her internal

---

[1] See Plato *Phaedrus* 244a–d for the association between prophecy and inspired madness.
[2] Cassandra received this curse after rejecting Apollo's sexual advances: see *Alexandra* 1454–1458.
    For an analysis of Cassandra's utterances in the *Agamemnon* (1072–1330) as a shift between
    ecstasy and rational mediation, see Mazzoldi 2002:145–154.
[3] The dating of the *Alexandra* and the identity of its author have incurred numerous difficulties.
    The ancient evidence (*Suda* λ 827) identifies the author of the *Alexandra* as Lycophron of Chalcis,
    a tragedian and member of the Pleiad working during the reign of Ptolemy II (283/282–246
    BCE). This date, however, does not fit with the two *Alexandra* passages concerned with the rise
    of Roman military might: 1226–1280 (Aeneas in Italy) and 1446–1450 (the ascendance of some
    unnamed wrestler who gains power over land and sea). One would not expect such an emphasis
    on Roman military power during the third century BCE (Σ *ad* 1226; Leone 2002:226). As a result,
    three different solutions have been proposed: (1) adhering to the ancient evidence and keeping
    Lycophron's *Alexandra* in the third century, (2) positing the existence of another Lycophron
    and dating the poem to the beginning of the second century BCE, or (3) retaining the third-
    century date and viewing the Roman sections as interpolations. The interpolation theory (3),
    as espoused by West 1984:127–151, rests on the assessment that the Roman passages are poorly
    integrated into what she views as the main theme of the later part of Cassandra's prophecy,
    the clash between the regions of "West" and "East" (1984:135–136). For arguments maintaining
    the unity of the poem and the third-century date, see Momigliano 1945:52, Lambin 2005:11–41,
    Hurst 2012c, and Fountoulakis 2014:103–124. While I likewise reject the interpolation theory, I

audience is in fact, for the author Lycophron and his extratextual audience, a condensation of the past, both mythological and historical.[4] The question of truth, as a result, must be addressed in terms of two agents: a fictional character inspired by Apollo and a real author using a variety of literary sources.[5] Both would evaluate truth differently.

Two characteristics of the poem further complicate the issue of truth. First, the poem lacks an external narrator to provide explicit comments on truth and falsehood, unlike the teacher personae in the *Phaenomena* and *Theriaca* and the poet-narrators in the *Aetia* and *Argonautica*. Instead, an unnamed messenger introduces and concludes the work. The work is entirely mimetic in its mode, containing the representation of the words of the messenger, who in turn replicates the discourse of the inspired and frenzied Cassandra.[6] The narrative thus is filtered through four levels, emanating from Apollo to the author Lycophron.[7] At the same time, Lycophron has Cassandra and the messenger employ cryptic language that obscures the intended referents of the poem.[8]

---

prefer the second-century date, following Ziegler 1927: col. 2365–2381, White 1997:51, Gigante Lanzara 1998:411, Kosmetatou 2000:51, Hornblower 2015 *passim*, and McNelis and Sens 2016:11. A useful chart of the varying opinions on both the date of the text and the identity of the wrestler, up until 1991, can be found in Schade 1999:220–228.

[4] Her prophecy can be roughly divided as follows: the events occurring before and immediately after the Trojan War (31–416), the homecomings undertaken by the Greek heroes (417–1282), and the clashes between Asia and Europe (1283–1450). I use Hornblower's 2015 text.

[5] For an overview of Lycophron's sources, which include both poetic works and prose texts, see Hornblower 2015:7–35. As West 2009:81–93 has demonstrated, Herodotus was an important influence. See also Priestly 2014:179–185.

[6] Although scholars have struggled to define the generic status of the *Alexandra*, the use of iambic trimeter, the meter employed in the spoken parts of drama, suggests an affinity with tragedy. Indeed, Lycophron makes numerous allusions to the tragedians, in particular Aeschylus and Euripides. However, as Cusset 2002/2003:138 points out, the *Alexandra* lacks the sung parts expected in a classical tragedy. Durbec 2011b:57 analyzes the structure in terms of a five-act drama. At the same time, the work displays numerous influences from epic, such as the rewriting of the *Odyssey* at 648–819. For this reason, Fusillo 1984:525 identifies in the work an interaction between an epic narrative and dramatic discourse. See also West 2000:164. For other discussions of genre, see Fountoulakis 1998:291–295 and Hurst 2012b:47–58. See also Sistakou 2016:168–192 for the *Alexandra*'s adoption and subversion of the tragic. Focusing on 1099–1119 (the death of Agamemnon), Molesworth 2018:173–199 argues that this passage evokes the performance of tragedy.

[7] Lowe 2004:308.

[8] The poem's obscurity has attracted much attention in its ancient and modern reception. The *Suda* refers to the work as τὸ σκοτεινὸν ποίημα ("the obscure poem"). For this reason, the *Alexandra* has a rich commentary tradition surrounding it. While Stephanus of Byzantium (50.12, 115.5, 399.7) in the *Ethnica* mentions a commentary by Theon (Augustan date), none of this work directly survives. The manuscripts transmit an ancient paraphrase, a later paraphrase, *scholia vetera*, and three versions of the twelfth-century commentary by Tzetzes. The two volumes of Scheer (1881–1908) contain the periphrases (vol. 1) and the *scholia vetera* and Tzetzean scholia (vol. 2). Leone 2002 includes the periphrases and *scholia vetera*. For discussion of the ancient

In this way, the *Alexandra* is allegorical in its presentation. Cassandra says one thing, but means something else,[9] "imitating," as the messenger observes, "the voice of the obscure Sphinx" (Σφιγγὸς κελαινῆς γῆρυν ἐκμιμουμένη, 7). Indeed, it is with this line that Lycophron encapsulates the dual characteristics of the work itself: its mimetic nature (ἐκμιμουμένη) and its allegorical dimension, as embodied by the obscure and riddling Sphinx.[10]

Yet this dual status of the work creates a paradox. While *mimesis* demands a correspondence between what is represented and its object, allegory involves a disjunction between what is stated and what is meant. Interpretation is necessary for both comprehending and assessing a truth expressed allegorically. In the proem to the *Alexandra*, the messenger explicitly requests the need for interpretation, urging the king Priam:

> τῶν ἄσσα θυμῷ καὶ διὰ μνήμης ἔχω,
> κλύοις ἄν, ὦναξ, κἀναπεμπάζων φρενὶ
> πυκνῇ διοίχνει δυσφάτους αἰνιγμάτων
> οἴμας τυλίσσων, ᾗπερ εὐμαθὴς τρίβος
> ὀρθῇ κελεύθῳ τὰν σκότῳ ποδηγετεῖ.

> Listen, O lord, to what I grasp in my heart and in my memory. Pondering with your clever mind, go through and unravel the obscure paths of her riddles, where a learned track, by a straight road, guides the things in the shadows.

> *Alexandra* 8–12

As Looijenga has observed, this request to assert mental energy applies also to the extratextual audience, who must navigate through the profusion of kennings, periphrases, new vocabulary, and obscure names.[11] Yet the question then arises: how does the combination of allegorical expression and a mimetic mode affect the criteria for evaluating truth? What kind of criteria do Cassandra, the messenger, and the author, Lycophron, favor? Do their criteria concentrate

---

sources about Lycophron's obscurity, see Berra 2009:259–318. Analyses of Lycophron's complex language and naming strategies can be found in Ciani 1973:132–148, Cusset 2001:61–72, Lambin 2005:233–260, Kalospyros 2009:209–219, and Sistakou 2009a:237–257. For analyses of the cult titles, see Cusset and Kolde 2012:1–30, Hornblower 2014:91–120, and McNelis and Sens 2016:38–46.

[9] It is in this sense that I interpret the poem as allegorical ("saying something else"). In many places Tzetzes rejects allegorical readings (see Σ *ad* 157; Scheer 2.75).

[10] Kossaifi 2009:147–148 notes the term does not have the same meaning as in Plato or Aristotle, arguing, "L'imitation se trouve ainsi déplacée, non sans humour, du concept idéal vers les profondeurs mystérieuses et terrifiantes que symbolisent ce monstre ambivalent."

[11] Looijenga 2009:75.

on an external existence that can be easily perceived and thus captured by *mimesis* or on a deeper essence, accessible only via sustained inquiry?

In this chapter, I will tackle this question by focusing on Cassandra's depiction of three mythological figures that reoccur in the work: Helen, Odysseus, and the Sirens. All three figures boast a rich mythological background, with particular relevance to the topic of truth and falsehood in myth and poetry. After their prominent roles in Homer's *Iliad* and *Odyssey*, Helen and Odysseus assumed many different guises in subsequent depictions. Absorbing these varying traditions, Cassandra demonstrates how falsity defines both of their identities. In the *Alexandra*, Helen is nothing but a destructive phantom, while Odysseus is a serial liar who is incapable of telling the truth and whose deceptions multiply his sufferings. By identifying Helen as a phantom in Troy, Cassandra deviates from Homer and deprives Helen of an existence, even while paradoxically retaining her culpability for causing the war. For Odysseus, Cassandra connects his innate deception not with resourcefulness and rhetorical prowess, as in Homer, but rather a degraded and dehumanized state. Furthermore, Cassandra's choice to rewrite his adventures at 648–819 constitutes an effort to assert her own truth over the existing tradition of Homer.

At the same time, while denigrating Helen and Odysseus as false and destructive, Cassandra offers a more positive portrayal of the Sirens, the deadly monsters of the *Odyssey* who enchanted sailors to death with their divine music. To signal the Sirens' importance, Cassandra devotes an extended section in the *Odyssey* portion (712–737) to describe the Sirens' death and the cults established in their honor. This section, replete with details about geography and cults, connects the Sirens with the world of the author's present. As I will argue, the Sirens attain a permanence and regularity, becoming integrated into the landscape and culture of Italy. Indeed, Cassandra grants these monsters a level of commemoration that is denied or undercut for most of the male heroes in the work.

In elevating the Sirens and emphasizing the falsity of Helen and Odysseus, Cassandra reveals that her criteria for truth are not based on surface appearances. Rather, her concern is focused on an inner essence, which cannot be immediately observed, but must be contemplated, questioned, and uncovered. An understanding of patterns and relationships, both familial and temporal, elucidates this inner essence, as Cassandra judges these characters in relation to their parents, as well as to herself and her personal experiences. The messenger, on the other hand, can only regard surface appearances, clouded by his limited mortal knowledge and inability to penetrate the obscurity of Cassandra's words. The poet Lycophron, who shares the characteristics of both prophetess and messenger, must mediate between these two different approaches.

1. Messenger Vs. Cassandra

A dive into Cassandra's cryptic utterances necessitates additional explication of the relationship between her and the messenger. Although both figures emanate from the poet Lycophron, the messenger's own words remain restricted to the beginning section (1–30) and to the epilogue (1461–1474). Despite the paucity of this sample, scholars and commentators have observed in the messenger an obscurity similar to the speech ascribed to Cassandra.[12] Indeed, the messenger's initial description of Paris' journey (22–27) features rare words and bold metaphors that assimilate the ships to young maidens and birds.[13] This lexical resemblance raises an important, albeit unanswerable question. Has Cassandra's mode of speaking seeped into his speech? Or has he imposed his way of speaking upon the words he has just heard, transforming inarticulate cries (ἄσπετον χέασα παμμιγῆ βοήν, 5) into something obscure yet intelligible?[14] In fact, he implies manipulation with τῶν ἄσσα θυμῷ καὶ διὰ μνήμης ἔχω ("what I grasp in my heart and in my memory," 8). He depends on his heart and memory for this material.[15] Such admitted selectivity clashes with his initial promise for exactness and totality: λέξω τὰ πάντα νητρεκῶς, ἅ μ' ἱστορεῖς / ἀρχῆς ἀπ' ἄκρας ("I will speak accurately all that you ask of me, from the very beginning," 1–2).[16]

The messenger's status engenders another paradoxical situation amid the confluence of *mimesis* and allegory. Cassandra's voice and viewpoint preponderate in the poem, yet the mimetic frame entraps and potentially distorts her discourse. In this reliance on Lycophron's messenger, we lack direct access to Cassandra's words, which themselves qualify as interpretations of Apollo's prophecies. Nevertheless, the desperate and frantic outpouring of her speech (28–30) encourages the reader to interpret the crux of the prophecy as ultimately

---

[12] See Wilamowitz-Moellendorff 1924.2:147, Hutchinson 1988:258n71, and Cusset 2006a:48–49. Looijenga 2009:61 also observes the riddling nature of the messenger's speech. For a refutation of this similarity, see Fountoulakis 1998:293, who argues for the relative intelligibility of the messenger's speech in 1–30 and 1461–1474.

[13] For discussion of the language in this section, see Looijenga 2009:61–62and McNelis and Sens 2016:19–22.

[14] On this difficulty of determining the direction of influence, see Cusset 2006a:49. According to Pillinger 2019:116, Cassandra "interpolates" the messenger's speech.

[15] McNelis and Sens 2016:57 see the juxtaposition of θυμός and μνήμη as a contrast between emotional and rational modes of poetic production. Looijenga 2009:70n19 suggests that line 8 can function as a metapoetic remark on the skills of the poet Lycophron. See also Kossaifi 2009:149–150. For discussion of the messenger's possible distortions, see Pillinger 2019:116n25.

[16] The adverb νητρεκῶς is an alternate form of ἀτρεκῶς. According to Durbec 2011e:13, its use has the strength of a poetic declaration. As Lambin 2005:209 notes, the first word λέξω announces that the poem is about language. McNelis and Sens 2016:53–54 point out that the promise for accuracy is a typical feature of tragic messenger speeches.

hers. Indeed, her prophetic power enables her to experience the events as though they are happening. Present tense verbs (e.g. λεύσσω, 52, 86) embody this sense of immediacy.[17] Yet, as befits her emulation of the riddling Sphinx (7), her ultimate truth is hidden, both by her cryptic language and the messenger's frame. Similarly, the pseudonym Alexandra (30) conceals her name,[18] while the dark stony prison encloses her body (348–351).[19]

These multiple confinements, verbal and literal, differentiate Cassandra from the messenger. Although unnamed and subordinate to Priam, he enjoys the ability of movement. In fact, after indicating the need for the audience's erudition (9–12), the messenger frames himself as a participant in a race:

ἐγὼ δ' ἄκραν βαλβῖδα μηρίνθου σχάσας,
ἄνειμι λοξῶν ἐς διεξόδους ἐπῶν,
πρώτην ἀράξας νύσσαν ὡς πτηνὸς δρομεύς.

But detaching the rope from the tip of the turning-point, I will enter the passages of her crooked words, having struck the starting-post, like a winged runner.

Alexandra 13–15

Aside from continuing the poetry as path metaphor, the expression ὡς πτηνὸς δρομεύς ("like a winged runner," 15) alights upon several other conventions. Since it connotes swiftness, πτηνός engages with the *topos* of the hasty messenger in tragedy.[20] At the same time, this adjective participates in the tradition of the flying poet, a trope spanning from archaic poetry to Callimachus' *Aetia* prologue (fr. 1.32).[21] For this reason, McNelis and Sens interpret the adjective πτηνός as connoting the messenger's aptness as a reporter.[22] Yet reporting does not necessarily equate to comprehension. As is clear from 9–12, this arduous task falls upon the audience, who must employ their clever minds to extricate the meaning of the obscure words. In shifting this undertaking to the audience,

---

[17] On the force of λεύσσω and other present tense verbs, see Cusset 2009:128, McNelis and Sens 2016:72, and Pillinger 2019:122. Sistakou 2012:137 views λεύσσω as conveying not "physical but spiritual sight."

[18] The scholiast (Σ *ad* 30; Leone 2002:7) explains this name by the fact that Cassandra "wards off men," since she is a virgin. Pausanias 3.26.5 records that Alexandra was an alternative name at Sparta. See Salapata 2002:131–159 for a discussion of this cult. Lambin 2005:212 proposes that A-lex-andra can be interpreted as "not speaking man."

[19] For discussions of this strange prison, see Hurst and Kolde 2008:152, Lambin 2005:252–253, 2009:165, Kossaifi 2009:148, and Rougier-Blanc 2009:552–553.

[20] See also Sens 2014:110n34.

[21] See Nünlist 1998:277–283.

[22] McNelis and Sens 2016:58.

the messenger signals a devotion to repetition and accuracy. This assiduous devotion obstructs a deeper understanding of Cassandra's cryptic utterances. Indeed, in likening himself to a runner with wings, I suggest, the messenger reveals that his movement through the speech remains restricted to the surface.

The messenger restates this interest in accuracy and repetition in the epilogue, which itself features numerous echoes of the prologue:

Τόσσ' ἠγόρευε καὶ παλίσσυτος ποσὶν
ἔβαινεν εἰρκτῆς ἐντός, ἐν δὲ καρδίᾳ
Σειρῆνος ἐστέναξε λοίσθιον μέλος,
Κλάρου Μιμαλλών, ἢ Μελαγκραίρας κόπις
Νησοῦς θυγατρός, ἤ τι Φίκιον τέρας,
ἑλικτὰ κωτίλλουσα δυσφράστως ἔπη.
ἐγὼ δὲ λοξὸν ἦλθον ἀγγέλλων, ἄναξ,
σοὶ τόνδε μῦθον παρθένου φοιβαστρίας,
ἐπεί μ' ἔταξας φύλακα λαΐνου στέγης
καὶ πάντα φράζειν κἀναπεμπάζειν λόγον
ἐτητύμως ἄψορρον ὤτρυνας τρόχιν.
δαίμων δὲ φήμας εἰς τὸ λῷον ἐκδραμεῖν
τεύξειεν, ὅσπερ σῶν προκήδεται θρόνων,
σῴζων παλαιὰν Βεβρύκων παγκληρίαν.

So many things she said, and she stepped back inside her enclosure. In her heart, she groaned the last song of the Siren, like a Mimallon of Clarus or the babbler of Melancraera, daughter of Neso, or some Phician monster, babbling twisted, difficult words. And I came, lord, announcing for you this oblique speech of the prophetic maiden, since you placed me as a guard of the stone prison and ordered me to come back as a messenger and to report and repeat the whole speech truthfully. But may the god make these utterances turn out for the better, he who cares for your rule, preserving the ancient realm of the Bebrycians!

Alexandra 1461–1474

After again remarking upon Cassandra's difficult words (δυσφράστως ἔπη, 1466), the messenger stresses his own accuracy with πάντα (1470) and the adverb ἐτητύμως (1471), which together parallel πάντα and νητρεκῶς in the first line. Similarly, κἀναπεμπάζειν (1470), translated here as "repeat," recalls κἀναπεμπάζων (9), where the verb is applied to Priam's and, by extension, the audience's contemplation of the poem. By restating this aspiration for accuracy, the messenger highlights its importance for his role as reporter. Yet suffused with this obsession lies a fundamental disbelief in Cassandra's words. While one would expect such disbelief because of Apollo's curse (1454–1458), the messenger's description of Cassandra (1461–1465) implicitly undermines her credibility. Not only does he describe her as groaning a Siren's song (1463), he also obliquely calls hers a Sphinx with τι Φίκιον τέρας ("some Phician monster," 1465), a designation that indicates this monster's paternity (*Theogony* 326). In equating her to a Siren and the Sphinx, the messenger fixates on Cassandra's monstrosity, while also echoing his initial comparison to the Sphinx in the prologue (7). Combined with the descriptions of her unbridled frenzy (5–6), such a fixation reflects her dehumanization. Cassandra, in fact, anticipates such dehumanization when she refers to her utterances with a verb fit for dog noises: βαύζω ("I bark," 1453).[23] At the same time, Cassandra's gender compounds the seeming falsity of her words, as the participle κωτίλλουσα ("babbling," 1466) combines the senses of feminine loquacity and flattery.[24] In the messenger's eyes, these elements coalesce to represent not a font of prophetic truth, but merely a monstrous, animalistic, and raving woman confined to a prison.

The messenger further implies his incredulity in the final three lines of the poem. Even though Cassandra warns that the prophecies will inevitably come true (1458), he still prays for a better outcome (1472–1473). In particular, his use of φήμας (1472), I argue, implies his disbelief. Although commentators have favored the translation "prophecies,"[25] it is difficult not to see the meaning "rumor" present here as well, as this meaning manifests a few lines above, in the conclusion of Cassandra's speech:

πίστιν γὰρ ἡμῶν Λεψιεὺς ἐνόσφισε,
ψευδηγόροις φήμαισιν ἐγχρίσας ἔπη,
καὶ θεσφάτων πρόμαντιν ἀψευδῆ φρόνιν,
λέκτρων στερηθεὶς ὧν ἐκάλχαινεν τυχεῖν.
θήσει δ' ἀληθῆ.

For the Lepsian deprived me of credibility when he smeared with false-speaking rumors my words and the unerring prophetic wisdom of my oracles. He was robbed of the sexual relations he yearned to acquire. He will render these things true.

Alexandra 1454–1458

---

[23] See Gigante Lanzara 2000:432–433.

[24] See Looijenga 2009:75n28.

[25] E.g. Ciani 1975:325, Fusillo, Hurst, and Paduano 1991:151 ("*le sue profezie*"), and Hornblower 2015:501. Hurst and Kolde 2008:84 translate as "*dires*"; Gigante Lanzara 2000:183 translates as "*le sue voce*."

Deprived of his sexual desire (1457), Apollo has debilitated Cassandra's credibility by anointing her utterances with ψευδηγόροις φήμαισιν ("false-speaking rumors," 1455). With this language that suggests the physical process of smearing, Cassandra constructs a distinction between surface and interiority. These rumors applied by Apollo overlie and obfuscate the words and the true prophetic thought that Apollo will render real. Thus, the messenger's discounting of her humanity and her speech indicates a dependence on surface appearances. He cannot discern the truth from the added rumors.

From this analysis, we can identify the crucial distinction between the messenger and Cassandra as a dichotomy between surface and depth. On the narrative level, this dichotomy maps upon the messenger's ability to move on the exterior and Cassandra's submersion within her strange gloomy prison. The framing device surrounding Cassandra's speech further embodies this sense of depth and interiority, as does her use of enigmatic allegorical speech. At the same time, the distinction between surface and depth corresponds to the two characters' respective knowledge. The messenger is devoted to accuracy and thus judges based on surface appearances, whereas Cassandra can access the deeper yet significantly more difficult prophetic truth. Such a truth not only deals with chains of causations, but encompasses a multiplicity of identities, all of which overlap to conceal a true essence. Cassandra, as I will demonstrate in the remainder of this chapter, assesses this true essence by comparing figures to their parents as well as to herself and to her own experiences.

2. Helen

As the cause of the Trojan War and so the atrocities produced in its wake, Helen occupies a critical place in Cassandra's prophecy. Indeed, we can observe Helen's role as a cause since Paris' departure from Troy to abduct Helen instigates Cassandra's frenzied utterances, as the messenger narrates at 20–27. While Cassandra does not divulge the purpose of Paris' trip until 86–89, her synoptic view of past, present, and future allows us to read Helen's presence here as well. Just the thought of Helen triggers Cassandra to recall the previous destruction of Troy by Heracles (31–34), an event that presages the final razing in the Trojan War.[26] Helen, as a result, possesses the power to evoke destruction, despite her absence. Yet, as Lycophron will highlight in Cassandra's subsequent portrayal, Helen's power and its deleterious effects transcend physical existence. Even

[26] See *Iliad* 5.640–642 for Heracles' destruction of Troy. According to Tzetzes (Σ *ad* 34; Scheer 2:29), Heracles sacks Troy because the king Laomedon breaks a promise and only gives Heracles mortal (not immortal) horses as a reward for killing the sea monster and saving Hesione.

as an εἴδωλον ("phantom"), Helen still instigates war. Whereas the εἴδωλον myth as recorded by Stesichorus and Euripides' *Helen* absolved the real Helen of blame,[27] Cassandra emphatically preserves this culpability. In the process, Helen, as filtered through Cassandra's point of view, represents a paradoxical figure, straddling the poles of nonexistence and guilt and appearing as both a victim and a destroyer. Through such paradoxes, however, Cassandra determines how Helen embodies the essence of destruction. It is through the irresistible power of her phantom appearance that Helen can inflict so much havoc. An understanding of Helen's lineage and behavior serves as the criterion for Cassandra's assessment of Helen.

The first extended mention of Helen occurs at 86–89, when Cassandra specifies the purpose of Paris' fateful departure:

λεύσσω θέοντα γρυνὸν ἐπτερωμένον
τρήρωνος εἰς ἅρπαγμα, Πεφναίας κυνός,
ἣν τόργος ὑγρόφοιτος ἐκλοχεύεται,
κελυφάνου στρόβιλον ὠστρακωμένην.

I see the winged firebrand rushing to seize the dove, the Pephnaean bitch, which the water-roaming vulture birthed, enclosed in the round covering of a shell.

Alexandra 86–89

Identifying Paris as the "winged firebrand" (γρυνὸν ἐπτερωμένον, 86),[28] Cassandra grants Helen two different designations within the span of the same line (87): Helen is a dove (τρήρωνος), as well as a "Pephnaean bitch" (Πεφναίας κυνός).[29] The first descriptor, dove, associates Helen with Aphrodite, the

---

[27] In Plato's *Phaedrus* (243a–b), Socrates claims that Stesichorus composed the *Palinode* after Helen blinded him for blaming her for the war. In the *Palinode*, Stesichorus denies that that Helen ever went to Troy (fr. 192 *PMGF* Davies). Rather, as we can learn from the reference at Plato *Republic* 586c, the war was fought over an εἴδωλον. According to a scholiast's comment on *POxy* 2506, fr. 26, the real Helen stayed with Proteus. Stesichorus' version influenced Euripides' *Helen*. This play not only involves the εἴδωλον going to Troy, but explicitly portrays Helen residing in Egypt with Proteus until Menelaus' return. The periphrasis to Lycophron on 822 (Leone 2002:330) claims that Hesiod (fr. 358 M/W) first introduced the εἴδωλον element.

[28] Cassandra calls Paris a firebrand, since Hecuba dreamed that she was giving birth to a firebrand. This dream portended the fall of Troy. See Apollodorus *Library* 3.12.5 and Euripides *Trojan Women* 922. The scholiast (Σ *ad* 86a, Leone 2002:20) also suggests that the "winged firebrand" refers to the ship. See *Alexandra* 1362 for another reference to Paris as a firebrand.

[29] According to the scholia (Σ *ad* 87c; Leone 2002:20), Pephne is a place in Laconia where Helen and Paris set off. An alternative interpretation given by the scholia is to read the adjective as not a geographic designation but as πεφναίας ("deadly"). See Negri 2009:189–190 for a discussion of this possibility.

goddess for whom doves are sacred.[30] The latter phrase, κυνός, evokes Helen's self-condemnation in the *Iliad* and *Odyssey*, thus providing a negative connotation and suggesting Helen's shamelessness and wanton sexuality.[31] Calling Helen, a dove, however, also casts her as a victim, since Cassandra frequently employs non-predatory bird names for female victims whom she pities.[32] Yet how can Helen simultaneously be a weak victim and someone worthy of blame? Does, rather, the inclusion of "Pephnaean bitch" serve as a correction of dove? Indeed, Cassandra acknowledges that, while Helen's capture by Paris does render her a victim and powerless, Helen remains responsible for the destruction of Troy.

The subsequent two lines, which deal with Helen's birth, shed further light on the topic of Helen's characterization. In 88, Cassandra identifies her as the offspring of the τόργος ὑγρόφοιτος ("water-roaming vulture"). This phrase, as a periphrasis for a swan, would refer to Zeus, who transformed into a swan to rape Leda and then produce Helen.[33] In calling Zeus a τόργος, properly a carrion bird, Cassandra imports deadly associations for Zeus and by extension his daughter Helen.[34] However, the water-roaming vulture could also refer to an alternate myth, in which Nemesis morphed into a goose to avoid Zeus' advances. The result of this sexual assault was the egg described in 89.[35] With Nemesis, the goddess of righteous indignation, as her mother,[36] Helen exemplifies the quintessential force of destruction, serving as her mother's proxy. Indeed, in the *Cypria*, Helen's sole purpose for existence is to bring death and enact Zeus' plan to depopulate the world (F1 West).

---

[30] See Σ *ad* 87b; Leone 2002:20.

[31] In Homer, Helen refers to herself as a bitch (*Iliad* 3.180, 6.344, 6.356, and *Odyssey* 4.145). In a survey of "dog" words in Homer, Graver 1995:53 determines that metaphors from this group act as a harsh form of abuse, "one which labels its object as greedy or potentially cannibalistic in the domain of material goods, or of fighting, sexuality, or speech."

[32] See Sistakou 2009a:242. For examples in Lycophron, see 103 (πελειαῖν, "doves" for Helen's daughters), 314 (διπλᾶς ἀηδόνας, "nightingales" for Laodice and Polyxena), and 357 (φάσσα, "dove" for Cassandra herself).

[33] For this version of Helen's birth, see Euripides *Helen* 17–21, 214–216, 256–259, 1144–1146, *Iphigenia at Aulis* 794–798, and *Orestes* 1385–1388. Although acknowledging the ambiguity of τόργος ὑγρόφοιτος, Fusillo, Hurst, and Paduano 1991:164 identify Zeus as the τόργος ὑγρόφοιτος. Hornblower 2015:143, however, points out that the verb ἐκλοχεύεται should refer to female parturition (Euripides *Helen* 258).

[34] For instance, Cassandra refers to Locrian Ajax, her rapist, as a "vulture" at 357.

[35] The *Cypria* featured this version (F 11 West = West 2013:82–83). Apollodorus *Library* 3.10.7 records that a shepherd found the egg produced by this union and gave it to Leda to rear.

[36] Pausanias (1.33.8) describes a scene at the temple of Nemesis at Rhamnus, in which Leda presents Helen to Nemesis. See Callimachus *Hymn to Artemis* 232 for a reference to Rhamnusian Helen.

In addition to suggesting two versions of Helen's birth, the periphrasis "water-roaming vulture" combines bird and water imagery and parallels the kenning for Paris at 86 (γρυνὸν ἐπτερωμένον). The participle ἐπτερωμένον ("winged") not only likens Paris to a bird but recalls the earlier description of his naval travel (20–27), which incorporated bird imagery: πελαργοχρῶτες ("stork-colored," 24) and πτίλα ("wings," 25).[37] By forming an analogy between Paris and Helen's avian parent (Zeus or Nemesis), Cassandra implies Helen's innate association with acts of sexual violation that in turn carry deadly ramifications. Just as the union of Zeus with either Leda or Nemesis creates Helen, so too will Helen and Paris birth the Trojan War from their illicit relations. Consequently, for Cassandra, familial relations represent a means of assessing an individual's behavior. In remarking on Helen's ominous parent, Cassandra can show that the term κύων ("bitch") is a more accurate reflection of Helen's character than τρήρων ("dove"). Moreover, in correcting this assessment, Cassandra reveals an ability to pierce through surface appearances. The egg contains not a bird, but a bitch.

After outlining Paris' journey in a second-person address (90–101), Cassandra describes the kidnapping itself, which occurs while Helen is sacrificing to the Thysae and Byne (Ino):

κ αὶ τὴν ἄνυμφον πόρτιν ἁρπάσας λύκος,
δυοῖν πελειαῖν ὠρφανισμένην γονῆς
καὶ δευτέραν εἰς ἄρκυν ὀθνείων βρόχων
λῆιτιν ἐμπταίσασαν ἰξευτοῦ πτερῷ,
Θύσηισιν ἁρμοῖ μηλάτων ἀπάργματα
φλέγουσαν ἐν κρόκαισι καὶ Βύνη θεᾷ...

And you, a wolf, will seize the unwedded heifer, who is bereaved of her two dove daughters. She will fall into the second net of foreign snares, made victim by the feathered trap of the fowler, just when on the shore she is burning the victims of the flocks to the Thysae and the goddess Byne.

Alexandra 102–107

As befits Lycophron's complex system of naming, Cassandra now employs two different designations for Paris and Helen to signify the dynamic between

---

[37] For the conflation between avian and nautical imagery, cf. *Agamemnon* 52: πτερύγων ἐρετμοῖσιν ἐρεσσόμενοι ("rowing with the oars of their wings," Trans: Fraenkel).

predator and victim. This time Paris appears as a wolf (λύκος, 102),[38] while Helen is the "unwedded heifer" (τὴν ἄνυμφον πόρτιν, 102), a phrase that seems paradoxical considering that Helen is currently married to Menelaus.[39] Cassandra heightens the paradox by applying the designation of dove not to Helen, as previously in 87, but rather to her two daughters (δυοῖν πελειαῖν).[40] Whereas the use of τρήρωνος for Helen calls attention to her dual role as victim and aggressor, the synonym πελειαῖν connotes the daughters' innocence.[41] In indicating the innocence of the daughters, Cassandra furthers her censure of Helen's capture. Not only has Helen forgotten her spousal duties, but her parental obligations as well.[42] In this way, the description of Helen as an unwedded heifer is accurate. Helen's choice to elope with Paris negates her current marital status.

In fact, as Cassandra shows with δευτέραν ("second," 104), Helen has a tendency for being taken by foreign predators. Prior to the abduction by Paris, Theseus carried Helen off while she was still a girl.[43] By obliquely referring to this previous capture, Cassandra emphasizes the inevitability of Helen's abductions. Just as Helen becomes caught within metaphorical nets (εἰς ἄρκυν ὀθνείων βρόχων, 104), so too is she ensnared by the serial kidnappings caused by her beauty. As Cusset observes, this imagery of the hunting net (ἄρκυν), which in classical tragedy occurred in the contexts of murder, is now transferred to the sphere of illegitimate relations.[44] Lycophron nevertheless retains this tragic connotation of murder, since the capture of Helen by Paris will cause death, albeit indirectly. For this reason, Cassandra can still insinuate blame, even while

---

[38] Cusset 2001:68 detects an anagram for Paris in πόρτιν ἁρπάσας. Other characters in the *Alexandra* called wolves include Theseus (147), Achilles (246), the Greeks (329), the Dioscuri (504), Idas and Lynceus (524), Heracles (871), Ares (938), the Achaeans at Siris (990), Elephenor (1034), Tarchon and Tyrrhenus (1248), the Phoenicians (1293), the Argonauts (1309), and Alexander the Great (1444).

[39] See Gigante Lanzara 2000:204 and Mari 2009:433. Hornblower 2015:145 rationalizes away the paradox of the unwedded heifer by noting that Helen is not married currently to Paris. Tzetzes (Σ *ad* 102; Scheer 2:54), however, interprets ἄνυμφον to mean πολύανδρον ("with many husbands").

[40] These two daughters are Hermione and Iphigenia. While the *Odyssey* (4.12–14) lists Hermione as Helen's only daughter, Stesichorus (*PMGF* 191 Davies) and Euphorion (fr. 86 Lightfoot) made Iphigenia Helen's daughter by Theseus. See Pausanias 2.22.6–7. According to other sources, Helen had a son Nicostratus (*Catalogue of Women* fr. 175 M/W = Apollodorus *Library* 3.11.1).

[41] See Sistakou 2009a:242.

[42] For Helen abandoning her child, see Sappho fr. 16.10.

[43] Theseus kidnapped Helen when she was seven years old. The evidence for this story is Stesichorus *PMGF* 191 Davies, Hellanicus 4 F 134 *FGrHist* (= Σ *ad Iliad* 3.144), Hellanicus 4 F 168 *FGrHist* (= Plutarch *Life of Theseus* 31), Pherecydes *FGrHist* 3 F 153 (= Athenaeus 13.557a), and Duris *FGrHist* 76 F 92 (= Tzetzes Σ *ad* Lyc. 102; Scheer 2:54–55).

[44] Cusset 2002/2003:150. For other uses of ἄρκυς in tragedy, see Aeschylus *Agamemnon* 1116, *Libation Bearers* 1000, *Eumenides* 460, Euripides *Medea* 1278, and *Heracles* 729.

framing Helen here as a victim (ληῖτιν, 105). Yet, in addition to this passive meaning, ληῖτις in the *Iliad* means "dispensing loot," applied as an epithet to Athena (*Iliad* 10.460). We can retain this sense here if we see Helen's descent into the trap (ἐμπταίσασαν, 105) as a conscious action, brought about for her desire for Paris. Helen is not just the loot, but in fact dispenses herself.

At 108–114, Cassandra recounts the aftermath of the abduction, describing Paris and Helen's journey to an island off the coast of Attica, where the couple has sex:[45]

θρέξεις ὑπὲρ Σκάνδειαν Αἰγίλου τ' ἄκραν,
αἴθων ἐπακτὴρ καγχαλῶν ἀγρεύματι.
νήσῳ δ' ἐνὶ δράκοντος ἐκχέας πόθον
Ἀκτῆς, διμόρφου γηγενοῦς σκηπτουχίας,
τὴν δευτέραν ἔωλον οὐκ ὄψει Κύπριν,
ψυχρὸν παραγκάλισμα κἀξ ὀνειράτων
κεναῖς ἀφάσσων ὠλέναισι δέμνια.

You [Paris] will rush beyond Scandeia and the cape of Aegilon, a fiery hunter exulting in your prey, and after you pour out your desire on the island of the Dragon, Acte, realm of the two-formed earthborn, you will not see a second day of sex, as you touch with empty arms a cold embrace and your bed in your dreams.

Alexandra 108–114

The adjective δευτέραν ("second") in 112 echoes the word in 104, and both instances appear as the second word in their respective lines. Yet while the word at 104 stressed the frequency of Helen's victimization, δευτέραν, when applied to a periphrasis for sex (ἔωλον Κύπριν, 112), produces an ironic undermining of Paris' purpose for stealing Helen in the first place. Despite his initial jubilation at the capture (ἐπακτὴρ καγχαλῶν ἀγρεύματι, 109) and one night of ejaculation (ἐκχέας πόθον, 110), Paris will not enjoy a second day of sex, but instead will experience a cold embrace (ψυχρὸν παραγκάλισμα, 113) and touch his bed with empty arms (κεναῖς ἀφάσσων ὠλέναισι δέμνια, 114). The collocation of

[45] At *Iliad* 3.445, Homer records that Helen and Paris had sex on the island Cranae. Ancient scholars identified three separate locations for this island: Cythera (Σ *ad Iliad* 3.445), an island off Gytheum (Pausanias 3.22.1), or an island known as Helene off the coast of Attica (Strabo 9.1.22, Stephanus of Byzantium 381.6). As Sens 2009:22 notes, Lycophron rejects the first option by making Paris pass by Scandeia (the port of Cythera; Stephanus of Byzantium 573.18). Since Acte is an alternate name for Attica (Euripides *Helen* 1673 and Stephanus of Byzantium 64.6), and the "two-formed earthborn" is a periphrasis for Cecrops (Apollodorus *Library* 3.14.1), the early king of Athens, we can see Lycophron as favoring Helene as the location for Paris and Helen's sexual acts.

ψυχρόν and παραγκάλισμα is a direct allusion to *Antigone* 649–651, where Creon associates a bad woman with a cold embrace: εἰδὼς ὅτι / ψυχρὸν παραγκάλισμα τοῦτο γίγνεται / γυνὴ κακὴ ξύνευνος ἐν δόμοις ("knowing that this embrace becomes cold, an evil woman as a bedmate in the house").[46] The fact that ψυχρὸν παραγκάλισμα occupies the same *sedes* in both authors sharpens the allusion. However, while Creon in the *Antigone* is referring to an actual evil woman, albeit in a hypothetical situation, the ψυχρὸν παραγκάλισμα of the *Alexandra* is in dreams (κἀξ ὀνειράτων, 113) and thus does not exist. Cassandra highlights the insubstantiality of this παραγκάλισμα by noting Paris' empty arms (κεναῖς ... ὠλέναισι, 114).[47] Yet, in mentioning Paris' attempt to touch (ἀφάσσων, 114) this specter, Cassandra paradoxically attaches a sense of corporality to the παραγκάλισμα. Despite not being real, the nonexistent object of an embrace still possesses a quality that encourages Paris' attempt to caress. Helen, even as an image, can elicit Paris' longing.

In the subsequent lines (115–131), Cassandra clarifies that the god Proteus took away the "real" Helen. While Proteus played some role in the various versions of the Helen myth, Lycophron diverges by making Proteus take Helen after she and Paris have already had sex. According to the account ascribed to the Egyptian priests in Herodotus (2.115), Proteus detained Helen in Egypt, while in the *Helen* of Euripides, Hermes snatched Helen and deposited her for safekeeping by Proteus, also in Egypt (44–48).[48] In the *Alexandra*, Proteus appears as an agent of divine vengeance, seeking to deprive Paris of the object of his desire:

κεῖνός σε, Γουνεὺς ὥσπερ, ἐργάτης δίκης,
τῆς θ' Ἡλίου θυγατρὸς Ἰχναίας βραβεύς,
ἐπεσβολήσας λυγρὰ νοσφιεῖ γάμων,
λίπτοντα κάσσης ἐκβαλὼν πελειάδος.

That one, just like Goneus, a worker of justice and the arbiter of the Ichnaean daughter of the Sun, will rebuke you harshly and deprive you of your marriage, when he drives you, lustful, from your slut dove.

Alexandra 128–131

The juxtaposition of κάσσης ("slut") and πελειάδος ("dove") recalls the pairing of κυνός and τρήρωνος at 87, thus emphasizing again Helen's dual status as victim

---

[46] Fusillo, Hurst, and Paduano 1991:168 note this allusion.
[47] Cf. Euripides *Helen* 35–36: καὶ δοκεῖ μ' ἔχειν / κενὴν δόκησιν, οὐκ ἔχων ("and he thinks he holds me, an empty phantom, when he does not").
[48] As West 2009:83 observes, "Helen is just as guilty as she was in Homer and Herodotus."

and sexual deviant. Moreover, the coupling of the participle λίπτοντα ("lustful," 131) for Paris and κάσσης creates an equivocation between the attacker, Paris, and his prey, Helen, to suggest the two are equally lecherous. Consequently, unlike in Euripides' *Helen*, Helen being in Proteus' custody does not maintain her chastity, nor does it absolve her of blame.

After upbraiding Paris for his transgressions against justice (132–138), Cassandra returns to focusing on Helen as an εἴδωλον:

> τοιγὰρ ψαλάξεις εἰς κενὸν νευρᾶς κτύπον,
> ἄσιτα κἀδώρητα φορμίζων μέλη.
> κλαίων δὲ πάτραν τὴν πρὶν ἠθαλωμένην
> ἵξῃ χεροῖν εἴδωλον ἠγκαλισμένος
> τῆς πενταλέκτρου θυιάδος Πλευρωνίας.

> For this reason, you will pluck the noisy string of the bow in vain, playing songs that bring no food or gifts. Weeping, you will come to your fatherland that was burned before, embracing in your arms the phantom of the five-times-wed Pleuronian Maenad.

> *Alexandra* 139–143

The vocabulary in this section echoes the wording in 111–114: κενόν in 139 echoes κεναῖς in 114, and the participle ἠγκαλισμένος ("holding," 142) repeats παραγκάλισμα (113).[49] Moreover, just as Cassandra implies the paradox of Paris attempting to touch the fake Helen in his dreams at 113–114, so too does she here stress the irony of Paris holding an image in his arms (χεροῖν εἴδωλον, 142). By commenting on the futility of Paris' physical interaction with a phantom, Cassandra again signals the power of Helen's image to stimulate desire, as well as the ultimate fruitlessness of Paris' quest.[50] His acknowledgment of this fruitlessness results in playing songs that bring no benefit (ἄσιτα κἀδώρητα φορμίζων μέλη, 140) and weeping (κλαίων, 141). Yet, while useless as an object of Paris' sexual longing, the phantom Helen nevertheless will cause the destruction of Troy. Cassandra subtly alludes to this fact by referring to the previous razing of Troy by Heracles with πάτραν τὴν πρὶν ἠθαλωμένην ("your fatherland that was burned before," 141). Indeed, the coordination of the participles ἠθαλωμένην and ἠγκαλισμένος, two five-syllable words beginning with the same letter (eta) in the same position at the end of the line, further suggests this causal link between Paris' capture of Helen and the annihilation of Troy.

---

49   McNelis and Sens 2016:73.
50   The scholiast (Σ *ad* 139b; Leone 2002:31), citing the proverb ("you will strike the lyre strings in vain," εἰς κενὸν κρούσεις τὰς χορδάς) sees an innuendo about male genitalia.

Even though Cassandra treats Helen as an εἴδωλον, the description "five-times-wed Pleuronian Maenad" (τῆς πενταλέκτρου θυιάδος Πλευρωνίας, 143) leads into a digression cataloguing Helen's five "husbands," as ordained by the Fates (144–145). Cassandra's choice to list these husbands corresponds to the emphasis on Helen's serial monogamy, while also evoking the catalogue format of pseudo-Hesiod's *Catalogue of Women*.[51] Moreover, unlike in the other instances, where Cassandra portrays her as an object of desire or capture,[52] Helen is the subject of verbs. The Fates decree that she "see the two greedy wolves" (δοιὼ μὲν ἁρπακτῆρας αὐγάσαι λύκους, 147), Theseus and Paris, and "the half-Cretan barbarian, an Epeian, not pure Argive by birth" (ἡμικρῆτα βάρβαρον / Ἐπειόν, οὐκ Ἀργεῖον ἀκραιφνῆ γοναῖς, 150–151), Menelaus.[53] She will behold (ὄψεται, 168) "the brother of the down-swooping falcon" (αὐθόμαιμον ... / κίρκου καταρρακτῆρος, 168–169), Deiphobus.[54] By making Helen the subject of verbs, after referring to her εἴδωλον status in 142, Cassandra ironically implies that Helen assumes greater agency in this phantom form.

The catalogue culminates in a description of the effects of this form on husband number five:

> ἐν δὲ δεμνίοις
> τὸν ἐξ ὀνείρων πέμπτον ἐστροβημένον
> εἰδωλοπλάστῳ προσκαταξανεῖ ῥέθει,
> τὸν μελλόνυμφον εὐνέτην Κυταϊκῆς...

And the fifth, disturbed by dreams, she will make waste away with her phantom-shaped form in his bed, the intended groom of the Cytaean woman.

Alexandra 171–174

This fifth husband is Achilles, whose designation is based on his eventual marital status (τὸν μελλόνυμφον εὐνέτην) to the woman of Cyta (Κυταϊκῆς, 174), i.e. Medea.[55] Achilles' marriage to Helen, however, takes places in a dream, as

---

[51] See Hornblower 2015:11. The catalogue of Helen's suitors appears in *Catalogue of Women* fr. 204 M/W.

[52] Aside from the catalogue of her husbands, Helen (or Helen as phantom) appears in the following cases: genitive in 131, 143, 505, 850, and 851, dative in 513, and accusative in 87, 102, 113, and 822.

[53] A digression about Menelaus' ancestor Pelops spans 152–167.

[54] Helen marries Hector's brother Deiphobus after the death of Paris. See *Odyssey* 4.276 and *Little Iliad* (Proclus Arg. 2e West).

[55] Cyta is a city in Colchis (Stephanus of Byzantium 398.14). Achilles and Medea marry in the after-life. See Σ *ad* Apollonius of Rhodes *Argonautica* 4.810–815 (Ibycus fr. 291 *PMGF* Davies).

Cassandra signifies with ἐξ ὀνείρων ("by dreams," 172).[56] At the same time, the placement of ὀνείρων near δεμνίοις ("bed," 171) parallels the coordination of κἀξ ὀνειράτων in 113 and δέμνια in 114, where Cassandra refers to Paris' attempt to embrace Helen in dreams. Likewise, the compound adjective εἰδωλοπλάστῳ ("phantom-shaped," 173) looks back to the εἴδωλον grasped by Paris in 142.[57] The accumulation of these verbal parallels signals an analogy between Paris and Achilles.[58] As Helen's husbands, both men become enchanted by the powers of her phantom form. Yet for Achilles, Cassandra lays particular emphasis on the violence of this dreamtime intercourse with the verb προσκαταξανεῖ ("will make waste away," 173) and the participle ἐστροβημένον ("disturbed," 172), which typically refers to physical movement but is used metaphorically here for emotional turmoil.[59] Indeed, Cassandra conveys Achilles' agony at the semantic level by positioning ἐξ ὀνείρων between the definite article (τόν) and the substantive adjective πέμπτον ("fifth," 172). These dreams, both verbally and literally, are tearing Achilles apart. That Helen, as an εἴδωλον, can unravel Achilles, the greatest of Greek heroes, attests to the ultimate power of this beauty. To Cassandra, Achilles is not the best of the Achaeans, but simply another man (the fifth) affected by Helen.[60]

After this predominance in the earlier sections of the prophecy, Helen is mentioned only a few more times in the poem. For instance, when dealing with the Dioscuri's invasion of Attica to retrieve Helen after her first abduction by Theseus, Cassandra calls Helen "the seized Maenad" (τῆς ἁρπαγείσης ... θυιάδος, 505), echoing θυιάδος at 143. Moreover, while praying that the Dioscuri never set foot in Troy (512–516), Cassandra repeats the bird imagery by calling Helen a δισαρπάγῳ κρεκί ("twice-snatched corncrake," 513). While both names underline Helen's status as a victim (ἁρπαγείσης and δισαρπάγῳ), θυιάδος in particular indicates Helen's sexual promiscuity,[61] and κρεκί connotes her disastrousness for marriage, as the bird was considered a bad omen for marriages.[62]

---

[56] According to Proclus' summary (Arg. 11b West) in the *Cypria*, Achilles desired to look upon Helen. Pausanias 3.19.11–13 records a story told by the Crotonites about how Achilles and Helen cohabitated on Leuce, an island in the Black Sea.

[57] For the formation of this compounded adjective, see Guilleux 2009:230, who translates the word as "*façonné comme un simulacre.*"

[58] See McNelis and Sens 2016:106.

[59] Gigante Lanzara 2009:100 points out that this verb is related to στρόβιλος ("ball"). The noun στρόβιλος occurs at 89 (Helen's egg) and at 506, in a description of the Dioscuri's egg-shaped helmets.

[60] For a discussion of the unfavorable depiction of Achilles in the *Alexandra*, see Sistakou 2008:166, Durbec 2011c: 35–54, and McNelis and Sens 2016:101–130.

[61] As Mari 2009:434 observes, Helen's sacrifice to the Thysae at 106 anticipates this designation.

[62] For literary evidence concerning the corncrake's status as an omen of bad marriages, Tzetzes (Σ *ad* 513; Scheer 2.186) cites Euphorion (fr. 6 Lightfoot) and Callimachus (fr. 428 Pf.)

Cassandra thus again points to the inextricable link between Helen's repeated victimization and the creation of conflict. Indeed, the Dioscuri's attack on Attica to retrieve Helen presages the Greeks' expedition to Troy.[63]

In addition to making men fight, Helen spurs Menelaus to look for her even after the war ends. Cassandra launches Menelaus' νόστος by referring to Helen as the "fatally married, captured wife":[64]

> ὁ δ' αἰνόλεκτρον ἁρπαγεῖσαν εὐνέτης
> πλᾶτιν ματεύων, κληδόνων πεπυσμένος,
> ποθῶν δὲ φάσμα πτηνόν, εἰς αἴθραν φυγόν,
> ποίους θαλάσσης οὐκ ἐρευνήσει μυχούς;
> ποίαν δὲ χέρσον οὐκ ἀνιχνεύσει μολών;

> And the husband, searching for his fatally married, captured wife, after he has learned from rumors, longing for a winged phantom that fled into the air, what sort of recesses of the sea will he not search? What sort of land will he not come to and investigate?

> *Alexandra* 820–824

As Cassandra indicates with the participial clause εἰς αἴθραν φυγόν ("that fled into the air," 822), Helen's φάσμα πτηνόν ("winged phantom," 822) has vanished at the end of the Trojan War.[65] As a result, Menelaus must rely on rumors (κληδόνων, 821) to recover his wife. Such rumors propel him to probe everywhere in the sea (θαλάσσης οὐκ ἐρευνήσει μυχούς, 823) and on land (χέρσον, 824), and Cassandra anticipates the magnitude of this journey by including two rhetorical questions, both introduced by ποίους and ποίαν and negated (οὐκ ... οὐκ). Yet, in noting this extensive scouring, Cassandra implies the futility of Menelaus' searches at sea and on land. The phantom Helen, in fleeing into the air, exists in neither.

Cassandra strengthens this emphasis on the futility of Menelaus' quest by forming a parallel between Menelaus and Odysseus. We can see this parallel most clearly by the fact that the section dedicated to Menelaus' νόστος (820–876) immediately succeeds Odysseus' (648–819). Verbal echoes, moreover, tie together the two heroes. The rhetorical questions employed for Menelaus at

---

[63] As Prioux and Pouzadoux 2014 note, the ramifications of this attack are significantly less than the Trojan War.

[64] As Cusset 2002/2003:144 observes, αἰνόλεκτρος is an Aeschylean *hapax* used at Aeschylus *Agamemnon* 712 to describe Paris.

[65] For similar language, see Euripides *Helen* 605–606, when the servant announces to Menelaus that the phantom Helen has disappeared into the sky. For other intertexts between the *Helen* and the *Alexandra*, see Gigante Lanzara 2010:257–264.

823–824 recall those for Odysseus at 668–669 (ποία … ποία),[66] while the collocation of ἐρευνήσει ("he will seek") and μυχούς ("recesses") in 823 reappears in a description of Odysseus at 1244–1245, which refers to Odysseus' meeting with Aeneas: πλάναισι πάντ᾽ ἐρευνήσας μυχὸν / ἁλός τε καὶ γῆς ("in his wanderings searching each recess of sea and land").[67] Just as Cassandra's account emphasizes Odysseus' journeys in the west, so too does Menelaus, unlike in Homer, end up in Taras, Croton, Sicily, and Elba (852–876) after Egypt.[68] In constructing this link between Menelaus and Odysseus, Cassandra demonstrates how both men struggle in their great wanderings, ultimately because of the nonexistent woman Helen. Yet, whereas Odysseus' prolonged νόστος is only indirectly caused by Helen, Menelaus amplifies his own travails by continuing to search for her purposefully.

In framing Menelaus' travels as a quest for a woman, Cassandra evokes another parallel, Achilles, who wanders in the Black Sea region to look for Iphigenia:

ἣν ὁ ξύνευνος Σαλμυδησίας ἁλὸς
ἐντὸς ματεύων, Ἑλλάδος καρατόμον,
δαρὸν φαληριῶσαν οἰκήσει σπίλον
Κέλτρου πρὸς ἐκβολαῖσι λιμναίων ποτῶν,
ποθῶν δάμαρτα, τήν ποτ᾽ ἐν σφαγαῖς κεμὰς
λαιμὸν προθεῖσα φασγάνων ἒκ ῥύσεται.

Her husband will look for her, the decapitator of Greece, within the Salmydesian sea. For a long time, he will inhabit the white rock near the outpouring of the marshy waters of the Celtic river, longing for his wife, whom one day at the sacrifice a deer will save from the knife when it offers its throat.

Alexandra 186–191

Several verbal echoes connect this section with the Menelaus passage: the participles ματεύων ("searching," 187) and ποθῶν ("longing," 190) occupy the

---

[66] See also McNelis and Sens 2016:154.

[67] Hellanicus *FGrHist* 4 F 84 (in Dionysius of Halicarnassus *Roman Antiquities* 1.72.2) mentions Odysseus founding Rome with Aeneas. At 1244, Cassandra calls Odysseus a νάνος ("dwarf"), which not only plays on Odysseus' short stature (*Iliad* 3.193 and *Odyssey* 6.230), but also the name of the Etruscan name Nanas. Hellanicus *FGrHist* 4 F 4 describes Nanas as a wandering leader of Pelasgians. According to the scholiast (Σ *ad* 1244a; Leone 2002:228), νάνος means "wanderer." See Phillips 1953:61 for discussion of this name.

[68] In the *Odyssey* (4.83–85), Menelaus claims that his travels after Troy included Cyprus, Phoenicia, Egypt, Libya, and the lands of the Ethiopians, the Sidonians, and the Erembi.

same *sedes* as in 821 and 822, respectively, while ξύνευνος ("husband," 186) for Achilles looks forward to εὐνέτης in 820.[69] By labeling Menelaus and Achilles as "husbands," Cassandra underscores the importance of erotic desires in driving their exertions. Indeed, Sistakou views the lovesick Achilles in the *Alexandra* as the prototype for the Romantic lover.[70] Yet from Cassandra's point of view, Menelaus and Achilles not only fall short as traditional heroes by striving for women, but specifically ones that cause harm for the larger community. Like Helen, who is "fatally married," (αἰνόλεκτρον, 820), Iphigenia is harmful to Greeks, as Cassandra signifies with the phrase Ἑλλάδος καρατόμον ("decapitator of Greece," 187), a reference to Iphigenia sacrificing Greeks as a priestess among the Taurians.[71] At the same time, just as both the real and phantom Helen vanish, Iphigenia disappears, first at Aulis when replaced with a deer (κεμὰς / λαιμὸν προθεῖσα φασγάνων ἒκ ῥύσεται, 190–191) and then at Tauris, where she transforms into an old woman who cooks human flesh: καὶ τὴν ἄφαντον εἶδος ἠλλοιωμένην / γραῖαν ("she who has vanished, changed into an old woman," 195–196). Iphigenia, as Helen's daughter by Theseus (Stesichorus *PMGF* 191 Davies), has inherited her mother's ability to disappear but still make men seek her out.

While the parallels with Odysseus and Achilles implicitly speak to the futility of Menelaus' quest, Cassandra, after describing Menelaus' time in Egypt, makes this point explicit at 850–851: καὶ πάντα τλήσεθ' οὕνεκ' Αἰγύας κυνὸς / τῆς θηλύπαιδος καὶ τριάνορος κόρης ("and he will endure all these things for the sake of an Aegyan bitch, a mother of female children and a maiden with three husbands"). With these particular labels, Cassandra recapitulates the reoccurring themes of Helen's representation: shamelessness (κυνός, 850), the fact that she gave birth to daughters (θηλύπαιδος, 851),[72] and finally her serial monogamy (τριάνορος, 851), which the scholiast construes as "many husbands" as opposed

[69] Durbec 2011c:43 also discerns this parallel.
[70] Sistakou 2012:158–161.
[71] As the scholiast (Σ *ad* 187a; Leone 2002:40–41) points out, the word can have two meanings, depending on the accentuation. If accented on the penult, καρατόμον is active in sense and means "decapitator." However, accentuation on the antepenult gives the adjective a passive meaning: "she is who is decapitated." The word, as a result, would refer to Iphigenia being sacrificed at Aulis. See also Sistakou 2009a:244n18.
[72] Holford-Strevens 2000:608–609 proposes that the compound adjective θηλύπαις means "female-boy girl" and would obliquely refer to Helen being used as Theseus' beloved boy, i.e. sodomized. This meaning, while it would suit Cassandra's vitriolic tone, lacks corroboration elsewhere in the text. Nowhere does Cassandra specify the nature of the sexual intercourse between Helen and Theseus. She does, however, mention Helen's dove daughters at 103, and for this reason, I adopt the meaning of Hornblower 2015.

to three.[73] Nevertheless, whatever the exact meaning of the word, the juxtaposition of τριάνορος with κόρης can generate a paradox, if κόρης is translated as "maiden." How can Helen be both promiscuous and a maiden? At the same time, κόρης contrasts with the pejorative κυνός in the previous line, and Cassandra calls attention to this disjunction by coordinating both words at the end of the line. Thus, within the span of these two lines, Cassandra can encapsulate the paradoxes that suffuse Helen's being, not only in the *Alexandra*, but in the literary tradition. Helen simultaneously constitutes a shameless bitch, a passive victim, and a phantom that induces men to fight and die for her sake (οὕνεκ', 850).[74]

In exploring these multiple aspects of Helen, Cassandra is attempting to isolate Helen's true identity and thus the cause of the war. Endowed with a synoptic view of past, present, and future, Cassandra can synthesize these varying manifestations to isolate a single Helen, one that ultimately does not exist but through her nonexistence inflicts devastation. Destruction is the true essence of Helen, as befits her birth from an act of sexual violence. Helen's incessant kidnappings by men substantiate these innate qualities. Yet for what reason does Cassandra underscore Helen's status as a phantom, while still ascribing culpability to Helen herself? On the one hand, the εἴδωλον element embodies the utter futility of the Trojan War. The Greek and Trojans fight and die for nothing. While this explanation for the εἴδωλον corresponds to Cassandra's pervasive denigration of masculine efforts, another reason is possible, if we consider the similar experiences of Helen and Cassandra. Indeed, like Helen, Cassandra is simultaneously a victim and a source of destruction. After Locrian Ajax assaults Cassandra in the temple of Athena (357–364), many Greeks perish at sea and wander in retribution for this outrage (365–366). Similarly, Cassandra associates Helen with Bacchic madness (Θύσῃσιν, 106; θυιάδος, 143), a characteristic that the messenger perceives in her own discourse (βακχεῖον στόμα, 28).

Of course, we would not expect a Trojan princess to express solidarity with a Greek woman, especially the one responsible for her own pain. At the same time, whereas Helen's phantom is an irresistible attraction to men, Cassandra tries to shun them, adhering to her alternate name Alexandra.[75] Yet interpreting Helen as a nonexistent force of doom makes it easier to avoid compassion for a

---

[73] See Σ *ad* 851c (Leone 2002:169). With this interpretation, the scholiast is attempting to harmonize this section with the description of Helen as five times wed (143). However, one could also argue that Theseus and Achilles do not count as husbands (e.g. Hornblower 2015:327), since Theseus abducted her, while Achilles only saw her in a dream. Cf. Prioux and Pouzadoux 2014, who count only Theseus, Menelaus, and Paris as the three husbands. For Helen described as "having many husbands" (πολυάνωρ), see Aeschylus *Agamemnon* 62.

[74] See Bergren 2008b:26 [1983] for a discussion of Helen's ambivalent nature. See Zeitlin 2010:263–282 for a similar assessment, with a focus on Helen in Euripidean tragedy.

[75] See Prioux and Pouzadoux 2014.

fellow victim of sexual assault. By Cassandra's harsh assessment, Helen is not even human, much less worthy of empathy. Indeed, Cassandra further minimizes Helen's existence by offering no reference to a reunion with Menelaus or her fate after death.[76] Discounting a reference to her shoes (855),[77] after 850–851, Helen vanishes from the text, just like the phantom she truly is.

3. Odysseus

Along with Helen, Odysseus plays a significant role in Cassandra's prophecy, as his νόστος takes up a large portion of the poem (648–819). While the *Odyssey* depicts him as a wily and resourceful trickster beset by struggles, later representations, particularly those in tragedy, framed Odysseus as an immoral and villainous rogue.[78] Within Cassandra's anti-Greek version, such a depiction is expanded, and as McNelis and Sens have demonstrated, Cassandra systematically deflates the heroism of Odysseus' deeds in order to undermine the κλέος granted to him by the epic tradition.[79] Rather, in her rendition, Cassandra focuses on his constant falsity, his passivity in his suffering, and the futility of his wanderings. By this, I argue, Cassandra not only challenges the epic tradition of Homer, but interrogates Odysseus' authority in assessing his own personal experiences. For her, Odysseus' lies do not attest to his skillful manipulation of language, but instead point to his inability to construe reality and be a source for his lived experiences. His natural propensity for falsity precludes any possibility for an accurate rendering, as does the multitude of his woes, which in many cases his deception causes and multiplies.

Before the section devoted to his νόστος, Odysseus is mentioned in relation to other characters. For instance, Cassandra dubs Sinon "the cousin of the wily Sisyphean fox" (τῆς Σισυφείας δ᾽ ἀγκύλης λαμπούριδος / ... αὐτανέψιος, 344–345), that is, the cousin of Odysseus. By pairing the adjective ἀγκύλης ("wily"), which connotes deception, with λαμπούριδος ("fox"), an animal known for its craftiness,[80] Cassandra emphasizes Odysseus' trickery. At the same time,

---

[76] For instance, in the *Odyssey* (4.561–569), Proteus informs Menelaus that he will live forever in the Elysian Fields. Cf. Euripides *Helen* 1667, where Castor tells Helen she will be called a "goddess." See Clader 1976:63–80.

[77] Menelaus dedicates Helen's shoes to Athena when arriving among the Iapygians in southern Italy.

[78] For an overview of these negative tragic depictions, see Stanford 1963:102–117. Particularly negative portrayals can be observed in Sophocles' *Philoctetes* and Euripides' *Hecuba*.

[79] McNelis and Sens 2016:129–154. See Pindar *Nemean* 7.20–23 for the thought that Homer was responsible for an exaggerated portrayal of Odysseus' sufferings.

[80] A λάμπουρις is a type of fox with a white tail (Σ *ad* 344c; Leone 2002:68). As Del Ponte 1981:116 observes, there is a verbal play with λάμπουρις and λάμψῃ in 345.

the choice to make Odysseus the son of the ultimate trickster, Sisyphus, rather than Laertes, suggests that this deception is an inherited trait.[81] Additionally, Odysseus' cousin Sinon shares this characteristic, as both figures employ trickery to achieve the destruction of Troy. According to the Cyclic tradition, Odysseus steals the Palladium, while Sinon signals for the Greeks to attack (344).[82]

Odysseus' deception, moreover, is referred to in another cameo appearance, when Cassandra calls the Cretan Idomeneus "the brother of Aethon in the fictitious writings" (Αἴθωνος αὐτάδελφον ἐν πλασταῖς γραφαῖς, 432). We can identify Odysseus as Aethon based on *Odyssey* 19, where Odysseus adopts this Cretan persona when concealing his identity to Penelope:

Δευκαλίων δ' ἐμὲ τίκτε καὶ Ἰδομενῆα ἄνακτα
ἀλλ' ὁ μὲν ἐν νήεσσι κορωνίσιν Ἴλιον εἴσω
ᾤχεθ' ἅμ' Ἀτρεΐδησιν· ἐμοὶ δ' ὄνομα κλυτὸν Αἴθων,
ὁπλότερος γενεῇ· ὁ δ' ἅμα πρότερος καὶ ἀρείων.
ἔνθ' Ὀδυσῆα ἐγὼν ἰδόμην καὶ ξείνια δῶκα.

Deucalion begat me and lord Idomeneus. But he went to Troy with the Atreids on his curved ships. My famed name is Aethon. I am younger by birth. He is both older and better. There I saw Odysseus and gave him guest gifts.

Odyssey 19.181–185

As with Odysseus' other Cretan lies (*Odyssey* 13.256–286 and 14.191–359), this fib serves to mask his identity.[83] With ἰδόμην ("I saw," 19.185), the Aethon persona cites autopsy and personal experience as the basis for his knowledge of Odysseus. To bolster the believability of the Aethon identity, Odysseus employs the Cretan Idomeneus as a frame of reference. In the *Alexandra*, on the other hand, Cassandra subverts the strategy, using the name Aethon to define Idomeneus and thus co-opting Odysseus' falsehood for her own purposes. By reframing Odysseus' lie, she deprives him of the agency he had in telling it. As Homer remarks at 19.203–209, such a lie seamlessly mixed truth and falsehood, causing Penelope to weep. Cassandra, however, can see past Odysseus' lies, as she indicates with the phrase ἐν πλασταῖς γραφαῖς ("in the fictitious writings," 432). This expression, as Hurst and Kolde observe, can refer both to the written

[81] The scholiast (Σ *ad* 344a; Leone 2002:68) clarifies that Anticlea (Odysseus' mother) slept with Sisyphus. Odysseus is Sinon's cousin because Anticlea is the sister of Aesimus, the father of Sinon. See also *Alexandra* 1030.
[82] For Sinon raising the signal, see Proclus' summary of the *Iliou Persis* (Proclus Arg. 2a West) and *Little Iliad* F 12 West (= Apollodorus *Epitome* 5.14–15).
[83] For an overview of Odysseus' Cretan lies, see Haft 1984:289–306.

text of the *Odyssey* as well as Odysseus' falsehoods within said text.[84] By pointing to the fictitious status of the work that records Odysseus' experiences, Cassandra calls into question the validity of all the utterances made by Odysseus, not just those explicitly marked as lies. As a result, while Cassandra's version does draw from the Homeric model for her treatment of Odysseus' wanderings, the entire Homeric account is subject to interrogation.

In the *Odyssey*, Odysseus' first-person account of his sufferings spans books 9–12, and while the Homeric poet does not explicitly comment on the truth and falsehood of this section, Odysseus' perpetual mendacity does raise suspicions of distortion (see chapter 1.1.3.2). [85] For Lycophron's Cassandra, however, there is no doubt concerning the falsity of Odysseus' version, and her reinterpretation goes to great lengths to recast Odysseus' experiences. The beginning of her version does so by placing more emphasis on his deceased comrades:

> τοὺς δ᾽ ἀμφὶ Σύρτιν καὶ Λιβυστικὰς πλάκας
> στενήν τε πορθμοῦ συνδρομὴν Τυρσηνικοῦ
> καὶ μιξόθηρος ναυτιλοφθόρους σκοπάς,
> τῆς πρὶν θανούσης ἐκ χερῶν Μηκιστέως
> τοῦ στερφοπέπλου Σκαπανέως Βοαγίδα,
> ἁρπυιογούνων κλώμακάς τ᾽ ἀηδόνων
> πλαγχθέντας, ὠμόσιτα δαιταλωμένους,
> πρόπαντας Ἅιδης πανδοκεὺς ἀγρεύσεται,
> λώβαισι παντοίαισιν ἐσπαραγμένους,
> ἕνα φθαρέντων ἄγγελον λιπὼν φίλων,
> δελφινόσημον κλῶπα Φοινίκης θεᾶς.

> Others will wander around Syrtis, the Libyan plains, the narrow convergence of the Tyrrhenian Strait, and the ship-destroying lookout places of the hybrid [Scylla] who previously died by the hands of Mecisteus,

---

84 Hurst and Kolde 2008:163. Tzetzes *ad* 432. (Scheer 2.159) deems γραφαῖς nonsense on the grounds that Odysseus did not write his account. See also Sens 2010:306 for a discussion of Cassandra attacking Odysseus' narrative authority.
85 See *Odyssey* 13.291–295, where Athena observes Odysseus' incessant trickery. As Richardson 1996:396 points out, since Homer does not go over this point in Odysseus' life, for the most part we cannot know what is the truth or a fabrication in 9–12. Pucci 1998b:143 notes that the Homeric narrator does reaffirm the contents of Odysseus' tale in a few places, such as at 1.68–71 (Zeus' reference to Polyphemus) and at 2.17–20 (a mention of the Cyclops eating the son of the Ithacan Aegyptius). In considering the effect of Odysseus' Phaeacian narrative, Goldhill 1991:55–56 states, "To recognize a possibility of uncertainty about the boundaries between truth and fiction in Odysseus' narrative (especially with regard to the importance of this narrative for understanding *nostos* and 'a/the man') is to recognize in Odyssean (*polumetis*) language an essential duplicitousness."

the hide-wearing Spademan, Cattle-Driver [Heracles], and the rocks of the harpy-legged nightingales [Sirens]. When they are eaten raw, the innkeeper Hades will take them all, as they are rent by all sorts of injuries. He will leave behind one [Odysseus], a messenger of his deceased friends, he of the dolphin sign, thief of the Phoenician goddess [Athena].

Alexandra 648–658

Over the course of nine lines (648–656), Cassandra condenses the adventures of Odysseus and his men, stressing the geographic extent and the various monsters faced. Before their reception by the inn-keeper Hades (655), i.e., dying, the crew encounters the Syrtes, Libya (648), and the Strait of Messina (649), and the dwellings of Scylla (650) and the Sirens (653). In all this, only Odysseus remains (657). As commentators have noted, the participle πλαγχθέντας ("wandering," 654) produces an allusion to πλάγχθη (*Odyssey* 1.2) in the *Odyssey* proem.[86] Yet whereas the *Odyssey* begins with Odysseus as a "man" (ἄνδρα, *Odyssey* 1.1), Cassandra focuses first on his comrades as a collective and delays mentioning him until 657 with ἕνα φθαρέντων ἄγγελον λιπὼν φίλων ("one, a messenger of his deceased friends").[87] By labeling Odysseus as a messenger (ἄγγελον, 657), Cassandra signifies his role in recounting his experiences wandering. The choice to introduce him as the messenger of his deceased friends, however, takes away Odysseus' individuality, instead framing him as the member of a group whom Hades happened to spare from death. Odysseus is not an active agent in his own experiences, but rather a passive reporter.

While the designation "messenger" is vague, Cassandra in the subsequent line gives hints that point to Odysseus' identity with δελφινόσημον and κλῶπα (658). The adjective δελφινόσημον refers to the dolphin sign he carried on his shield,[88] and κλῶπα Φοινίκης θεᾶς alludes to his theft of the Palladium, the statue of Athena upon which the safety of Troy depended.[89] Since neither of these stories comes from the Homeric tradition, the pairing of these monikers reflects a conscious blending of sources. Instead of characterizing Odysseus as πολύτροπον ("much-turning," *Odyssey* 1.1), an ambivalent adjective that

---

[86] For instance, see Hurst and Kolde 2008:193 and McNelis and Sens 2016:135.

[87] Hurst 2012a:101.

[88] According to the scholiast, the sources for this story are Stesichorus (225 *PMGF* Davies) and Euphorion (fr. 87 Lightfoot). Odysseus chose this animal as a sign because a dolphin saved the baby Telemachus from drowning (Plutarch *On the Intelligence of Animals* 985b–c).

[89] In the *Little Iliad* (Proclus Arg. 4e F 11 West), Diomedes and Odysseus steal the Palladium. In the *Iliou Persis* (F 4 West = Dionysius of Halicarnassus *Roman Antiquities* 1.69.3), however, a fake version is stolen.

embodies his versatility,[90] Cassandra associates him with a sign, which Cusset interprets as reflecting the link between Odysseus and representation.[91] Indeed, the *Odyssey* portrays Odysseus as acutely concerned with his self-representation, especially when he disguises his identity or when recounting his adventures. The phrase κλῶπα Φοινίκης θεᾶς, however, casts Odysseus' deceptive skills in a distinctly negative light. Not only does the word signify the theft that enables the destruction of Troy, through a verbal play, κλῶπα, also anticipates the Cyclops, whose blinding occurs because of Odysseus' deception.[92] At the same time, the decision to call Athena the Phoenician, an epiclesis for her among the Corinthians according to the scholiast, evokes the deceitful Phoenician who figured in Odysseus' lie to Eumaeus at *Odyssey* 14.288.[93] As a result, with κλῶπα Φοινίκης θεᾶς, Cassandra expresses Odysseus' falsity in a variety of respects, suggesting both his deceitful actions and his lying words. Moreover, by coordinating ἄγγελον and κλῶπα, Cassandra implies that Odysseus' status as messenger is marked by deceit.

In the subsequent lines, Cassandra summarizes Odysseus' adventures at sea. Although covering many of the incidents included in the *Odyssey*, her account does not follow the same order,[94] and for some episodes, such as the Sirens and Scylla, she refers to them multiple times. The result is a broad, impressionistic sweep that underscores the constancy of Odysseus' toils.[95] As recorded in Cassandra's version, Odysseus experiences the Cyclops (659–661), Laestrygonians (662–665), Charybdis (668), Scylla (669), the Sirens (670–672), Circe (673–680), the Underworld (681–687), Pithecusae (688–693), Campania (694–711), the Sirens again (712–737), the winds of Aeolus (738–741), Charybdis (742–743), Calypso (744), and being tossed at sea on his raft (745–761) (see Table 2 for comparison). Within this whirlwind catalogue of so many struggles, Odysseus' role is minimized. Cassandra frames his involvement in terms

---

[90] See Pucci 1998a:23–27 for a discussion of the meaning of πολύτροπος. In addition to the meanings "of many journeys" or "many turns of the minds," Pucci proposes the notion of "many turns of speech."

[91] Cusset 2007:207.

[92] Cusset 2007:207.

[93] Σ *ad* 658b; Leone 2002:133. See Hornblower 2015:277.

[94] See Schade 1999:55–56 for a comparison of the ordering in the Homeric account and the version in the *Alexandra*. Hurst 2012a:103–109 [2002] also provides an overview of Lycophron's engagement with the *Odyssey*, listing agreements, contradictions, and innovations. See Tzetzes *ad.* 740 (Scheer 2.238) for the complaint about the disjointed order of Lycophron's version. In Euripides *Trojan Women* (431–443), Cassandra gives an overview of Odysseus' journeys.

[95] Gigante Lanzara 1997:45 observes, "Sulla base di un itinerario in parte diverso da quello omerico il racconto procede con ritmo sussultorio, avviluppato in se stesso come un spirale, toccando più volte gli stessi temi: duo volte Scilla, tre volte le Sirene, mentre l'esposizione diacronica ricorre solo saltuariamente nelle digressioni."

of seeing (ὄψεται, 659; ἐπόψεται, 662 and 673) and suffering (ταλάσσει, 746). Instead of achieving great deeds in his wanderings with his craftiness, Odysseus remains passive, wretched (τάλας, 746) and buffeted by the incessant stream of monsters and storms.

Finally, after being saved by Ino (757–758), Odysseus will arrive among the Phaeacians:

> νῆσον δ᾽ εἰς Κρόνῳ στυγουμένην
> Ἄρπην περάσας, μεζέων κρεανόμον,
> ἄχλαινος ἵκτης πημάτων λυγρῶν κόπις,
> τὸν μυθοπλάστην ἐξυλακτήσει γόον,
> ἀρὰς τετικὼς τοῦ τυφλωθέντος δάκους.

He will come to the island hated by Cronus, the Sickle, cutter of genitals. As a suppliant without a cloak and a babbler of his painful woes, he will bark out a groan that produces tales, after he has paid for the curses of the blinded monster.

Alexandra 761–765

Indicating Scherie (also Drepane, see chapter 3.2), the home of the Phaeacians, as the Sickle island hated by Cronus (εἰς Κρόνῳ στυγουμένην, 761),[96] Cassandra concentrates on Odysseus' degraded state when arriving on the island. He is a "suppliant without a cloak" (ἄχλαινος ἵκτης, 763) and a "babbler of his painful woes" (πημάτων λυγρῶν κόπις, 763). As commentators have noted, the noun κόπις appears in Euripides' *Hecuba* in a description of Odysseus as an evil smooth talker (132).[97] The word, if related to the verb κόπτω ("cut"), as the scholiast and Tzetzes suggest, not only carries the sense of deception, but specifically that of "logic-chopping."[98] Odysseus, by botching the logic of his own painful experiences, shows an inability to express them accurately. Rather, Odysseus "will bark out a groan that produces tales" (τὸν μυθοπλάστην ἐξυλακτήσει γόον, 764).[99] With the compound adjective μυθοπλάστην, which looks back to πλασταῖς at 432, Cassandra calls attention to the fabricated status of Odysseus' utterances among the Phaeacians.[100] Yet by coupling it with the noun γόον, Cassandra

---

[96] According to Timaeus (*FGrHist* 566 F 79 from Σ *ad* Apollonius Rhodes *Argonautica* 4.982), Zeus cut off Cronus' genitals, and the sickle ended up beneath Scherie/Drepane/Corcyra.

[97] Schade 1999:167 and Gigante Lanzara 2009:112.

[98] Σ *ad* 763 (Leone 2002:154).

[99] Ciani 1975:196.

[100] West 1983:116 sees a contradiction in Cassandra calling Odysseus' Phaeacian tales false, since Cassandra also includes much of this same information. For this reason, West suggests transposing 763–764 to follow 788 (μόνος πρὸς οἴκους ναυτίλων σωθεὶς τάλας), where Cassandra

implies the incomprehensibility of such an expression, which she likens to that of an animal with the verb ἐξυλακτήσει ("will bark out"). Instead of crafting a speech that induces the Phaeacians' wonder and amazement (*Odyssey* 13.1–2), Odysseus in this version speaks in a way that signals his degraded and animalistic state.[101] As Cassandra implies by immediately referring to Polyphemus' curses in 765 (ἀρὰς ... τοῦ τυφλωθέντος δάκους), Odysseus' experience of this condition is a consequence of blinding the Cyclops. By attacking the monster, Odysseus has become like him: a desperate animal.

Cassandra's humiliation of Odysseus continues even during his return to Ithaca (768–771). She heightens his suffering by portraying Penelope as a wasteful harlot (771–773), a sharp contrast from the faithful and prudent Penelope of Homer.[102] Since returning to a stable household and wife was Odysseus' goal in his νόστος, the depiction of the house as depleted by Penelope renders such exertions futile. Cassandra, in fact, notes that Odysseus undergoes more misery at home than at Troy:

αὐτὸς δὲ πλείω τῶν ἐπὶ Σκαιαῖς πόνους
ἰδὼν μολοβρὸς τλήσεται μὲν οἰκετῶν
στυγνὰς ἀπειλὰς εὐλόφῳ νώτῳ φέρειν
δέννοις κολασθείς. τλήσεται δὲ καὶ χερῶν
πληγαῖς ὑπείκειν καὶ βολαῖσιν ὀστράκων.

After he has seen more struggles than at the Scaean Gates, he, a greedy knave, will endure bearing the hateful threats of the slaves on his patient back, castigated by rebukes. He will endure submitting to blows of the fists and thrown pottery shards.

Alexandra 774–778

In this case, Odysseus' suffering happens because he has assumed the outward appearance of a beggar with Athena's help (*Odyssey* 13.397–403), as Cassandra indicates obliquely with μολοβρός ("greedy knave," 775). This word appears in

---

deals with Odysseus' return home. As a result, τὸν μυθοπλάστην ... γόον would refer to the lies Odysseus tells on Ithaca, and ἄχλαινος would allude to the tale that Odysseus spins to acquire a cloak from Eumaeus at 14.462–506. For a rejection of this transposition, see Schade 1999:166, who follows Holzinger 1895:282–283 in seeing γόον as referencing Odysseus' groan among the Phaeacians after listening to Demodocus (*Odyssey* 8.540). Hornblower 2015:308, however, suggests that the phrase τὸν μυθοπλάστην ... γόον represents Odysseus' Phaeacian tales in general.

[101] Gigante Lanzara 2000:329.

[102] For evidence for Penelope's promiscuity, the scholiast (Σ *ad* 772e; Leone 2002:155) cites Duris of Samos (*FGrHist* 76 F 21). In the *Odyssey*, Penelope is described as πινυτή (11.445), περίφρων (11.446), and ἐχέφρων (13.406, 16.130, etc.).

the *Odyssey* twice, both times when other disreputable characters (Melanthius, 17.219; the beggar Irus, 18.26) insult the disguised Odysseus.[103] By repeating this word, Cassandra lends validity to their perceptions. For her, Odysseus, although not truly a beggar, has become so well assimilated with this lowly persona that he brings about sufferings for himself that exceed those experienced in the Trojan War. Indeed, unlike at Troy, at home in Ithaca he is constantly bombarded by physical attacks, not with weapons by other warriors, but with mundane household items.[104] The repetition of the τλήσεται ("he will endure") in 775 and 777 reflects the constancy of such attacks.

This reference to Odysseus' abasement at Ithaca causes Cassandra to recall another instance of his willingness to be tormented:

οὐ γὰρ ξέναι μάστιγες, ἀλλὰ δαψιλὴς
σφραγὶς μενεῖ Θόαντος ἐν πλευραῖς ἔτι,
λύγοισι τετρανθεῖσα, τὰς ὁ λυμεὼν
ἐπεγκολάπτειν ἀστένακτος αἰνέσει,
ἑκουσίαν σμώδιγγα προσμάσσων δομῇ,
ὅπως παλεύσῃ δυσμενεῖς, κατασκόποις
λώβαισι καὶ κλαυθμοῖσι φηλώσας πρόμον.

For whips will not be foreign to him, but the broad seal of Thoas will still remain on his side, incised with switches. Without a groan, the destroyer will allow these wounds to be engraved, as he takes a voluntary welt on his body, so that he can overthrow his enemies, tricking our leader with the wounds of a spy and tears.

Alexandra 779–785

For this incident, the scholiast supplies further context. Wishing to enter Troy as a spy, Odysseus allows Thoas to whip him until the point of being unrecognized.[105] While indicating Odysseus' willingness with ἀστένακτος αἰνέσει ("will allow without a groan," 782) and ἑκουσίαν ("willing," 783), Cassandra stresses the brutality of this beating by remarking that a seal (σφραγίς, 780), the mark of the beating, will remain. Such a σφραγίς not only symbolizes Odysseus' submission to Thoas' violence, but Odysseus' ulterior motive, that is, deceiving Priam (πρόμον, 785) and the Trojans. In causing himself brutal damage, Odysseus

---

[103] See Rengakos 1994b:124 for a discussion of this word's meaning.

[104] In the *Odyssey*, Odysseus has a footstool (17.462) and a cow hoof (20.299) hurled at him. In the *Bone Gatherers* of Aeschylus (fr. 180 Radt), a chamber pot is flung at him.

[105] Σ *ad* 780 (Leone 2002:156). This episode occurred in the *Little Iliad* (Proclus Arg. 4b West). See West 2013:195–197 for discussion. At *Odyssey* 4.244–250, Helen recounts how Odysseus snuck into Troy in disguise.

ultimately seeks to harm the Trojans (ὅπως παλεύσῃ δυσμενεῖς, 784), using the outward manifestation of his pain and his weeping as a part of this deception. Indeed, Cassandra personifies the wounds by labeling them "spies" (κατασκόποις, 784).[106] Thus, as in her description of Ithaca earlier, Cassandra envisions Odysseus' suffering as connected to his falsehood. In doing so, she calls into question the veracity of all of Odysseus' claimed experiences. For a person willing to employ weeping as a means of trickery, how could one trust any expression of his woe and pain?

After this allusion to Odysseus' trickery at Troy, Cassandra offers a recapitulation of Odysseus' birth, wanderings, return home, and finally death:

> ὃν Βομβυλείας κλιτὺς ἡ Τεμμικία
> ὕψιστον ἡμῖν πῆμ' ἐτέκνωσέν ποτε,
> μόνος πρὸς οἴκους ναυτίλων σωθεὶς τάλας.
> λοῖσθον δὲ καύηξ ὥστε κυμάτων δρομεὺς
> ὡς κόγχος ἅλμῃ πάντοθεν περιτριβεὶς
> κτῆσίν τε θοίναις Πρωνίων λαφυστίαν
> πρὸς τῆς Λακαίνης αἰνοβακχεύτου κιχὼν
> σῦφαρ θανεῖται, πόντιον φυγὼν σκέπας,
> κόραξ σὺν ὅπλοις Νηρίτων δρυμῶν πέλας.
> κτενεῖ δὲ τύψας πλευρὰ λοίγιος στόνυξ
> κέντρῳ δυσαλθὴς ἔλλοπος Σαρδωνικῆς.
> κέλωρ δὲ πατρὸς ἄρταμος κληθήσεται.

He, whom the Temmician hill of Bombyleia [Athena] once bore as the greatest pain for us, wretched and the only one of the sailors will come safely home. At last, like a sea swallow running in the waves or a shell worn down on all sides by the sea, he will come upon his property devoured in the feasts of the Pronians because of the dread Bacchic Laconian woman. He will die, although he fled the refuge of the sea, a wrinkled armed crow near the oaks of Neriton. Striking his sides, a spear-point, deadly and incurable with the barb of the Sardonian fish will kill him, and the son will be called the butcher of his father.

Alexandra 786–797

Beginning with Odysseus' birth (ἐτέκνωσέν ποτε, 787) and culminating in his death (θανεῖται, 793), Cassandra characterizes Odysseus' life as one of decay. Though a source of misery for the Trojans (ὕψιστον ἡμῖν πῆμα, 787), Odysseus

---

[106] See Hornblower 2015:311.

causes agony for himself, as Cassandra signifies with the adjective τάλας ("wretched," 788), which picks up τλήσεται at 775 and 777 and τλήμονος at 773. At the same time, the comparison to a shell worn down by the sea in 790 accentuates Odysseus' degradation and loss of humanity. Just as the feasts of the suitors and Penelope have depleted his property at home (791–792), so too has his identity been eroded at sea. However, while the *Odyssey* features Odysseus regaining both his property and identity by murdering the suitors and reuniting with Penelope and his father Laertes, Cassandra denies Odysseus this reintegration into society, instead focusing on his death in 794–800 and 805–807.[107] Unlike the gentle demise predicted by Tiresias in the *Odyssey* (11.134–137), Odysseus perishes when his son by Circe, Telegonus, stabs him with the barb of a stingray (795–797).[108] Not only does this death constitute a shameful end for Odysseus, but it is caused by Telegonus' inability to recognize him. Odysseus' old age has rendered him a wrinkled crow (σῦφαρ ... / κόραξ, 793–794), unrecognizable to even his son.

After elaborating on the aftermath of Odysseus' death (799–811),[109] Cassandra concludes this portion devoted to Odysseus with a final assessment of his experiences:

χὼ μὲν τοσούτων θῖνα πημάτων ἰδὼν
ἄστρεπτον Ἅιδην δύσεται τὸ δεύτερον,
γαληνὸν ἦμαρ οὔποτ' ἐν ζωῇ δρακών.

And he who has seen a heap of so many struggles, for a second time will sink down to Hades, from whence there is no return, after he has never in his life beheld a peaceful day.

Alexandra 812–814

Cassandra conceptualizes Odysseus' sufferings (πημάτων, 812) as a metaphorical heap (θῖνα, 812), recalling this word's use in Homer's *Odyssey* (12.45) and Aeschylus' *Persians* (818) to refer to the countless piles of corpses in the sea. By stressing the constancy and multitude of these struggles, Cassandra suggests the impossibility of Odysseus describing them all accurately. Indeed, when he has never seen a peaceful day in his life (814), how could he distinguish between all the terrible ones? Which experiences are truly awful, and are they simply

---

[107] See McNelis and Sens 2016:149–150.

[108] This version (Arg. 3 F5 West; F5 West) is derived from the *Telegony* of Eugammon of Cyrene (sixth century BCE).

[109] For instance, at 805–806, Odysseus' body ends up in Etruria, near the mountain of Perge. See Malkin 1998:174.

embellished by his account? At the same time, how many of these woes were the result of his deception, such as the beatings he endured willingly at Troy and Ithaca while disguised?

Since falsehood is so tied up with Odysseus' experiences, Cassandra determines, with bitter irony, that it would have been better for him to remain in Ithaca while assuming the guise of a mad person:

> ὦ σχέτλι᾽, ὥς σοι κρεῖσσον ἦν μίμνειν πάτρᾳ
> βοηλατοῦντα καὶ τὸν ἐργάτην μύκλον
> κάνθων᾽ ὑπὸ ζεύγλαισι μεσσαβοῦν ἔτι
> πλασταῖσι λύσσης μηχαναῖς οἰστρημένον
> ἢ τηλικῶνδε πεῖραν ὀτλῆσαι κακῶν.

> O miserable one, how it would have been better for you to remain in your fatherland, as you were driving oxen, and to attach the lusty working donkey beneath the yoke, while still goaded by the fabricated devices of madness, than to have endured a test of such great evils.

Alexandra 815–819

According to the scholiast, Odysseus attempts to evade the Trojan War by pretending to be mad and yoke asses.[110] Palamedes exposes this ruse by dropping the baby Telemachus in the way of the plow, forcing Odysseus to abandon the ruse and save his son. For Cassandra, however, this feigned experience of madness is ultimately less deleterious than Odysseus' decision to go to war in Troy and practice his deception there. Odysseus in Troy will not only provoke the annihilation of the city, but also suffering for himself and the death of all his comrades. By staying in Ithaca, on the other hand, only Telemachus dies, while Odysseus is engaged in the useless task of driving donkeys. By framing such a futile task as preferable to a life of war and adventure, Cassandra offers the ultimate repudiation of the heroic experience, which, as McNelis and Sens have observed, echoes Achilles' denigration of the heroic life in the *Odyssey* (11.489–491).[111] At the same time, in revealing the futility of Odysseus' exertions, Cassandra demonstrates her superior understanding of causation, specifically the effect of Odysseus' innate deception. Since, as she has shown, such falsehood inevitably leads to suffering, Cassandra bitterly proposes an option that minimizes such pain, both for him and more importantly for Troy.

---

[110] Σ *ad* 815a (Leone 2002:163). See *Cypria* Arg. 5b West (= Apollodorus *Epitome* 3.7) for a similar version. Sophocles' *Odysseus Gone Mad* covered this incident.

[111] See McNelis and Sens 2016:153.

By touching upon Odysseus' phony madness, Cassandra invites a comparison between Odysseus and her experiences. Indeed, her frenzied speech leads others, such as the messenger, to perceive her as mad.[112] In fact, just as she associates animalistic utterances with herself: βαΰζω (1453), so too does she attribute barking to Odysseus (ἐξυλακτήσει, 764). Furthermore, as Cusset observes, both receive veneration after death: Cassandra in Daunia (1126–1140) and Odysseus as a seer among the Eurytanians (799).[113] Finally, both Cassandra and Odysseus suffer because of Helen. Just as Odysseus loses his property and identity after the war, Cassandra has her virginity robbed by Locrian Ajax. However, while Cassandra possesses knowledge about her and others' future woes, Odysseus, with his limited human knowledge, can be a source only for his past experiences.[114] Yet, as Cassandra's hostile representation has stressed, Odysseus fails even in that respect. His natural propensity for falsehood results in more anguish for himself and others, and in turn this multitude of pains has divested Odysseus of his ability to report accurately. Cassandra, in challenging the Homeric account, is not necessarily arguing against *what* happened during Odysseus' journeys, but rather *how* it happened, that is, the correct interpretation of Odysseus' actions in each event. For her, crafty heroism has dissolved into pure knavery. Moreover, by calling Odysseus a κόπις (763), the same word the messenger uses when comparing her to the Sibyl (Μελαγκραίρας κόπις, 1464),[115] Cassandra reveals that Odysseus truly is what others mistakenly perceive her to be: an unreliable babbler.

4. Sirens

Just as Cassandra's recasting of the *Odyssey* takes up a large portion of the prophecy (648–819), so too does the description of the Sirens' death at 712–737 feature predominantly in the *Odyssey* section.[116] In fact, as observed by Hurst and Kolde's analysis of the poem's structure, the Siren section occupies the

---

[112] See *Alexandra* 28, where the messenger refers to her "Bacchic mouth" (βακχεῖον στόμα). See Looijenga 2009:69.

[113] Cusset 2009:137. The scholiast cites Aristotle's *Constitution of the Ithacans* (fr. 508 Rose) as evidence for an oracular cult for Odysseus among the Eurytanians, a tribe of Aetolians.

[114] See Pillinger 2019:133.

[115] Μελαγκραίρα is another name for the Sibyl of Cumae (pseudo-Aristotle *On Marvelous Things Heard* 95). For an analysis of the parallels between Cassandra and the Cumaean Sibyl, see Cusset 2004:53–60 and Pillinger 2019:139–141.

[116] West 1984:140–141 targets the Siren section as an interpolation based on the assumption that the Italian place names are too obscure for Lycophron or his readers to know. As a result, she posits that this passage was added later to appeal to an Italian audience. The weakness of her argument lies in the fact that these passages, metrically and stylistically, do not differ from the rest of the poem. On this point, see Schade 1999:9.

very center of the poem.[117] In addition to this structural centrality, the Sirens boast thematic importance, as they mirror Cassandra and her experiences in multiple respects. Like Cassandra, the Sirens are virgins, dwelling at the margins of society.[118] Just as the Sirens live upon a cliff in the middle of the sea (653),[119] Cassandra languishes inside of a stone prison (348–351, 1462). The Homeric Sirens, moreover, also possess divine omniscience in their songs, proclaiming to Odysseus:

ἴδμεν γάρ τοι πάνθ᾽, ὅσ᾽ ἐνὶ Τροίῃ εὐρείῃ
Ἀργεῖοι Τρῶές τε θεῶν ἰότητι μόγησαν,
ἴδμεν δ᾽ ὅσσα γένηται ἐπὶ χθονὶ πουλυβοτείρῃ.

For we know all the toils the Argives and Trojans endured in wide Troy by the will of the gods. We know everything that happens on the fruitful earth.

Odyssey 12.189–191

The Sirens' preternatural awareness of the atrocities of Trojan War parallels Cassandra's prophetic knowledge.[120] Yet with this divine enchanting truth of the Sirens comes death for the listeners. According to Homer's Circe (12.45–46), πολὺς δ᾽ ἀμφ᾽ ὀστεόφιν θὶς / ἀνδρῶν πυθομένων, περὶ δὲ ῥινοὶ μινύθουσιν ("around them is a giant heap of the bones of moldering men, and around the bones the skin is shriveling"). Cassandra's speech, though not directly causing death, does frequently focus on death and destruction, particularly of the Greeks at sea who die because of her rape by Locrian Ajax.

These points of intersection between the Sirens and Cassandra constitute the crux of Cassandra's character: a marginalized know-it-all virgin who wreaks havoc upon men. At the end of the poem, the messenger makes this comparison explicit, equating Cassandra's speech with a Siren song: Σειρῆνος ἐστέναξε λοίσθιον μέλος ("she groaned the last song of the Siren," 1463). Moreover, we may also detect another parallel between Cassandra and the Sirens at 670–672, when Cassandra lists them as one of the dangers encountered by Odysseus:

---

[117] Hurst and Kolde 2008:xxvii. Likewise, as Pillinger 2019:134 notes, the Siren episode occurs in the center portion of the *Odyssey*.

[118] See Biffis 2016:70 for similar observations. For Cassandra's virginity, see *Alexandra* 348–356. According to the scholion on *Odyssey* 12.39, Aphrodite became angered at the Sirens' choice to remain virgins and transformed them into birds.

[119] In Homer, the Sirens live in a meadow (*Odyssey* 12.45). Strabo (1.2.12) records a tradition that places the Sirens on the Sirenussae, a three-peaked rock between the gulf of Cumae and Paestum. For the Sirens' island, see also pseudo-Aristotle *On Marvelous Things Heard* 103.

[120] See McNelis and Sens 2016:62.

179

τίς οὐκ ἀηδὼν στεῖρα Κενταυροκτόνος
Αἰτωλὶς ἢ Κουρῆτις αἰόλῳ μέλει
πείσει τακῆναι σάρκας ἀκμήνους βορᾶς;

What barren Centaur-slaying nightingale, Aetolian or Curetid, will not,
with her varied song, persuade their flesh to waste away starving?

Alexandra 670–672

Labeled a nightingale (ἀηδών, 670; cf. 653), as befits their musicality, the Sirens
exert their power by means of their "varied song" (αἰόλῳ μέλει, 671). Not only
does the noun μέλει look forward to μέλος for Cassandra at 1463, the adjec-
tive αἰόλῳ recalls the messenger's description of Cassandra's utterances at 3–4:
οὐ γὰρ ἥσυχος κόρη / ἔλυσε χρησμῶν, ὡς πρίν, αἰόλον στόμα ("for not peace-
fully, as before, did she loosen the varied mouth of her oracles"). Since the
scholiast equates the adjective αἰόλος with ποικίλος ("varied"),[121] we can see
the messenger characterizing Cassandra by the same kind of variegated and
complex speech she ascribes to the Sirens.

Despite the messenger's perceived analogy between Cassandra and the
Sirens, they differ in the effects of their speech. The divine truth sung by the
Sirens induces men to fall into a state of forgetfulness and consequently nonex-
istence.[122] Indeed, Cassandra frames this ability as persuading (πείσει, 672),
and the assonance (A̲ἰτωλί̲ς, α̲ἰόλ̲ῳ) and repetition of lambdas (Αἰτωλί̲ς, αἰόλῳ
μέλει) in 671 replicate the musicality of their song. Cassandra, on the other
hand, lacks the ability to sway people with her words: πίστιν γὰρ ἡμῶν Λεψιεὺς
ἐνόσφισε ("the Lepsian deprived us of credibility," 1454). In the case of Odysseus,
however, the Sirens' power fails, and for this reason they commit suicide, as
Cassandra recounts at 712–737.[123] These deaths, I argue, while terminating
the performance of an enchanting divine truth, enable the Sirens to acquire
a different relationship to truth. Instead, the Sirens become transmuted into
permanent fixtures of the Italian landscape and Italian cult. In this way, the
Sirens can symbolize the poem's pervading focus on Italy.

---

[121] For the equation between αἰόλος and ποικίλος, see Σ *ad* 3a–4a (Leone 2002:2). At Plato *Cratylus*
409a Socrates equates ποικίλλειν and αἰολεῖν. Looijenga 2009:65 proposes that αἰόλος could also
denote "false," in addition to "ambiguous." See Aeschylus *Prometheus Bound* 661 for the adjective
αἰολοστόμους.

[122] See *Odyssey* 12.39–46.

[123] In the *Odyssey*, Odysseus and his men manage to escape death by following Circe's instructions.
As the men row with wax stuffed in their ears, Odysseus listens to the songs while tied to the
mast. For the Sirens' suicide as caused by Odysseus, see Apollodorus *Epitome* 7.19 and Hyginus
Stories 125.

Before describing each Siren's death in detail, Cassandra introduces them as a group:

κτενεῖ δὲ κούρας Τηθύος παιδὸς τριπλᾶς,
οἴμας μελῳδοῦ μητρὸς ἐκμεμαγμένας,
αὐτοκτόνοις ῥιφαῖσιν ἐξ ἄκρας σκοπῆς
Τυρσηνικὸν πρὸς κῦμα δυπτούσας πτεροῖς,
ὅπου λινεργὴς κλῶσις ἑλκύσει πικρά.

He will kill the three maiden daughters of the child of Tethys, who imitated the songs of their melodious mother. With suicidal leaps they will dive on their wings from the top of their lookout place toward the Tyrrhenian wave, where the bitter linen thread will draw them.

Alexandra 712–716

In 712–713, Cassandra indicates the Sirens' status as maidens (κούρας), their number (τριπλᾶς), and their lineage (Τηθύος παιδός).[124] While Cassandra frequently refers to characters in terms of parentage,[125] she here alludes to both the father and mother of the Sirens. Their father, called the child of Tethys (Τηθύος παιδός, 712), is the river-god Achelous.[126] Cassandra previously alluded to the Sirens' descent from Achelous with the designation Αἰτωλὶς ἢ Κουρῆτις at 671. As the scholiast points out, these two geographic labels allude to the fact that the river Achelous separates Aetolia and Acarnania, the home of the Curetes.[127] As a result, on their father's side, the Sirens possess a connection to the physical landscape, specifically bodies of water. Their musical ability, however, derives from their mother, as Cassandra indicates with the participial phrase οἴμας μελῳδοῦ μητρὸς ἐκμεμαγμένας ("imitating the songs of their melodious mother," 713). This mother, according to the scholiast, is the Muse Terpsichore.[128] In mimicking the songs (οἴμας) of a Muse, the Sirens likewise have access to the divine knowledge of the Muses. Indeed, the Sirens' claim to divine omniscience (*Odyssey* 12.189–191) echoes Homer's description of the

---

[124] In the *Odyssey*, there are two Sirens, as indicated by the dual Σειρήνοιϊν at 12.52. Since Σειρήνοιϊν appeared at the end of the line, Hurst 2012d:98 points out that τριπλᾶς, also at the end of the line, directs the reader to the *Odyssey* passage. See Zwicker 1927:291–293 for a discussion of the various names of the Sirens.

[125] For a list of names based on lineage, see Ciani 1973:138–139.

[126] Σ *ad* 712b (Leone 2002:143). See *Argonautica* 4.895–896.

[127] Σ *ad* 671 (Leone 2002:136). Sens 2009:23 sees the description Αἰτωλὶς ἢ Κουρῆτις as bringing up an academic question.

[128] Σ *ad* 712a (Leone 2002:142). Other sources (Apollodorus *Epitome* 7.18 and Hyginus *Stories* 141) list Melpomene as the Sirens' mother. In the Sophoclean fragment (fr. 861 Radt), the Sirens are the children of Phorcys.

Muses at *Iliad* 2.485.[129] Thus, through their parentage, the Sirens straddle two spheres: the physical world in which they sing and a transcendent sphere of divine knowledge not available to humans, which, when performed by the Sirens, results in death.

Cassandra immediately follows this reference to the Sirens' singing by clarifying the nature of their demise. The Sirens dive into the Tyrrhenian Sea (Τυρσηνικὸν πρὸς κῦμα, 715), committing their bodies to the threads of the Fates. This self-committed act reconfigures the Sirens' relationship to their parents. By dying, they will no longer sing the strains of their mother, and through the submersion into water they acquire a closer association with their paternal side. At the same time, they shift from a conspicuous location on the top of a hill (ἐξ ἄκρας σκοπῆς, 714) to being hidden, first by the waves, then later when they are buried on land.

Cassandra specifies this geographic shift when describing the tomb of Parthenope, the first dead Siren:

τὴν μὲν Φαλήρου τύρσις ἐκβεβρασμένην
Γλάνις τε ῥείθροις δέξεται τέγγων χθόνα.
οὗ σῆμα δωμήσαντες ἔγχωροι κόρης
λοιβαῖσι καὶ θύσθλοισι Παρθενόπην βοῶν
ἔτεια κυδανοῦσιν οἰωνὸν θεάν.

The tower of Phalerus and Glanis, watering the earth with its streams, will receive one of them, when she is cast on the shore. There the inhabitants will construct a tomb for the maiden and will honor Parthenope, the bird goddess, with yearly libations and the sacrifices of oxen.

Alexandra 717–721

Initially referring to Parthenope as "the one cast ashore" (τὴν ... ἐκβεβρασμένην, 717), Cassandra in 717–718 includes two geographic markers to demarcate this Siren's final destination: the tower of Phalerus and the river Glanis. Although interpreters have struggled with these two references, particularly Φαλήρου τύρσις, it is certain that Lycophron is referring to the region of Naples.[130] According to Strabo, Parthenope received a cult there.[131] The river Γλάνις, (Latin

---

[129] See Pucci 1998c:7. For discussion of the similarities and differences between the Muses and Sirens, see Doherty 1995:83–85.

[130] The scholiast (Σ *ad* 717b; Leone 2002:143) states that Parthenope ended up at Naples and identifies Phalerus as the founder of Naples. Stephanus of Byzantium (656.20) records that Phalerum is the city where Parthenope was cast ashore. However, as Raviola 2006:139 observes, this material does not make a direct correlation between a Φαλήρου τύρσις and Naples.

[131] Strabo 1.2.18 and 5.4.7.

Clanius), while not directly near Naples, nevertheless runs in Campania.[132] This mention of a river emphasizes Parthenope's descent from the river Achelous,[133] in addition to marking her current fixed placement in Campania. It is in this place where the inhabitants (ἔγχωροι, 719) construct a tomb (σῆμα, 719) and honor her with yearly libations and sacrifices (ἔτεια κυδανοῦσιν, 721). Parthenope, in the process, has transformed into a "bird goddess" (οἰωνὸν θεάν, 721), a designation that fits her appearance as a woman-bird hybrid.[134]

In describing the establishment of Parthenope's cult, Cassandra evokes two other recipients of cult: Philoctetes at 929 and Hector at 1213.[135] Indeed, both male heroes receive the same verb κυδανοῦσιν, which appears in the identical metrical position in 721, 929, and 1213. However, in contrast with the description of the cults of Philoctetes and Hector, Cassandra features Parthenope's real name in 720. This decision is highly unusual considering Lycophron's predilection for pseudonyms and periphrases. Even Cassandra herself is designated by the alternate name Alexandra at 30. Sistakou and Hornblower explain this choice to name the Sirens as due to their status as "secondary characters."[136] I, however, contend that the centrality of their placement in the poem prevents us from classing them as "secondary characters." Although not appearing as crucial as Helen, Odysseus, or other major players like Paris and Achilles, the Sirens do receive a lengthy section as well as multiple mentions. At the same time, the Sirens as a group are famous, unlike the two Cypriot heroes Cepheus and Praxandrus named at 586.[137] For Parthenope and the other two Sirens, on the other hand, the use of real names corresponds to the association of their names with places in Italy. Indeed, Parthenope, whose name reflects her virginity and her voice, becomes closely associated with Naples, with Parthenope acting as an eponym for the settlement before Naples.[138]

The next Siren, Leucosia, does not receive a cult like Parthenope but acquires commemoration in a different way:

---

[132] For a discussion of the name Glanis, see Schade 1999:130–131. The Clanius river is mentioned in the *Georgics* (2.225). Citing the Lycophron passage, Stephanus of Byzantium (208.12) identifies it as a river of Cumae.

[133] See Aston 2011:69.

[134] While Homer does not specify the Sirens' appearance, later literary and pictorial depictions portrayed them as bird-women hybrids. See Euripides *Helen* 167 and Apollonius *Argonautica* 4.898–899. For an overview of Siren iconography, see Neils 1995:178–181.

[135] Philoctetes is venerated at Croton and Hector is worshipped at Thebes.

[136] Sistakou 2009a:249 and Hornblower 2015:293.

[137] According to the scholiast (Σ *ad* 586; Leone 2002:116–117), Lycophron gives the names of these two Cypriots because they are not kings nor are they in the Homeric Catalogue of Ships.

[138] For the relevance of Parthenope's name, see Breglia Pulci Doria 1987:88. See Pliny *Natural History* 3.62.

ἀκτὴν δὲ τὴν προὔχουσαν εἰς Ἐνιπέως
Λευκωσία ριφεῖσα τὴν ἐπώνυμον
πέτραν ὀχήσει δαρόν, ἔνθα λάβρος Ἴς
γείτων θ' ὁ Λᾶρις ἐξερεύγονται ποτά.

Leucosia, hurled toward the projecting headland of Enipeus, will occupy for a long time the rock that bears her name, where the rushing Is and neighboring Laris discharge their streams.

Alexandra 722–725

As with Parthenope, Cassandra gives the geographic destination of this Siren. Since Ἐνιπέως is a cult title for Poseidon,[139] the "projecting headland of Enipeus" (ἀκτὴν ... τὴν προὔχουσαν εἰς Ἐνιπέως, 722) indicates Poseidonia. Moreover, Cassandra mentions two rivers, the Is and the Laris, to delineate further this location, as well as repeating the emphasis on bodies of water.[140] Leucosia, through the act of hurling herself (ριφεῖσα, 723), becomes incorporated into this landscape, granting her name to the πέτραν, which scholars have identified with the Punta Licosa between Poseidonia/Paestum and Elea/Velea.[141] Though hidden beneath the ground and silent in death, Leucosia will have her name memorialized for a long time (δαρόν, 724).

The final Siren, Ligeia, meets her demise at Tereina:[142]

Λίγεια δ' εἰς Τέρειναν ἐκναυσθλώσεται,
κλύδωνα χελλύσσουσα, τὴν δὲ ναυβάται
κρόκαισι ταρχύσουσιν ἐν παρακτίαις,
Ὠκινάρου δίναισιν ἀγχιτέρμονα.
λούσει δὲ σῆμα βούκερως νασμοῖς Ἄρης
ὀρνιθόπαιδος ἴσμα φοιβάζων ποτοῖς.

---

[139] The scholiast (Σ *ad* 722a; Leone 2002:144) reveals that Enipeus is a cult title for Poseidon at Miletus. This name also alludes to a story preserved in the *nekyia* section of the *Odyssey* (11.235–259). Poseidon took the form of the river Enipeus in Thessaly to seduce Tyro. See Cusset and Kolde 2013:181.

[140] The scholiast (Σ *ad* 724f–725a; Leone 2002:145) identifies the Is and Laris as rivers in Italy. While the Laris is unattested elsewhere, the Is is mentioned in association with Paestum (Parthax *FGrHist* 825 F 1). See Holzinger 1895:279 for the suggestion that Is and Laris form a wordplay of Silaris (a river near Paestum mentioned by Strabo 5.4.13).

[141] According to the scholiast (Σ *ad* 724a; Leone 2002:145), πέτρα means "island." See Coviello 2006:157 for the argument that the promontory of Enipeus is the Punta Licosa.

[142] Tereina is a Crotonite foundation in Bruttium. Its exact location, however, is uncertain. See Stephanus of Byzantium 617.5.

Ligeia will disembark at Tereina, spitting out a wave, and the sailors will bury her on the stony seashore near the eddies of Ocinarus. The bull-horned Ares will wash the tomb with its streams, purifying the foundation of the bird-child with its waters.

Alexandra 726–731

In contrast with Parthenope and Leucosia, Ligeia's name appears as the first word of her respective section. Indeed, this name, meaning "sweet-sounding," is connected closely with the enchanting beauty of the Sirens' song.[143] Yet, as Ligeia "disembarks" (ἐκναυσθλώσεται, 726), her singing ability becomes debilitated, when she spits out waves (κλύδωνα χελλύσσουσα, 727). This participial phrase, while referring to the muffling of this Siren's song, in fact displays the sonority that one would expect from a singer. κλύδωνα and χελλύσσουσα both contain lambdas and upsilons, and in 728 the sense of musicality is sustained by the coordination of κρόκαισι ("stony seashore") with κλύδωνα and ταρχύσουσιν ("they will bury") with χελλύσσουσα. When dead and buried, however, Ligeia's mellifluous voice becomes forever silenced, and we can detect an irony in the fact that those who bury her here, sailors, are the same people she and her sisters would have caused to perish at sea without proper burial. Ligeia, on the other hand, receives such rites, and Cassandra emphasizes the permanence of this tomb placement by using two similar words for the structure: σῆμα ("tomb," 730) and ἴσμα ("foundation," 731).[144] At the same time, as with Parthenope and Leucosia, Ligeia is associated with bodies of waters, such as the Ocinarus river and the Ares river,[145] which purifies (φοιβάζων, 731) her tomb.

Before concluding this digression about the Sirens, Cassandra returns to Parthenope to mention the rites performed for this Siren at Naples:

πρώτη δὲ καί ποτ' αὖθι συγγόνων θεᾷ
κραίνων ἁπάσης Μόψοπος ναυαρχίας
πλωτῆρσι λαμπαδοῦχον ἐντυνεῖ δρόμον
χρησμοῖς πιθήσας, ὅν ποτ' αὐξήσει λεὼς

---

[143] For a description of the sweet-sounding song of the Sirens, see *Odyssey* 12.44 and 12.183. Cf. Alcman fr. 30 *PMGF* Davies.

[144] Holzinger 1895:279, however, argues that σῆμα refers to the island Ligeia, while the ἴσμα is the city Tereina.

[145] The Ocinarus reoccurs at 1009. It has been identified with the San Biase (Bérard 1957:161), Fiumi dei Bagni, Savuto, and Zinnavo. See also Amiotti 1999:89 for this identification. For the Ares river, the scholiast (Σ *ad* 730b; Leone 2002:146) notes that it is not a river around Tereina and gives alternate readings: Ἔρης and Ἔρις, both of which are rivers in the area. Holzinger 1895:279 proposes an allusion to the union of the god Ares and the nymph Terina (Antoninus Liberalis *Metamophoses* 21.1).

Νεαπολιτῶν, οἳ παρ᾿ ἄκλυστον σκέπας
ὅρμων Μισηνοῦ στύφλα νάσσονται κλίτη.

And hereafter one day, for the first of the sister goddesses, the leader
of the entire fleet of Mopsops will institute a torch race for the sailors,
obeying the oracles. This custom the people of Naples will expand,
those who will dwell upon the rough cliffs next to the peaceful refuge
of the harbor Misenum.

Alexandra 732–737

As Hornblower observes, this passage offers an allusion to one of the more
securely attested historical individuals mentioned in the poem.[146] According to
the scholiast, the commander of the fleet of Mopsops (κραίνων ἁπάσης Μόψοπος
ναυαρχίας, i.e. Athenian fleet) is the fifth-century commander Diotimus.[147] In
making this reference to a real historical personage, Cassandra establishes a
link between the mythical Sirens and the contemporary world of Lycophron.
Parthenope, as the recipient of the torch race ritual, shapes human actions,
spurring not only Diotimus' decision to obey the oracles and establish the ritual,
but also the people of Naples, who continue and expand the custom. Yet what
about a torch race is significant? Edlund points out that torch races were a major
feature of the Panathenaic festival at Athens.[148] Since Strabo (5.4.7) stresses the
Athenian role in the foundation of Naples, the establishment of a torch race
by Diotimus would symbolize the ties between Athens and Naples. Such a
political interest in connecting mainland Greece with the Greek West does fit
within the poem's overall design, which not only emphasizes the western loca-
tions spatially, but also portrays the rise of Roman power as the chronological
telos.[149] Because it was instituted by an Athenian general and still observed by
the Neapolitans in Lycophron's day, Parthenope's torch race participates in this
spatial and temporal progression, connecting East and West as well as past and
present.

---

[146] Hornblower 2015:297.
[147] The scholiast (Σ *ad* 732; Leone 2002:147) cites Timaeus (*FGrHist* 566 F 98). In Thucydides (1.45),
Diotimus is one of the Athenian leaders sent to Corcyra.
[148] Edlund 1987:47.
[149] See McNelis and Sens 2011:78–80; 2016:11. For the prevalence of western locations, see
Hornblower 2018:49, who calculates 457 lines in the prophecy (out of the 1429 spoken by
Cassandra) devoted to western areas. When interpreting 1446–1450, the rise of the Roman
power, scholars have struggled with the identification of the wrestler, as well as the date and
context of the poem. For an overview of this issue, see Hornblower 2015:491–493, who identi-
fies the wrestler as Titus Quinctius Flamininus, the victor at the Battle of Cynoscephalae in 197
BCE. Jones 2014:41–55 argues that the Roman passages refer to the time of the Antiochene War
(192–188 BCE).

While reinterpreting the Sirens as recipients of cultic worship in Italy, Cassandra anticipates her own cult, also in Italy, at Daunia:[150]

οὐ μὴν ἐμὸν νώνυμνον ἀνθρώποις σέβας
ἔσται, μαρανθὲν αὖθι ληθαίῳ σκότῳ.
ναὸν δέ μοι τεύξουσι Δαυνίων ἄκροι
Σάλπης παρ' ὄχθαις, οἵ τε Δάρδανον πόλιν
ναίουσι, λίμνης ἀγχιτέρμονες ποτῶν.
κοῦραι δὲ παρθένειον ἐκφυγεῖν ζυγὸν
ὅταν θέλωσι, νυμφίους ἀρνούμεναι,
τοὺς Ἑκτορείοις ἠγλαϊσμένους κόμαις,
μορφῆς ἔχοντας σίφλον ἢ μῶμαρ γένους,
ἐμὸν περιπτύξουσιν ὠλέναις βρέτας
ἄλκαρ μέγιστον κτώμεναι νυμφευμάτων,
Ἐρινύων ἐσθῆτα καὶ ῥέθους βαφὰς
πεπαμέναι θρόνοισι φαρμακτηρίοις.
κείναις ἐγὼ δηναιὸν ἄφθιτος θεὰ
ῥαβδηφόροις γυναιξὶν αὐδηθήσομαι.

My worship will not be nameless among men, withered hereafter by the shadow of oblivion. The best of the Daunians will build a temple for me next to the banks of the Salpe and those who dwell in the Dardanian city, near the waters of the marsh. Girls will embrace my image in their arms, acquiring the greatest defense against marriage. This will be whenever they wish to flee the yoke of maidens and refuse their grooms, those adorned with the hairstyle of Hector, but possessing some blemish in their appearance or fault in lineage. The girls will take up the garb of the Erinyes and dye their faces with magic herbs. For a long time, I shall be called an undying goddess by those rod-bearing women.

Alexandra 1126–1140

Cassandra's description of her own cult comes after the mention of the worship of Agamemnon (1123–1125), her Greek captor with whom she will be murdered (1099–1122).[151] As with the cults of Parthenope and Ligeia, Cassandra specifies the creators of her temple (Δαυνίων ἄκροι, 1128), as well as its geographic location near a river (Σάλπης, 1129). Moreover, the section contains several verbal

[150] For a discussion of this cult, see Mari 2009:415–427 and Biffis 2014. Mari 2009:422 argues that this cult was most likely a prenuptial ritual and not actually intended to prevent marriage.
[151] See Durbec 2011d:17–25 for a list of the verbal echoes of Aeschylus' *Agamemnon* in this section.

echoes of the Siren passages. For instance, νώνυμνον ("nameless") in 1126 recalls ἐπώνυμον for Leucosia in 723, and αὖθι ("hereafter") in 1127 appears in the same position as it does for Parthenope in 732. The collocation ἀγχιτέρμονες ποτῶν ("near the streams") in 1130 echoes ἀγχιτέρμονα in 729 and ποτοῖς in 731 for Ligeia. Finally, θεά ("goddess") at the end of 1139 for Cassandra looks back to θεάν in 721 and θεᾷ in 732, both applied to Parthenope. This accumulation of verbal echoes attests to the importance of the Sirens as models for Cassandra. For these marginalized female voices, death allows for the preservation of their names and fame, as well as integration into society. The deceased Sirens acquire honor from sailors instead of causing them to die. Similarly, Cassandra, as a θεά, aids other maidens in evading marriage, a task she could not achieve in her own life when enslaved by her "husband" Agamemnon (1118).

Cast originally as deadly monsters endured by Odysseus (653, 670–672), the Sirens are unable to destroy him and in the process gain a new existence in death. No longer singers of an enchanting and deadly divine truth, the Sirens instead become symbols, marking parts of the Italian landscape. Parthenope and Ligeia have tombs (σῆμα), while Leucosia is assimilated to her eponymous rock. In construing the deceased Sirens as constructive elements of Italian society, Cassandra resolves the numerous dualities surrounding them. Just like Helen, the hybrid Sirens are simultaneously beautiful and lethal, luring men to forgetfulness and death. Yet, whereas Cassandra reconciled Helen's paradoxical nature by reducing her to a nonexistent image and depriving her of commemoration after death, in an Italian context the Sirens retain their actual names and association with rivers, as suits their patrilineal descent. The mention of these bodies of waters, moreover, lends a level of verisimilitude by situating the Sirens in concrete locations. In this way, these mythical *femmes fatales*, although silent and hidden beneath the ground, have become solid and real, more so than the specter Helen or their killer Odysseus, creator of fabricated stories.

5. Conclusion

In mimicking the speech of the cryptic Sphinx (7), Cassandra utters complex language that initially veils its referent only to reveal a deeper essence. The multiplicity of obscure designations corresponds to the complexity of the figures discussed. Indeed, for Helen and Odysseus especially, literary sources grappled with the ambiguous nature of these two figures. Stesichorus and Euripides (*Helen*) remade the Homeric Helen into a phantom at Troy, while Attic tragedy reinterpreted the Homeric Odysseus' clever trickery as knavery. In the *Alexandra*, Cassandra's representation of Helen and Odysseus expands and amplifies such depictions to elucidate the falsity entailed in both characters. Helen, with her "phantom-shaped form" (εἰδωλοπλάστῳ ... ῥέθει, 173), causes longing as well as death. Odysseus, with his laments producing stories (τὸν μυθοπλάστην ... γόον, 764), manufactures pain for himself, and in doing so loses his ability to express his experiences accurately. Thus, a disjunction between appearance and reality exists for both. Helen is split between a real and a phantom Helen, and the duplicitous Odysseus' words distort his lived experiences, just as his disguises mask his appearance. Odysseus may have seen and suffered many woes, but through these he lacks any capacity to tell them truthfully.

Cassandra's comprehension of this deeper truth derives from two major types of criteria. First, in presenting characters with reference to lineage, Cassandra demonstrates the close relationship between parent and child. As a source of destruction, Helen takes after her menacing avian parent (swan-Zeus or goose-Nemesis), and Odysseus assumes the traits of his crafty father Sisyphus. At the same time, Cassandra subtly assesses these characters in comparison to herself and her experiences. Both Helen and Cassandra endure sexual victimization and in turn wreak devastation. Moreover, Cassandra shares Odysseus' wretchedness and suffering after the destruction of Troy. Like Odysseus, Cassandra behaves as a messenger, but of the future in addition to the past. Yet Cassandra's omniscience distinguishes her from these two characters. Although lacking Odysseus' ability to persuade others,[152] Cassandra can situate her sufferings in a larger context, realizing that cultic worship constitutes the compensation for her pain and the silencing of her voice in death. The same applies to the Sirens, who, as deadly half-avian monsters, straddled the realms of divine knowledge (from their Muse mother) and the physical world (from their river-god father Achelous). In death, however, the Sirens become reinterpreted by Cassandra as symbols, absorbed into the geography of Italy and commemorated by their real names, an honor denied to most of the characters in the *Alexandra*. Enclosed in the very center of the prophecy by both Odysseus (648–711, 738–819, and 1244–1245) and Helen (86–173, 513, 820, and 850–851), these deceased feminine monsters represent the ultimate truth, one that is concealed and must be interpreted.

Just as Helen and Odysseus surround the Siren suicide section, so too does the messenger's frame envelop Cassandra's utterances. His attempt to report with perfect accuracy does not exclude the possibility of distortion and bias. Even if he were to achieve his goal, his reliance on surface appearances still prevents an acquisition of a deeper comprehension necessary to penetrate the labyrinthine words. As an imperfect reporter, moreover, the messenger corresponds to

---

[152] For this contrast between Cassandra and Odysseus, see Biffis 2021:52.

the faulty narrator Odysseus.[153] Not only does Cassandra identify Odysseus as a messenger (ἄγγελον, 657), the simile καύηξ ὥστε κυμάτων δρομεύς ("like a sea swallow running in the waves," 789) echoes the messenger's simile ὡς πτηνὸς δρομεύς ("like a winged runner") at 15. Since both ἄγγελον and δρομεύς occur in descriptions of Odysseus' failures and degradation, the shared language for Odysseus and the messenger points to the similar limitations of the two. Indeed, the messenger's actual lowly status is not unlike Odysseus' convincing guises as beggar. At the same time, as was the case with Odysseus' reported adventures in *Odyssey* 9–12, we are at the mercy of the messenger's efforts for Cassandra's speech. What precisely he is distorting or omitting cannot be known.

Behind the omniscient Cassandra and ignorant messenger is their creator, the real author Lycophron, whose Apollo (source of inspiration) is the profusion of literary and historical sources used to produce the poem. However, as is clear from the lengthy footnote at the beginning this chapter, his identity and date have occupied over a century of scholarship. Nevertheless, existing in his present (most likely the second century BCE) and clearly interested in Italy,[154] Lycophron possesses Cassandra's knowledge up until that point. Yet, like the messenger, he too is subject to human limitations, confronted by the variety of conflicting accounts, which become condensed and reconciled, often paradoxically, in the replication of Cassandra's oracular speech. Moreover, as a male who assumes her voice, Lycophron further parallels the male messenger, subjecting and possibly distorting female speech for his poetic project. In doing so, however, Lycophron uses Cassandra and her experiences during the Trojan War to encapsulate the complex nexuses of causation that connect past, present, and future in the Greek literary and historical tradition. It is only through the voice of a victim of the Trojan War that we can comprehend the true ramifications of violence, sexuality, war, and death.

---

[153] Cf. Sistakou 2012:138n19, who sees a parallel between the messenger and "Homer."

[154] For arguments regarding Lycophron's associations with Italy, see Amiotti 1982:452–460 and most recently Linant de Bellefonds, Pouzadoux, and Prioux 2017:199–246. While maintaining the second-century date of the poem and the pseudonymous Lycophron, Hornblower 2018:48 similarly posits Italian connections for the author.

5

Conclusion
Fabricated for Truth

Just as I began this monograph by examining Callimachus' *Hymn to Zeus*, it is useful to preface the conclusion with a second look at the other *locus classicus* for the issue of truth and falsehood in Hellenistic poetry: Theocritus' *Idyll* 7.43–48. In this *Idyll,* the narrator Simichidas, while traveling to a harvest festival on Cos, encounters a goatherd named Lycidas (11–20). Wishing to engage Lycidas in a singing contest (35–36), Simichidas speaks "with purpose" (ἐπίταδες, 42), claiming that he is not yet worthy to compete with Sicelidas (Asclepiades) and Philitas (35–36). This calculated display of modesty in turn elicits Lycidas' laughter (γελάσσας, 42), which is followed with the promise of a gift, an enigmatic assessment regarding Simichidas' honesty, and his views toward poetic pretensions:

> 'τάν τοι' ἔφα 'κορύναν δωρύττομαι, οὕνεκεν ἐσσὶ
> πᾶν ἐπ' ἀλαθείᾳ πεπλασμένον ἐκ Διὸς ἔρνος.
> ὥς μοι καὶ τέκτων μέγ' ἀπέχθεται, ὅστις ἐρευνῇ
> ἶσον ὄρευς κορυφᾷ τελέσαι δόμον Ὠρομέδοντος,
> καὶ Μοισᾶν ὄρνιχες, ὅσοι ποτὶ Χῖον ἀοιδὸν
> ἀντία κοκκύζοντες ἐτώσια μοχθίζοντι.'

> "I will gift you this staff," he said, "since you are a sapling fabricated by Zeus entirely for truth. For I greatly despise the builder, who seeks to construct a house equal to the peak of Mount Oromedon, and I greatly despise the Muses' roosters who toil in vain while crowing against the Chian singer."

> Theocritus *Idyll* 7.43–48

As I mentioned in the first chapter (1.5), the juxtaposition of ἐπ' ἀλαθείᾳ ("for truth") and the participle πεπλασμένον ("fabricated") in 44 creates an immediate paradox. While the former word encompasses the overlapping spheres of truth, reality, honesty, and realism, πλάσσω and its related words (e.g. πλάσμα) connote manipulation and hence falsehood.[1] Thus, in this paradoxical formulation that recalls the Muses' "falsehoods like real things" at *Theogony* 27–28, Simichidas is simultaneously a fabrication yet one intended in some way for "truth."[2] While some commentators emphasize the irony suffusing Lycidas' statement, such a contradictory identity befits Simichidas' status as a fictive character in a poem replete with allusions to earlier poems (e.g. Hesiod's meeting with the Muses) and statements concerning the nature and practice of poetry (e.g. 7.45–48).[3]

Yet for the purposes of this monograph, this section contains additional points of interest along with the emphatic juxtaposition of truth and falsehood. Specifically, Lycidas' assessment that Simichidas constitutes "a sapling fabricated by Zeus entirely for truth" involves multiple processes. Not only has Simichidas been "fabricated," he has been done so in a complete way (πᾶν), and for a particular purpose, truth. At the same time, Simichidas' status as a sapling (ἔρνος) suggests his youthfulness and thus potential for development. Though a mere sapling, Simichidas can improve to render himself worthy of the gifted staff. Likewise, Lycidas' assessment about Simichidas represents a process, as it arose from the encounter between the two figures and Simichidas' affectation of modesty (ἐπίταδες, 42). Indeed, the phrase ἐπίταδες ("on purpose,"42) calls attention to the likely speciousness of this Simichidas' modesty. Finally, not only does Lycidas compare poetic composition to the process of house construction (45–46), the entire poem thematizes the process of a journey.[4]

Similarly, in interpreting selected passages in five poems (*Phaenomena*, *Theriaca*, *Aetia*, *Argonautica*, and *Alexandra*), I have emphasized the processes represented in the evaluation of truth and falsehood. Adapting the concept of "the criterion of truth" from Hellenistic philosophical debates, I have identified multiple types of criteria depicted within the studied poems. The main three criteria are (1) visibility, (2) personal experience, and (3) genealogy. This finding of multiple criteria is not unexpected, since the Epicureans and Stoics proposed

---

[1]   LSJ πλάσσω (V) and πλάσμα (II).

[2]   For analysis and translation of this enigmatic phrase, see Gow 1952.2:142, Puelma 1960:159–160, Dover 1971:154, Serrao 1971:47–52, Segal 1974:131–132, Walsh 1985:19, Goldhill 1986:50–51n81, Gutzwiller 1991:166, Plazenet 1994:85, Hunter 1999:163–164, and Klooster 2011:202–204.

[3]   For observations about the mocking tone, see, for instance, Williams 1971:144 and Segal 1974:132. For discussions of this poem's programmatic nature, see Goldhill 1991:225–240 and Klooster 2011:195–208. Krevans 1983:201–220 demonstrates how the poem's geographic allusions contribute to ideas about poetry and poetic inspiration.

[4]   On this point, see Goldhill 1986:35.

multiple types of criteria, e.g. αἰσθήσεις ("perceptions") for the Epicureans and the φαντασία καταληπτική ("the apprehensible presentation") for the Stoics.

While none of the criteria identified in the poem correspond directly to the philosophic criteria, visibility and personal experience fall under the rubric of "perceptions". Constellations are seen in the sky, while snake bites are felt. Yet perception is often deficient, particularly for the remote mythical past or for figures as multifaceted as Helen or Medea. Indeed, in comprising a diverse array of subject matter, the five poems strike upon multiple kinds of truths: scientific, historical, and mythical, while also covering the past, present, and even future. Each kind of truth necessitates a different mode of assessment and thus different criteria for truth. The different poetic personae further influence this process of assessment. While personae of teachers speak in the *Phaenomena* and *Theriaca*, the *Aetia* and *Argonautica* feature self-conscious narrators personally involved in the narrative. Lycophron's *Alexandra*, however, removes any such narrator, instead making an unnamed messenger report the words of the inspired prophetess Cassandra.

The teacher of the *Phaenomena* and the unnamed messenger of the *Alexandra* both gravitate toward visibility as the main criterion for assessing truth. In the case of the former, this choice makes sense. As suits its title *Phaenomena*, the poem deals with celestial and terrestrial signs that appear as expected and are thus conducive to interpretation. Humans, however, must perceive this divine regularity, imposing order by forming the stars into recognizable shapes, giving names, and assigning mythical narratives. As I argued, the extended myths (e.g. *Phaenomena* 30–35, 96–136, and 216–224) in this poem model this process of interpretation by emphasizing the correlation between visible signs and definite consequences. The irregularity that does exist in this world, such as the movements of the planets (*Phaenomena* 454–461), does not matter, and it is in that narrow area where the teacher professes uncertainty.

In the *Alexandra*, however, visibility, at least based on surface appearances, represents a defective criterion. Not only do Cassandra's raving and cryptic utterances obfuscate the identity of the referents, but she deals with the intricate and hidden chains of causation that lead to a destructive and chaotic future. Unable to comprehend Cassandra's words and to understand this future, the messenger instead bases his judgment of Cassandra solely on her external appearance as an animalistic raving woman. In this way, he can discount her words, fulfilling Apollo's curse. At the same time, the messenger thrusts the task of interpretation upon the audience.

Along with visibility, personal experience reoccurs as a criterion in three of the studied works: the *Theriaca*, *Aetia*, and *Alexandra*. Yet, just as personal experience varies in actual life, so too does the representation of personal experience differ in these three works. In the *Theriaca* and particularly in the extended myths (8–12, 13–20, 309–319, 343–354, 541–549), Nicander recreates scenes of dangerous encounters. In doing so, he demonstrates how direct experience enables understanding and discovery amid a chaotic and hidden world. Despite the speaker's ostensibly confident tone in the proem, a level of uncertainty remains.

While personal experience in Nicander's chaotic world entails a degree of doubt, for Callimachus' childlike narrative persona in the *Aetia*, it produces certainty. In collating obscure information about rituals and customs from all over the Greek world, the Callimachean speaker can confidently assess sources and information, due to a close relationship with the Muses. Indeed, as figments of a dream, they are a part of him. At the same time, the conversation format in books 1–2 enables the speaker to ask questions and thus shape the discourse. Even with the frame dropped in the final two books, the juxtaposition of separate narratives continues. The result is a disjointed narrative with different voices (e.g. Berenice's Lock in fr. 110), connected, however, by thematic links and by the ironic personal voice of the Callimachean persona. Callimachus, through this childlike speaker, has created his truth, one derived from prose sources but ultimately reconfigured to be his own.

Finally, for the character Cassandra in the *Alexandra*, personal experience, paradoxically of the future, empowers her to interrogate the complex nature of figures like Helen, Odysseus, and the Sirens. Through her awareness and direct experience of future consequences, Cassandra can pierce through the false appearances to establish Helen's destructive nonexistence and Odysseus' incessant and self-harming mendacity. The deleterious and enchanting Sirens, by contrast, are reinterpreted as symbols of Roman power. The ascendance of Roman military power represents the ultimate truth of the poem (1446–1450), which for Cassandra is the future, but for her creator Lycophron the present and the past.

Combined with personal experience, genealogy functions as the other major criterion for Cassandra in the *Alexandra*. For instance, emphasizing Sisyphus as Odysseus' actual father (*Alexandra* 344) calls attention to Odysseus' innate deception. Similarly, Helen's violent birth (*Alexandra* 88) encodes her destructiveness. Genealogy, moreover, plays a role in the other studied works. According to the myth at *Theriaca* 8–12, the genesis of deadly creations from Titans' blood attests to their viciousness. In the *Aetia*, however, Theogenes' Ician birth (fr. 178.8) strengthens his credibility as a source about Ician customs. In all three cases, genealogy enables not just an understanding of identity, but also causation. Whereas Lycophron's Helen and Nicander's deadly creatures will breed destruction, the Ician Theogenes, as a humanized source, will generate knowledge.

Conversely, in Apollonius' *Argonautica*, these three criteria—visibility, personal experience, and genealogical descent—are not definite. Rather, the narrator displays an escalating level of uncertainty over the progression of the narrative, assimilating himself to his uncertain characters. Confronted with the complexity of the subject matter in the final two books and the difficulty of defining character motivations, the uncertain narrator at places consults his sources, the Muses. Yet, as I have shown, even their authority can be dubious, as the Muse in book four does not fully elucidate the nature of Medea's motivations at the beginning of the book. Neither does the Apollonian narrator, and as a result, we are left with two simultaneous manifestations of Medea, just as the narrator provides two conflicting legends about the sickle beneath Drepane (*Argonautica* 4.982–992). In both cases, the narrator's inability to decide implies the dearth of a solid criterion for truth.

Along with the multiple criteria in the five works, these Hellenistic poets allude to multiple fonts of authority. In addition to the unnamed sources of stories ("they say," "it is said"), Zeus in the *Phaenomena*, Hesiod in the *Theriaca*, Xenomedes and the Ician Theogenes in the *Aetia*, the Muses in the *Phaenomena*, *Aetia*, and *Argonautica*, and Apollo in *Alexandra* function as sources. Yet the poems' personae evaluate their sources differently with the contrasting criteria. Certainty arises when perceiving the signs produced by Zeus (*Phaenomena* 10–13) and shown by the Muses (*Phaenomena* 18), and Callimachus' speaker can deftly extract and critique information from his Muses, the Ician Theogenes, and Xenomedes. Nicander's Hesiod and Apollonius' Muses, on the other hand, represent questionable sources, despite their traditional authority. For Lycophron's Cassandra, Apollo grants her oracular vision but deprives her of credibility (*Alexandra* 1454–1458). In this way, Cassandra as a source constitutes the inversion of the Hesiodic Muses. Instead of uttering falsehoods like true things (*Theogony* 27–28), she speaks things, both true and real, that seem like falsehood. In this way, Lycophron's Cassandra nicely encapsulates the paradox of being "fabricated for truth."

In fact, we may interpret all five poems as entities "fabricated for truth." Although it is difficult to apply modern notions of fiction to ancient works,[5] the five poems nevertheless present constructed personae participating in

---

[5]   Scholars have debated to what extent one can detect early ideas about fictionality in Greek literature and what poetic work or genre constitutes the beginnings of Greek fiction. For discussions of this issue and bibliography, see Bowie 1993:1–37 (on earlier poetry) and Halliwell 2011:10–15, especially, 10n19. Payne 2007:1 argues that Theocritus' pastoral poems count as the first example of "fully fictional" worlds in Greek poetry.

constructed scenarios, just like the Lycidas and Simichidas encounter in *Idyll* 7. The second two words ("for truth"), however, require additional qualification and consideration. In what way are these poems made "for" truth? What, moreover, is "truth" in a cultural and intellectual context in which prose had long usurped the domain of purveying truth, while poetry was assessed primarily on aesthetic criteria?

The "truth" represented in these poems, I propose, involves wrestling with the nexuses between identity and causation. Such an aspiration makes sense amid the influx of aetiological concerns in Hellenistic verse. Names and rituals defined the identity of peoples and places, yet some factor caused these names and rituals at some point in the distant past. Even the divine and eternal constellations had received names and shapes. Yet, aside from the difficulty of learning about the remote past, the proliferation of often conflicting prose sources further heightened the difficulty of establishing any truth. Finally, certain mythological figures, especially Helen and Medea, elicited debate. Not only were they deemed the causes of intercultural conflict (e.g. Herodotus *Histories* 1.2–1.4),[6] Helen and Medea possessed disparate identities. Indeed, while Nicander presents a helpful Helen who avenges and protects her crew by debilitating an evil snake (*Theriaca* 309–319), Lycophron's Cassandra reduces her existence to that of a detrimental simulacrum. Medea, for the Apollonian narrator, is simultaneously the cause of the narrative's completion (*Argonautica* 3.3) and a source of ἀπορία, one corresponding to the Skeptic tendencies of the narrator and his characters.

Let us now return to the first of the two previously posed questions. That is, in what way are these five poems fabricated *for* truth? In early poetry, truth is conceptualized as a target to be hit or missed (e.g. νημερτής). Falsehood, while a distortion from truth, can assume a similarity to true things by the power of the Muses (*Theogony* 27). For Parmenides, truth became a more rigorous journey combining revelation and reasoning to access the true reality. Of course, none of the five studied poems offers this road map to the true reality. Nor are the poems equivalent to the Platonic dialogues, which, though fictional, model the dialectical processes involved in uncovering the true reality.[7] Rather, as I have demonstrated, Aratus, Nicander, Callimachus, Apollonius, and Lycophron subtly represent the processes of interrogating truth and falsehood through poetic language, myths, allusions, and etymologies.

---

[6] For the relationship between Helen and Medea as sources of conflict, see Hunter 1987:138 and Priestly 2014:178.
[7] Gill 1993:68.

The contrasting processes depicted in the poems result in the representations of different spatial relationships to truth. Of all the personae in the five poems, the Apollonian narrator casts himself as deviating the most from truth, not unlike the far-flung remnants of the Argo (*Argonautica* 4.555) and the increasingly distant Muses. Likewise in the *Alexandra*, Lycophron constructs a messenger who fails at divining the deeper truth, despite an obsession with surface accuracy. Of the two personae claiming to teach, Aratus' persona appears closer to truth than that of Nicander's. The clarity and regularity of celestial and terrestrial signs enable greater certainty, despite their multiplicity and distance in the sky. Nicander's subject matter, by contrast, is concealed and thus marked by greater ambiguity. Finally, the Callimachean narrator in all his guises and Lycophron's Cassandra are characterized as inching closest to the truth. Yet, whereas Callimachus' narrator frequently flaunts his controlled and chosen truth, Cassandra obfuscates her true oracular speech in ambiguity and paradox. In doing so, both personae have fabricated truths that are their own.

Tables

1) circumstances of Orion on Chios;
2) attempted assault;
3) preparation of scorpion
4) appearance of scorpion;
5) slaying of Orion;
6) predecessors speaking in the past;
7) present time

Greek and Line Number	Order in Narrative
καμπαὶ ... Ὠρίωνα (634–636)	7) present time
προτέρων λόγος (637)	7) present time
οἵ μιν ἔφαντο (637)	6) predecessors speaking in the past
ἑλκῆσαι πέπλοιο (638)	2) attempted assault
Χίῳ ... Οἰνοπίωνι (638–640)	1) circumstances of Orion on Chios
ἡ δέ οἱ ... σκορπίον (641–643)	3) preparation of scorpion
ὅς ῥά μιν ...ἐόντα (643)	5) slaying of Orion
πλειότερος προφανείς (644)	4) appearance of scorpion
ἐπεὶ .... ἤκαχεν αὐτήν (644)	2) attempted assault
τοὔνεκα ... φεύγειν (645–646)	7) present time

Table 1: Chronology of Events at *Phaenomena* 634–646

Tables

Passage in the *Alexandra* (in order)	Corresponding Episode in *Odyssey* 9-12
Libya (648)	9.82–104
Scylla (649)	12.234–259
Sirens (653)	12.166–200
Death of Companions (654–658)	12.403–446
Cyclops (659–661)	9.105–566
Laestrygonians (662–665)	10.80–132
Scylla and Charybdis (668)	12.234–259
Circe (673–680)	10.133–574
the Underworld (681–687)	11.12–640
the Sirens again (712–737)	12.166–200
the winds of Aeolus (738–741)	10.1–79
Charybdis (742–743)	12.234–259
Calypso (744)	12.447–450

Table 2: Odysseus' Adventure Time: *Alexandra* Vs. *Odyssey*

Bibliography

Abbreviations of Reference Works Consulted

LSJ = Liddell, Scott, and Jones, 1940. *An English-Greek Lexicon*. Ninth Edition. Oxford

Smyth = Smyth, H. W. 1956. *Greek Grammar*. Cambridge, MA.

Works Cited

Acosta-Hughes, B. 2010. *Arion's Lyre: Archaic Lyric into Hellenistic Poetry*. Princeton.

Acosta-Hughes, B., L. Lehnus, and S. Stephens, eds. 2011. *Brill's Companion to Callimachus*. Leiden.

Acosta-Hughes, B., and S. Stephens. 2002. "Rereading Callimachus' *Aetia* Fragment 1." *Classical Philology* 97:238–255.

———. 2012. *Callimachus in Context: From Plato to the Augustan Poets*. Cambridge.

Adkins, A. W. H. 1972. "Truth, ΚΟΣΜΟΣ, and ΑΡΕΤΗ in the Homeric Poems." *Classical Quarterly* 22:5–18.

Albis, R. 1996. *Poet and Audience in the* Argonautica *of Apollonius*. Lanham.

Allan, W. 2008. *Euripides:* Helen. Cambridge.

Allen, K. 2001. *Inference from Signs: Ancient Debates about the Nature of Evidence*. Oxford.

Ambühl, A. 2005. *Kinder und junge Helden: Innovative Aspekte des Umgangs mit der literarischen Tradition bei Kallimachos*. Leuven.

Amiotti, G. 1982. "Lico di Reggio e l'*Alessandra* di Licofrone." *Athenaeum* 60:452–460.

———. 1999. "La sirena Ligea, Licofrone e il territorio lametino." In *Tra l'Amato e il Savuto*. Vol. 2. *Studi sul Lametino antico e tardo-antico*, ed. G. De Sensi Sestito, 87–92. Soveria Mannelli.

Andrews, N. E. 1998. "Philosophical Satire in the *Aetia* Prologue." In Harder, Regtuit, and Wakker 1998:1–19.

Angiò, F. 2002. "Filita di Cos in bronzo (Ermesianatte, fr.7, 75–78 Powell—*P.Mil. Vogl.VIII* 309, col. X 16–25)." *Archiv für Papyrusforschung* 48:17–24.

Annas, J. 1980. "Truth and Knowledge." In Schofield, Burnyeat, and Barnes 1980:84–104.

Arnott, W. G. 1976. "Two Functions of Ambiguity in Callimachus' *Hymn to Zeus*." *Rivista di cultura classica e medioevale* 18:13–17.

Asmis, E. 2007. "Myth and Philosophy in Cleanthes' *Hymn to Zeus*." *Greek, Roman, and Byzantine Studies* 47:413–429.

Asper, M. 1997. *Onomata Allotria: Zur Genese, Struktur und Funktion poetologischer Metaphern bei Kallimachos*. Stuttgart.

———. 2001. "Gruppen und Dichter: Zu Programmatik und Adressatenbezug bei Kallimachos." *Antike und Abendland* 47:84–116.

———. 2008. "Apollonius on Poetry." In Papanghelis and Rengakos 2008:167–197.

———. 2011. "Callimachean Geopoetics and the Ptolemaic Empire." In Acosta-Hughes, Lehnus, and Stephens 2011:155–177.

Aston, E. 2011. Mixanthrôpoi: *Animal-Human Hybrid Deities in Greek Religion*. Liège.

Austin, N. 1994. *Helen of Troy and Her Shameless Phantom*. Ithaca.

Barigazzi, A. 1981. "Esiodo e la chiusa degli 'Aitia' di Callimacho." *Prometheus* 7:97–107.

Barnes, M. 2003. *Inscribed* Kleos: *Aetiological Contexts in Apollonius of Rhodes*. PhD diss., University of Missouri.

Bassi, K. 1993. "Helen and the Discourse of Denial in Stesichorus' Palinode." *Arethusa* 26: 51–75.

Belfiore, E. 1985. "'Lies unlike Truth': Plato on Hesiod, *Theogony 27*." *Transactions of the American Philological Association* 115:47–57.

———. 1992. *Tragic Pleasures: Aristotle on Plot and Emotion*. Princeton.

———. 2006. "A Theory of Imitation in Plato's *Republic*." In Laird 2006:87–114.

Bénatouïl, T. 2005. "Les signes de Zeus et leur observation dans les *Phénomènes* d'Aratos." In *Signe et prédiction dans l'Antiquité*, ed. J. Turpin, 129–144. Saint-Étienne.

Bérard, J. 1957. *La colonisation grecque de l'Italie méridionale et de la Sicile dans l'antiquité: L'histoire et la légende*. 2nd ed. Paris.

Bergren, A. 2008a. "Helen's Good Drug." In Bergren 2008c:111–130. Orig. pub. in *Contemporary Literary Hermeneutics and the Interpretation of Classical Texts*, ed. S. Kresic, 200–214. Ottawa, 1981.

———. 2008b. "Language and the Female in Early Greek Thought." In Bergren 2008c:13–40. Orig. pub. *Arethusa* 16:69–95, 1983.

———. 2008c. *Weaving Truth: Essays on Language and the Female in Greek Thought*. Hellenic Studies 19. Washington, DC.

Berkowitz, G. 2004. *Semi-Public Narration in Apollonius'* Argonautica. Leuven.

Bernays, J. 2006. "Aristotle on the Effect of Tragedy." In Laird 2006: 158–175. Trans. J. Barnes. Orig. pub. as "Grundzüge der verlorenen Abhandlung des Aristoteles über Wirkung der Tragödie," *Abhandlungen der historisch-philosophischen Gesellschaft in Breslau* 1:135–202, 1857.

Bernsdorff, H. 2002. "Anmerkungen zum neuen Poseidipp (*P. Mil. Vogl. VIII* 309)." *Göttinger Forum für Altertumswissenschaft* 5:11–45.

Berra, A. 2009. "*Obscuritas lycophronea*: Les témoignages anciens sur Lycophron." In Cusset and Prioux 2009:259–318.

Bett, R. 1994. "What Did Pyrrho Think about 'The Nature of the Divine and the Good?'" *Phronesis* 39:303–337.

Beye, C. R. 1982. *Epic and Romance in the* Argonautica *of Apollonius*. Carbondale.

Biffis, G. 2014. "Can Iconography Help to Interpret Lycophron's Description of the Ritual Performed by Daunian Maidens (Alexandra 1126–1140)?" *Aitia. Regards sur la culture hellénistique au XXIe siècle* 4. http://journals.openedition.org/aitia/1025.

———. 2016. "Sirene in Licofrone, tra culto e concettualizzazione letteraria." In *Sulle sponde dello Ionio: Grecia occidentale e Greci d'Occidente*, ed. G. Sesisto and M. Intrieri, 67–78. Pisa.

———. 2021. "Lycophron's Cassandra, A Powerful Female Voice." In *Women and Power in Hellenistic Poetry*, ed. M. A. Harder et al., 35–57. Leuven.

Bing, P. 1988a. "A Note on the New 'Musenanruf' in Callimachus' *Aetia*." *Zeitschrift für Papyrologie und Epigraphik* 74:273–275.

———. 1988b. *The Well-Read Muse: Present and Past in Callimachus and the Hellenistic Poets*. Göttingen.

———. 1990. "A Pun on Aratus' Name in Verse 2 of the *Phainomena*?" *Harvard Studies in Classical Philology* 93:281–285.

———. 1993. "Aratus and His Audiences." In Mega Nepios: *Il destinatario nell'epos didascalio = The Addressee in Didactic Epic*, ed. A. Schiesaro, P. Mitsis, and J. Clay, 99–109. Pisa.

———. 2003. "The Unruly Tongue: Philitas of Cos as Scholar and Poet." *Classical Philology* 98:330–348.

Blondell, R. 2013. *Helen of Troy: Beauty, Myth, Devastation*. Oxford.

Blum, R. 1991. *Kallimachos: The Alexandrian Library and the Origins of Bibliography*. Trans. H. Wellisch. Madison.

Borgogno, A. 2002. "Le Muse di Apollonio Rodio." *Res Publica Litterarum* 25:5–21.

Bowie, E. L.1986. "Early Greek Elegy, Symposium and Public Festival." *Journal of Hellenic Studies* 106:13–35.

———. 1993. "Lies, Fiction and Slander in Early Greek Poetry." In Gill and Wiseman 1993:1–37.

Boys-Stones, G. R., ed. 2003a. *Metaphor, Allegory, and the Classical Tradition: Ancient Thought and Modern Revisions*. Oxford.

———. 2003b. "The Stoics' Two Types of Allegory." In Boys-Stones 2003a:189–216.

Breglia Pulci Doria, L. 1987. "Le Sirene: Il canto, la morte, la polis." *AION Annali di archeologia e storia antica* 9:65–98.

Brillante, C. 1990. "History and the Historical Interpretation of Myth." In Edmunds 1990a:93–138.

Brink, K. O. 1946. "Callimachus and Aristotle: An Inquiry into Callimachus' ΠΡΟΣ ΠΡΑΞΙΦΑΝΗΝ." *Classical Quarterly* 40:11–26.

Brumbaugh, M. 2019. *The New Politics of Olympos: Kingship in Kallimachos'* Hymns. Oxford.

Brunschwig, J. 1999. "Introduction: The Beginnings of Hellenistic Epistemology." In *Cambridge History of Hellenistic Philosophy*, ed. K. Algra et al., 229–259. Cambridge.

Bruss, J. S. 2004. "Lessons from Ceos: Written and Spoken Word in Callimachus." In Harder, Regtuit, and Wakker 2004:49–70.

Burnyeat, M. F. 1980. "Tranquillity without Stop: Timon, Fr. 68." *Classical Quarterly* 30:86–93.

Byre, C. S. 1991. "The Narrator's Addresses to the Narratee in Apollonius Rhodius' *Argonautica*." *Transactions of the American Philological Association* 121:215–227.

———. 2002. *A Reading of Apollonius Rhodius'* Argonautica—*The Poetics of Uncertainty*. Lewiston.

Cameron, A. 1992. "Genre and Style in Callimachus." *Transactions of the American Philological Association* 122:305–312.

———. 1995. *Callimachus and His Critics*. Princeton.

Campbell, M. 1983. *Studies in the Third Book of Apollonius'* Argonautica. Hildesheim.

Carlisle, M. 1999. "Homeric Fictions: Pseudo-Words in Homer." In *Nine Essays on Homer*, ed. M. Carlisle and O. Levaniouk, 55–91. Lanham.

Cazzaniga, I. 1975. "Per Nicandro Colofonio la Titanomachia fu opera autentica di Esiodo?" *Rendiconti dell'Istituto Lombardo* 109:173–180.

Cerri, G. 2007. "Apollonio Rodio et le Muse *hypophetores*: Tre interpretazioni a confronto." *Quaderni urbinati di cultura classica* 85:159–165.

Chantraine, P. 2009. *Dictionnaire étymologique de la langue grecque: Histoire des mots*. New edition. Paris.

Cherubin, R. 2009. "*Alêtheia* from Poetry into Philosophy: Homer to Parmenides." In Wians 2009:51–72.

Ciani, M. 1973. "Scritto con mistero: Osservazioni sull'oscurità di Licofrone." *Giornale italiano di filologia* 25:132–148.

———. 1975. *Lexikon zu Lycophron*. Hildesheim.

Clader, L. 1976. *Helen: The Evolution from Divine to Heroic in the Greek Epic Tradition*. Leiden.

Clare, R. J. 2002. *The Path of the Argo: Language, Imagery, and Narrative in the* Argonautica *of Apollonius Rhodius*. Cambridge.

Clauss, J. J. 1986. "Lies and Allusions: The Addressee and Date of Callimachus' *Hymn to Zeus.*" *Classical Antiquity* 5:155–170.

———. 1993. *The Best of the Argonauts: The Redefinition of the Epic Hero in Book 1 of Apollonius's* Argonautica. Berkeley.

———. 1997. "Conquest of the Mephistophelian Nausicaa: Medea's Role in Apollonius' Redefinition of the Epic Hero." In *Medea: Essays on Medea in Myth, Literature, Philosophy, and Art*, ed. J. J. Clauss and S. I. Johnston, 149–177. Princeton.

———. 2006. "*Theriaca*: Nicander's Poem of the Earth." *Studi italiani di filologia classica* 4:160–182.

Clauss, J. J., and M. Cuypers, eds. 2010. *A Companion to Hellenistic Literature.* Chichester.

Clayman, D. L. 1977. "The Origins of Greek Literary Criticism and the *Aitia* Prologue." *Wiener Studien* 90:27–34.

———. 1988. "Callimachus' *Iambi* and *Aitia.*" *Zeitschrift für Papyrologie und Epigraphik* 74:277–286.

———. 2000. "The Scepticism of Apollonius." In Harder, Regtuit, and Wakker 2000:33–53.

———. 2009. *Timon of Phlius: Pyrrhonism in Poetry.* Berlin.

Cohen, B., ed. 1995. *The Distaff Side: Representing the Female in Homer's* Odyssey. Oxford.

Cole, T. 1983. "Archaic Truth." *Quaderni urbinati di cultura classica* 13:7–28.

Coughlan, T. Forthcoming. "The Viper's Mouth and Hound's Howl: Discovery, Remedy and Polysemy at Nicander *Th.* 233 and 671."

Coviello, G. 2006. "Commento storico a Licofrone (*Alex.* 722–725)." *Hesperìa* 21:151–170.

Coxon, A. H. 2009. *The Fragments of Parmenides: A Critical Text with Introduction and Translation, the Ancient* Testimonia *and a Commentary*. Las Vegas.

Cozzoli, A. T. 2006. "L'*Inno* a Zeus: Fonti e modelli." In *Callimachea* Vol. 1, ed. A. Martina and A. T. Cozzoli, 115–136. Rome.

———. 2011. "The Poet as a Child." In Acosta-Hughes, Lehnus, and Stephens 2011:407–428.

Crane, G. 1986. "Tithonus and the Prologue to Callimachus' *Aetia.*" *Zeitschrift für Papyrologie und Epigraphik* 66:269–278.

Crugnola, A. 1971. *Scholia in Nicandri Theriaka cum Glossis.* Milan.

Cusset, C. 1999. *La Muse dans la Bibliothèque: Réécriture et intertextualité dans la poésie alexandrine.* Paris.

———. 2001. "Le bestiaire de Lycophron: Entre chien et loup." *Anthropozoologica* 33–34:61–72.

———. 2002. "Poétique et onomastique dans les *Phénomènes* d'Aratos." *Pallas* 59:187–196.

———. 2002-2003. "Tragic Elements in Lycophron's *Alexandra*." *Hermathena* 173/174:137–153.

———. 2004. "Cassandra et/ou la Sibylle: Les voix dans l'*Alexandra* de Lycophron." In *La Sibylle: Parole et representation,* ed. M Bouquet and F. Morzadec, 53–60. Rennes.

———. 2006a. "Dit et non-dit dans l'*Alexandra* de Lycophron." In Harder, Regtuit, and Wakker 2006:43–60.

———. 2006b. "Les images dans la poésie scientifique alexandrine: Les *Phénomènes* d'Aratos et les *Thériaques* de Nicandre." In Cusset 2006c:49–104.

———. ed. 2006c. Musa docta: *Recherches sur la poésie scientifique dans l'antiquité.* Saint-Étienne.

———. 2007. "Les détournements du nom propre: L'exemple de Lycophron." *Lalies* 27:199–212.

———. 2009. "L'*Alexandra* dans l'*Alexandra*: Du récit spéculaire à l'œuvre potentielle." In Cusset and Prioux 2009:119–139.

———. 2011. "Aratos et le stoïcisme." *Aitia. Regards sur la culture hellénistique au XXIe siècle* 1. http://journals.openedition.org/aitia/131.

———. 2018. "Y a-t-il des modalités particulières de la performance vocale féminine dans la poésie hellénistique? Une parole contrainte." In Harder, Regtuit, and Wakker 2018:75–97.

Cusset, C., and A. Kolde. 2012. "Rôle et représentation des dieux traditionnels dans l'*Alexandra* de Lycophron." In Harder, Regtuit, and Wakker 2012:1–30.

———. 2013. "The Rhetoric of the Riddle in the *Alexandra* of Lycophron." In Kwapisz, Petrain, and Syzmánski 2013:168–183.

Cusset, C., and É. Prioux, eds. 2009. *Lycophron: Éclats d'obscurité.* Saint-Étienne.

Cuypers, M. 2004a. "Apollonius of Rhodes." In De Jong, Nünlist, and Bowie 2004:43–62.

———. 2004b. "Prince and Principle: The Philosophy of Callimachus' *Hymn to Zeus*." In Harder, Regtuit, and Wakker 2004:95–116.

———. 2005. "Interactional Particles and Narrative Voice in Apollonius and Homer." In Harder and Cuypers 2005:35–69.

———. 2010. "Historiography, Rhetoric, and Science: Rethinking a Few Assumptions on Hellenistic Prose." In Clauss and Cuypers 2010:317–336.

Dawson, D. 1992. *Allegorical Readers and Cultural Revision in Ancient Alexandria.* Berkeley.

DeForest, M. 1994. *Apollonius' Argonautica: A Callimachean Epic.* Leiden.

de Jong, I. J. F. 1987. *Narrators and Focalizers: The Presentation of the Story in the Iliad.* Amsterdam.

———. 2004. "Narratological Theory on Narrators, Narratees, and Narrative." In De Jong, Nünlist, and Bowie 2004:1–10.

de Jong, I. J. F., and R. Nünlist, eds. 2007. *Time in Ancient Greek Literature: Studies in Ancient Greek Narrative.* Vol. 2. Leiden.

de Jong, I. J. F., R. Nünlist, and A. Bowie, eds. 2004. *Narrators, Narratees, and Narratives in Ancient Greek Literature: Studies in Ancient Greek Narrative.* Vol. 1. Leiden.

DeLacy, P. 1948. "Stoic Views of Poetry." *American Journal of Philology* 69:241–271.

Del Ponte, A. 1981. "Lycophronis *Alexandra*: La versificazione e il mezzo espressivo." *Studi italiani di filologia classica* 53:101–133.

De Marco, V. 1963. "Osservazioni su Apollio Rodio, I.1–22." In *Miscellanea di studi alessandrini in memoria di Augusto Rostagni*, ed. L. Ferrero et al., 350–355. Torino.

Denniston, J. D. 1950. *The Greek Particles.* 2nd ed. Oxford.

Depew, M. 1993. "Mimesis and Aetiology in Callimachus' *Hymns*." In Harder, Regtuit, and Wakker 1993:57–77.

———. 2004. "Gender, Power, and Poetics in Callimachus' Book of *Hymns*." In Harder, Regtuit, and Wakker 2004:117–137.

———. 2007. "Springs, Nymphs, and Rivers: Models of Origination in Third-Century Alexandrian Poetry." In *Literatur und Religion 2: Wege zu einer mythisch-rituellen Poetik bei den Griechen*, ed. A. Bierl, R. Lämmle, and K. Wesselman, 141–171. Berlin.

Depew, M., and D. Obbink, eds. 2000. *Matrices of Genres: Authors, Canons, and Society.* Cambridge, MA.

De Stefani, C. 2005. "La poesia didascalica di Nicandro: Un modello prosastico." *Incontri triestini di filologia classica* 5:55–72.

Detienne, M. 1967. *Les maîtres de vérité dans la Grèce archaïque.* Paris.

Dettori, E. 2004. "Appunti sul 'Banchetto di Pollis' (Call. fr.178 Pf.)." In Pretagostini and Dettori 2004:33–63.

Diels, H., and W. Kranz, eds. 1951. *Die Fragmente der Vorsokratiker.* 3 vols. 6th ed. Berlin.

Doherty, L. 1995. "Sirens, Muses, and Female Narrators in the *Odyssey*." In Cohen 1995:81–92.

Domaradzki, M. 2017. "The Beginnings of Greek Allegoresis." *Classical World* 110:299–321.

Dover, K. J. ed. 1971. *Theocritus: Select Poems.* Bristol.

Durbec, Y. 2011a. *Essais sur l'Alexandra de Lycophron.* Amsterdam.

———. 2011b. "L'*Alexandra* de Lycophron, un drama en cinq actes: Analyse métrique et questions de structure." In Durbec 2011a:55–62.

———. 2011c. "Le pire des Achéens: Le blâme d'Achille dans l'*Alexandra* de Lycophron." In Durbec 2011a:35–54.

———. 2011d. "Lycophron, *Alexandra* 1099–119, la mort d'Agamemnon et de Cassandra." In Durbec 2011a: 17–25.

———. 2011e. "Lycophron et la poétique de Callimaque: Le prologue de l'*Alexandra*, 1–15." In Durbec 2011a:12–16.

Dyck, A. 1989. "On the Way from Colchis to Corinth: Medea in Book 4 of the 'Argonautica.'" *Hermes* 117:455–470.

Edlund, I. 1987. "The Sacred Geography of Southern Italy in Lycophron's *Alexandra*." *Opuscula Romana* 16:43–49.

Edmunds, L., ed. 1990a. *Approaches to Greek Myth*. Baltimore.

———. 1990b. "Introduction: The Practice of Greek Mythology." In Edmunds 1990a:1–20.

Effe, B. 1970. "Προτέρη γενεή: Eine stoische Hesiod-interpretation in Arats *Phainomena*." *Rheinisches Museum für Philologie* 113:167–182.

———. 1974a. "Der Aufbau von Nikanders *Theriaka* und *Alexipharmaka*." *Rheinisches Museum für Philologie* 117:53–66.

———. 1974b. "Zum Eingang von Nikanders *Theriaka*." *Hermes* 102:119–121.

———. 1977. *Dichtung und Lehre: Untersuchungen zur Typologie des antiken Lehrgedichts*. Munich.

———. 1988. "Die Funktionen narrativ-fiktionaler Digressionen im antiken Lehrgedicht." In *Acta conventus neo-latini Guelpherbytani: Proceedings of the Sixth International Congress of Neo-Latin Studies; Wolfenbuttel, 12 August to 16 August 1985*, ed. S. P. Revard, F. Rädle, and M. A. Di Cesare, 403–407. Binghamton, NY.

———. 2005. "Typologie und literarhistorischer Kontext: Zur Gattungsgeschichte des griechischen Lehrgedichts." In Horster and Reitz 2005:27–44.

Erren, M. 1967. *Die Phainomena des Aratos von Soloi: Untersuchungen zum Sach- und Sinnverständnis*. Wiesbaden.

Fabian, K. 1992. "Il Banchetto di Pollis: Callimachi frr. 178–185 Pf. (Icus)." In OINHPA TEYXH: *Studi triestini di poesia conviviale*, ed. K. Fabian, E. Pellizer, and G. Tedeschii, 131–166. Alessandria.

Fakas, C. 2001a. "Arat und Aristoteles' Kritik am Lehrgedicht." *Hermes* 129:479–483.

———. 2001b. *Der hellenistische Hesiod: Arats Phainomena und die Tradition der antiken Lehrepik*. Wiesbaden.

Fantuzzi, M. 1996. "Aetiologie." In *Neue Pauly Enzyklopaedie der Antike. Altertum.* Vol. 1, ed. H Cancik and H. Schneider. Stuttgart. 369–371.

———. 2011. "Speaking with Authority: Polyphony in Callimachus' *Hymns*." In Acosta-Hughes, Lehnus, and Stephens 2011:429–453.

Fantuzzi, M., and R. Hunter. 2004. *Tradition and Innovation in Hellenistic Poetry.* Cambridge.

Faulkner, A. 2015. "The Female Voice of Justice in Aratus' *Phaenomena*." *Greece and Rome* 62:75–86.

Feeney, D. C. 1991. *The Gods in Epic: Poets and Critics of the Classical Tradition.* Oxford.

Ferrari, G. 1988. "Hesiod's Mimetic Muses and the Strategies of Deconstruction." In *Post-Structuralist Classics*, ed. A. Benjamin, 45–78. London.

———. 1989. "Plato and Poetry." In Kennedy 1989: 92–148.

———. 1999. "Aristotle's Literary Aesthetics." *Phronesis* 44:181–198.

Finkelberg, M. 1998. *The Birth of Literary Fiction in Ancient Greece.* Oxford.

Floridi, L. 2004. "Mendacità del mito e strategie encomiastiche nell' *Inno a Zeus* di Callimacho." In Pretagostini and Dettori 2004:65–75.

Ford, A. 1992. *Homer: The Poetry of the Past.* Ithaca.

———. 1999. "Performing Interpretation: Early Allegorical Exegesis of Homer." In *Epic Traditions in the Contemporary World: The Poetics of Community*, ed. M. H. Beissinger, J. Tylus, and S. L. Wofford, 33–55. Berkeley.

———. 2002. *The Origins of Criticism: Literary Culture and Poetic Theory in Classical Greece.* Princeton.

———. 2015. "The Purpose of Aristotle's *Poetics*." *Classical Philology* 110:1–21.

Fountoulakis, A. 1998. "On the Literary Genre of Lycophron's *Alexandra*." *Acta Antiqua Academiae Scientiarum Hungaricae* 38:291–295.

———. 2014. "Poet and Prophetess: Lycophron's *Alexandra* in Context." In Harder, Regtuit, and Wakker 2014:103–124.

Fowler, D. 2000. "The Didactic Plot." In Depew and Obbink 2000:205–219.

Fränkel, H. 1968. *Noten zu den* Argonautika *des Apollonios.* Munich.

Fraser, P. M. 1972. *Ptolemaic Alexandria.* 3 vols. Oxford.

Frede, M. 1987a. *Essays in Ancient Philosophy.* Minneapolis.

———. 1987b. "Stoics and Skeptics on Clear and Distinct Impressions." In Frede 1987a:151–176.

———. 1987c. "The Ancient Empiricists." In Frede 1987a:243–260.

Fuhrer, T. 1988. "A Pindaric Feature in the Poems of Callimachus." *American Journal of Philology* 109:53–68.

Fusillo, M. 1984. "L'*Alessandra* di Licofrone: Racconto epico e discorso 'drammatico.'" *Annali della Scuola Normale Superiore di Pisa* 14:495–525.

———. 1985. *Il tempo delle Argonautiche.* Rome.

Fusillo, M., A. Hurst, and G. Paduano. 1991. *Alessandra.* Milan.

Garriga, C. 1996. "The Muses of Apollonius of Rhodes: The Term ΥΠΟΦΗΤΟΡΕΣ." *Prometheus* 22:105–114.

Gatz, B. 1967. *Weltalter, goldene Zeit und sinnverwandte Vorstellungen.* Hildesheim.

Gee, E. 2000. *Ovid, Aratus and Augustus: Astronomy in Ovid's* Fasti. Cambridge.

———. 2013. *Aratus and the Astronomical Tradition*. Oxford.

George, E. 1977. "Apollonius, *Argonautica* 4.984–85: Apology for a Shameful Tale." *Rivista di Studi Classici* 25:360–364.

Gerson, L. 2009. *Ancient Epistemology*. Cambridge.

Giangrande, G. 1967. "'Arte Allusiva' and Alexandrian Epic Poetry." *Classical Quarterly* 17:85–97.

Gigante Lanzara, V. 1997. "Il νόστος di Odisseo et la prospezione della memoria: Lycophr. *Alex.* 648–819." *Maia* 49:43–68.

———. 1998. "Il tempo dell'*Alessandra* e i modelli ellenistici di Licofrone." *La parola del passato* 53:401–418.

———. 2000. *Licofrone:* Alessandra. Milan.

———. 2009. "Ἔστι μοι μυρία παντᾷ κέλευθος (Pind. Isthm. IV 1)." In Cusset and Prioux 2009:95–115.

———. 2010. "Echi dell'*Elena* euripidea nell'*Alessandra*." *La parola del passato* 65:257–264.

Gill, C. 1993. "Plato on Falsehood—Not Fiction." In Gill and Wiseman 1993:38–87.

Gill, C., and T. P. Wiseman, eds. 1993. *Lies and Fiction in the Ancient World*. Exeter.

Giubilo, B. 2009. "Note su ΕΤΥΤΗΜΟΣ in Apollonio Rhodio e in Callimaco." In *οὐ πᾶν ἐφήμερον. Scritti in memoria di Roberto Pretagostini*, ed. C. Braidotti, E. Dettori, and E. Lanzillotta, 247–258. Rome.

Goldhill, S. 1986. "Framing and Polyphony: Readings in Hellenistic Poetry." *Proceedings of the Cambridge Philological Society* 32:25–52.

———. 1991. *The Poet's Voice: Essays on Poetics and Greek Literature*. Cambridge.

González, J. M. 2000. "*Musai Hypophetores*: Apollonius of Rhodes on Inspiration and Interpretation." *Harvard Studies in Classical Philology* 100:268–292.

Gow, A. S. F. 1952. *Theocritus*. 2 vols. 2nd ed. Cambridge.

Gow, A. S. F., and A. F. Scholfield. 1953. *Nicander: The Poems and Poetical Fragments*. Cambridge.

Graver, M. 1995. "Dog-Helen and Homeric Insult." *Classical Antiquity* 14:41–61.

Green, P. 1997. *The* Argonautika. Berkeley.

Greene, R. 2017a. "Callimachus and New Ancient Histories." *Aitia. Regards sur la culture hellénistique au XXIe siècle* 7.1. https://journals.openedition.org/aitia/1706.

———. 2017b. "Recollecting Histories: Herodotus and Thucydides in Callimachus' *Aetia*." *Phoenix* 71:21–43.

Grillo, A. 1988. *Tra filologia e narratologia*. Rome.

Guilleux, N. 2009. "La fabrique des *hapax* et des *prôton legomena* dans l'*Alexandra*, entre connivence et cryptage." In Cusset and Prioux 2009:221–236.

Gummert, P. H. 1992. *Die Erzählstruktur in den* Argonautika *des Apollonios Rhodios*. Frankurt.

Gutzwiller, K. J. 1991. *Theocritus' Pastoral Analogies: The Formation of a Genre.* Madison.

———. 1992. "The Nautilus, the Halcyon, and Selenaia: Callimachus's *Epigram* 5 Pf. = 14 G.-P." *Classical Antiquity* 11:194–209.

———. 1998. *Poetic Garlands: Hellenistic Epigrams in Context.* Berkeley.

———. 2002a. "Art's Echo: The Tradition of Hellenistic Ecphrastic Epigram." In *Hellenistic Epigram,* ed. M. A. Harder, R. F. Regtuit, and G. C. Wakker, 85–112. Leuven.

———. 2002b. "Posidippus on Statuary." In *Il papiro di Posidippo un anno dopo,* ed. G. Bastianini and A. Casanova, 41–60. Florence.

———. ed. 2005. *The New Posidippus: A Hellenistic Poetry Book.* Oxford.

———. 2010. "Literary Criticism." In Clauss and Cuypers 2010:337–365.

Haft, A. 1984. "Odysseus, Idomeneus and Meriones: The Cretan Lies of *Odyssey* 13–19." *Classical Journal* 79:289–306.

Halliwell, S. 1986. *Aristotle's* Poetics. Chicago.

———. 1992. "Pleasure, Understanding, and Emotion in Aristotle's *Poetics*." In Rorty 1992:241–260.

———. 2002. *The Aesthetics of Mimesis: Ancient Texts and Modern Problems.* Princeton.

———. 2011. *Between Ecstasy and Truth: Interpretations of Greek Poetics from Homer to Longinus.* Oxford.

Hanses, M. 2014. "The Pun and the Moon in the Sky: Aratus' ΛΕΠΤΗ Acrostic." *Classical Quarterly* 64:609–614.

Harder, M. A. 1988. "Callimachus and the Muses: Some Aspects of Narrative Technique in *Aetia* 1–2." *Prometheus* 14:1–14.

———. 1990. "Untrodden Paths: Where Do They Lead?" *Harvard Studies in Classical Philology* 93:287–309.

———. 1992. "Insubstantial Voices: Some Observations on the Hymns of Callimachus." *Classical Quarterly* 42: 384–394.

———. 1993a. "Aspects of the Structure of Callimachus' *Aetia*." In Harder, Regtuit, and Wakker 1993:99–110.

———. 1993b. "Between 'Prologue' and 'Dream' (Call.fr. 1a, 19ff.)." *Zeitschrift für Papyrologie und Epigraphik* 96:11–13.

———. 1994. "Travel Descriptions in the *Argonautica* of Apollonius Rhodius." In *Travel Fact and Travel Fiction: Studies on Fiction, Literary Tradition, Scholarly Discovery and Observation in Travel Writing,* ed. Z. von Martels, 16–29. Leiden.

———. 1998. "'Generic Games' in Callimachus' *Aetia*." In Harder, Regtuit, and Wakker 1998:95–113.

———. 2002. "Intertextuality in Callimachus' *Aetia*." In Montanari and Lehnus 2002:189–223.

———. 2003. "The Invention of Past, Present and Future in Callimachus' *Aetia*." *Hermes* 131:290–306.

———. 2004. "Callimachus." In De Jong, Nünlist, and Bowie 2004:63–82.

———. 2007a. "Callimachus." In De Jong and Nünlist 2007:81–96.

———. 2007b. "To Teach or Not to Teach … ? Some Aspects of the Genre of Didactic Poetry in Antiquity." In *Calliope's Classroom: Studies in Didactic Poetry from Antiquity to the Renaissance*, ed. M. A. Harder, A. A. MacDonald, and G. J. Reinink, 23–48. Leuven.

———. 2010. "Callimachus' *Aetia*." In Clauss and Cuypers 2010:92–105.

———. 2012. *Callimachus: Aetia*. 2 vols. Oxford.

———. 2013. "From Text to Text: The Impact of the Alexandrian Library on the Work of Hellenistic Poets." In *Ancient Libraries*, ed. J. König, K. Oikonomopoulou, and G. Woolf, 96–108. Cambridge.

———. 2014. "Spiders in the Greek Wide Web?" In Hunter, Rengakos, and Sistakou 2014:259–271.

Harder, M. A., and M. Cuypers, eds. 2005. *Beginning from Apollo: Studies in Apollonius Rhodius and the Argonautic Tradition. Caeculus* 5. Leuven.

Harder, M. A., R. F. Regtuit, and G. C. Wakker, eds. 1993. *Callimachus*. Groningen.

———. 1998. *Genre in Hellenistic Poetry*. Groningen

———. 2000. *Apollonius Rhodius*. Leuven.

———. 2004. *Callimachus II*. Leuven.

———. 2006. *Beyond the Canon*. Leuven.

———. 2009. *Nature and Science in Hellenistic Poetry*. Leuven.

———. 2012. *Gods and Religion in Hellenistic Poetry*. Leuven.

———. 2014. *Hellenistic Poetry in Context*. Leuven.

———. 2018. *Drama and Performance in Hellenistic Poetry*. Leuven.

Haslam, M. W. 1993. "Callimachus' *Hymns*." In Harder, Regtuit, and Wakker 1993:111–125.

Hatzimichali, M. 2009. "Poetry, Science and Scholarship: The Rise and Fall of Nicander of Colophon." In Harder, Regtuit, and Wakker 2009:19–40.

Heath, M. 1985. "Hesiod's Didactic Poetry." *Classical Quarterly* 35:245–263.

Heidegger, M. 1927. *Sein und Zeit*. Tübingen.

Heiden, B. 2007. "The Muses' Uncanny Lies: Hesiod, *Theogony* 27, and Its Translators." *American Journal of Philology* 128:153–175.

Hinds, S. 1998. *Allusion and Intertext: Dynamics of Appropriation in Roman Poetry*. Cambridge.

Holford-Strevens, L. 2000. "θηλύπαις in Lycophron 850-51." *Classical Quarterly* 50:606–610.

Holmberg, I. 1995. "Euripides' *Helen*: Most Noble and Most Chaste." *American Journal of Philology* 116:19–42.

Holzinger, C. 1895. *Lykophrons* Alexandra. Leipzig.

Hopkinson, N. 1984. "Callimachus' *Hymn to Zeus*." *Classical Quarterly* 34:139–148.

———. 1988. *A Hellenistic Anthology*. Cambridge.

Hornblower, S. 2014. "Lykophron and Epigraphy: The Value and Function of Cult Epithets in the *Alexandra*." *Classical Quarterly* 64:91–120.

———. 2015. *Lykophron:* Alexandra. Oxford.

———. 2018. *Lykophron's* Alexandra, *Rome, and the Hellenistic World*. Oxford.

Horster, M., and C. Reitz, eds. 2005. *Wissensvermittlung in dichterischer Gestalt*. Stuttgart.

Hunter, R. L. 1987. "Medea's Flight: The Fourth Book of the *Argonautica*." *Classical Quarterly* 37:129–139.

———. 1988. "'Short on Heroics': Jason in the *Argonautica*." *Classical Quarterly* 38:436–453.

———. 1989a. *Apollonius of Rhodes:* Argonautica; *Book III*. Cambridge.

———. 1989b. "Winged Callimachus." *Zeitschrift für Papyrologie und Epigraphik* 76:1–2.

———. 1993. *The* Argonautica *of Apollonius: Literary Studies*. Cambridge.

———. 1996a. "Callimachus Swings (frr. 178 and 43 Pf.)." *Ramus* 25:17–26.

———. 1996b. "The Divine and Human Map of the *Argonautica*." *Syllecta Classica* 6:13–27.

———. 1999. *Theocritus: A Selection*. Cambridge.

———. 2008a. "The Poetics of Narrative in the *Argonautica*." In Papanghelis and Rengakos 2008:115–146.

———. 2008b. "Written in the Stars: Poetry and Philosophy in the *Phaenomena* of Aratus." In *On Coming After: Studies in Post-Classical Greek Literature and its Reception* Vol. 1, ed. R. Hunter, 153–188. Berlin.

———. 2014. *Hesiodic Voices: Studies in the Ancient Reception of Hesiod's* Works and Days. Cambridge.

———. 2015. *Apollonius of Rhodes:* Argonautica; *Book IV*. Cambridge.

Hunter, R., A. Rengakos, and E. Sistakou, eds. 2014. *Hellenistic Studies at a Crossroads: Exploring Texts, Contexts and Metatexts*. Berlin.

Hunter, R., and T. Fuhrer. 2002. "Imaginary Gods? Poetic Theology in the *Hymns* of Callimachus." In Montanari and Lehnus 2002:143–175.

Hurst, A. 1967. *Apollonios de Rhodes, manière et coherence*. Rome.

———. 1998. "Géographes et poètes: Le cas d'Apollonios de Rhodes." In *Sciences exactes et sciences appliquées à Alexandrie*, ed. G. Argoud and J.-Y. Guillaumin, 279–288. Saint-Étienne.

———. 2012a. "L'*Odyssée* de Lycophron." In Hurst 2012d:97–110.

———. 2012b. "Lycophron: La condensation du sens, le comique et l'*Alexandra*." In Hurst 2012d:47–58.

———. 2012c. "Sur la date du Lycophron." In Hurst 2012d:15–22.

———. 2012d. *Sur Lycophron.* Geneva.

Hurst, A., and A. Kolde, ed. 2008. *Lycophron:* Alexandra. Paris.

Hutchinson, G. O. 1988. *Hellenistic Poetry.* Oxford.

———. 2003. "The *Aetia:* Callimachus' Poem of Knowledge." *Zeitschrift für Papyrologie und Epigraphik* 145:47–59.

———. 2009. "Read the Instructions: Didactic Poetry and Didactic Prose." *Classical Quarterly* 59:196–211.

———. 2014. "Hellenistic Poetry and Hellenistic Prose." In Hunter, Rengakos, and Sistakou 2014:31–51.

Huxley, G. 1965. "Xenomedes of Keos." *Greek, Roman, and Byzantine Studies* 6:235–245.

Jacques, J.-M. 1960. "Sur un acrostiche d' Aratos. *Phén.*,783–787." *Revue des études anciennes* 62:48–61.

———. 1969. "Aratos et Nicandre. ΝΩΘΗΣ et ʽΑΜΥΔΡΟΣ." *Revue des études anciennes* 71:38–56.

———. 2002. *Nicandre, Œuvres.* Vol. 2. Les Thériaques: *Fragments iologiques antérieurs à Nicandre.* Paris.

———. 2006. "Nicandre de Colophon: Poète et médecin." In Cusset 2006:19–48.

James, A. W. 1972. "The Zeus Hymns of Cleanthes and Aratus." *Antichthon* 6:28–38.

Janko, R. 2000. *Philodemus: On Poems; Book 1.* Oxford.

Jones, K. 2014. "Lycophron's *Alexandra,* the Romans, and Antiochus III." *Journal of Hellenic Studies* 134:41–55.

Kaesser, C. 2005. "The Poet and the 'Polis.' The *Aetia* as Didactic Poem." In Horster and Reitz 2005:95–114.

Kaibel, G. 1894. "Aratea." *Hermes* 29:82–123.

Kalospyros, N. A. E. 2009. "Literary Syntactic Patterns in Lycophron's *Alexandra.*" In Cusset and Prioux 2009:209–219.

Kambylis, A. 1965. *Die Dichterweihe und ihre Symbolik: Untersuchungen zu Hesiodus, Kallimachos, Properz und Ennius.* Heidelberg

Kannicht, R. 1988. *The Ancient Quarrel between Philosophy and Poetry: Aspects of the Greek Conception of Literature.* Christchurch.

Katz, J., and K. Volk. 2000. "Mere Bellies? A New Look at *Theogony* 26–8." *Journal of Hellenic Studies* 120:122–131.

Kennedy, G. A. ed. 1989. *The Cambridge History of Literary Criticism.* Vol. 1. Cambridge.

Kerkhecker, A. 1988. "Ein Musenanruf am Anfang der *Aitia* des Kallimachos." *Zeitschrift für Papyrologie und Epigraphik* 71:16–24.

Kidd, D. A. 1981. "Notes on Aratus, *Phaenomena.*" *Classical Quarterly* 31:355–362.

———. 1997. *Aratus:* Phaenomena. Cambridge.

Kirichenko, A. 2012. "Nothing to Do with Zeus? The Old and the New in Callimachus' First *Hymn*." In Harder, Regtuit, and Wakker 2012:181–201.

Klein, T. M. 1983. "Apollonius' Jason: Hero and Scoundrel." *Quaderni urbinati di cultura classica* 13:115–126.

Klooster, J. 2007. "Apollonius of Rhodes." In De Jong and Nünlist 2007:63–80.

———. 2011. *Poetry as Window and Mirror: Positioning the Poet in Hellenistic Poetry.* Leiden.

———. 2012. "Apollonius of Rhodes." In *Space in Ancient Greek Literature*, ed. I. J. F. de Jong, 55–76. Leiden.

———. 2013. "Apostrophe in Homer, Apollonius and Callimachus." In *Über die Grenze: Metalepse in Text- und Bildmedien des Altertums*, ed. U. E. Eisen and P. von Möllendorff, 151–173. Berlin.

Klooster, J., M. A. Harder, R. F. Regtuit, and G. C. Wakker, eds. 2019. *Callimachus Revisited: New Perspectives in Callimachean Scholarship.* Peeters.

Knight, V. 1995. *The Renewal of Epic: Responses to Homer in the* Argonautica *of Apollonius.* Leiden.

Knoefel, P. K., and M. C. Covi. 1991. *A Hellenistic Treatise on Poisonous Animals: The* Theriaca *of Nicander of Colophon. A Contribution to the History of Toxicology.* Lewiston, NY.

Knox, P. 1993. "The Epilogue to the *Aetia*: An Epilogue." *Zeitschrift für Papyrologie und Epigraphik* 96:175–178.

Koenen, L. 1993. "The Ptolemaic King as a Religious Figure." In *Images and Ideologies: Self-Definition in the Hellenistic World*, ed. A. Bulloch, E. Gruen, and A. Stewart, 25–115. Berkeley.

Köhnken, A. 2008. "Hellenistic Chronology: Theocritus, Callimachus, and Apollonius of Rhodes." In Papanghelis and Rengakos 2008:73–94.

Komornicka, A. 1972. "Quelques remarques sur la notion d'ἀλάθεια et de ψεῦδος chez Pindare." *Eos* 60:235–253.

Kosmetatou, E. 2000. "Lycophron's *Alexandra* Reconsidered: The Attalid Connection." *Hermes* 128:32–53.

———. 2004. "Vision and Visibility: Art Historical Theory Paints a Portrait of New Leadership in Posidippus' *Andriantopoiika*." In *Labored in Papyrus Leaves: Perspectives on an Epigram Collection Attributed to Posidippus (P.Mil. Vogl. VIII 309)*, ed. B. Acosta-Hughes, E. Kosmetatou, and M. Baumbach, 187–211. Hellenic Studies 2. Washington, DC.

Kossaifi, C. 2009. "Poétique messager. Quelques remarques sur l'incipit et l'épilogue de l'*Alexandra* de Lycophron." In Cusset and Prioux 2009:141–159.

Kotwick, M. 2020. "Allegorical Interpretation in Homer: Penelope's Dream and Early Greek Allegoresis." *American Journal of Philology* 141:1–26.

Kouremenos, T., G. M. Parássoglou, and K. Tsantsanoglou. 2006. *The Derveni Papyrus: Edited with Introduction and Commentary*. Florence.

Kraus, M. 1987. *Name und Sache: Ein Problem im frühgriechischen Denken*. Amsterdam.

Krevans, N. 1983. "Geography and Literary Tradition in Theocritus 7." *Transactions of the American Philological Association* 113:201–220.

———. 1984. *The Poet as Editor: Callimachus, Virgil, Horace, Propertius, and the Development of the Poetic Book*. PhD diss., Princeton University.

———. 1991. "'Invocation' at the End of the *Aetia* Prologue." *Zeitschrift für Papyrologie und Epigraphik* 89:19–23.

———. 2000. "On the Margins of Epic: The Foundation-Poems of Apollonius." In Harder, Regtuit, and Wakker 2000:69–84.

———. 2004. "Callimachus and the Pedestrian Muse." In Harder, Regtuit, and Wakker 2004: 173–184.

Krischer, T. 1965. "ΕΤΥΜΟΣ und ΑΛΗΘΗΣ." *Philologus* 109:161–174.

Kroll, W. 1924. *Studien zum Verständnis der römischen Literatur*. Stuttgart.

Kühlmann, W. 1973. *Katalog und Erzählung: Studien zu Konstanz und Wandel einer literarischen Form in der Antiken Epik*. PhD diss., Universität Freiburg.

Kwapisz, J., and K. Pietruczuk. 2019. "Your Own Personal Library of Alexandria: Callimachus' Scholarly Works and their Readers." In Klooster, Harder, Regtuit, and Wakker 2019:221–247.

Kwapisz, J., D. Petrain, and M. Syzmánski, eds. 2013. *The Muse at Play: Riddles and Wordplay in Greek and Latin Poetry*. Berlin.

Kyriakou, P. 1995. *Homeric Hapax Legomena in the Argonautica of Apollonius of Rhodes: A Literary Study*. Stuttgart.

———. 2018. "Narrator and Poetic Divinities in Apollonius Rhodius' *Argonautica*." *Trends in Classics* 10:367–391.

Lachenaud, G., ed. 2010. *Scholies à Apollonios de Rhodes*. Paris.

Laird, A., ed. 2006. *Oxford Readings in Ancient Literary Criticism*. Oxford.

Lambin, G. 2005. *L'Alexandra de Lycophron*. Rennes.

———. 2009. "L'auteur dans *Alexandra*." In Cusset and Prioux 2009:161–169.

Landolfi, L. 1996. *Il volo di Dike: Da Arato a Giovenale*. Bologna.

Lausberg, M. 1990. "Epos und Lehrgedicht. Ein Gattungsvergleich am Beispiel von Lucans Schlangenkatalog." *Würzburger Jahrbücher für die Altertumswissenschaft* 16:173–203.

Lear, J. 1988. "Katharsis." *Phronesis* 33:297–326.

Ledbetter, G. 2003. *Poetics before Plato*. Princeton.

Lefkowitz, M. R. 1980. "The Quarrel between Callimachus and Apollonius." *Zeitschrift für Papyrologie und Epigraphik* 40:1–19.

Lelli, E. 2011. "Proverbs and Popular Sayings in Callimachus." In Acosta-Hughes, Lehnus, and Stephens 2011:384–403.

Leone, P. 2002. *Scholia Vetera et Paraphrases in Lycophronis* Alexandram. Galatina.

Levet, J.-P. 1976. *Le vrai et le faux dans la pensée grecque archaïque: Étude de vocabulaire. Présentation Générale; Le vrai et le faux dans les épopées homériques.* Paris.

———. 2008. *Le vrai et le faux dans la pensée grecque archaïque d'Hésiode à la fin du Ve siècle.* Paris.

Linant de Bellefonds, P., C. Pouzadoux, and É. Prioux. 2017. "Lycophron l'Italien?" In Linant de Bellefonds and Prioux 2017:199–246.

Linant de Bellefonds, P., and É. Prioux, eds. 2017. *Voir les mythes: Poésie hellénistique et arts figurés.* Paris.

Livrea, E. 1973. *Apollonii Rhodii* Argonauticon *Liber IV.* Florence.

Lobel, E. 1928. "Nicander's Signature." *Classical Quarterly* 22:114–115.

Lombardi, M. 1998. "Callimaco H. Zeus 65 ψευδοίμην, ἀίοντος ἅ κεν πεπίθοιεν ἀκουήν: La poetica della verità e le menzogne credibili." *Rivista di cultura classica e medioevale* 40:165–172.

Long, A. A. 2006. "Stoic Readings of Homer." In Laird 2006:211–237.

Long, A. A., and D. Sedley, eds. 1987. *The Hellenistic Philosophers.* 2 vols. Cambridge.

Looijenga, A. 2009. "Unrolling the *Alexandra*: The Allusive Messenger-Speech of Lycophron's Prologue and Epilogue." In Cusset and Prioux 2009:59–80.

Lovatt, H. 2018. "Apollonius Rhodius *Argonautica* 4 and the Epic Gaze: There and Back Again." In *Gaze, Vision, and Visuality in Ancient Greek Literature,* ed. A. Kampakoglou and A. Novokhatko, 88–112. Berlin.

Lowe, N. J. 2004. "Lycophron." In De Jong, Nünlist, and Bowie 2004:307–314.

Lüddecke, K. L. G. 1998. "Contextualizing the Voice in Callimachus' 'Hymn to Zeus.'" *Materiali e discussioni per l'analisi dei testi classici* 41:9–33.

Ludwig, W. 1963. "Die *Phainomena* Arats als hellenistische Dichtung." *Hermes* 91:425–448.

Luther, W. 1935. *"Wahrheit" und "Lüge" im ältesten Griechentum.* Leipzig.

Lynn, J. K. 1995. *Narrators and Narration in Callimachus.* PhD diss., Columbia University.

Maass, E. 1892. *Aratea.* Berlin.

Magnelli, E. 2005. "Callimaco, fr. 75 Pf., et la tecnica narrative dell'elegia ellenistica." In Κορυφαίῳ ἀνδρί: *mélanges offerts à André Hurst,* ed. A. Kolde, A. Lukinovich, and A.-L. Rey, 203–212. Geneva.

———. 2006. "Nicander's Chronology: A Literary Approach." In Harder, Regtuit, and Wakker 2006:185–204.

Malkin, I. 1998. *The Returns of Odysseus: Colonization and Ethnicity.* Berkeley.

Malomud, A. 2015. "Интерпретация Αἰνελένη в Nic. Ther. 310." *Indo-European Linguistics and Classical Philology* 19:534–537.

Malten, L. 1918. "Ein neues Bruchstück aus den Aitia des Kallimachos." *Hermes* 53:148–179.

Mari, M. 2009. "Cassandra et le altre: Riti di donne nell'*Alessandra* di Licofrone." In Cusset and Prioux 2009:405–440.

Martin, J., ed. 1974. *Scholia in Aratum vetera*. Stuttgart.

———. 1979. "Les *Phénomènes* d'Aratos. Étude sur la composition du poème." In *L'astronomie dans l'antiquité classique. Actes du colloque tenu à l'Université de Toulouse-le-Mirail les 21–23 octobre 1977*, ed. G. Aujac and J. Soubiran, 91–104. Paris.

———. 1998. *Aratos* Phénomènes. 2 vols. Paris.

Massimilla, G. 1996. *Callimacho* AITIA *Libri Primo e Secondo*. Pisa.

———. 2000. "Nuovi elementi per la cronologia di Nicandro." In *La letteratura ellenistica: Problemi e prospettive di ricerca*, ed. R. Pretagostini, 127–137. Rome.

———. 2011. "The *Aetia* through Papyri." In Acosta-Hughes, Lehnus, and Stephens 2011:39–62.

Mazzoldi, S. 2002. "Cassandra's Prophecy between Ecstasy and Rational Mediation." *Kernos* 15:145–154.

McLennan, G. R. 1977. *Callimachus,* Hymn to Zeus: *Introduction and Commentary*. Rome.

McNelis, C., and A. Sens. 2011. "Trojan Glory: *Kleos* and the Survival of Troy in Lycophron's *Alexandra*." *Trends in Classics* 3:56–82.

———. 2016. *The* Alexandra *of Lycophron. A Literary Study*. Oxford.

Meijering, R. 1987. *Literary and Rhetorical Theories in Greek Scholia*. Groningen.

Meyer, D. 1993. "Nichts Unbezeugtes singe ich. Die fiktive Darstellung der Wissenstradierung bei Kallimachos." In *Vermittlung und Tradierung von Wissen in der griechischen Kultur*, ed. W. Kullmann and J. Althoff, 317–336. Tübingen.

———. 2008. "Apollonius as Hellenistic Geographer." In Papanghelis and Rengakos 2008:267–285.

Mitsis, P., and C. Tsagalis, eds. 2010. *Allusion, Authority, and Truth: Critical Perspectives on Greek Poetic and Rhetorical Praxis*. Berlin.

Molesworth, K. 2018. "Watching Tragedy in Lycophron's *Alexandra*." In Harder, Regtuit, and Wakker 2018:173–199.

Momigliano, A. 1945. "The Locrian Maidens and the Date of Lycophron's *Alexandra*." *Classical Quarterly* 39:49–53.

Montanari, F., and L. Lehnus, eds. 2002. *Callimaque*. Geneva.

Morgan, K. A. 2000. *Myth and Philosophy: From the Presocratics to Plato*. Cambridge.

Mori, A. 2008. *The Politics of Apollonius Rhodius'* Argonautica. Cambridge.

Morrison, A. D. 2007. *The Narrator in Archaic Greek and Hellenistic Poetry*. Cambridge.

———. 2011. "Callimachus' Muses." In Acosta-Hughes, Lehnus, and Stephens 2011:329–348.

Most, G. W. 2011. "What Ancient Quarrel between Philosophy and Poetry?" In *Plato and the Poets,* ed. P. Destrée and F.-G. Hermann, 1–20. Leiden.

Murray, J. 2005. "The Constructions of the Argo in Apollonius' *Argonautica.*" In Harder and Cuypers 2005:88–106.

———. 2014. "Anchored in Time: The Date in Apollonius' *Argonautica.*" In Harder, Regtuit, and Wakker 2014:247–283.

———. 2018. "Silencing Orpheus: The Fiction of Performance in Apollonius' *Argonautica.*" In Harder, Regtuit, and Wakker 2018:201–224.

Mühll, P. von der. 1962. *Homeri* Odyssea. Basel.

Murray, P. 1981. "Poetic Inspiration in Early Greece." *Journal of Hellenic Studies* 101:87–100.

———. ed. 1996. *Plato on Poetry.* Cambridge.

Naddaf, G. 2009. "Allegory and the Origins of Philosophy." In Wians 2009:99–131.

Naddaff, R. 2009. "No Second Troy: Imagining Helen in Greek Antiquity." In Wians 2009:73–97.

Nagy, G. 1989. "Early Greek Views of Poets and Poetry." In Kennedy 1989:1–77.

———. 1999. *The Best of the Achaeans: Concepts of the Hero in Archaic Greek Poetry.* Revised edition. Baltimore.

———. 2010. "The Meaning of *Homoios* (ὁμοῖος) in *Theogony* 27 and Elsewhere." In Mitsis and Tsagalis 2010:153–167.

Natzel, S. 1992. Κλέα γυναικῶν: *Frauen in den "Argonautika" des Apollonios Rhodios.* Trier.

Negri, M. 2009. "Oscurità et identità: Strategie licofronee di innovazione semantica nel lessico sportivo (αὐλός, νύσσα) et paternità dell'*Alessandra.*" In Cusset and Prioux 2009:171–191.

Neils, J. 1995. "*Les Femmes Fatales*: Skylla and the Sirens in Greek Art." In Cohen 1995:175–184.

Neitzel, H. 1980. "Hesiod und die lügenden Musen: Zur Interpretation von *Theogonie* 27f." *Hermes* 108:387–401.

Newman, J. K. 1985. "Pindar and Callimachus." *Illinois Classical Studies* 10:169–189.

Nisetich, F. 2001. *The Poems of Callimachus.* Oxford.

Nünlist, R. 1998. *Poetologische Bildersprache in der frühgriechischen Dichtung.* Stuttgart.

Nussbaum, M. 1992. "Tragedy and Self-Sufficiency: Plato and Aristotle on Fear and Pity." In Rorty 1992:261–290.

O'Hara, J. J. 1996. *True Names: Vergil and the Alexandrian Tradition of Etymological Wordplay.* Ann Arbor.

Overduin, F. 2009. "The Fearsome Shrewmouse: Pseudo-science in Nicander's *Theriaca.*" In Harder, Regtuit, and Wakker 2009:79–93.

———. 2013. "A Note on Alcibius and the Structure of Nicander's *Theriaca*." *The Classical World* 107:105–109.

———. 2014. "The Anti-bucolic World of Nicander's *Theriaca*." *Classical Quarterly* 64:623–641.

———. 2015. *Nicander of Colophon's* Theriaca: *A Literary Commentary*. Leiden.

———. 2017. "Beauty in Suffering: Disgust in Nicander's *Theriaca*." In *The Ancient Emotion of Disgust*, ed. D. Lateiner and D. Spatharas, 141–155. Oxford.

———. 2019. "The Didactic Callimachus and the Homeric Nicander: Reading the *Aetia* Through the *Theriaca*?" In Klooster, Harder, Regtuit, and Wakker 2019:265–283.

Paduano Faedo, L. 1970. "L'inversione del rapporto poeta-musa nella cultura ellenistica." *Annali della Scuola Normale Superiore di Pisa* 39:377–386.

Papadopoulou, M. 2009. "Scientific Knowledge and Poetic Skill: Colour Words in Nicander's *Theraica* and *Alexipharmaca*." In Harder, Regtuit, and Wakker 2019:95–119.

Papanghelis, T. D., and A. Rengakos, eds. 2008. *Brill's Companion to Apollonius Rhodius*. 2nd ed. Leiden.

Park, A. 2013. "Truth and Genre in Pindar." *Classical Quarterly* 63:17–36.

Parsons, P. 1977. "Callimachus: *Victoria Berenices*." *Zeitschrift für Papyrologie und Epigraphik* 25:1–51.

Pasquali, G. 1913. "I due Nicandri." *Studi italiani di filologia classica* 20:55–111.

Payne, M. 2007. *Theocritus and the Invention of Fiction*. Cambridge.

Pendergraft, M. L. B. 1990. "On the Nature of the Constellations: Aratus, *Ph.* 367–85." *Eranos* 88:99–106.

———. 1995. "Euphony and Etymology: Aratus' *Phaenomena*." *Syllecta Classica* 6:43–67.

Pfeiffer, R. 1928. "Ein Neues Altersgedicht des Kallimachos." *Hermes* 63:302–341.

———. ed. 1953. *Callimachus*. Vol. 2, *Hymni et Epigrammata*. Oxford.

———. 1968. *History of Classical Scholarship: From the Beginnings to the End of the Hellenistic Age*. Oxford.

Phillips, E. D. 1953. "Odysseus in Italy." *Journal of Hellenic Studies* 73:53–67.

Phillips, T. 2020. *Untimely Epic: Apollonius Rhodius'* Argonautica. Oxford.

Phinney, E. 1967. "Narrative Unity in the *Argonautica*, the Medea-Jason Romance." *Transactions of the American Philological Association* 98:327–341.

Pillinger, E. 2019. *Cassandra and the Poetics of Prophecy in Greek and Latin Literature*. Cambridge.

Plazenet, L. 1994. "Théocrite: *Idylle* 7." *L'Antiquité Classique* 63:77–108.

Porter, H. N. 1946. "Hesiod and Aratus." *Transactions of the American Philological Association* 77:158–170.

Possanza, M. D. 2004. *Translating the Heavens: Aratus, Germanicus, and the Poetics of Latin Translation*. New York.

Pratt, L. 1993. *Lying and Poetry from Homer to Pindar: Falsehood and Deception in Archaic Greek Poetics*. Ann Arbor.

Prauscello, L. 2006. "Sculpted Meanings, Talking Statues: Some Observations on Posidippus 142.12 A-B (= XIX G-P) ΚΑΙ ΕΝ ΠΡΟΘΥΡΟΙϹ ΘΗΚΕ ΔΙΔΑϹΚΑΛΙΗΝ." *American Journal of Philology* 127:511–523.

Prescott, H. W. 1921. "Callimachus' Epigram on the Nautilus." *Classical Philology* 16:327–337.

Pretagostini, R. 1984. *Ricerche sulla poesia alessandrina: Teocrito, Callimaco, Sotade*. Rome.

———. 1995. "L'incontro con le Muse sull'Elicona in Esiodo e in Callimaco: Modificazioni di un modello." *Lexis* 13:157–172.

Pretagostini, R., and E. Dettori, eds. 2004. *La cultura ellenistica: L'opera letteraria e l'esegesi antica*. Rome.

Priestly, J. 2014. *Herodotus and Hellenistic Culture: Literary Studies in the Reception of the* Histories. Oxford.

Prioux, É. 2007. *Regards alexandrins: Histoire et théorie des arts dans l' épigramme hellénistique*. Leuven.

———. 2009. "On the Oddities and Wonders of Italy: When Poets Look Westward." In Harder, Regtuit, and Wakker 2009:121–148.

———. 2017. "Posidippe: L'évidence et l'occasion." In Linant de Bellefonds and Prioux 2017:13–51.

Prioux, É., and C. Pouzadoux. 2014. "Entre histoires de familles et histoire universelle: Liens générationnels, parentés et mariages dans la représentation de la trame temporelle entourant le conflit troyen." *Aitia. Regards sur la culture hellénistique au XXIe siècle* 4. https://journals.openedition.org/aitia/923#ftn6.

Pucci, P. 1977. *Hesiod and the Language of Poetry*. Baltimore.

———. 1998a. "The Proem of the *Odyssey*." In Pucci 1998b:11–29.

———. 1998b. *The Song of the Sirens: Essays on Homer*. Lanham.

———. 1998c. "The Song of the Sirens." In Pucci 1998b:1–9.

Puelma, M. 1960. "Die Dichterbegegnung in Theokrits 'Thalysien.'" *Museum Helveticum* 17:144–164.

———. 1989. "Der Dichter und die Wahrheit in der griechischen Poetik von Homer bis Aristoteles." *Museum Helveticum* 46:65–100.

Race, W. H. 1982. "Aspects of Rhetoric and Form in Greek Hymns." *Greek, Roman, and Byzantine Studies* 23:5–14.

Ramelli, I., and G. Lucchetta. 2004. *Allegoria*. Milan.

Raviola, F. 2006. "Commento storico a Licofrone (*Alex.* 712–721; 732–737)." *Hesperìa* 21:135–149.

Reeve, M. D. 1996–1997. "A Rejuvenated Snake." *Acta Antiqua Academiae Scientiarum Hungaricae* 37:245–258.

Reinsch-Werner, H. 1976. *Callimachus Hesiodicus: Die Rezeption der hesiodischen Dichtung durch Kallimachos von Kyrene.* Berlin.

Rengakos, A. 1994a. *Apollonios Rhodios und die antike Homererklärung.* Munich.

———. 1994b. "Lykophron als Homererklärer." *Zeitschrift für Papyrologie und Epigraphik* 102:111–130.

Richardson, N. J. 2006. "Homeric Professors in the Age of the Sophists." In Laird 2006:62–86.

Richardson, S. 1996. "Truth in the Tales of the *Odyssey.*" *Mnemosyne* 49:393–402.

Romano, A. J. 2011. "Callimachus and Contemporary Criticism." In Acosta-Hughes, Lehnus, and Stephens 2011:309–328.

Rorty, A. O. ed. 1992. *Essays on Aristotle's* Poetics. Princeton.

Rosenmeyer, T. G. 1955. "Gorgias, Aeschylus, and *Apate.*" *American Journal of Philology* 76:225–260.

Rösler, W. 1980. "Die Entdeckung der Fiktionalität in der Antike." *Poetica* 12:283–319.

Rostropowicz, J. 2003. "Zeus and Men in the *Phaenomena* by Aratus of Soli." *Eirene* 39:219–228.

Rougier-Blanc, S. 2009. "Espaces, architecture, et métaphores dans l' *Alexandra* de Lycophron." In Cusset and Prioux 2009:539–558.

Russell, D. 2003. "The Rhetoric of the *Homeric Problems.*" In Boys-Stones 2003a:217–234.

Salapata, G. 2002. "Myth into Cult: Alexandra/Kassandra in Lakonia." In Oikistes: *Studies in Constitutions, Colonies, and Military Power in the Ancient World, Offered in Honor of A. J. Graham*, ed. B. Gorman and E. Robinson, 131–159. Leiden.

Sandbach, F. H. 1971. "Phantasia Kataleptike." In *Problems in Stoicism*, ed. A. A. Long, 9–21. London.

Scarborough, J. 1977. "Nicander's Toxicology I: Snakes." *Pharmacy in History* 19:3–23.

Schade, G. 1999. *Lykophrons 'Odyssee':* Alexandra *648–819.* Berlin.

Scheer, E. 1881–1908. *Lycophronis* Alexandra. 2 vols. Berlin.

Schiesaro, A. 1996. "Aratus' Myth of *Dike.*" *Materiali e discussioni per l'analisi dei testi classici* 37:9–26.

Schmitz, T. 1999. "'I Hate All Common Things': The Reader's Role in Callimachus' *Aetia* Prologue." *Harvard Studies in Classical Philology* 99:151–178.

Schneider, O. 1856. *Nicandrea,* Theriaca *et* Alexipharmaca. Leipzig.

Schofield, M., M. Burnyeat, and J. Barnes, eds. 1980. *Doubt and Dogmatism: Studies in Hellenistic Philosophy.* Oxford.

Schroeder, C. M. 2012. "'To Keep Silent Is a Small Virtue': Hellenistic Poetry and the Samothracian Mysteries." In Harder, Regtuit, and Wakker 2012:307–334.

Schwabl, H. 1972. "Zur Mimesis bei Arat: *Prooimium* und *Parthenos.*" *In* ANTIDOSIS: *Festschrift für W. Kraus*, ed. R. Hanslik, A. Lesky, and H. Schwabl, 336–356. Vienna.

Schwinge, E. 1986. *Künstlichkeit von Kunst: Zur Geschichtlichkeit der alexandrinischen Poesie.* Munich.

Scodel, R. 1980. "Wine, Water, and the Anthesteria in Callimachus Fr. 178 Pf." *Zeitschrift für Papyrologie und Epigraphik* 39:37–40.

Scully, S. 2015. *Hesiod's* Theogony: *From Near Eastern Creation Myths to* Paradise Lost. Oxford.

Sedley, D. 2003. *Plato's* Cratylus. Cambridge.

Segal, C. 1962. "Gorgias and the Psychology of the Logos." *Harvard Studies in Classical Philology* 66:99–155.

———. 1974. "Simichidas' Modesty: Theocritus, *Idyll* 7.44." *American Journal of Philology* 95:128–136.

Selden, D. 1998. "Alibis." *Classical Antiquity* 17:289–412.

Semanoff, M. 2006a. "Astronomical Ecphrasis." In Cusset 2006c:157–177.

———. 2006b. "Undermining Authority: Pedagogy in Aratus' *Phaenomena*." In Harder, Regtuit, and Wakker 2006:303–318.

Sens, A. 2000. "The Particle HTOI in Apollonian Narrative." In Harder, Regtuit, and Wakker 2000:173–193.

———. 2005. "The Art of Poetry and the Poetry of Art: The Unity and Poetics of Posidippus' Statue-Poems." In Gutzwiller 2005:206–225.

———. 2009. "Lycophron's *Alexandra*, The Catalog of Ships and Homeric Geography." In Cusset and Prioux 2009:19–37.

———. 2010. "Hellenistic Tragedy and Lycophron's *Alexandra*." In Clauss and Cuypers 2010:297–313.

———. 2014. "Narrative and Simile in Lycophron's *Alexandra*." In Hunter, Rengakos, and Sistakou 2014:97–111.

Serrao, G. 1971. *Problemi di Poesia Alessandrina.* Vol. I, *Studi su Teocrito.* Rome.

Sider, D. 2014. "Didactic Poetry: The Hellenistic Invention of a Pre-existing Genre." In Hunter, Rengakos, and Sistakou 2014:13–29.

Silverman, A. 1992. "Plato's *Cratylus*: The Naming of Nature and the Nature of Naming." In *Oxford Studies in Ancient Philosophy*, volume X, ed. J. Annas, 25–73. Oxford.

Sistakou, E. 2008. *Reconstructing the Epic: Cross-Readings of the Trojan Myth in Hellenistic Poetry.* Leuven.

———. 2009a. "Breaking the Name Codes in Lycophron's *Alexandra*." In Cusset and Prioux 2009:237–257.

———. 2009b. "Callimachus Hesiodicus Revisited." In *Brill's Companion to Hesiod*, ed. F. Montanari, A. Rengakos, and C. Tsagalis, 219–252. Leiden.

———. 2012. *The Aesthetics of Darkness: A Study of Hellenistic Romanticism in Apollonius, Lycophron and Nicander.* Leuven.

———. 2014a. "From Emotion to Sensation: The Discovery of the Senses in Hellenistic Poetry." In Hunter, Rengakos, and Sistakou 2014:135–156.

———. 2014b. "Mapping Counterfactuality in Apollonius' *Argonautica*." In *Geography, Topography, Landscape: Configurations of Space in Greek and Roman Epic*, ed. M. Skempis and I. Ziogas, 161–180. Berlin.

———. 2016. *Tragic Failures: Alexandrian Responses to Tragedy and the Tragic.* Berlin.

———. 2017. "From Present to Presence: Modes of Presentification in Hellenistic Poetry." In *Past and Present in Hellenistic Poetry*, ed. M. A. Harder, R. F. Regtuit, and G. C. Wakker, 1–22. Leuven.

———. 2019. "Denarrating the Narratable in the *Aetia*: A Postmodern Take on Callimachean Aesthetics." In Klooster, Harder, Regtuit, and Wakker 2019:329–357.

Snell, B. 1978. *Der Weg zum Denken und zur Wahrheit: Studien zur frühgriechischen Sprache.* Göttingen.

Solmsen, F. 1966. "Aratus on the Maiden and the Golden Age." *Hermes* 94:124–128.

Spatafora, G. 2005. "Riflessioni sull'arte poetica di Nicandro." *Giornale italiano di filologia* 57:231–262.

———. 2008. "I *Theriakà* di Nicandro: Digressioni mitologiche e ostilità tra animali." *Giornale italiano di filologia* 60:49–58.

Spentzou, E. 2002. "Stealing Apollo's Lyre: Muses and Poetic ἆθλα in Apollonius' *Argonautica* 3." In *Cultivating the Muse: Struggles for Power and Inspiration in Classical Literature*, ed. E. Spentzou and D. Fowler, 93–116. Oxford.

Stanford, W. B. 1963. *The Ulysses Theme: A Study in the Adaptability of a Traditional Hero.* 2nd ed. Oxford.

Steiner, D. 2007. "Feathers Flying: Avian Poetics in Hesiod, Pindar, and Callimachus." *American Journal of Philology* 128:177–208.

Stephens, S. A. 1998. "Callimachus at Court." In Harder, Regtuit, and Wakker 1998:167–185.

———. 2000. "Writing Epic for the Ptolemaic Court." In Harder, Regtuit, and Wakker 2000:195–215.

———. 2003. *Seeing Double: Intercultural Poetics in Ptolemaic Alexandria.* Berkeley.

———. 2010. "Ptolemaic Alexandria." In Clauss and Cuypers 2010:46–61.

———. 2015a. "Callimachus and His Narrators." In *Hymnic Narrative and the Narratology of Greek Hymns*, ed. A. Faulkner and O. Hodkinson, 49–68. Leiden.

———. 2015b. *Callimachus: The* Hymns. Oxford.

Stewart, A. 2005. "Posidippus and the Truth in Sculpture." In Gutzwiller 2005:183–205.

Stinton, T. W. C. 1976. "'Si Credere Dignum Est': Some Expressions of Disbelief in Euripides and Others." *Proceedings of the Cambridge Philological Society* 22:60–89.

Striker, G. 1996a. *Essays on Hellenistic Epistemology and Ethics*. Cambridge.

———. 1996b. "Epicurus on the Truth of Sense Perceptions." In Striker 1996a:77–91. Orig. pub. in *Archiv für Geschichte der Philosophie* 59:125–142, 1977.

———. 1996c. "κριτήριον τῆς ἀληθείας." In Striker 1996a:22–76. Orig. pub. in *Nachrichten der Akademie der Wissenschaften zu Göttingen* 2:48–110, 1974.

———. 1996d. "Sceptical Strategies." In Striker 1996a:92–115. Orig. pub. in Schofield, Burnyeat, and Barnes 1980:54–83.

———. 1996e. "The Problem of the Criterion." In Striker 1996a:150–165. Orig. pub. in *Epistemology*, ed. S. Everson, 143–160. Cambridge, 1990.

Stroh, W. 1976. "Hesiods lügende Musen." In *Studien zum antiken Epos*, ed. H. Görgemanns and E. A. Schmidt, 85–112. Meisenheim.

Strootman, R. 2010. "Literature and Kings." In Clauss and Cuypers 2010:30–45.

Struck, P. 1995. "Allegory, Aenigma, and Anti-Mimesis: A Struggle Against Aristotelian Rhetorical Literary Theory." In *Greek Literary Theory After Aristotle*, ed. J. G. J. Abbenes, S. R. Slings, and I. Sluiter, 215–234. Amsterdam.

———. 2004. *Birth of the Symbol: Ancient Readers at the Limits of their Texts*. Princeton.

Sullivan, M. B. 2013. "Nicander's Aesopic Acrostic and Its Antidote." In Kwapisz, Petrain, and Syzmánski 2013:225–245.

Suzuki, M. 1989. *Metamorphoses of Helen: Authority, Difference, and the Epic*. Ithaca.

Svavarsson, S. H. 2002. "Pyrrho's Dogmatic Nature." *Classical Quarterly* 52:248–256.

Svenbro, J. 1976. *La parole et le marbre: Aux origines de la poétique grecque*. Lund.

Tarán, L. 1965. *Parmenides: A Text with Translation, Commentary, and Critical Essays*. Princeton.

Tate, J. 1929. "Plato and Allegorical Interpretation." *Classical Quarterly* 23:142–154.

———. 1934. "On the History of Allegorism." *Classical Quarterly* 28:105–114.

Taylor, C. C. W. 1980. "'All Perceptions Are True.'" In Schofield, Burnyeat, and Barnes 1980:105–124.

Thalmann, W. 1984. *Conventions of Form and Thought in Early Greek Epic Poetry*. Baltimore.

———. 2011. *Apollonius of Rhodes and the Spaces of Hellenism*. Oxford.

Toohey, P. 1996. *Epic Lessons: An Introduction to Ancient Didactic Poetry.* London.

Touwaide, A. 1991. "Nicandre, de la science à la poésie. Contribution à l'exégèse de la poésie médicale grecque." *Aevum* 65:65–101.

Valverde Sánchez, M. 1989. *El Aition en las* Argonáuticas *de Apolonio de Rodas: Estudio Literario.* Murcia.

van Dijk, G. J. 1997. *ΑΙΝΟΙ, ΛΟΓΟΙ, ΜΥΘΟΙ: Fables in Archaic, Classical, and Hellenistic Greek Literature; with a Study of the Theory and Terminology of the Genre.* Leiden.

van Noorden, H. 2009. "Aratus' Maiden and the Source of Belief." In Harder, Regtuit, and Wakker 2009:255–275.

———. 2015. *Playing Hesiod: The "Myth of the Races" in Classical Antiquity.* Cambridge.

van Tress, H. 2004. *Poetic Memory: Allusion the Poetry of Callimachus and the Metamorphoses of Ovid.* Leiden.

Verdenius, W. J. 1972. "Notes on the Proem of Hesiod's *Theogony.*" *Mnemosyne* 25:225–260.

Veyne, P. 1988. *Did the Greeks Believe in Their Myths? An Essay on Constitutive Imagination.* Trans. P. Wissing. Chicago.

Vian, F. 1978. "ΙΗΣΩΝ ΑΜΗΧΑΝΕΩΝ." In *Studi in onore di Anthos Ardizzoni*, ed. E. Livrea and A. Privitera, 1025–1041. Rome.

Vian, F., and E. Delage, eds. 1974. *Apollonios de Rhodes:* Argonautiques, Chants I–II. Paris.

———. 1980. *Apollonios de Rhodes:* Argonautiques, Chants II. Paris.

———. 1981. *Apollonios de Rhodes:* Argonautiques, Chant IV. Paris.

Volk, K. 2002. *The Poetics of Latin Didactic: Lucretius, Vergil, Ovid, and Manilius.* Oxford.

———. 2010. "Aratus." In Clauss and Cuypers 2010:197–210.

———. 2012. "Reading the Signs in Aratus' *Phaenomena.*" *American Journal Philology* 133:209–240.

Walcot, P. 1977. "Odysseus and the Art of Lying." *Ancient Society* 8:1–19.

Walsh, G. B. 1984. *The Varieties of Enchantment: Early Greek Views of the Nature and Function of Poetry.* Chapel Hill.

———. 1985. "Seeing and Feeling: Representation in Two Poems of Theocritus." *Classical Philology* 80:1–19.

Weber, G. 2011. "Poet and Court." In Acosta-Hughes, Lehnus, and Stephens 2011:225–244.

West, M. L. 1966. *Hesiod:* Theogony. Oxford.

———. 1974. *Studies in Greek Elegy and Iambus.* Berlin.

———. 1978. *Hesiod* Works and Days. Oxford.

———. 1998. *Homerus* Ilias. 2 vols. Stuttgart.

———. 2013. *The Epic Cycle: A Commentary on the Lost Troy Epics.* Oxford.

West, S. 1983. "Notes on the Text of Lycophron." *Classical Quarterly* 33:114–135.

———. 1984. "Lycophron Italicised." *Journal of Hellenic Studies* 104:127–151.

———. 2000. "Lycophron's *Alexandra*: Hindsight as Foresight Makes No Sense?" In Depew and Obbink 2000:153–166.

———. 2009. "Herodotus in Lycophron." In Cusset and Prioux 2009:81–93.

Wheeler, G. 2002. "Sing, Muse … : The Introit from Homer to Apollonius." *Classical Quarterly* 52: 33–49.

White, H. 1987. *Studies in the Poetry of Nicander*. Amsterdam.

———. 1997. "An Interpretative Problem in Lycophron's *Alexandra*." *Habis* 28:49–51.

Whitman, J. 1987. *Allegory: The Dynamics of an Ancient and Medieval Technique*. Cambridge, MA.

Wians, W., ed. 2009. *Logos and Muthos: Philosophical Essays in Greek Literature*. Albany.

Wilamowitz-Moellendorff, U. von. 1924. *Hellenistische Dichtung in der Zeit des Kallimachos*, Vol. 2. Berlin.

Williams, F. 1971. "A Theophany in Theocritus." *Classical Quarterly* 21:137–145.

———. 1993. "Callimachus and the Supranormal." In Harder, Regtuit, and Wakker 1993:217–225.

Williams, M. F. 1991. *Landscape in the Argonautica of Apollonius Rhodius*. Frankfurt.

Wilson, K. D. 2015. *Signs in the Song: Scientific Poetry in the Hellenistic Period*. PhD diss., University of Pennsylvania.

———. 2018a. "Avenging Vipers: Tragedy and Succession in Nicander's *Theriaca*." *Classical Journal* 113:257–280.

———. 2018b. "Reading and Performing Didactic Poetry in the Hellenistic Period." In Harder, Regtuit, and Wakker 2018:317–332.

Woodruff, P. 1992. "Aristotle on *Mimēsis*." In Rorty 1992:73–95.

Wray, D. 2000. "Apollonius' Masterplot: Narrative Strategy in *Argonautica* 1." In Harder, Regtuit, and Wakker 2000:239–265.

Zanker, G. 1979. "The Love Theme in Apollonius Rhodes' *Argonautica*." *Wiener Studien* 92:52–75.

Zeitlin, F. 2010. "The Lady Vanishes: Helen and Her Phantom in Euripidean Drama." In Mitsis and Tsagalis 2010:263–282.

Zetzel, J. E. G. 1981. "On the Opening of Callimachus, *Aetia* II." *Zeitschrift für Papyrologie und Epigraphik* 42:31–33.

Ziegler, K. 1927. "Lykophron der Tragiker und die *Alexandra* Frage." *Realencyclopädie der classischen Altertumswissenschaft* 13:2316–2381.

Zwicker, F. 1927. "Sirenen." *Realencyclopädie der classischen Altertumswissenschaft* 3:288–308.

Index Locorum

Acusilaus
FGrHist 2 F 14, 57n66
Aelian
On the Nature of Animals 6.51, 65n87,
66; 9.21, 88
Various Histories 9.14, 31n133
Aeschylus
Agamemnon 52, 156n37; 62, 166n73;
688–689, 84; 712, 84n128, 163n64;
1072–1330, 145n2; 1116, 157n44
Eumenides 225–234, 58n69; 460,
157n44; 584, 17n79
Libation Bearers 1000, 157n44
Persians 818, 176
Prometheus Bound 661, 180n121
Fragments, fr. 55 Radt, 2n2; fr. 180
Radt, 174n104
Alcman
Fragments, fr. 30 Davies, 185n143;
fr. 77 Davies, 84n128
Antagoras
Fragments, fr. 1 Powell, 29
Anthologia Graeca 7.42, 112n66; AP
16.120.1, 32; AP 16.120.4, 32
Antoninus Liberalis
Metamorphoses 21.1, 185n145
Apollodorus (pseudo-Apollodorus)
Epitome 3.7, 177n110; 5.14–15,
168n82; 7.18, 181n128
Library 3.10.7, 155n35; 3.11.1, 157n40;
3.12.5, 154n28; 3.14.1, 158n45

Apollonius
Argonautica
Book 1: 1.1, 106, 121–122; 1.1–2,
106; 1.5, 106; 1.8, 106, 123;
1.18–22, 122–123; 1.21–22, 131;
1.22, 122, 124, 128; 1.23–34,
107n44; 1.26–27, 125n108;
1.27, 124; 1.28, 129; 1.31, 124;
1.30–31, 125n108; 1.111–114,
112n94; 1.145, 129n123; 1.460,
108n52; 1.638, 108n52; 1.648–
649, 107n48; 1.661, 131n130;
1.722–724, 112n94; 1.774–780,
10n42; 1.797, 129n124; 1.916–
921, 134; 1.953–960, 98n5;
1.988, 129n125; 1.1053, 108n52;
1.1061, 98n4; 1.1141, 129n123;
1.1213–1219, 106; 1.1220, 106;
1.1233, 108n52; 1.1286, 108;
1.1295, 3n9
Book 2: 2.218–239, 35n145; 2.311–
312, 107; 2.312, 131n130; 2.317–
407, 107; 2.334–345, 107; 2.409,
126n113; 2.410, 108n52; 2.500,
129n125; 2.526–527, 98n4; 2.578,
108n52; 2.598–600, 107; 2.681,
108n52; 2.693, 107n44; 2.708–
709, 107n44; 2.845, 121n93;
2.853, 129n123; 2.860, 108n52;
2.885, 108n52; 2.1015–1029, 107;
2.1140, 108n52; 2.1223, 133

Index of Greek Words

Index of Subjects